God's Solution for America

~ and the Nations of the World ~

This is a Spiritual Revolution!

David Carl Hertler
Jean Hallahan Hertler

Verily, verily, I say unto you, Except a corn of wheat fall into the ground and die, it abideth alone: but if it die, it bringeth forth much fruit. ~ John 12:24

God's Solution for America
~ and the Nations of the World ~
This is a Spiritual Revolution!

Copyright © 2024 David Carl Hertler and Jean Hallahan Hertler
All Rights reserved

Copyright Notice: All rights reserved. This book is protected by the copyright laws of the United States of America and international copyright law. This book may not be copied or reprinted for commercial gain or profit. The use of quotations or page copying for personal, or group study is permitted and encouraged. Permission for any other use will be granted upon request. Unless otherwise identified, Scripture quotations are from the King James Version of the Bible.

ISBN: 978-0-5782963-0-2 (paperback), ISBN: 978-0-5782963-2-6 (EPUB)
First Edition February, 2024

Disclaimer

Please read this disclaimer carefully. Your reading of this book will constitute and be deemed an acceptance of the terms of this disclaimer. If you do not agree with any of the terms below, discontinue reading this book immediately. The information and content provided in this book are the opinions of David Carl Hertler and Jean Hallahan Hertler and is being provided for entertainment purposes only. The information provided herein may not be suitable for your situation. The authors and publisher assume no responsibility for errors, omissions or contrary interpretation of the subject matter herein. Although the authors and publisher have made every effort to ensure the information in this book was correct at press time, the authors and publisher do not assume and hereby disclaim any liability to any party for any loss, damage, or disruption caused by errors or omissions, whether such errors or omissions result from negligence, accident, or any other cause.

For more information visit www.ReinhabitedRepublic.com

Fair Use Notice

The material in this book is provided for educational and informational purposes. It may contain copyrighted material, the use of which has not always been specifically authorized by the copyright owner. It is being made available in an effort to advance the understanding of historical issues. It is believed that this constitutes a 'fair use' of any such copyrighted material as provided for in Section 107 of the US Copyright Law. In accordance with Title 17 U.S.C. Section 107. If you wish to use copyrighted material from this book for purposes of your own that go beyond 'fair use', you must obtain permission from the copyright owner. The information in this book does not constitute legal advice.

Heritage Endeavors
Forestville, Wisconsin

DEDICATION

Above all, to God the Father, God the Son, and God the Holy Spirit who revealed and inspired this opus. Yᵉhovah, may Your Name be praised and remain here forever, along with Your eyes and Your heart.
(2 Chronicles 7:16)

With meekness, to the American people in all 50 States that they would project "a city on a hill" and in the nation's capital that America would be "a city on a hill" to the rest of the world.

To our forefathers and foremothers, who embraced Biblical Christianity, the "religion of Liberty," and fulfilled their prophetic calling by birthing a nation in covenant with the *Creator of the universe* resulting in civil and religious liberty.

To the patriots and lovers of Liberty, both seen and unseen, who have given their lives, fortunes, and sacred honor for its cause.

To those of other nations who recognized the prophetic calling and destiny of the American people to be a blessing to all the families of the earth (*Genesis 12:3*), and who have sacrificed much in obedience to Almighty God in order for America to fulfill that mandate.

To our posterity: our children, our grandchildren, and their grandchildren.

And finally, to the remnant in the Body of Christ that believes that they must do their duty to their country as part of their duty to God. Who believe that politics are a part of Biblical Christianity in such a country as the American Republic.

ACKNOWLEDGMENTS

The brave Pilgrims, Puritans, early Americans, those who loved the Lord with all their hearts, souls, and minds, guided by the hand of Creator God in the *New World* while fulfilling their prophetic destiny as a unique people that would come to birth forth "one nation under God." A description of their inspiration in this work is beyond words.

Those who shed their blood for the cause of Liberty, known and unknown, both Americans and those of other nations. A description of the inspiration created by the gift of their lives would require a heavenly language to communicate sufficiently.

Our teachers from both this current time and those of the past, who invested their inspired work as a legacy. It is the work of our teachers that "put the ink in the well" for the Holy Spirit to be able to draw from and compose a panoramic-like picture across the American Republic's timeline.

In loving memory of Senator Donald Mack Adams, Wisconsin free State, distinguished former United States Marine and publisher of the 2-volume *Re-inhabited* book series. His labor of love has produced much good fruit in the world. His beloved wife Lisa Kitchenmaster who has wholeheartedly supported this legacy.

President James Buchanan Geiger, who has knowledge of the Truth as it relates to both the natural and spiritual realms, three years earlier requested that this book be written bringing forth a greater depth in knowledge and understanding of the American Republic that interfaces a greater dimension of Truthful world history. This work could not and would not have been achieved without his guidance.

President James Timothy Turner and Mrs. Karen Turner, who sacrificed their lives to the ultimate in answering the call of the Lord toward the restoration of His government and the jurisdiction of Liberty on earth known as the American Republic. "Thank you" with all that is within us.

Governor James Carpenter, Colorado free State, who was gifted from heaven with "a download of the keys to the kingdom" that was opened to Jean with understanding that resulted in Chapter One.

Dave Mook for his ever so welcomed encouragement and feedback in this journey.

Rev. Steve Loopstra, Director, www.yourservantinchristministries.org for his kind encouragement and prayer assistance in publishing this work.

Christie Kaderabek and Holly Baer for their feedback and guidance in this work.

Betsy St. Peter and Elodee Kroll for their loving encouragement and intercessory gifting.

Gary and Karen Kuchta for their loving support and belief in us and our ministry.

Pete and Lynn Allard for their loving support, prayers, and beloved friendship in likemindedness in these days that are like no other.

CONTENTS

Dedication	iii
Acknowledgements	iv
Contents	v
Foreword – President James Buchanan Geiger	vi
Foreword – Former President James Timothy Turner	viii
Foreword – Chaplain Dr. Wade King Butler	xi
Foreword – Governor James E. Carpenter, Colorado free State	xii
Preface	xv
Introduction	xvii

<u>Chapter</u>

One ~ The American Republic: Foundational Principles and Insight with an Accurate Historical Outlook on its Founding and Objective	1
Two ~ The Biblical View on the American Revolution With Nathaniel Whitaker, D.D. in 1775	31
Three ~ American Republic vs. Corporate Democracy: The Counterfeit Begins	57
Four ~ Worshipers of Satan Setup Their Corporate Democracy	125
Five ~ God's Solution for America	153
Six ~ Conclusion	191

FOREWORD

This work identifies the enemies of the American People, the ones referred to by President Washington in his farewell address:

"…cunning, ambitious, and unprincipled men will be able to subvert the Power of the People and to usurp for themselves the reins of Government; destroying afterwards the very engines which have lifted them to unjust dominion…The spirit of encroachment tends to consolidate the powers of all departments in one, and thus to create, whatever the form of government, a real despotism…" George Washington, Farewell Address, 1796

America, take heed that you read and understand the history of the takeover of our Republic by these *"unprincipled men."* Once the Republic is restored we must be diligent to never let this happen again. As Americans what can we do to combat this behemoth? Simply stated, we must appeal to the same Heavenly Father, the same One to Whom our Fore Fathers appealed. Then, we must put on the helmet of salvation, and enter the battle to restore our Republic. It was by their confidence in God and their faith in Him that they were able to proceed against overwhelming odds towards victory.

What did their appeal, faith and works accomplish? Some would say that they laid the foundation for a Biblical Republic, the forerunner to the Kingdom of God on earth, the beginning stages, if you will, to the answer to the prayer of the ages, namely:

"Thy kingdom come. Thy will be done in earth, as it is in heaven."
Matthew 6:10, KJV

Dear reader let it be said that you joined in that effort by your prayers, faith and actions.

This work goes into the details by documenting how and why the control of money was used to steal that control from the American People and place it into the hands of *"unprincipled men."* This is one of the most important concepts for the American People to understand because, once you read this book, you will fully comprehend why the control of money of a country equals the control of said country. You will learn that this control was stolen via war, assassinations, secret proceeding and the like.

The authors make a point that all governments spring forth from law forms. Where do law forms come from you make ask? They make a compelling argument that law forms come from religion and therefore all governments have, as their foundation, a religion. Upon what religion was our country founded? Christianity. The authors do a great job of documenting this fact. Why is this important? Once you read the book you will understand that our Fore Fathers intended for their children to be educated to have a Biblical world view, and that without those foundational principles the continuance of the Republic could not be guaranteed. In other words, this is the very foundation of our civil and religious liberties.

So why should the American People care about our government?

First of all, in this country, the People are supposed to be the government themselves, unlike any other nation that ever existed. So, when someone quotes the verse about obey those who have the rule over you (higher powers) and try to say to blindly obey them then they do not understand our form of government. We are supposed to be "self-governing."

"Let every soul be subject unto the higher powers. For there is no power but of God: the powers that be are ordained of God."
Romans 13:1, KJV

Does that mean we are free to promote lawlessness? The short answer is no, especially since the People, themselves formed a binding covenant with God Almighty when we appealed to heaven for help in establishing liberty upon this land via the Declaration of Independence.

In short the American People made God the HIGHER POWER in this country, not any other entity; that includes our government. Our government officials are supposed to be the servants of the People, not the other way around.

Start getting involved. If you understand the implications of what I have just shared with you then you will begin to understand that it is not only your right to fix your own government, it is your duty.

Let there be liberty and justice for all.

> James Buchanan Geiger
> President
> Republic for the United States of America

FOREWORD

I am honored that David and Jean Hertler have asked me to write the Foreword to their book. David and Jean are dear friends that are in tune with God our Creator's revelation for the American People of our time. The book you are about to read is truth. It reveals knowledge from GOD our Creator that the People of a nation cannot enjoy true and complete life, liberty, and pursuit of happiness without following the moors of morality.

America is in serious trouble. The American People have been enslaved link by link by invisible chains forged by the very elected leaders who are sworn to serve in your best interest.

They routinely lie to the People by trying to convince them that they are free. The elected officials at the local, state, and national levels work tirelessly to steal your wealth, create unsustainable debt for you and your posterity and force you, against your will, into a socialist/communist society. The very agencies of these corporate governments are being weaponized against the American People. If you believe you still have freedom of speech, freedom of religion or the right to bear arms, try exercising those rights. When you do you will be declared an enemy of the State. Remember January 6th, 2020. A number of peaceful protestors exercising a constitutionally protected right, are today in prison. The current administration will not hesitate to prosecute anyone who speaks or acts out against their socialist policies. If this agenda is not stopped now, it will get much worse.

I have heard it expressed many times that voters only have a choice between the best of two evils on election day. I agree that this is often true. This is not the fault of political candidates. It is our own fault for not offering a better selection of candidates. The situation will not change until the American People who have knowledge and integrity campaign and are elected to political offices. We need statesmen and stateswomen to serve in these offices, not corrupt career politicians. If you are waiting for someone else to do this, you are out of time. The current leaders at all levels of our nation are now planning to install a socialist/communist government in America. The current leaders have no choice. They have already accepted the bribes, emoluments, and other benefits over the years and now they are obligated. To refuse to cooperate with the socialist/communist leaders who own them would lead to public exposure and possibly their deaths. Our enemies in times past were foreign but today they inhabit various public offices across America.

I am concerned that the corruption in our political offices will soon lead to societal collapse and civil war in America. A war will result in the loss of millions of American lives. I, nor any sane person wants to see that happen. Collapse and war can be avoided if the American People unite and replace these immoral career politicians with people who have knowledge and integrity. We must begin at the local government levels and progress to state and national levels. We have millions of Americans that are much more capable than these corrupt career politicians that have never done an honest day's work in their lives. If you know a capable person, ask them to become a candidate or maybe you can do it yourself. There are about 316 million Americans and less that one percent are elected and/or appointed to public offices. It is time to make our voices heard. Our battle will be won at the ballot box.

We must create Political Action Committees to support and raise funds for our political candidates in every county in America. Expose the public voting records of incumbent politicians. The public will vote them out of office once they discover what they are really supporting. Churches need to withdraw from the 501c3 incorporation so ministers and officers can once again get involved in electing men and women of good moral character to public office. As it stands today a minister can be arrested and criminally charged for supporting a political candidate. The assets of a 501c3 incorporated church may be seized by the Internal Revenue Service for violations of this rule. A pastor of a 501c3 church is obligated to spy on and report any member who may have a negative opinion of the government.

Our liberty cannot and will not be secured by immoral career politicians. It is up to us, the American People to act and act now. We have an obligation not only to our countrymen but also to God our Creator to take action to protect our God given liberties. We will be judged by our actions or by our failure to act.

Our Founding Fathers risked ALL to secure our freedoms. They only succeeded because of divine intervention by our Father in heaven. If we unite and act, He will also come to our aid. He will not do it without our participation. If you fail to act due to fear of retaliation or lack of concern you do not deserve to be called an American or share in the blessings when we win this struggle. You will be counted as our enemy. An angel of God cursed Meroz, the ancient tribes of Israel that failed to support their brothers in battle. May the angel of God curse all who fail to act to help those Americans that stand and defend their liberties.

As for me, I will give all to support those brave souls who stand with me. Will you be one of them as well. With my dying breath I will bless God my Creator and ask for God to bless America and her People.

Sincerely,

James Timothy Turner
Founding Father and Former President
Republic for the United States of America

FOREWORD

Several years ago, I had a vision of Jean writing three books for the education of the populace of the nation concerning the truth and background of the Republic for the United States of America. It was an exhausting task which created a great burden on Jean and David to research every available book and paper they could find yet proved to be some of the most important fundamental teachings the nation has ever seen. As they were recovering, I said to Jean there is one more book you are called to write on religion and its fundamental part of building America. It is a shame that the powers of darkness always try to counter the Word of God and HIS purposes. Once again Jean and David have captured the essence of the founding of a nation, what the enemy has done and what we must do as Sons and Daughters of GOD to correct the problems.

Our struggles have never been and will never be about the political form of republican or democratic process but rather about the Kingdom of God verses the kingdom of darkness. Kingdom thinking for the hope of our nation is critical for our survival. I have made that stand with several of our national leaders, lobbyists, and educators. It can be quite a debate yet at the same time without Kingdom thinkers expressing Spiritual, Emotional, Economic and Governmental Liberty we surrender our nation and future to the communistic form of thinking lead by luciferins with the intent of destroying all that we stand for as free people, one nation under God.

To quote a dear friend, Dr. Marlene McMillan, we must understand that "Divine Governmental Authority is divided into four parts, Individual Self Government, Home Government, Church Government, and Civil Government all which are subject to HIS accountability." Each are included in the 'Ecclesia' our LORD instructed us to walk in as the appropriate form of Governance.

I pray that you will soak the teaching of this work into your very being and gain an understanding of your history that you pass on to your children and children's children for generations to come. What we have needs to be guarded with our very lives otherwise future generations will only become slaves to societies bent on the very destruction of all mankind.

Dr. Wade King Butler
Secretary of State, Presiding Chaplain
Republic for the United States of America

FOREWORD

Understanding the Times in which we live, an analyzed approach to life... let's step back and look at curses and blessings.

In the light of the Laws of Nature, and of Nature's God which is the Divine revealed written Word known as the Holy Bible, is based the foundation for the following assessment.

We find ourselves here in early 2023 amid worldwide destruction. Manmade: bioweapons, self-inflicted famine, supply chain disruptions. The list goes on and on... I would call that a curse, so let's examine curses.

Let's examine what the Holy Scripture has to say about this. In Exodus 20:3 it states that "You shall have no other gods before me." In *Matthew 4:10* is stated, "You shall worship the Lord thy God, and him only shall you serve."

So, in our world today we find that we have as stated in the Declaration of Independence as the American Republic's law form, the Laws of Nature and of Nature's God of which are infallible, as having been secretly overlaid by the laws of man who have appointed themselves as our "ruling class." This usurpation of dominion by carnal man has caused a collision in the Heavens. I call that a curse.

What does the Holy Bible say about being doubleminded? Jesus declared, "No one can serve two masters. Either he will hate the one and love the other, or he will be devoted to the one and despise the other" (*Matthew 6:24*). Creator God and "the things of this world" (*1 John 2:15-17*) are of such opposite natures that it is impossible to love either one completely without hating the other (*James 4:4*).

What happened to the Old Testament Jews? They desired a king...oops! They got one...Saul! The Bible teaches that there's only one King... So, when they asked for man's kingdom to have rule over them, they regrettably got what they asked for. Again, the blessings and curses.

When our country was founded, it was established on being able to worship our God in heaven, according to the Holy Bible, and being ruled by the Laws of Nature and of Nature's God creating a jurisdiction of Civil and Religious Liberty. So when America moved away from that law form (common law), and came under men's dominion or rule of law known as corporate law or Uniform Commercial Code (UCC — codes and statutes) making it superior to God's Laws and the Laws of Nature and of Nature's God which includes His Divine revealed written Word, it has resulted in bringing us to the precipice of where we are today, and the curse is the result of that collision. The Organic Act of 1871, passed by Congress of that era, is the who and how our law form was changed.

At that same time, Congress also passed the Federal Dictionary Act of 1871 of which changed the meaning of words that came to be used in a law language owned by the Law Merchants (judges) in their secret and newly established law form. Once the States adopted the Uniform Commercial Code, this became the rule of law tied to the commercial/monetary system in exchange for "the good faith and credit of the American people" — by an organization of crooks.

In 2021, in this oppressive jurisdiction, the Church, God's People, were mandated by this unrighteous law form as to when, where, and how to worship. Blessings and curses….

Now that we have figured out and understand where we as a nation of People came from by the intent of our Founding Fathers to live in a jurisdiction of Civil and Religious Liberty, and then in the astounding realization of where we're currently at and how we got here, we need to know where to go to correct it and how to get there. Let's examine what the Holy Bible and the Laws of Nature and of Nature's God have to say. As a Child of God, and according to the Holy Bible also known as Nature's God, I expect to possess my Blessings.

Welcome to God's Solution for America.

God Bless Our Republic.

James E. Carpenter
Governor
Colorado free State

PREFACE

The god of this world, the prince of the air, blinded the first Adam's race to where even the second Adam's elect have fallen prey. There has been, and there is, a counterfeit king. This "angel of light" has used a "black pope" as a mediator throughout the long list of the papacy in Vatican to an unsuspecting people who thought they were worshipping and obeying the one true God, the *Creator of the universe*.

A counterfeit king, "monarch of monarchs," with two keys of the world's kingdom being spiritual and temporal, the papacy has his own disciples and evangelists to carry out his deeds of darkness through lies and deception. Lucifer has a secret militia that has been in place since shortly after the Light of the Gospel began to shine through a long period of *Dark Ages*, beginning with the *English Reformation* in the 14th century and then to William Tyndale's and Martin Luther's *European Reformation*, the start of Protestantism in 1517.

Lucifer, through his *Money Changers* and their "Illuminized" secret society agents, have infiltrated, built, and formed tyrannical governments throughout time. His lust for all-power has strategically pursued a *Counter-Reformation* and *One World Government*. The objective has included a Luciferian "New World Order," currently renamed as a "Global Reset," as Lucifer and his sons have ardently sought to continue dominion and domination through the next thousand years, attempting to thwart the coming *Millennial Reign* of Christ the King.

Satan has created a matrix of illusion, a Great Deception, by stripping God's absolutes and demoralizing the world. His objective and goals have been to usurp and destroy America, a people in nation who had covenanted with the *Creator of the universe*. The first Christian settlers in America, the Pilgrims and Puritans, arrived on this continent of the western hemisphere in the early 1600s, referring to this yet unknown wilderness as the "New World." *God's Solution for America ~ and the Nations of the World* exposes how the Kingdom of Darkness has been secretly usurping the heritage of those in covenant with Almighty God. Why was America the greatest nation in the world? Because the foundation of government was established on God's laws and the teachings of Christ. Our forefathers, the Pilgrims, created a Biblical culture; their culture was one of holiness and virtue which led to *Civil and Religious Liberty*.

We are now at the end of the Age and, as prophesied in the *Word of God*, the two kingdoms — the Kingdom of Light/Heaven and the Kingdom of Darkness/Hell, are in the final curtain call in the climax of the Great Drama. The goal of the Kingdom of Darkness, and its *New World Order* Democracy, is to exalt Satan's plan and agenda while at the same time in acceleration mode seeking to destroy the American Republic and that which gives glory to Yᵉhovah God, the Creator.

God's Solution for America ~ and the Nations of the World brings to light the only hope for America as well as the world. We find the recipe for hope in looking back in time through America's truthful history and to those who came to the *New World* to live out the scriptures of the Holy Bible they had learned from the *Protestant Reformation*. The journey back in time tracing America's heritage reveals a Birthright that projects a unique identity in "No King but King Jesus." With this identity America realizes a National Purpose which leads to a Prophetic Destiny which is yet to be fulfilled.

Where Christ came the first time for the Scepter, He will come the second time for the Birthright.

David and Jean Hertler

INTRODUCTION

Our forefathers, the Pilgrim Separatists, came to the *New World* on the North American continent seeking the freedom to live out the Holy Scriptures. They came to "the Lord's table in the wilderness" (*Hosea 2:14*) with an objective of seeking liberty of conscience while also endeavoring to advance the Gospel of the Kingdom of Christ and of God.[1] Christ taught us to pray to the Father "*Thy Kingdom come*," so the kingdom belongs to God the Father and the King is none other than Jesus, ("Yeshua" in the Hebrew language), the expressed image of the Father. It was in the *New World* where Biblical republicanism began, modeled after the ancient Hebrew Republic — God's government, providing a jurisdiction of Liberty for His people in covenant with Him and with each other.

When the Pilgrims arrived on the northeastern seaboard of America, on November 11, 1620 while yet aboard the *Mayflower,* they wrote the *Mayflower Compact*, a set of rules for self-governance for these settlers who would come to be known as the Plymouth Colony. On November 20, 1620 they set foot on land at Plymouth Rock (in what came to be Massachusetts). From their studies while living in Holland for the 12 years they were exiled from England, they brought along with them knowledge of *Civil and Religious Liberty*. They knew how to build a Biblical culture. They knew how to create a model Christian government. They lived seven days a week in a commonwealth, God's commonwealth.

They taught their children how to read from the Holy Bible. They also taught one another principles of Biblical virtue. They developed family virtue, church society virtue, and civil virtue. They enjoyed living with Biblical Godly character in being trustworthy, in being upright and prudent. They learned respectability, worth, honor, and integrity. They also practiced moral excellence, goodness, Godly character, and faith in God. They learned how to be kind and show love while practicing purity. It was nothing short of monumental that from living the principles they learned in studying the *Word of God*, they understood and knew they were righteous by faith in Christ. They learned about merit and charity. They also learned about faithfulness, justice, innocence, temperance, and honesty. All of these characteristics were pursued to become like Christ and to display His power.

They enjoyed learning about God's virtue not only in their families but in church fellowship. This wonderful God-fearing community enjoyed liberty and happiness because they made a covenant with God to become His people and live in His commonwealth. Righteousness exalted their community.

Because of a tyrannical-pagan monarch, tens of thousands of British subjects boarded ships from the *Old World* and came to "the city upon a hill" seeking *Civil and Religious Liberty* in America. The Puritans learned this Biblical model of government from the Pilgrims. Several covenants were made in commonwealth going forward that germinated into the covenant of the *Declaration of Independence*. The Founding Fathers,

---
[1] *Ephesians 5:5 ~ For this ye know, that no whoremonger, nor unclean person, nor covetous man, who is an idolater, hath any inheritance in the kingdom of Christ and of God.*
2 Peter 1:1 ~ For so an entrance shall be ministered unto you abundantly into the everlasting kingdom of our Lord and Saviour Jesus Christ.
Revelation 1:9 ~ I John, who also am your brother, and companion in tribulation, and in the kingdom and patience of Jesus Christ, was in the isle that is called Patmos, for the word of God, and for the testimony of Jesus Christ.

delegates of the People which had grown into 13 American Colonies, united together and crafted God's government, what they referred to as "the model government," to form a more perfect union with a law form based on "the Laws of Nature and of Nature's God." This describes the Creator's will in how His *cosmos* (universe) is to operate by the immutable laws of the sciences and the written *Word of God*, the Holy Bible, of which governs this jurisdiction of Liberty, the Kingdom of Heaven on earth.

Matthew 6:9-10 ~ After this manner therefore pray ye: Our Father which art in heaven, Hallowed be thy name. Thy kingdom come, Thy will be done in earth, as it is in heaven.

It had been 156 years from the arrival of the Pilgrims and then the Puritans when their descendants, the Founding Fathers, wrote the *Declaration of Independence* based on the *Laws of Nature and of Nature's God*. This government enjoyed a foundation based on Biblical Christianity. Creator God was invoked four times in the *Declaration*. Going forward in time, there was much study in the book of *Deuteronomy* that bore fruit in 1787 when the *Constitution for the united States* was framed to answer the *Declaration of Independence* and George Washington became the first President under this *Constitution* on April 30, 1789. America became the greatest nation in the world, "a light to the nations" *(Isaiah 49:6; 42:6-8)*, up until the assassination of President Abraham Lincoln in 1865.

The downfall of America spiraled under the evil leading of President Andrew Johnson (1865-1869), Lincoln's successor, who opened the gateway to bring in the worshippers of Satan through *Illuminized Freemasonry* and their masters, the International Bankers (namely, the House of Rothschild), who align with what the Holy Bible refers to as the "Money Changers."[2]

The ultimate controlling body that runs the world at the top remain behind the scene as the *High Priests of the Luciferian Creed*. They work in darkness from the *Synagogue of Satan* while their agenturs occupy high positions within governmental structures orchestrating policy and manipulating governments and corporations throughout the world toward their goal of domination in a *One World Government-New World Order*.

Having secreted the American Republic into dormancy when the nation was war-torn, the Freemasons established a Corporate Democracy and wickedness ruled our country while masquerading as the American Republic in this heinous and great deception. Going off course from the original *Constitution* and *Bill of Rights*, managing to hide the original *Thirteenth Article of Amendment*,[3] those Amendments passed by the (*de facto*[4]) Corporate Congress thereafter, and of which also violate the covenant of the *Declaration of*

---

[2] *John 2:14-16 ~ 14 And found in the temple those that sold oxen and sheep and doves, and the <u>changers of money</u> sitting: 15 And when he had made a scourge of small cords, he drove them all out of the temple, and the sheep, and the oxen; and poured out the changers' money, and overthrew the tables; 16 And said unto them that sold doves, Take these things hence; make not my Father's house an house of merchandise.*

[3] The Original Thirteenth Article of Amendment To The Constitution For The United States:
   "If any citizen of the United States shall accept, claim, receive, or retain any <u>title of nobility or honour</u>, or shall without the consent of Congress, accept and retain any present, pension, office, or emolument of any kind whatever, from any emperor, king, prince, or foreign power, <u>such person shall cease to be a citizen of the United States, and shall be incapable of holding any office of trust or profit under them, or either of them</u>." [Emphasis added]
   Sourced from: www.amendment-13.org [Recovered through Wayback Machine website, http://web.archive.org/web/20220903022952/http://www.amendment-13.org/index.html]

[4] *Noah Webster's First Edition of An American Dictionary of the English Language, 1828:*

Independence, were instituted by these Luciferians as they worked together as a brotherhood through their secret societies to destroy the government of Liberty and the Christian religion from which the American Republic was derived.[5]

Abraham Lincoln was elected President of the United States in November 1860. By the pernicious design of the *Rulers of Evil* in the international banking cartel and their pawns in the secret occult societies, division and growing tension had surmounted in the United States Congress between the Northern and Southern (*Slave Power*) congressmen. Before Lincoln was inaugurated on March 4, 1861, eleven Southern States (so-called) seceded from the Union and the *War Between the States* was fomented on April 9, 1861.

Wars are expensive and throughout recorded history have proven to be a chief tool of the international *Money-Lenders*, the banking elite, of which we refer to as the *Money Changers,* in their goal of gaining control through legalized usury and other tactics of manipulation that include deception and bribes.[6]

The system of dealing in money is the medium of exchange for labor and commodities of a country. When money is loaned for interest or usury or for increase, it is thereby taken out of its normal, natural use as a medium of exchange and becomes a commodity to be trafficked in and a profit made from it, making a slave of it, to gain an unearned profit for its owner, making its possession desirable, and attractive in an unnatural way.[7] "*Babylonian Black Money-Magick*" is the secret art of making money from nothing also using the power of pernicious usury to accumulate interest.[8]

Our Founding Fathers well-understood the critical nature in retaining Liberty in a nation included its own control of its medium of exchange and volume of money in circulation and made provision for its security when framing the new *Constitution* in 1787. *Article 1, Section 8, Clause 5* stipulates,

> "*The CONGRESS shall have power to … coin money [and] regulate the value thereof….*" [Emphasis added]

Founding Father, author of the *Declaration of Independence*, and third President of the United States, Thomas Jefferson (1743-1826) stated,

> "*I sincerely believe… that [private] banking establishments are more dangerous than standing armies; & that the principle of spending money [debt] to be paid by posterity, under the name of funding, is but swindling futurity on a large scale.*"[9]

Jefferson also stated,

"*De facto:* [L.] actually; in fact; existing; as a king *de facto*, distinguished from a king *de jure,* or by right.
[5] William Guy Carr, *Pawns In the Game, (*Willowdale, Ontario: Federation of Christian Laymen, 3rd ed., 1958) Ch 3
[6] Carr, *Pawns in the Game,* Intro
[7] Publius Melton Butler, Dr. R. E. Search, *Lincoln: Money Martyred,* (Seattle: Lincoln Publishing Company, 1935), 12
[8] Preston James, Mike Harris, "Hidden History of the Incredibly Evil Khazarian Mafia," March 11, 2015, https://geopolitics.co/2015/03/11/hidden-history-of-the-incredibly-evil-khazarian-mafia/
[9] Thomas Jefferson's letter to John Taylor, 28 May 1816, https://founders.archives.gov/documents/Jefferson/03-10-02-0053

> *"Bank-paper [paper money issued by private banks without honest value] must be suppressed, and the circulating medium must be restored to the nation [the People] to whom it belongs.[10]"*

James Madison (1751-1836) was known as the "Chief Architect of the Constitution" and was the fourth President of the United States. He was also a member of the First U.S. Congress, where he introduced the *Bill of Rights*. James Madison said,

> *"History records that the money changers have used every form of abuse, intrigue, deceit, and violent means possible to maintain their control over governments by controlling money and its issuance."*[11]

Just like our Founding Fathers, Lincoln understood the importance of money as a key element in control and power of a nation. The power of issue and control of the value and volume of money and credit is considered the life blood of a country.[12]

In his State of the Union Address before Congress on December 3, 1861, Abraham Lincoln responded to the bankers' argument that the people could not be trusted with their constitutional power and the political, monetary system of free enterprise our Founding Fathers conceived by saying:

> *"No men living are more worthy to be trusted than those who toil up from poverty – none less inclined to take or touch aught which they have not honestly earned. Let them beware of surrendering the political power which they already possess which if surrendered will surely be used to close the door of advancement against such as they and fix new disabilities upon them till all liberty shall be lost."*[13]

Lincoln and his Secretary of the Treasury, Salmon P. Chase, went to the New York bankers and applied for loans in order that the Federal Government had the means to fund the war. The bankers were willing to lend it but only under terms of a staggering 24 to 36 percent interest, an amount that is equivalent to extortion and would bankrupt the North.

Lincoln consulted a trusted friend, Colonel Dick Taylor of Chicago and asked for advice. In what may indeed be the best piece of advice ever given to a President, Colonel Taylor responded that the solution was easy; the Union had the power under the *Constitution* to solve its financing problem by printing its money as a sovereign government. Colonel Taylor advised President Lincoln to *"just get Congress to pass a bill authorizing the printing of full legal tender treasury notes or greenbacks and pay your soldiers with them and go ahead and win your war with them also."*[14]

Lincoln followed Colonel Taylor's advice and funded the war by printing paper notes backed by the credit of the government. These legal-tender U.S. Notes or "Greenbacks" represented receipts for labor and goods delivered to the United States. They were paid to soldiers and suppliers and were exchangeable for goods

---

[10] Thomas Jefferson'a letter to John Wayles Eppes, 11 September 1813, https://founders.archives.gov/documents/Jefferson/03-06-02-0388

[11] TheMoneyMasters.com, "Famous Quotations on Banking," (accessed 12/21/2013), http://www.themoneymasters.com/the-money-masters/famous-quotations-on-banking/

[12] Butler, Search, *Lincoln Money Martyred*, 9, 11, 110, 111

[13] Abraham Lincoln: "First Annual Message," December 3, 1861. Online by Gerhard Peters and John T. Woolley, The American Presidency Project. Accessed September 2, 2014, http://www.presidency.ucsb.edu/ws/?pid=29502

[14] Butler, Search, *Lincoln Money Martyred*, 44-45

and services of a value equivalent to their service to the community. The Greenbacks aided the Union not only in winning the war but in funding a period of unprecedented economic expansion.

Lincoln's government was blessed in creating the greatest industrial giant the world had yet seen. The steel industry was launched, a continental railroad system was created, a new era of farm machinery and inexpensive tools were promoted, free higher education was established, government support was provided to all branches of science, the Bureau of Mines was organized, and labor productivity was increased by 50 to 75 percent.

The Greenback was not the only currency used to fund these achievements; but they could not have been accomplished without it, and they could not have been accomplished on money borrowed at the outrageous rates of interest/usury the bankers were attempting to extort from the North.[15]

President Lincoln later wrote Colonel Taylor to express gratitude and stated that following through on his advice resulted in giving *"the people of this Republic the greatest blessing they every had – their own paper money to pay their own debts."*[16]

*A $1 Legal Tender Note
from the Series 1862-1863 greenback issue* [17]
Engraved signatures of Lucius E. Chittenden (Register of the Treasury) and Francis E. Spinner (Treasurer of the United States)

President Lincoln explained his monetary policy just before the close of the Civil War in 1865:

> *"…The government should create, issue, and circulate all the currency and credit needed to satisfy the spending power of the government and the buying power of the consumers. The privilege of creating and issuing money is not only the supreme prerogative of government, but it is the government's greatest creative opportunity. By the adoption of these principles the long felt want for a uniform medium will be satisfied. The taxpayers will be saved immense sums of interest, discounts, and exchanges. The financing of all public enterprise, the maintenance of stable government and ordered progress, and the conduct of the Treasury will become matters of practical administration. The people can and will be furnished with a currency as safe as their own government. Money will cease to be master and become the servant of humanity…."*[18]

Lincoln succeeded in restoring the government's power to issue the national currency, but his revolutionary monetary policy was vehemently opposed by powerful forces. The threat to "established interests"

---

[15] Ellen Hodgson Brown, J.D., "Revive Lincoln's Monetary Policy: an Open Letter to President Obama," April 8, 2009, http://www.webofdebt.com/articles/lincoln_obama.php
[16] Butler, Search, *Lincoln Money Martyred*, 46
[17] *Wikimedia Commons*, s.v. "US-$1-LT-1862-Fr-16c.jpg," This work is in the public domain
[18] Butler, Search, *Lincoln Money Martyred*, 47

stimulated an editorial in *The London Times* explaining the (Rothschild's privately owned) Bank of England's attitude towards it:

> *"If this mischievous financial policy which has had its origin in the North American Republic [greenback issue of money] during the late [civil] war should become indurated down to a fixture, then that Government will furnish its own money without cost. It will pay off its debts and be without debts. It will have all the money necessary to carry on its commerce. It will become prosperous beyond precedent in the history of the world. The brains and wealth of all countries will go to North America. That government must be destroyed or it will destroy every monarchy [of the money lenders] on the globe."* [19] [Emphasis added]

In order to cast discredit on the Greenbacks, in February 1862, the *Money Barons* "persuaded" Congress to vote in favor of the "Exception Clause" which stipulated that the Greenbacks could not be used to pay the interest on the national debt, nor to pay taxes, excises, or import duties. Then in 1863 having financed the election of enough compromised Senators and Representatives, the *Money Changers* succeeded in getting Congress to revoke the Greenback Law and instead enact the *National Banking Act* which ensured that money would be issued as interest-bearing by privately-owned banks.

The *National Banking Act* also stipulated that the Greenbacks should be retired from circulation as soon as they came back to the Treasury in payment of taxes. Lincoln heatedly protested though his most urgent objective was to win the war and save the Union of States of which obligated him to put off the banking battle until after the war when he could put his energy into the challenge of the bankers, the *Money Changers*. President Lincoln said that he,

> *"...could not fight two wars at the same time, the Confederates at the front and the bankers in the rear, and of the two the Confederates were the more honorable."*[20]

In 1864, Lincoln was re-elected to a second term as President, and he made it very clear that he would attack the power of the bankers once the war was over. The *Civil War* ended on April 9, 1865, and Lincoln was assassinated five days later. The *Money Changers* used their *Babylonian Black Money-Magick* as they always do by means of restriction of credit organized by the banks and also reducing the volume of currency in circulation which caused hardship for the American People along with massive numbers of business failures into the tens of thousands.

Had Lincoln's monetary policy been implemented, it would have ushered in a worldwide economic renewal. Because he "defied" the bankers in proposing to print constitutional interest-free money to pay for the war debt, Lincoln was assassinated a few weeks after his monetary policy was introduced and before he could complete his *Reconstruction Plan* to reestablish constitutional government in a restored Republic, in a reconciled Union of States.

From then on there were no further issues of Greenbacks, and they were eventually removed from circulation. Unbeknownst to the American People, the "government" continued to operate but under the

---

[19] Ibid. 47
[20] Ibid. 49

private authority dictate of an "oligarch" of creditor financiers — also known as *"cunning, ambitious, and unprincipled men."*[21]

In just a few decades, in 1913-1914, the *Money Barons* managed to manipulate their way into controlling position by creating and establishing the Federal Reserve, a privately-owned central bank. By means of their agenturs, their pawns in the Luciferian secret societies, bribery of compromised and traitorous members of Congress (and murder when they deem necessary), their *Babylonian Black Money-Magick* manifested through printing Federal Reserve Notes (dollar bills) and loaning them to the government of which the American People are responsible for payment <u>with interest</u>. The government has been submerged in debt that has grown exponentially ever since, until it is now reported an un-repayable amount in the quadrillions.[22]

Proverbs 22:7 ~ The rich ruleth over the poor, and the borrower is servant to the lender.

According to a 2013 study conducted by a university economics professor, the (*de facto*[23]) Federal Government had accumulated over $70 trillion in unreported debt, an amount nearly six times the declared figure.[24] The miscalculation of what it owed was derived by leaving out certain unfunded liabilities that include government loan guarantees, deposit insurance, and actions taken by the Federal Reserve Banking System as well as the cost of other government trust funds. Factoring in those figures brings the total amount the government owed at that time in 2013 to a staggering $70 trillion.[25]

The debt has continued to grow into the quadrillions of dollars and insolvency looms in the fraudulent financial system as well as the Corporate (all-capital-letter business name) THE UNITED STATES OF AMERICA, INC. (Incorp Delaware Stock Co.).[26] which has masqueraded as the American Republic since 1781. Disguises, masquerading, make-believe, and confusion are other chief tools used by the *Illuminatists* in their love of money, lust for power, and objective to bring about their secret plans for a Luciferian *One World Governmennt-New World Order*.[27] [28]

---

[21] *George Washington's Farewell Address to the People of the United States,* September 17, 1796, Archiving Early America as sourced from *The Independent Chronicle,* September 26, 1796, accessed November 1, 2014,
http://www.earlyamerica.com/milestone-events/george-washingtons-farewell-address-full-text/
President George Washington, gave warning in his *Farewell Address* to the People of the United States, 1796:
"...**cunning, ambitious, and unprincipled men** will be enabled to subvert the power of the people, and to usurp for themselves the reins of government; destroying afterwards the very engines which have lifted them to unjust dominion... The spirit of encroachment tends to consolidate the powers of all the departments in one, and thus to create, whatever the form of government, a real despotism..." [Emphasis added]

[22] Melissa Melton, "HOLY SH*T: U.S. National Debt Has Officially Hit $18 Trillion," December 8, 2014,
http://www.dcclothesline.com/2014/12/08/holy-sht-u-s-national-debt-officially-hit-18-trillion/

[23] *Noah Webster's First Edition of An American Dictionary of the English Language,* 1828:
"*De facto*: [L.] actually; in fact; existing; as a king *de facto,* distinguished from a king *de jure,* or by right.

[24] Robert Bridge, "US debt six times greater than declared – study," *RT News,* August 6, 2013 http://rt.com/usa/us-debt-study-hamilton-economy-103/

[25] "California economist says real US debt $70 trillion," August 15, 2013, *Fox News,*
http://www.foxnews.com/politics/2013/08/15/california-economist-says-real-us-debt-70-trillion-not-16-trillion-government/

[26] Delaware.gov, Department of State: Division of Corporations: Entity Details, "Entity Name: THE UNITED STATES OF AMERICA, INC," File Number 4525682, https://delecorp.delaware.gov/tin/controller

[27] Butler, Search, *Money Martyred,* 34, 37, 50, 82, 99, 103

[28] Carr, *Pawns in the Game,* Intro

"For nearly a century, Lincoln's statue at the Lincoln Memorial has gazed out pensively across the reflecting pool toward the Federal Reserve building, as if pondering what the bankers had wrought since his death and how to remedy it." [29]

So, we now have understanding that it was in the *Reconstruction Era* of the Civil War years when great deception was perpetrated on the American People as these *"cunning, ambitious, and unprincipled men"* [30] secreted the American Republic and God's government on the earth into dormancy while a Corporate Democracy, "the devil's own government," [31] proceeded forward in great masquerade.

2 Corinthians 11:14 ~ And no marvel; for Satan himself is transformed into an angel of light.

According to former intelligence agent of the British MI-6, researcher, historian, author, and lecturer, Dr. John Coleman, the *Committee of 300* was established early in the 18th century although it did not take on its present form until around 1897 (when the China opium trade was legalized).[32] The *Committee of 300* are the ultimate controlling body that runs the world and are the inheritors of the modern-day *Illuminati*. They occupy high positions within the (*de facto*) governmental structure and at the same time often hold several offices in various organizations and corporations who are dedicated to the goal of *One World Government*.[33]

Son of the founder of the mammoth German electrical engineering company (AEG), industrialist, Socialist politican, writer and financial advisor to the Kaiser of Germany as well as to the Rothschilds, Walther Rathenau (1867-1922) writing in the Wiener Press (Dec. 24, 1921) said,

> *"Only 300 men, each of whom knows all others govern the fate of Europe. They select their successors from their own entourage. These men have the means in their hands of putting an end to the form of State which they find unreasonable."* [34] [35]

Exactly six months after publication, Rathenau was assassinated.

William Guy Carr (1895-1959) was a Canadian Naval Commanding Officer who served in WWI and WWII in a distinguished career that included the Canadian Intelligence Service. He was also an author and lecturer that presented from documented evidence the fact that there are two *Illuminati* councils above the *Committee of 300*. Carr exposed the executive body of *The Council of Thirty Three*, and above them *The Supreme*

---

[29] Brown, "Revive Lincoln's Monetary Policy"
[30] President George Washington, gave warning in his *Farewell Address* to the People of the United States, 1796:
   "...**cunning, ambitious, and unprincipled men** will be enabled to subvert the power of the people, and to usurp for themselves the reins of government; destroying afterwards the very engines which have lifted them to unjust dominion... The spirit of encroachment tends to consolidate the powers of all the departments in one, and thus to create, whatever the form of government, a real despotism..." [Emphasis added]
[31] Dr. Benjamin Rush, quote "*A simple democracy, or an unbalanced republic, is one of the greatest of evils. I think with Dr. Zubly that 'a democracy (with only one branch) is the Devil's own government.*'" The Founders' Constitution, Volume 1, Chapter 4, Document 30, http://press-pubs.uchicago.edu/founders/documents/v1ch4s30.html, The University of Chicago Press; Letters of Benjamin Rush. Edited by L. H. Butterfield. 2 vols. Memoirs of the American Philosophical Society, vol. 30, parts 1 and 2. Princeton: Princeton University Press, for the American Philosophical Society, 1951.
[32] Dr. John Coleman, *The Conspirators' Hierarchy: The Committee of 300,* (WIR, 4th ed, Jan 1, 1997) 51
[33] Ibid., Intro
[34] Carr, *Pawns in the Game,* Ch 16, endnote 6
[35] Wes Penre, "The Black Nobility," Illuminati-News.com, Jan 13, 2004, https://www.bibliotecapleyades.net/sociopolitica/esp_sociopol_blacknobil01.htm

Council of Thirteen. These *High Priests of the Luciferian Creed* that direct the *Synagugue of Satan* at the top work from darkness behind the scenes. They form an association of brothers in all points of the globe working in unison as a powerful force dedicated to the goal of a *One World Government* and when the time is ripe at the *End of the Age*, they seek to crown their dark prince, the *god of this world*,[36] the *son of perdition* as the *New World Order's* ruling Monarch and totalitarian dictator. We can perceive such an individual to describe antichrist.[37] [38]

In the *Holy Scriptures*, Christ referred to these immoral men as being of *the Synagogue of Satan*.

Revelation 2:9 ~ I know thy works, and tribulation, and poverty, (but thou art rich) and I know the blasphemy of them which say they are Jews, and are not, but are the synagogue of Satan. [Emphasis added]

Revelation 3:9 ~ Behold, I will make them of the synagogue of Satan, which say they are Jews, and are not, but do lie; behold, I will make them to come and worship before thy feet, and to know that I have loved thee. [Emphasis added]

It was in 2010, when enlightened men and women led by God's Holy Spirit served notice on the (*de facto*) Corporate UNITED STATES as well as the nations and organizations of the world as stipulated in the *Law of Nations*, that the *de jure*[39] American Republic has been restored in law. As prophesied in the *Word of God*, it is time for the restoration of all things (*Acts 3:20-21*), and Dominion is to transfer to the saints of the Most High (*Daniel 7:27*).

Acts 3:20-21 ~ And he shall send Jesus Christ, which before was preached unto you: Whom the heaven must receive until the times of restitution of all things, which God hath spoken by the mouth of all his holy prophets since the world began.

Daniel 7:27 ~ And the kingdom and dominion, and the greatness of the kingdom under the whole heaven, shall be given to the people of the saints of the most High, whose kingdom is an everlasting kingdom, and all dominions shall serve and obey him.

As pointed out in the fourth chapter, "Worshipers of Satan Setup Their Corporate Democracy," much corruption was crafted and put into play with an objective to demoralize America. America lost her liberty, virtue, and happiness because wickedness ruled a limping, bleeding America. *God's Solution for America* is to bring politics, "the divine science of [God's] government,"[40] back in the pulpit and to stand up the Republic "commonwealth" to bring back His government based on Biblical Christianity as it had been for the first three centuries of this nation. It is not religious, it is governmental.

Isaiah 33:22 ~ For the Lord is our judge [Judicial], the Lord is our lawgiver [Legislature], the Lord is our king [Executive]; he will save us. [Emphasis added]

---

[36] *2 Corinthians 4:4 ~ In whom the god of this world hath blinded the minds of them which believe not, lest the light of the glorious gospel of Christ, who is the image of God, should shine unto them.*
[37] *2 Thessalonians 2:3 ~ Let no man deceive you by any means: for that day shall not come, except there come a falling away first, and that man of sin be revealed, the son of perdition;*
[38] Carr, *Pawns in the Game*, Intro
[39] *Webster's 1913 Dictionary*: "*De jure*: By right; of right; by law; - often opposed to *de facto*"
[40] John Adams, *Thoughts on Government: applicable to The Present State of the American Colonies* (Philadelphia: John Dunlop, 1776)

VIRTUE must be practiced in America to once again become "a city on a hill" (*Matthew 5:14*) as Puritan leader John Winthrop preached before the Massachusetts Bay colonists in 1630 — and so that "We the People" will be able to enjoy liberty and happiness because *Civil and Religious Liberty* is restored! This is the means for America to be healed and enabled to stand right-side up, as righteousness will exalt America when the people practice virtue, and by cause-to-effect, result in the enjoyment of *Civil and Religious Liberty*! Let's do it God's way! This is God's Solution for America!

Matthew 5:14 ~ Ye are the light of the world. A city that is set on an hill cannot be hid.

In this modern era, the Church wonders why their prayer isn't answered. The reason why is found in the *Word of God* precisely at *Isaiah chapters 58 and 59*. The Church hasn't done its civil duty of Liberty as well as caring for others, which is described in these scriptures as Justice. When the Church obeys the *Word of God* and does their civil duty, then the Lord will answer — and He will intervene and reward His people for their obedience in fulfilling this duty. His people will restore what was ruined throughout the generations and repair the breach in order to renew the national covenant with Creator God.

The Sabbath observance of God's holy day is what separated the people of God from other peoples. We must acknowledge and understand that observing the Sabbath with delight is a cause of our heritage. America must once again heed the ordinances of God as had been practiced for centuries in this nation.

The "high places" in the scriptures refers to government — He will reward us with His government and laws as was given to our forefathers allowing us to live in the jurisdiction of Liberty — both Civil and Religious, which are inseparable.

Though sin in the nation has separated us from the blessings of obedience (*Deuteronomy 28:1-14*), we have hope that *Divine Providence* will once again intervene. Because His people have not called for justice and truth, they are in a dangerous place. It's a place lacking safety and is full of anarchy and destruction. There is no peace or right judgment because of ignorance and lack of knowledge. For this reason there is no justice and though we have waited and yearned for it, the land has progressed into gross darkness. We feel despair as sin abounds and we're separated as apostate from the goodness of God.

Hosea 4:6 ~ My people are destroyed for lack of knowledge: because thou hast rejected knowledge, I will also reject thee, that thou shalt be no priest to me: seeing thou hast forgotten the law of thy God, I will also forget thy children.

The days are evil because there is no judgment and justice. Truth has been thwarted in our nation and so there cannot be equity in law pertaining to the scales of justice. Those who love God and have separated themselves unto Him in following His Word have become prey for the wicked. God watches over His beloved with a jealous eye so at a point in time when He determines, He will intervene with Divine vengeance and recompense causing His enemies to fear Him with trepidation — and when they retaliate, the Spirit of the Lord will battle them with fury. God will redeem those who repent and turn to Him. They will enter into His covenant and His Spirit will be on them as His Word is in them by a renewed mind. As they speak His Word it will be done for them and their offspring forever. His Word will not return void.

Our Founding Fathers were well studied in world history and were certainly familiar with the writings of Cicero. Marcus Tullius Cicero (106 BC - 43 BC) was a Roman statesman, orator, lawyer and philosopher.

Cicero is considered one of Rome's greatest orators and his influence on the Latin language was immense in style even in European languages up to the 19th century. Cicero comprehended the magnificence of the first great commandment to love, respect, and obey the all-wise Creator. He believed that for a nation to prosper it must put God in first place. He fixed this precept in proper perspective by saying that God's law is "right reason." When perfectly understood it is called "wisdom." When applied by government in regulating human relations it is called "justice." When people come together and unite in a covenant or compact under this law, they become a true "commonwealth," and since they intend to administer their affairs under God's law, they belong to His commonwealth.

Isaiah 58:6 ~ Is not this the fast that I have chosen? to loose the bands of wickedness, to undo the heavy burdens, and to let the oppressed go free, and that ye break every yoke?"

Those who act upon this type of fast that God has chosen in restoring the Kingdom government and its ordinances of justice in caring for the people in the nation will be known as and called "the repairer of the breach," "the re-inhabitation," "the restorer of the original paths to dwell" in the Kingdom of God on earth under His covenant protection and provision (*Isaiah 58:12*).

Isaiah 58:12 ~ And they that shall be of thee shall build the old waste places: thou shalt raise up the foundations of many generations; and thou shalt be called, The repairer of the breach, The restorer of paths to dwell in.

Daniel 2:44 ~ And in the days of these kings [in the end times of the Last Days] shall the God of heaven set up a kingdom, which shall never be destroyed: and the kingdom shall not be left to other people, but it shall break in pieces and consume all these kingdoms, and it shall stand for ever. [Emphasis added]

Daniel 7:18 ~ But the saints of the most High shall take the kingdom, and possess the kingdom for ever, even for ever and ever.

Daniel 7:22 ~ Until the Ancient of days came, and judgment was given to the saints of the most High; and the time came that the saints possessed the kingdom.

Daniel 7:27 ~ And the kingdom and dominion, and the greatness of the kingdom under the whole heaven, shall be given to the people of the saints of the most High, whose kingdom is an everlasting kingdom, and all dominions shall serve and obey him.

Please read *Isaiah chapter 59*. Here Isaiah speaks of the remnant, or those within the nation of the Kingdom who are enlightened to understand that the Kingdom's government was set aside resulting in its demise (government and law: transfer of sovereignty) and destruction (dormancy). And about how this remnant will restore the original Kingdom government that had been lost because of neglecting God's laws, His government jurisdiction made through Covenant with Him.

Early Americans viewed themselves as the New Covenant people of God and identified themselves in His Word.

Psalm 125:1-2 ~ ¹ They that trust in the Lord shall be as mount Zion, which cannot be removed, but abideth for ever. ² As the mountains are round about Jerusalem, so the Lord is round about his people from henceforth even for ever.

Early Americans believed that this new nation was to be the fulfillment of *Isaiah 2:2-3* and their intention was to set up a political and social order that would be an example of righteous laws so the other nations of the world could also have God's moral government and reside in His jurisdiction of Liberty.[41]

Isaiah 2:2-3 ~ 2 And it shall come to pass <u>in the last days</u>, that the mountain [i.e., kingdom government] of the Lord's house shall be established in the top of the mountains, and shall be exalted above the hills [lesser kingdoms]; and all nations shall flow unto it. 3 And many people shall go and say, Come ye, and let us go up to the mountain of the Lord, to the house of the God of Jacob; and he will teach us of his ways, and we will walk in his paths: for out of Zion shall go forth the law, and the word of the Lord from [New] Jerusalem. [Emphasis added]

Prophecy is simply history that has not yet happened. What is described in the prophetic *Word of God* points to <u>now</u> being the time. Let us receive the knowledge of our true history, our heritage, our identity as a nation of people, our birthright, and proceed forward in the restoration of God's American Republic. Then we will fulfill our destiny in pointing the way for the other nations of the world to expand the Kingdom of Christ and of God and live in the jurisdiction of Liberty.

It was after the Continental Congress voted for independence and before the signing of the *Declaration of Independence* occurred when Samuel Adams, "Father of the American Revolution" said,

> *"We have this day restored the Sovereign, to whom alone men ought to be obedient. He reigns in Heaven, and with a propitious eye beholds his subjects assuming that freedom of thought and dignity of self-direction [self-government] which he bestowed on them. From the rising to the setting sun, may his kingdom come."*[42]
>
> [Emphasis added]

Luke 19:13b ~ Occupy till I come.

This book is not about us at all. We are vessels of the Lord. This book was written with great meekness because this is God's solution for America. It is also His solution for the nations of the world. Great truths and documented evidence have been revealed and shown to us so that we can write about them and share with others the knowledge of our true history and how to reverse the curse and bring true knowledge to the People. This is a spiritual revolution!

---

[41] Dr. Stephen Jones, *The Seven Churches*, "Chapter 7: The Church of Philadelphia (1776-1914 A.D.)," (Fridley: God's Kingdom Ministries, 1997 Rev. 2004) 66
[42] Samuel Adams, "American Independence," August 1, 1776, *Masterpieces of American Eloquence*, (New York: The Christian Herald, 1900) 24

God's Solution for America

~ and the Nations of the World ~

This is a Spiritual Revolution!

Chapter One

The American Republic

Foundational Principles and Insight
with an Accurate Historical Outlook on its Founding and Objective

Liberty is the object and life of all republican (commonwealth) governments, as it encompasses the jurisdiction of Christ's government on earth always in accord with the Creator's laws. First, Christ set His people free from bondage of sin and guilt which had kept them slaves.[43] Internal liberty, accomplished through faith in Christ's atoning death and victorious ascension, made men free. This internal liberty came to external manifestation in society and culture, and it was the *Word of God* unleashed in the hands of the individual that would, in time, liberate every area of life both internal and external. This was Christ's mission. [44][45]

Dr. Benjamin Rush, 1783[46]

Dr. Benjamin Rush (1745-1813) was a signer of the *Declaration of Independence*, a physician, "father of public schools" and a principal promoter of the American Sunday School Union. He also served as the Surgeon General of the Continental Army, helped to write the Pennsylvania constitution, and was the treasurer of the U.S. Mint. In 1786, Dr. Rush established the first free medical clinic and later helped found the first American anti-slavery society.[47] In 1798, after the adoption of the *Constitution for the United States*,[48] he declared:

---

[43] *John 8:32-36 ~ 32 And ye shall know the truth, and the truth shall make you free. 33 They answered him, We be Abraham's seed, and were never in bondage to any man: how sayest thou, Ye shall be made free? 34 Jesus answered them, Verily, verily, I say unto you, Whosoever committeth sin is the servant of sin. 35 And the servant abideth not in the house for ever: but the Son abideth ever. 36 If the Son therefore shall make you free, ye shall be free indeed.*

[44] *Luke 4:18 ~ The Spirit of the Lord is upon me, because he hath anointed me to preach the gospel to the poor; he hath sent me to heal the brokenhearted, to preach deliverance to the captives, and recovering of sight to the blind, to set at liberty them that are bruised,*

[45] Marshall Foster, Mary Elaine Swanson, *The American Covenant: The Untold Story, (Thousand Oaks: The Mayflower Institute, 1992)* 52, 81

[46] Wikimedia, s.v., Benjamin Rush Painting by Peale 1783, This work is in the public domain

[47] William J. Federer, America's *God and Country Encyclopedia of Quotations,* "Benjamin Rush," (Coppell: FAME Publishing, Inc., 1994) 543

[48] Clarification of **"of"** and **"for"** in referencing our *Constitution* correctly and considering the Corporate UNITED STATES' version of the name used for its constitution: In review of the use of the words by our Founding Fathers in the Founding Documents, it was concluded that the two are the same. Reasoning – the *Constitution **for** the United States* became the *Constitution **of** the United States* upon adoption by the several States. In other words, it was put up **"for"** adoption, but once it was adopted became ours, **"of."** In further, the First Congress of the *Republic for the United States of America* claimed ownership of all forms of our nation's name – both "of" and "for" in the re-inhabiting document, *Declaration of Sovereign Intent (c2010)*. In effort to dispel confusion and to aid the reader the word "for" is used throughout this work. Where original *de jure* documents use the word "of" and are quoted in this work, the original citing is quoted as lawfully recorded in government archives.

> *"[T]he only foundation for a useful education in a republic is to be laid in religion. Without this there can be no virtue, and without virtue there can be no liberty, and <u>liberty is the object and life of all republican governments</u>... But the religion I mean to recommend in this place, is <u>the religion of Jesus Christ</u>."* [49]
> [Emphasis added]

Historical records tell the story throughout time of men who sought domination over others believing they were bestowed of Creator God to be His ruling agents in the temporal world. In this doctrine known as the *Divine Right of Kings*, a nation of people were often in the hands and at the mercies of despotic totalitarian rulers who held a pagan idea of man and government.[50]

When Christ made the way for His Kingdom on earth, those who by faith entered this jurisdiction came to understand that the Kingdom of Heaven and the Kingdom of God are translated from Greek phrases that are referring to the right to be ruled by God rather than ruled by men who think they are gods.[51] The American story is one such story of which is imperative to know and comprehend in order to capture her National Purpose and Prophetic Destiny. Let us review and reason together.

The earliest permanent settlers in the *New World* of the western hemisphere are recorded as those of Jamestown, landing on May 13, 1607, moving forward on the historical timeline to the Pilgrims, arriving at Cape Cod on November 9, 1620, and the Puritans 300 of which arrived in 1628 at Massachusetts to prepare for the arrival of 1,500 more in 1630.[52] With the exception of a few in the Virginia Colony, planted in 1607 and whose primary purpose was mainly business ventures for economic prosperity, the colonial settlements were largely Christian.[53]

They were primarily Christians who were seeking the freedom to live out the Holy Scriptures that they learned because of what "the morning star of the Reformation," John Wycliffe (1320s-1384), accomplished in having translated the Holy Bible into their English language, making it possible for the common people to read the *Word of God* for themselves. Up until then the Holy Bible had been available only in Latin and therefore only the educated clergy and those of nobility could read it.
Wyclif Giving 'The Poor Priests' His Translation of the Bible by William Frederick Yeames, published before 1923[54]

---

[49] Dr. Benjamin Rush, "Thoughts, Upon the Mode of Education Proper in a Republic," *A Plan for the Establishment of Public Schools and the Diffusion of Knowledge in Pennsylvania; to Which Are Added, Thoughts upon the Mode of Education Proper in a Republic*, (Philadelphia: Thomas Dobson, 1786). Reproduced in *Essays on Education in the Early Republic*, ed. Frederick Rudolph, (Cambridge, MA: The Belknap Press of Harvard University Press, 1965) 9-23
[50] Marshall Foster, Mary Elaine Swanson, *The American Covenant: The Untold Story*, (Thousand Oaks: The Mayflower Institute, 1992) 5
[51] Gregory Williams, "About His Holy Church," hisholychurch.org
[52] J. Olney, A.M., *A History of the United States, on a New Plan; Adapted to the Capacity of Youth. To which is Added, the Declaration of Independence, and the Constitution of the United States*, "Period II: Comprises the events that occurred from the settlement of Jamestown, 1607, to the Declaration of Independence, 1776" (New-Haven: Durrie & Peck, 1839) pp 35-136
[53] Dr. Stephen Jones, *The Prophetic History of the United States*, (Fridley: God's Kingdom Ministries, 2006), 36
[54] *Wikimedia Commons*, s.v. "File:WycliffeYeamesLollards 01.jpg," This work is in the public domain

John Wycliffe in his General Prologue to the Bible translation of 1384 (and paraphrased by President Abraham Lincoln in his Gettysburg Address during the Civil War):

"The Bible is for the Government of the People, by the People, and for the People."[55]

The *English Reformation* occurred 130 years before Martin Luther and the *European Reformation* he stirred in Germany in 1517.[56]

The "Sword of the Word of God," [57] the Holy Bible, was "sharpened" when William Tyndale (1494-1536), an English scholar, translated the first English Bible from the original Hebrew and Greek texts. Tyndale, a scholar in the principles of grammar and philology (knowledge of the etymology or origin and combination of words), birthed the very first accurate English transcript of the Bible to be mass reproduced in the 16th century. He's come to be known as the true father of our present-day English Bible.

William Tyndale[58] *Picture source: Foxe's Book of Martyrs*

William Tyndale became a leading figure, along with Martin Luther, in the *European Reformation* and the start of *Protestantism* that posed a religious and political challenge to the Catholic Church—particularly papal authority in perceived errors, abuses, and discrepancies. For 1,260 years, Catholicism reigned as the only Christianity in Europe. This "protest" and revealing of Truth by authority of source in the *Word of God* can be viewed as a spiritual asteroid impacting the earth with a Light that had not been seen with such brilliance since Christ's *First Coming*.

It was in the *New World* where this Biblical republicanism began, modeled after the ancient Hebrew Republic of which the Pilgrims studied and learned in depth while exiled in Leyden, Holland (1608-1620) before their pilgrimage across the Atlantic to the wilderness of the unsettled North American continent.[59]

---

[55] World History Institute staff, "The Reformation of All Things," *Freedom Journal,* Oct MMXXIII
[56] Marshall Foster, Mary Elaine Swanson, *The American Covenant: The Untold Story, (Thousand Oaks: The Mayflower Institute, 1992)* 46, 54, 55; Rosalie J. Slater, M.A., *Teaching and Learning America's Christian History,* (San Francisco: Foundation for American Christian Education, 1965/1969) 166-168; Verna M. Hall, *The Christian History of the Constitution of the United States of America: Christian Self-Government,* (San Francisco: Foundation for American Christian Education, 1960 rev 1975) 28B, 29
[57] *Hebrews 4:12 ~ For the word of God is quick, and powerful, and sharper than any two edged sword, piercing even to the dividing asunder of soul and spirit, and of the joints and marrow, and is a discerner of the thoughts and intents of the heart.*
[58] *Wikimedia Commons,* s.v. "William Tyndale," This work is in the public domain
[59] Marshall Foster, Mary Elaine Swanson, *The American Covenant: The Untold Story, (Thousand Oaks: The Mayflower Institute, 1992)* 54, 74

The pilgrims signing the compact, on board the May Flower, Nov. 11th, 1620 [60]

painted by T.H. Matteson (1813-1884) / engraved by Gauthier 1859

Rosalie J. Slater (1919-2006)[61]

Rosalie J. Slater, author of *Teaching and Learning America's Christian History*, published in 1965, speaks into the character, beliefs, and pursuits of our forefathers, the Pilgrim Separatists, in their pursuit of leaving the comforts of civilization in the *Old World* settling on the shores of a vast unsettled wilderness in the *New World*.

> *"The Pilgrim Separatists established the beginnings of our Christian Republic – the United States of America. They came to New England for liberty of conscience – and because 'they had a great hope and inward zeal' for 'ye propagating and advancing ye gospel of ye kingdom of Christ in those remote parts of ye world.'*
>
> *Fleeing both ecclesiastical and civil tyranny, the valiant Pilgrims of Plymouth Plantation brought to these shores Primitive Christianity. Like their counterparts of the first century of Christianity, they witnessed by their lives the consistency of their faith. Not one went back. In the record of Plymouth Colony we find the parenthood of our Republic. Here can be found the seed of all our important institutions. Here begins our precious record of <u>Christian Character</u>, <u>Christian Self-Government</u>, <u>Christian Economics</u>, <u>Christian Education</u> and <u>Biblical Christian Unity</u>. <u>For it is what constitutes the character of individual Americans that determines whether our government, economics, education and unity are Christian or pagan</u>."* [62] [Emphasis added]

Because meanings of words have changed over time, along with the demoralization of our modern culture and society – along with it the influence "the world" has had on the organized Church – we pause for clarification and point out that the word "Christian" in its character and ideology as portrayed today does <u>not</u> reflect the character and citizenry of its original presence in America. Our intent is to articulate our

---

[60] Library of Congress, "The pilgrims signing the compact, on board the May Flower, Nov. 11th, 1620 / painted by T.H. Matteson; engraved by Gauthier, Digital Id ppmsca 07842, This media file is in the public domain

[61] Rosalie J. Slater, Cofounder, Courtesy of The Foundation for American Christian Education, https://face.net/our-founders/

[62] Rosalie J. Slater, M.A., *Teaching and Learning America's Christian History,* (San Francisco: Foundation for American Christian Education, 1965/1969) 178

history in truth and original meaning of Christianity to depict following *the Way, the Truth and the Life*, who is Christ,[63] in a surrendered lifestyle of worship as its pure original meaning and sense in lifestyle.[64]

May our friends of the bloodline of Judah of whom we share a rich Hebrew heritage as children of Abraham, Isaac, and Jacob, recognize our intent in conveyance and differentiate with us between what was once sacred in lifestyle from that of this current state of which has been perverted or paganized. The intent of our use of the word, "Christian," is as a disciplined follower of Christ. Disciples of *the Way, the Truth, and the Life* whose *First Coming* as Savior of mankind and who led *the Way* in how to live in the Kingdom and its jurisdiction of Liberty[65] by pointing out the difference between what was written in the Oracles of Creator God from the traditions of men and rudiments of the world.[66]

He, being the Messiah, fulfilled what was written of Himself so that He is now *the Hope* of <u>all</u> Mankind.[67] His disciples, *in Truth,* follow His Example, *His Way* of Living with ability because of having been "born again,"[68] and filled with His Holy Spirit as He promised.[69] This manner of Kingdom-living likewise in turn, is for His disciples to show *the Way* by teaching others both *The Way of Life* and *His Way of Walking*. Christianity in effect is not a new religion, but the implantation of the *Word of God* upon the heart instead of on tablets of stone. [70] [71] Not a religion, but *the Way of Life*.

In the early American story, because our forefathers felt that they were called by God to pick up where Moses left off, there was an incredible sense of compelling as a nation to identify with the Hebrew Children of ancient Israel. This inclination was exhibited in the rapidly growing popularity of university courses in the Hebrew language. People wanted to read and comprehend the *Old Testament* in the original tongue. Many colleges made the study of Hebrew a requirement. There was even a suggestion that Hebrew be adopted as the national language in place of English.[72]

May it serve well in historical note that there was a Jewish presence in Newport, Rhode Island dated to the arrival of fifteen Sephardic Jewish families in 1658. Religious services were held in private homes until property for a synagogue was purchased in 1759 and a building was completed and dedicated in 1763. At least twenty-five Jewish families lived in Newport by the time of the Revolution, making it the largest Jewish community in the colonies. Many left during the British occupation of the town, and the Jewish community

---

[63] *John 14:6 ~ Jesus saith unto him, I am the way, the truth, and the life: no man cometh unto the Father, but by me.*
[64] *Romans 12:1-2 ~ ¹ I beseech you therefore, brethren, by the mercies of God, that ye present your bodies a living sacrifice, holy, acceptable unto God, which is your reasonable service. ² And be not conformed to this world: but be ye transformed by the renewing of your mind, that ye may prove what is that good, and acceptable, and perfect, will of God.*
[65] *2 Cor. 3:17 ~ "Now the Lord is that Spirit: and where the Spirit of the Lord is, there is liberty."*
[66] *Col 2:8 ~ Beware lest any man spoil you through philosophy and vain deceit, after the tradition of men, after the rudiments of the world, and not after Christ.*
[67] *Matthew 5:17 ~ Think not that I am come to destroy the law, or the prophets: I am not come to destroy, but to fulfil.*
[68] *John 3:5-6 ~ 5 Jesus answered, Verily, verily, I say unto thee, Except a man be born of water and of the Spirit, he cannot enter into the kingdom of God. 6 That which is born of the flesh is flesh; and that which is born of the Spirit is spirit.*
[69] *John 14:26 ~ But the Comforter, which is the Holy Ghost, whom the Father will send in my name, he shall teach you all things, and bring all things to your remembrance, whatsoever I have said unto you.*
[70] *Jeremiah 31:33 ~ But this shall be the covenant that I will make with the house of Israel; After those days, saith the Lord, I will put my law in their inward parts, and write it in their hearts; and will be their God, and they shall be my people.*
[71] *2 Corinthians 3:3 ~ Forasmuch as ye are manifestly declared to be the epistle of Christ ministered by us, written not with ink, but with the Spirit of the living God; not in tables of stone, but in fleshy tables of the heart.*
[72] W. Cleon Skousen, *The Majesty of God's Law, It's Coming to America*, (Salt Lake City: Ensign Publishing, 1996), 23

in Newport had only begun to recover its former prominence at the time of President Washington's visit in August 1790. The Hebrew Congregation of Newport reached out to President Washington with a letter:

> *"Deprived as we heretofore have been of the invaluable rights of free Citizens, we now (with a deep sense of gratitude to the Almighty disposer of all events) behold a Government, erected by the Majesty of the People – a Government, which to bigotry gives no sanction, to persecution no assistance – but generously affording to All liberty of conscience, and immunities of Citizenship: deeming every one, of whatever Nation, tongue, or language, equal parts of the great governmental Machine: This so ample and extensive Federal Union whose basis is Philanthropy, Mutual Confidence and Publick Virtue, we cannot but acknowledge to be the work of the Great God, who ruleth in the Armies Of Heaven and among the Inhabitants of the Earth, doing whatever seemeth him good."* [73]

President Washington promptly responded with an endearing and affirming response:

> *"…May the Children of the Stock of Abraham, who dwell in this land, continue to merit and enjoy the good will of the other Inhabitants; while every one shall sit in safety under his own vine and figtree, and there shall be none to make him afraid. May the father of all mercies scatter light and not darkness in our paths, and make us all in our several vocations useful here, and in his own due time and way everlastingly happy."* [74]

George Washington (1732-1799) [75]
First President under the
  Constitution for the united States of America
"Father of His Country"

May all people of the families of the earth sense an inclusion of welcome to the gift of Heaven provided on earth and find safe haven in that which is meant for them too.

Our forefathers and mothers educated their children using the Geneva Bible (first published 1557-1560) and succeeding generations came to include the *New-England Primer* which was the first textbook printed in America, published between 1687-1690. Many of the Founding Fathers and their children learned to read from *The New-England Primer*. Full of moral Bible verses, *The New-England Primer* taught children to spell

---

[73] "From George Washington to the Hebrew Congregation in Newport, Rhode Island, 18 August 1790," Founders Online, National Archives, https://founders.archives.gov/documents/Washington/05-06-02-0135 [Original source: The Papers of George Washington, Presidential Series, vol. 6, 1 July 1790 – 30 November 1790, ed. Mark A. Mastromarino. Charlottesville: University Press of Virginia, 1996, pp. 284–286.]
[74] Ibid.
[75] *Wikimedia Commons*, s.v. "George Washington by Gilbert Stuart, 1795-96.png," This work is in the public domain

and was used in schools from 1692 until after the Progressive Era beginning in 1900 when "progressives" endeavored to steer Americans contrary while embarking upon a path of socialism.[76]

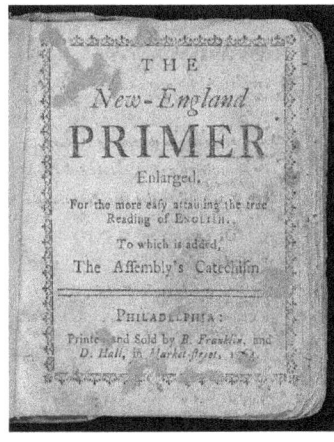

The New-England primer:
Enlarged: For the more easy attaining the true reading of English:
To which is added, the Assembly's Catechism:
Philadelphia: Printed and sold by
B. Franklin, and D. Hall,
in Market-street, 1764. [77]

Verna M. Hall (1912-1987)[78]

Verna M. Hall is the author of the landmark book on the Christian foundations of our nation. *The Christian History of the Constitution for the United States of America: Christian Self-Government* traces historically the *Chain of Christianity* moving westward to America. It examines the importance of <u>the Holy Bible as the great political textbook</u> and documents the appearance, appreciation, and application of Biblical principles of government in how they were used to construct the American Christian republic.[79] Stated in the preface of Mrs. Hall's book compiled from archives of vintage original source material and first published in 1960:

"For about twenty years the compiler of these volumes searched for the fundamental reason why America embarked upon a path of socialism, and why Americans continue to travel this ever-increasing and widening road. About four years ago the answer became an obvious one; a scheduled talk before a small P-TA meeting was cancelled by the Trustees of the school when they learned I was to speak on the religious nature of the Constitution and the Declaration of Independence. It seemed to me that this incident revealed a startling fact; that Americans evidently had forgotten the Christian foundation upon which this nation is reared and the importance of its relation to the form of government established by the Constitution. We as a people, were allowing ourselves to become separated from the <u>keystone</u> of our national structure – our <u>Christian heritage</u> – through such occurrences as had happened at this small school. By omission, America had deflected into socialism. The keystone in the arch of our national structure has been loosened."[80] [Emphasis added]

---

[76] Jean Hallahan Hertler with David Carl Hertler, *Re-inhabited: Republic for the United States of America,* Vol. I, "America's Truthful History," (ValleyAssetsPublishing.com, 2016) 258
[77] *Wikimedia Commons,* s.v. "The New England Primer Enlarged printed and sold by Benjamin Franklin," This work is in the public domain
[78] Verna M. Hall, Cofounder, Courtesy of The Foundation for American Christian Education, https://face.net/our-founders/
[79] Marshall Foster, Mary Elaine Swanson, *The American Covenant: The Untold Story,* (Thousand Oaks: The Mayflower Institute, *1992)* xi
[80] Verna M. Hall, *The Christian History of the Constitution of the United States of America: Christian Self-Government,* (San Francisco: Foundation for American Christian Education, 1960 rev 1975) Preface II

Throughout history, man has erected monuments in effort to preserve and perpetuate the memory of a person or people who raised it, or of a remarkable event. The *National Monument to the Forefathers* is located in Plymouth, Massachusetts. It is a forgotten tribute and memorial to the Mayflower Pilgrims dedicated on August 1, 1889. The Monument was initially proposed as far back as 1794 and when the Pilgrim Society was founded in 1820, the bicentennial of the landing of the Mayflower Pilgrims, plans for the Monument advanced.

Formerly known as the *Pilgrim Monument*, the cornerstone was laid in 1859 just prior to the *War Between the States*, also referred to as *The Great Rebellion* and *Civil War*. It is thought to be the world's largest solid granite monument, originally imagined to be 153-feet tall though later was reduced to 81-feet probably due to lack of funds war-related. The Monument was designed to remind all citizens, both North and South, of their collective heritage in the cause of preserving national unity because of a shared heroic origin by the Pilgrims. In our generation, some refer to the monument as the "Matrix of Liberty" because it was left behind by our forefathers as a recipe and strategy in case their descendants would ever forget how Liberty is obtained, we would have a roadmap to restore it.[81]

National Monument to the Forefathers[82]
(formerly known as the Pilgrim Monument)
Erected 1888, Dedicated 1889
Plymouth, Massachusetts
courtesy of T.S. Custadio

"The Matrix of Liberty"

Inscribed on the front panel of the monument is:

"National Monument to the Forefathers. Erected by a grateful people in remembrance of their labors, sacrifices and sufferings for the cause of civil and religious liberty."

Inscribed on the back panel of the monument is a quote by William Bradford, Pilgrim leader and elected Governor of the Plymouth Colony, taken from his famous historical work, *Of Plymouth Plantation*:

"Thus out of small beginnings greater things have been produced by His hand that made all things of nothing, and gives being to all things that are; and, as one small candle may light a thousand, so the light here kindled

---

[81] Jean Hallahan Hertler with David Carl Hertler, *Re-inhabited: Republic for the United States of America,* Vol. II, "The Story of the Re-inhabitation," (ValleyAssetsPublishing.com, 3rd ed. 2018) III
[82] *Wikimedia Commons,* s.v. "File:Monument to the Forefathers 1.jpg." Author: T.S. Custadio aka ToddC4176 at en.wikipedia, Permission granted.

hath shone unto many, yea in some sort to our whole nation; let the glorious name of Jehovah have all the praise."

It is clear to us that the objective of early Christian Americans in the *New World* on the North American continent was to achieve a jurisdiction where they could live in Christian Liberty—both civil and religious. We assert that it is from Biblical Christianity where Liberty and self-government is derived. Our forefathers taught their children Christian self-government which contributed to family government which in turn, affected church government/polity. This body of believers in Christ formed a "mini-republic" and it is from here that the Biblical republican form of government germinated into civil government.[83]

In the Founding Era, approximately 98-percent of the colonists were Protestants, with the remaining 1.9 percent being Roman Catholics.[84] Most of society was cloaked in virtue because a virtuous people was necessary in order to achieve their goal which was to live in Liberty, the jurisdiction of Creator God's government. The character trait of virtue emulates moral excellence and Godly character that stems from having a holy heart. Those character traits include trustworthiness, uprightness, prudence, respectability, worth, honor, integrity, goodness, faith, kindness, love, purity, righteousness, merit, charity, faithfulness, justice, innocence, and temperance. All of these virtuous traits describe "Love's conduct" and are prerequisite in achieving self-government in this very unique Biblical republicanism of "self-government in union." It's about loving the Creator and then loving thy neighbor as thyself.

Matthew 22:36-40 ~

> *Master, which is the great commandment in the law? Jesus said unto him, Thou shalt love the Lord thy God with all thy heart, and with all thy soul, and with all thy mind. This is the first and great [most important] commandment. And the second is like unto it, Thou shalt love thy neighbour as thyself. On these two commandments hang all the law and the prophets.* [Emphasis added]

2 Peter 1:1-11 ~

> *Simon Peter, a servant and an apostle of Jesus Christ, to them that have obtained like precious faith with us through the righteousness of God and our Saviour Jesus Christ: Grace and peace be multiplied unto you through the knowledge of God, and of Jesus our Lord, According as his divine power hath given unto us all things that pertain unto life and godliness, <u>through the knowledge of him that hath called us to glory and virtue:</u>*

> *Whereby are given unto us exceeding great and precious promises: that by these ye might be partakers of the divine nature, having escaped the corruption that is in the world through lust.*

> *And beside this, giving all diligence, <u>add to your faith virtue; and to virtue knowledge;</u> And to knowledge temperance; and to temperance patience; and to patience godliness; And to godliness brotherly kindness; and*

---

[83] W. Cleon Skousen, *The Majesty of God's Law, It's Coming to America*, (Salt Lake City: Ensign Publishing, 1996), 494-527
[84] Barry A. Kosmin and Seymour P. Lachman, *One Nation Under God: Religion in Contemporary American Society,* (New York: Harmony Books, 1993), pp. 28–29 as cited by Mark David Hall, "Did America Have a Christian Founding?," June 7, 2011, heritage.org

to brotherly kindness charity. For if these things be in you, and abound, they make you that ye shall neither be barren nor unfruitful in the knowledge of our Lord Jesus Christ.

<u>But he that lacketh these things is blind</u>, and cannot see afar off, and hath forgotten that he was purged from his old sins.

Wherefore the rather, brethren, give diligence to make your calling and election sure: for if ye do these things, ye shall never fall: For so an entrance shall be ministered unto you abundantly into the everlasting kingdom of our Lord and Saviour Jesus Christ. [Emphasis added]

As we ponder the phenomenal depth of Godly character in virtue—and of which is the very means to attain and maintain Liberty, we realize that it requires immediate and serious attention in order to recover and restore our heritage in the jurisdiction of Liberty, with a law form established in Christian self-government with voluntary union.

Proverbs 14:34 ~

"Righteousness exalteth a nation: but sin is a reproach to any people."

We look to the wisdom of our fathers for direction and guidance.

Samuel Adams[85]

Samuel Adams (1722-1803), is known as the "Father of the American Revolution." Along with his cousin John Adams, Samuel Adams labored over 20 years as a patriot and leader, both having come to achieve their signatures on our nation's Founding Document, the *Declaration of Independence*. Samuel Adams said:

> "A general dissolution of principles and manners will more surely overthrow the liberties of America than the whole force of the common enemy. <u>While the people are virtuous they cannot be subdued; but when they lose their virtue they will be ready to surrender their liberties to the first external or internal invader…. If virtue and knowledge are diffused among the people, they will never be enslaved. This will be their great security</u>."[86] [Emphasis added]

---

[85] *Wikimedia Commons, s.v.* "J S Copley - evid.jpg," by artist John Singleton Copley, This work isi in the public domain
[86] William J. Federer, *America's God and Country Encyclopedia of Quotations*, "Samuel Adams," (Coppell: FAME Publishing, Inc., 1994) 23 as citing from Rosalie J. Slater, *Teaching and Learning America's Christian Heritage* (San Francisco: Foundation for American Christian Education, American Revolution Bicentennial edition, 1975) 251; Verna M. Hall, *The Christian History of the Constitution of the United States of America—Christian Self-Government with Union* San Francisco: Foundation for American Christian Education, 1976) 4; et al.

"Neither the wisest constitution nor the wisest laws will secure the liberty and happiness of a people whose manners are universally corrupt."[87]

"<u>He therefore is the truest friend to the liberty of his country who tries most to promote its virtue</u>, and who, so far as his power and influence extend, will not suffer a man to be chose into any office of power and trust who is not a wise and virtuous man....<u>The sum of all is, if we would most truly enjoy this gift of Heaven, let us become a virtuous people.</u>"[88] [Emphasis added]

We realize that virtue is a matter of national security, and that knowledge is the safety zone of preservation for a nation of people who hold conviction in maintaining the government of God, both internal individually and external into civil society.

James Madison (1751-1836) was a Founding Father and is known as the *"Chief Architect of the Constitution,"* our nation's Operating Document. Considered one of its brilliant defenders, Madison identified the leading reason for its success. Writing in *The Federalist*, and speaking first regarding the form of a republic, he asserted:

"It is evident that no other form would be reconcilable with the genius of the people of America; with the fundamental principles of the Revolution; or with that honorable determination which animates every votary [vow] of freedom: To rest all our political experiments on <u>the capacity of mankind for self-government</u>."[89] [Emphasis added]

President James Madison, 1816 [90]

"The capacity of mankind for self-government." This famous phrase of Madison has echoed through American history for over two centuries. What is it that produces mankind's capacity or ability to be self-governed? History shows that mankind's ability to govern itself is in direct proportion to the relationship of the individual to Creator God, to Christ. There were challenges enough in early America where most of the nation were Bible-believers who lived out their beliefs in obedience to Christ, the *Word of God*.[91] Through

---

[87] William J. Federer, *America's God and Country Encyclopedia of Quotations*, "Samuel Adams," (Coppell: FAME Publishing, Inc., 1994) 23 as citing from Samuel Adams. A political essay, printed in *The Public Advisor*, p. 1749; William V. Wells, *The Life and Public Services of Samuel Adams* (Boston: Little Brown, & Co., 1865), Vol. I, p. 22; et al.

[88] William J. Federer, *America's God and Country Encyclopedia of Quotations*, "Samuel Adams," (Coppell: FAME Publishing, Inc., 1994) 23 as citing from Samuel Adams. Statement. William V. Wells, *The Life and Public Services of Samuel Adams* (Boston: Little, Brown & Co., 1865); Rosalie J. Slater, *Teaching and Learning America's Christian Heritage* (San Francisco: Foundation for American Christian Education, American Revolution Bicentennial edition, 1975); et al.

[89] Verna M. Hall, Rosalie J. Slater, *The Bible and the Constitution of the United States of America: A Primer of American Liberty*, (Chesapeake: The Foundation for American Christian Education, 2nd ed. 201) 14

[90] *Wikimedia Commons*, s.v. "James Madison.jpg," This work is in the public domain

[91] *John 1:1, 14 ~ 1 In the beginning was the Word, and the Word was with God, and the Word was God. 14 And the Word was made flesh, and dwelt among us, (and we beheld his glory, the glory as of the only begotten of the Father,) full of grace and truth.*

the years a gradual change in education away from Biblical principles contributed to a famine of the *Word of God* as well as in the pulpit failing to preach the whole counsel of God. [92]

Saul Alinsky[93]

The reality of our culture today includes the rising of a generation that was not taught the principles and absolutes of Liberty and Christian self-government. From cause-to-effect, their teachers were students in the 1960s that were steeped in the philosophy of Socialism as presented by their mentor, Saul Alinsky (1909-1972).[94] This anti-American ideology was further magnified with an evil tactic of revising American history to a false narrative, and again, from cause-to-effect, left us with a rebellious generation that is steeped in paganism, the religion whose government is a jurisdiction of death and destruction.[95]

Everyone has a philosophy or belief system with a religious premise — even if they are atheist/agnostic. [96] In 1961 the U.S. Supreme Court acknowledged that *Secular Humanism* is a religion.[97]

Hosea 4:6 ~

> <u>My people are destroyed for lack of knowledge</u>: *because thou hast rejected knowledge, I will also reject thee, that thou shalt be no priest to me: seeing thou <u>hast forgotten the law of thy God</u>, I will also forget thy children.* [Emphasis added]

The wisdom, knowledge, and understanding of our forefathers and Founding Fathers was rooted in the Holy Bible and they expected that premise of the Christian religion and its civil polity, the government of the Kingdom of Heaven, to remain with their posterity, their children, their inheritance from the Lord — and His inheritance from them.[98]

At the opening of the *Thirty-third Congress* in 1854, a debate arose as to whether or not to elect chaplains, as had been customary from the beginning of the *First Federal Congress* in 1789. On March 27, 1854,

---

[92] *Amos 8:11 ~ Behold, the days come, saith the Lord God, that I will send a famine in the land, not a famine of bread, nor a thirst for water, but of hearing the words of the Lord:*
[93] *Wikimedia*, s.v. "Saul Alinsky," Permission granted by author, Pierre869856
[94] Mike Ford, "Opinion: Now is Our Chance to Remake Public Education," August 11, 2020, redstate.com
[95] Marshall Foster, Mary Elaine Swanson, *The American Covenant: The Untold Story*, (Thousand Oaks: The Mayflower Institute, 1992) 8-10
[96] Dr Marlene McMillian, *Five Pillars of Liberty*, (Fort Worth: Liberty View Media 2011) 44-45
[97] Torcaso v. Watkins, 367 U.S. 488 (1961), "11 <u>Among religions in this country</u> which do not teach what would generally be considered a belief in the existence of God are Buddhism, Taoism, Ethical Culture, <u>Secular Humanism</u> and others. See Washington Ethical Society v. District of Columbia, 101 U.S.App.D.C. 371, 249 F.2d 127; Fellowship of Humanity v. County of Alameda, 153 Cal.App.2d 673, 315 P.2d 394; II Encyclopaedia of the Social Sciences 293; 4 Encyclopaedia Britannica (1957 ed.) 325 327; 21 id., at 797; Archer, Faiths Men Live By (2d ed. revised by Purinton), 120—138, 254—313; 1961 World Almanac 695, 712; Year Book of American Churches for 1961, at 29, 47." https://www.law.cornell.edu/supremecourt/text/367/488
[98] ▪*Psalm 127:3 ~ Lo, children are an heritage of the Lord: and the fruit of the womb is his reward.*
  ▪*1 Corinthians 3:9 ~ For we are labourers together with God: ye are God's husbandry, ye are God's building.*
  ▪ *Matthew 19:14 ~ But Jesus said, Suffer little children, and forbid them not, to come unto me: for of such is the kingdom of heaven.*

Representative James Meacham (1810-1856, Vermont), who served as spokesman of the *U.S. House Committee on the Judiciary,* spoke in favor of continuing the practice of appointing chaplains:[99]

Congressman James Meacham[100]

"What is an establishment of religion? It must have a creed, defining what a man must believe; it must have rites and ordinances, which believers must observe; it must have ministers of defined qualifications, to teach the doctrines and administer the rites; it must have tests for the submissive and penalties for the non-conformist. There never was an established religion without all these….

At the adoption of the Constitution…every State…provided as regularly for the support of the Church as for the support of the Government….

Down to the Revolution, every colony did sustain religion in some form. It was deemed peculiarly proper that the religion of liberty should be upheld by a free people.

Had the people, during the Revolution, had a suspicion of any attempt to war against Christianity, that Revolution would have been strangled in its cradle.

At the time of the adoption of the Constitution and the amendments, the universal sentiment was that Christianity should be encouraged, not any one sect [denomination]. Any attempt to level and discard all religion would have been viewed with universal indignation. The object was not to substitute Judaism or Mohammedanism, or infidelity, but to prevent rivalry among the sects [Christian denominations] to the exclusion of others.

It [Biblical Christianity] must be considered as the foundation on which the whole structure rests. Laws will not have permanence or power without the sanction of religious sentiment, -- without a firm belief that there is a Power above us that will reward our virtues and punish our vices.

In this age there can be no substitute for Christianity: that, in its general principles, is the great conservative element on which we must rely for the purity and permanence of free institutions. That was the religion of the founders of the republic, and they expected it to remain the religion of their descendants. There is a great and very prevalent error on this subject in the opinion that those who organized this Government did not legislate on religion."[101] [Emphasis added]

---

[99] Lorenzo D. Johnson, *Chaplains of the General Government, with Objections to Their Employment Considered,* (New York: Sheldon, Blakeman & Co., 1856) 9
[100] *Wikimedia Commons,* s.v. "James Meacham.jpg," This work is in the public domain
[101] Federer, *America's God and Country Encyclopedia of Quotations,* "Congress of the United States of America," (Coppell: FAME Publishing, Inc, 1994), 169-170 as citing from Congress of the United States of America. March 27, 1854, Mr. Meacham giving report of the House Committee on the Judiciary. Benjamin Franklin Morris, *The Christian Life and Character of the Civil Institutions of the United States* (Philadelphia: George W. Childs, 1864) 317, 320-327; et al.

Two months later in May 1854, *Congress of the United States of America* passed a resolution in the House which declared:

> *"The great vital and conservative element in our system is the belief of our people in the pure doctrines and divine truths of the gospel of Jesus Christ."*[102]

Where it appears as impossible to redeem an ungodly, pagan generation—and nation—to the Biblical Christian religion, the religion of our forefathers and Founding Fathers in its civil polity and *Providential worldview*, we remember and have hope in that all things are possible in Christ.[103]

One of our four founding documents, the *Northwest Ordinance*, enacted July 13, 1787, and codified as law by the *First Congress* as *1 Statute 50* on August 7, 1789, created the Northwest Territory, the first organized territory of the united States from lands beyond the Appalachian Mountains, between British North America and the Great Lakes to the north and the Ohio River to the south. The upper Mississippi River formed the territory's western boundary, Pennsylvania was the eastern boundary.

Drafted by Founding Father Thomas Jefferson, who also authored our nation's Founding Document, the *Declaration of Independence*, here appears evidence of our Founder's intent on the importance of education and moral absolutes as fundamental in maintaining this unique government.

> *Northwest Ordinance (1787)*[104]
>
> <u>Sec. 14. It is hereby ordained and declared by the authority aforesaid, That the following articles shall be considered as articles of compact between the original States and the people and States in the said territory and forever remain unalterable, unless by common consent, to wit:</u>
>
> <u>Art. 3. Religion, morality, and knowledge, being necessary to good government and the happiness of mankind, schools and the means of education shall forever be encouraged.</u> *The utmost good faith shall always be observed towards the Indians; their lands and property shall never be taken from them without their consent; and, in their property, rights, and liberty, they shall never be invaded or disturbed, unless in just and lawful wars authorized by Congress; but laws founded in justice and humanity, shall from time to time be made for preventing wrongs being done to them, and for preserving peace and friendship with them.*

Religion and morality had to be the basis of their culture, Biblical principles and moral absolutes were the core curriculum in the schools. The objective was to create virtue in their posterity, their children. They

---

[102] Federer, *America's God and Country Encyclopedia of Quotations*, "Congress of the United States of America," (Coppell: FAME Publishing, Inc, 1994), 170 as citing from Congress of the United States of America. May 1854, A Resolution passed in the House. Benjamin Franklin Morris, *The Christian Life and Character of the Civil Institutions of the United States* (Philadelphia: George W. Childs, 1864) 328; et al.

[103] *Matthew 19:26 ~ "But Jesus beheld them, and said unto them, With men this is impossible; but with God all things are possible."*

[104] "Northwest Ordinance; July 13, 1787," accessed at *The Avalon Project,* Lillian Goldman Law Library, Yale Law School, Source: Documents Illustrative of the Formation of the Union of the American States. Government Printing Office, 1927. House Document No. 398. Selected, Arranged and Indexed by Charles C. Tansill,

understood from the *Holy Scriptures* that without virtue there cannot be liberty *"...and liberty is the object and life of all republican governments."*[105]

Today we hear the word "freedom" being associated with America. Let it be clear that Liberty is much more than freedom.

<u>Liberty = freedom + morality & comes with responsibility</u>.

After being administered the oath of office prescribed by the *Constitution for the United States of America* and inaugurated as President, George Washington kissed the Bible held for him as he gave his oath, and then proceeded to the Senate Chamber where he read his Inaugural Address before the members of Congress. He expressed his love and devotion to his country and spoke indepth about...

> *"...that Almighty Being who rules over the universe, who presides in the councils of nations, and whose providential aids can supply every human defect, that His benediction [blessing] may consecrate [to make to be sacred; to set apart] to the liberties and happiness of the people of the United States a Government instituted by themselves for these essential purposes, and may enable every instrument employed in its administration to execute with success the functions allotted to his charge."*[106] [Emphasis added]

*George Washington's inauguration
as the first President of the United States
under the
Constitution for the United States of America
which took place on April 30, 1789
Oil painting circa 1899*[107]

President Washington spoke about *"the Invisible Hand which conducts the affairs of men"* and Divine Providence that distinguished the United States in having become an independent nation. He said that the foundation of our national policy must be laid in the pure and absolute principles of morality as he also spoke into what this Government must depend on for success. He admonished that it would be up to the

---

[105] Dr. Benjamin Rush, "Thoughts, Upon the Mode of Education Proper in a Republic," *A Plan for the Establishment of Public Schools and the Diffusion of Knowledge in Pennsylvania; to Which Are Added, Thoughts upon the Mode of Education Proper in a Republic*, (Philadelphia: Thomas Dobson, 1786). Reproduced in *Essays on Education in the Early Republic*, ed. Frederick Rudolph, (Cambridge, MA: The Belknap Press of Harvard University Press, 1965) 9-23
[106] George Washington's First Inaugural Address; 4/30/1789; (SEN 1A-E1); Presidential Messages, 1789 - 1875; Records of the U.S. Senate, Record Group 46; National Archives Building, Washington, DC.
[107] *Wikimedia Commons*, s.v., File:Washington's Inauguration.jpg, This work is in the public domain

American People to maintain the principles of morality as the means to carefully preserve "<u>the sacred fire of liberty</u>." He stated,

> *"...that the foundation of our national policy will be laid in the pure and immutable principles of private morality, and the preeminence [superiority in excellence] of free government be exemplified by all the attributes which can win the affections of its citizens and command the respect of the world. I dwell on this prospect with every satisfaction which an ardent love for my country can inspire, since there is no truth more thoroughly established than that there exists in the economy and course of nature an indissoluble union between virtue and happiness; between duty and advantage; between the genuine maxims of an honest and magnanimous policy and the solid rewards of public prosperity and felicity [happiness]; since we ought to be no less persuaded that the propitious [gracious or merciful] smiles of Heaven can never be expected on a nation that disregards the eternal rules of order and right which Heaven itself has ordained; <u>and since the preservation of the sacred fire of liberty and the destiny of the republican model of government are justly considered, perhaps, as deeply, as finally, staked on the experiment entrusted to the hands of the American people</u>."*[108] [Emphasis added]

George Washington was President of the Convention that wrote the *Constitution*. He was President of the United States of America who oversaw the formation of the *Bill of Rights* and its ratification. He gave 45 years of his life to public service to see America become strong and established as an independent nation. He is known as the "Father of his country."

President Washington, in his *Farewell Address* after serving two terms as President (1789-1797) under the *Constitution for the United States,* included several very succinct, clear warnings and counsels to the American People on what they must do to stay on track and preserve their Liberty. President Washington's warnings and counsels were so important, that for over a century in America his *Farewell Address* was published as a complete textbook, and students were required to memorize it in full. It was studied thoroughly because American children were taught that it was the most significant political speech ever delivered by a U.S. President. Prior to World War II, this *Farewell Address* could be found in every textbook.[109]

Broadside print for distribution of President George Washington's Farewell Address [110]

---

[108] George Washington's First Inaugural Address; 4/30/1789; (SEN 1A-E1); Presidential Messages, 1789 - 1875; Records of the U.S. Senate, Record Group 46; National Archives Building, Washington, DC.
[109] The John Ankerberg Show with David Barton, "Was America Founded on Christian Principles?" (1992)
[110] Library of Congress, Religion and the Founding of the American Republic, VI. Religion and the Federal Government, "The Farewell Address," This work is in the public domain

One of President Washington's warnings pertained to religion and morality. He said,

> *"Of all the dispositions [setting in order; regulating; governing] and habits which lead to political prosperity, religion [Biblical Christianity] and morality are indispensable supports. In vain would that man claim the tribute of patriotism, who should labor to subvert these great pillars of human happiness, these firmest props of the duties of men and citizens. The mere politician, equally with the pious [Godly] man, ought to respect and to cherish them. A volume could not trace all their connections with private and public felicity [happiness]. Let it simply be asked: Where is the security for property, for reputation, for life, if the sense of religious obligation desert the oaths which are the instruments of investigation in courts of justice? And let us with caution indulge the supposition [imagining as true] that morality can be maintained without religion [Biblical Christianity]. Whatever may be conceded to the influence of refined education on minds of peculiar [particular; special] structure, reason and experience both forbid us to expect that national morality can prevail in exclusion of religious principle.*
>
> *It is substantially true that virtue or morality is a necessary spring of popular [pertaining to the common people] government. The rule, indeed, extends with more or less force to every species of free government. Who that is a sincere friend to it can look with indifference upon attempts to shake the foundation of the fabric?*
>
> *Promote then, as an object of primary importance, institutions for the general diffusion [spreading] of knowledge. In proportion as the structure of a government gives force to public opinion, it is essential that public opinion should be enlightened [instructed; furnished with clear views]."*[111] [Emphasis added]

Sir William Blackstone[112]

Following are some basic foundational principles of the American Republic gleaned from original source material inclusive of writings and teachings of William Blackstone (1723-1780, England). Blackstone's *Commentaries on the Laws of England* was the manual for law students in the united States during and after the revolutionary period and the drafting of the *Constitution for the united States*.

~ All government springs from religion. [113][114]

~ This nation birthed forth from Biblical Christianity which is "the religion of Liberty." [115][116]

---

[111] George Washington's Farewell Address to the People of the United States, September 17, 1796, Archiving Early America as sourced from The Independent Chronicle, September 26, 1796
[112] *Wikimedia*, s.v. "SirWilliamBlackstone.jpg," This work is in the public domain
[113] S. D. Baldwin, *Armageddon: or, The Overthrow of Romanism and Monarchy; The Existence of the United States Foretold in the Bible, Its Future Greatness; Invasion by Allied Europe; Annihilation of Monarchy; Expansion into the Millennial Republic, and its Dominion Over the Whole World,* (Cincinnati: Applegate & Co., Publishers, 1864) 20
[114] Verna M. Hall, *The Christian History of the Constitution of the United States of America: Christian Self-Government,* (San Francisco: Foundation for American Christian Education, 1960 rev 1975) Preface III
[115] *Galatians 5:1 ~ "Stand fast therefore in the liberty wherewith Christ hath made us free, and be not entangled again with the yoke of bondage."*
[116] *2 Cor. 3:17 ~ "Now the Lord is that Spirit: and where the Spirit of the Lord is, there is liberty."*

~ Civil and religious liberty are inseparable[117]

~ The law form of the nation's republican form of government acknowledges and abides by "the Laws of Nature and of Nature's God."[118]

~ "The Laws of Nature" is the Creator's will in how His universe operates (consider the immutable laws of the sciences)[119]

~ "Nature's God" is the Divine revealed *Word of God*.[120]

~ Any human law that disagrees with or contradicts Creator God's law is no law, it is void.[121]

~ Should a human law (legal) violate the Natural and the Divine laws (lawful), we are bound to transgress that human law or else offend both the Natural and the Divine.[122]

~ The Creator is the *Supreme Judge of the world* [123] Who rules from His throne in heaven above, issuing sentences to both individuals and nations according to the blessings of obedience or curses of disobedience to His Laws which are universal.[124]

~ Mankind is created in the image of God.[125] In the Creator's design, each individual is unique and of great value.[126]

~ The jurisdiction of Liberty in this model of government affords its citizens to abide by the Creator's Laws and worship with their life according to the dictates of their conscience, known as "liberty of conscience."[127]

---

[117] Verna M. Hall, Rosalie J. Slater, *The Bible and the Constitution of the United States of America: A Primer of American Liberty*, (Chesapeake: The Foundation for American Christian Education, 2nd ed. 2012) 26
[118] Preamble of the Declaration of Independence
[119] William Blackstone, *Commentaries on the Laws of England,* Section the Second, Of the Nature of Laws in General
[120] Ibid.
[121] Ibid. 42-43
[122] Ibid.
[123] Preamble of the Declaration of Independence
[124] *Deuteronomy 28:1-68*
[125] *Genesis 1:26-27 ~ "And God said, Let us make man in our image, after our likeness: and let them have dominion over the fish of the sea, and over the fowl of the air, and over the cattle, and over all the earth, and over every creeping thing that creepeth upon the earth. So God created man in his own image, in the image of God created he him; male and female created he them."*
[126] Marshall Foster, Mary Elaine Swanson, *The American Covenant: The Untold Story*, Chapter 4, "The Individual Set Free," (Thousand Oaks: The Mayflower Institute, 1992) 63-76
[127] *Romans 12:1-2 ~ "I beseech you therefore, brethren, by the mercies of God, that ye present your bodies a living sacrifice, holy, acceptable unto God, which is your reasonable service. And be not conformed to this world: but be ye transformed by the renewing of your mind, that ye may prove what is that good, and acceptable, and perfect, will of God."*

> ~ Conscience is the faculty within a human where the "voice of Nature" speaks of power and principle as a moral compass. [128] [129]
>
> ~ Liberty of conscience did not exist until Christianity appeared in the world.[130]
>
> ~ We have a property in our rights—the right to conscience is the most sacred of all property.[131]

Much becomes obvious as we realize and recognize some very foundational truths in our nation's historical beginning that has been recovered from archived treasures, preserved by heaven; our ancestor's writings indicate that education is considered as a vital forefront in securing Liberty. This education must be premised on a *Providential worldview* and the scope and sequence of curriculum be Biblical in nature. This is our heritage that was secured by our Founders in pledging their lives, fortunes, and sacred honor.[132] This is the foundation, and these are the moorings on which America must return in order to preserve the American Republic and her Christian liberties afforded by education and knowledge of Biblical Christian Self-Government.

Again, we look to the wisdom of our fathers. Signer of the *Declaration of Independence* and second President of the United States, John Adams (1735-1826), said:

> "Be it remembered, however, that <u>liberty must at all hazards be supported. We have a right to it, derived from our Maker</u>! But if we had not, our fathers have earned and bought it for us at the expence of their ease, their estates, their pleasure, and their blood.
>
> —<u>And liberty cannot be preserved without a general knowledge among the people</u>, who have a right, from the frame of their nature, to knowledge, as their great Creator, who does nothing in vain, has given them understandings, and a desire to know; but besides this, they have a right, an indisputable, unalienable, indefeasible, divine right to that most dreaded and envied kind of <u>knowledge</u>, I mean, of the characters and conduct of their rulers."[133] [Emphasis added]

John Adams[134]
"The Statesman"

---

[128] Acts 24:16 ~ "And herein do I exercise myself, to have always a conscience void to offence toward God, and toward men."
[129] *Noah Webster's First Edition of An American Dictionary of the English Language,* 1828: "<u>Conscience</u>: The principle within us, which decides on the lawfulness or unlawfulness of our own actions and affections, and instantly approves or condemns them."
[130] Rosalie J. Slater, M.A., *Teaching and Learning America's Christian History*, (San Francisco: Foundation for American Christian Education, 1965/1969) 228 referencing the writings of Dr. Augustus Neander (1789-1850)
[131] Ibid.
[132] Declaration of Independence
[133] John Adams, Essay on Canon and Feudal Law (1765), thefederalistpapers.org
[134] Carole Bos, "John Adams" AwesomeStories.com. giving media credit to Image online, courtesy of the abigailadams.org website

Professor Gordon S. Wood is an American historian and professor at Brown University. He is a recipient of the 1993 Pulitzer Prize for History for *The Radicalism of the American Revolution* (1992). His 1969 book *The Creation of the American Republic, 1776–1787* won a 1970 Bancroft Prize. In 2010, he was awarded the National Humanities Medal. Professor Wood describes what the Founding Fathers meant by a "virtuous" people.

> *"Each man must somehow be persuaded to submerge his personal wants into the greater good of the whole. This willingness of the individual to sacrifice his private interest for the good of the community – such patriotism or love of country – the eighteenth century termed <u>public virtue</u>… The eighteenth century mind was thoroughly convinced that a popularly based government 'cannot be supported without <u>virtue</u>."* [135]

Sometimes we experience a greater understanding when we consider the opposite of, or absence of a matter.

Edmund Burke [136]

Edmund Burke (1729-1797) was an Irish statesman and philosopher. He served as a member of parliament in the House of Commons of Great Britain, the mother country of the British colonists in America. In that era, Burke was an advocate of reinforcing virtues with manners in society and of the importance of religious institutions for the moral stability and good of the State. He said:

> *"What is liberty without wisdom and without virtue? It is the greatest of all possible evils; for it is folly, vice, and madness, without restraint.*
>
> *Men are qualified for civil liberty in exact proportion to their disposition to put moral chains upon their appetites…*
>
> *Society cannot exist, unless a controlling power upon will and appetite be placed somewhere and the less of it there is within, the more there must be without.*
>
> *It is ordained in the eternal constitution of things that men of intemperate minds cannot be free. Their passions forge their fetters"* [137]

Now that we've viewed historical evidence and have sound knowledge of our true heritage and founding as a nation, we are able to envision a model for restoring the means to Liberty and the blessings (*Deuteronomy 28:1-13*) that come from obeying and heeding *"the Laws of Nature and of Nature's God,"* the Creator's laws as acknowledged in the preamble of the *Declaration of Independence*. Almighty God's "Natural Laws" are acknowledged and preserved in our nation's Founding Document, the *Declaration of Independence*, as well

---

[135] W. Cleon Skousen, *The Majesty of God's Law, It's Coming to America*, (Salt Lake City: Ensign Publishing, 1996), 475
[136] Wikimedia s.v., "EdmundBurke1771," This work is in the public domain
[137] Edmund Burke, 1791, in "A Letter to a Member of the National Assembly," The *Works of the Right Honourable Edmund Burke,* Vol. III. (of 12) (London: John C. Nimmo, 1887) 560

as the Operating Document, the *Constitution for the United States* of which is declared as "the supreme law of the land."[138]

Having gained knowledge and understanding of why our Fathers considered education with a Providential worldview of primary importance, ability is then within scope and sequence to perceive the vision of the restoration of education in Biblical Christian liberty, the result of which affects and interconnects with nearly every other facet in life, to be as "the keys to the kingdom." Those familiar with the *Word of God* know that the keys to the kingdom relate to our spiritual authority in Christ.

> *Matthew 16:19 ~ And I will give unto thee the keys of the kingdom of heaven: and whatsoever thou shalt bind on earth shall be bound in heaven: and whatsoever thou shalt loose on earth shall be loosed in heaven.*

Because the people of God are destroyed for lack of knowledge and that knowledge consists inclusive of the Creator's laws,[139] we reason that "the keys to the kingdom" represent the authority to open the way for people to "enter into the Kingdom of God" and live in its jurisdiction "on earth as it is in heaven."[140] The Messiah gave His disciple, Peter, "the keys of the Kingdom of the heavens" and along with them, the authority to unlock information/knowledge about how the people of God by faith in Christ Jesus, Yeshua HaMashiach, can live in Christian liberty as citizens of heaven on earth.[141] Authority comes with the responsibility to establish righteousness in the earth.[142] The Kingdom is here for those who covenant to follow the path of liberty.[143]

The keys, the authority to enter and live in the Kingdom of heaven on earth, necessitates education to gain knowledge of how to live in Liberty,[144] the result which preserves not only religious liberty, but civil liberty and its institutions, government/civic inclusive. Failure to establish righteousness brings divine judgment which cause-to-effect leads to bondage and captivity in a jurisdiction of evil rulers who command the people to sin in gross violation of *"the Laws of Nature and of Nature's God."*[145]

---

[138] *Constitution for the united States, Article VI, Clause 2, "This Constitution, and the Laws of the United States which shall be made in Pursuance thereof; and all Treaties made, or which shall be made, under the Authority of the United States, shall be the supreme Law of the Land; and the Judges in every State shall be bound thereby, any Thing in the Constitution or Laws of any State to the Contrary notwithstanding." [Emphasis added]*

[139] *Hosea 4:6 ~ My people are destroyed for lack of knowledge: because thou hast rejected knowledge, I will also reject thee, that thou shalt be no priest to me: seeing thou hast forgotten the law of thy God, I will also forget thy children.*

[140] *Matthew 6:10 ~ Thy kingdom come. Thy will be done in earth, as it is in heaven.*
Acts 14:22 ~ Confirming the souls of the disciples, and exhorting them to continue in the faith, and that we must through much tribulation enter into the kingdom of God.

[141] *Philippians 3:20 (NASB) ~ For our citizenship is in heaven, from which also we eagerly wait for a Savior, the Lord Jesus Christ;*

[142] *Dr Stephen Jones, "Mystery Babylon's lawful Obligation," Sept 18, 2018, godskingdom.org*

[143] *Matthew 6:9-10 ~ ⁹ Our Father which art in heaven, Hallowed be thy name. ¹⁰ Thy kingdom come, Thy will be done in earth, as it is in heaven.*

[144] *Luke 1:77 ~ To give knowledge of salvation unto his people by the remission of their sins,*

[145] *Luke 11:52 ~ Woe unto you, lawyers! for ye have taken away the key of knowledge: ye entered not in yourselves, and them that were entering in ye hindered.*

Hope does indeed abound, for when the people turn to Creator God with wholeness of heart, He will remove the vail of ignorance that blinds and obstructs and in turn enlighten their understanding with eyes to see the manifestation of the Kingdom of heaven on earth along with its jurisdiction of Liberty.[146]

John Knox (c1514-1572) was a Scottish minister, Reformed theologian, and founder of the Presbyterian Church of Scotland. John Knox was the leader of the remarkable *Protestant Reformation* in Scotland. Four generations later, his descendant John Witherspoon (1723-1794) followed in Reverend Knox's legacy as a Scottish Presbyterian minister. Reverend Witherspoon immigrated to America by invitation to become the president of the College of New Jersey (today known as Princeton University). John Witherspoon was a signer of the *Declaration of Independence* and a member of the Continental Congress.

Portrait of John Knox[147]

Reverend Witherspoon's emphasis of Biblical principles impacting government and nation-building was tremendously felt in the Colonies during the foundation of America. His influence continued through his students, who remarkably included a U.S. President (James Madison), a U.S. Vice-President (Aaron Burr), three Supreme Court Justices, 10 Cabinet members, 13 Governors, 28 Senators, 49 Congressmen, 37 judges, 114 ministers, as well as 12 members of the *Continental Congress* and 9 of the 55 writers of the *Constitution for the United States*.

John Witherspoon discipled his new nation by training the leaders, just as his ancestor John Knox had done in Scotland 200 years earlier. Because of his impact on our Founding Fathers, he is known as "the father of fathers."[148]

---

[146] *2 Corinthians 3:12-18 ~ 12 Seeing then that we have such hope, we use great plainness of speech: 13 And not as Moses, which put a veil over his face, that the children of Israel could not stedfastly look to the end of that which is abolished: 14 But their minds were blinded: for until this day remaineth the same vail untaken away in the reading of the old testament; which vail is done away in Christ. 15 But even unto this day, when Moses is read, the vail is upon their heart. 16 Nevertheless when it shall turn to the Lord, the vail shall be taken away. 17 Now the Lord is that Spirit: and where the Spirit of the Lord is, there is liberty. 18 But we all, with open face beholding as in a glass the glory of the Lord, are changed into the same image from glory to glory, even as by the Spirit of the Lord.*

[147] *Wikimedia Commons* s.v., "File:Portrait of John Knox (4671577).jpg, This work is in the public domain

[148] Bill Federer, American Minute blog postAmerican Minute with Bill Federer, "A Republic must either reserve its Virtue or lose its Liberty—Rev. John Witherspoon, Signer of Declaration of Independence," Nov 10, 2020,

John Witherspoon, c1790 [149]

In a fiery sermon on July 31, 1776, John Witherspoon challenged his congregation:

> *"I beseech you to make a wise improvement of the present threatening aspect of public affairs, and to remember that your duty to God, to your country, to your families, and to yourselves is the same. True religion is nothing else but an inward temper and outward conduct suited to your state and circumstance in procidence [to fall down] at any time. And as peace with God and conformity to him adds to the sweetness of created comforts while we possess them, so in times of difficulty and trial, it is in the man of piety [reverence for God] and inward principle, that we may expect to find the uncorrupted patriot, the useful citizen, and the invincible soldier. God grant that in America, <u>true religion and civil liberty</u> may be <u>inseparable</u>, and that the unjust attempts to destroy the one, may in the issue tend to the support and establishment of both."*[150] [Emphasis added]

Joseph Story[151]

Joseph Story (1779-1845) was Chief Justice of the U. S. Supreme Court and also a professor at Harvard Law School. He wrote influential works of which included *Commentaries on the Constitution*. In his commentary of the First Amendment's original meaning, Justice Story insures:

> *"There is not a truth to be gathered from history more certain, or more momentous, than this: that <u>civil liberty</u> cannot long be separated from <u>religious liberty</u> without danger, and ultimately without destruction to both. Wherever <u>religious liberty</u> exists, it will, first or last, bring in and establish <u>political liberty</u>."* [152]

---

[149] *Wikimedia Commons* s.v., "File:Peale, Charles Willson, John Witherspoon (1723-1794), President (1768-94)," This work is in the public domain

[150] Federer, *America's God and Country Encyclopedia of Quotations,* "John Witherspoon," (Coppell: FAME Publishing, Inc, 1994) 702-703 as citing from John Witherspoon. May 17, 1776, in his sermon entitled, "The Dominion of Providence over the Passions of Men." Vanum Lansing Collins, *President Witherspoon* (New York: Arno Press and *The New York Times,* 1969), I:197-198; et al.; World History Institute staff, "The Reformation of All Things," *Freedom Journal,* Oct MMXXIII

[151] *Wikimedia Commons* s.v., "Joseph Story," This work is in the public domain

[152] Federer, America's God and Country Encyclopedia of Quotations, "Joseph Story," (Coppell: FAME Publishing, Inc, 1994) 702-575 as citing from Joseph Story. Tryon Edwards, D.D., *The New Dictionary of Thoughts–A Cyclopedia of Quotations* Garden City, NY: Hanover House, 1852; revised and enlarged by C.H. Catrevas, Ralph Emerson Browns, and Jonathan Edwards [descendent along with Tryon, of Jonathan Edwards (1703-1758), president of Princeton], 1891; The Standard Book Company, 1955, 1963) 337

By restoring our education model to our heritage in Christian liberty, from cause-to-effect, the major ills of our current society will be corrected. For example…

One. With big government in concert with corrupt unions and associations having infiltrated our schools and pushing the carrot incentive of Federal moneys, schools are obligated to teach curriculum which, if American history is even taught, has been revised to a contemporary false narrative known as "revisionist history." Coupled with curriculum that teaches Socialism — which espouses dogma that removes the Creator and Biblical principles of which are moral absolutes, while making the State "god" and resulting in the curses of disobedience (*Deuteronomy 28:15-68*). Restoration of Christian self-government in education will bring our nation the blessings of obedience (*Deuteronomy 28:1-13*).

Two. When self-government is established among the People, they will participate in their representative form of government in a less structured and limited government at the national/federal level as well as in the States.[153]

Three. America transitioned in jurisdiction from a God-centered republic to a man-centered corporate democracy.[154] During the *Reconstruction Era* of the Civil War years, this *de facto* government made advances in its plan for world domination and enslavement of the people by creating a for-profit Prison Industry which has been designed so that a percentage of today's school children are guaranteed as tomorrow's workers in their for-profit Prison Industry.[155] Restoring the American Republic will end this "merchandising" in the "souls of men."[156]

Four. Today's illiteracy will be cured. In the Founding Era 100% were literate.[157] Americans were the awe of Europe.[158] Today the illiterate (if not State welfare-dependent), fill inferior jobs resulting in the Creator's design for the destiny of the unique individual to be thwarted. By conquering illiteracy and presenting Christian liberty to school-aged children, there will also be a reduction in crime.[159]

---

[153] Republic for the United States of America, *Executive Summary with Historical Addendum*, Aug 23, 2019, RepublicForTheUnitedStatesOfAmerica.org

[154] Rosalie J. Slater, M.A., *Teaching and Learning America's Christian History*, (San Francisco: Foundation for American Christian Education, 1965/1969) xiii

[155] Vicky Pelaez, "The Prison Industry in the United States: Big Business or a New Form of Slavery?," *Global Research,* March 31, 2014, as cited by Jean Hallahan Hertler with David Carl Hertler, *Re-inhabited: Republic for the United States of America*, Vol. I, "America's Truthful History," (ValleyAssetsPublishing.com 2016) 262

[156] *Revelation 18:12-13 ~ "The merchandise of gold, and silver, and precious stones, and of pearls, and fine linen, and purple, and silk, and scarlet, and all thyine wood, and all manner vessels of ivory, and all manner vessels of most precious wood, and of brass, and iron, and marble, And cinnamon, and odours, and ointments, and frankincense, and wine, and oil, and fine flour, and wheat, and beasts, and sheep, and horses, and chariots, and slaves, and souls of men."*

[157] Marshall Foster, Mary Elaine Swanson, *The American Covenant: The Untold Story*, (Thousand Oaks: The Mayflower Institute, 1992) 8-9 as citing Rosalie J. Slater, M.A., *Teaching and Learning America's Christian History*, (San Francisco: Foundation for American Christian Education, 1965/1969) 89

[158] Alexis de Tocqueville, *Democracy in America,* (Rochelle, NY: Arlington House, 1840 Heirloom Edition) 1:326-327 as cited by W. Cleon Skousen, *The Majesty of God's Law, It's Coming to America*, (Salt Lake City: Ensign Publishing, 1996) 520

[159] Phyllis Schlafly, "Big Brother Education, 1994:Out-based Education Nonsense," *The Phyllis Schlafly Report,* May 1994, eagleforum.org as cited by Jean Hallahan Hertler with David Carl Hertler, *Re-inhabited: Republic for the United States of America,* Vol. I, "America's Truthful History," (ValleyAssetsPublishing.com 2016) 256-261

Five. The curses of disobedience (*Deuteronomy 28:15-68*) currently being experienced in this nation will be corrected by teaching Biblical Christian self-government and our unique republican form of government that results in the blessings of obedience (*Deuteronomy 28:1-13*).

A summary of the Biblical covenanted blessings of obedience sanctioned for a nation in keeping and obeying God's Law, include:

> Becoming the greatest nation on earth.
>
> Being blessed with an abundance of food, clothing, and comfortable homes.
>
> Being blessed with good health and strong children.
>
> Being blessed with great military strength so that no nation would dare attack them, and in case of war they would be blessed with victory.
>
> Being blessed with abundant rains and flourishing crops.
>
> Being blessed with so much wealth that other nations would come to borrow, but they would never have need to borrow from others.

A more narrowed summary of the blessings for obedient performance are national independence, individual life, liberty, and the pursuit of happiness.[160]

A summary of the Biblical covenanted curses of disobedience sanctioned for a nation in not keeping and obeying God's Law, include:

> Becoming a wandering, scattered, homeless, poverty-stricken people.
>
> Being cursed, despised, and abused wherever they went.
>
> Suffering terrible diseases, plagues, pestilences, famine, thirst, and, in time of siege, they would eat their own dead.
>
> Being weak, vulnerable, and continually conquered by their enemies. Their land would be confiscated, their crops devoured, their wives ravished, and their daughters carried away into slavery.
>
> Among the nations of the world, they would never be the head but always the tail.
>
> In the end, there would be pitifully few of them left compared to the vast multitude they might have been.

A more narrowed summary of the curses for disobedience in non-performance are: tyranny, oppression, and even death.[161]

---

[160] W. Cleon Skousen, *The Majesty of God's Law, It's Coming to America*, (Salt Lake City: Ensign Publishing, 1996) 162-163
[161] Ibid., 163

We must see clearly while also holding a holy conviction before Almighty God to impart knowledge by educating the American people concerning our heritage and true history that secures the keystone of our Christian heritage.

The American people must also be diligent and move quickly in this most important command of the Lord in training up our children.[162]

Knowledge of our Christian heritage and the ways of blessing by our Creator to know safety and happiness—Liberty—is in our power to determine our future and that of our posterity, our seed, our inheritance of the Lord, and His inheritance from us.[163]

Again, we revert to the wisdom of our early fathers.

Lyman Beecher (1775-1863) was a distinguished Presbyterian preacher and revivalist before the Civil War. Having become well known as a reformer, educator, and central figure in theological controversies, Reverend Beecher later became the president and professor at Lane Theological Seminary. In 1831, Lyman Beecher wrote in the newspaper, *The Spirit of the Pilgrims:*

> *"The government of God is the only government which will hold society, against depravity within and temptation without; and this it must do by the force of its own law written upon the heart. This is that unity of the Spirit and that bond of peace which can alone perpetuate national purity and tranquility – that law of universal and impartial love by which alone nations can be kept back from ruin. There is no safety for republics but in self-government, under the influence of a holy heart, swayed by the government of God."* [164]

Lyman Beecher[165]

James 1:25 ~

> *"But whoso looketh into the perfect law of liberty, and continueth therein, he being not a forgetful hearer, but a doer of the work, this man shall be blessed in his deed."*

---

[162] *Proverbs 22:6 ~ Train up a child in the way he should go, And when he is old he will not depart from it.*
[163] *Psalm 127:3 ~ Lo, children are an heritage of the LORD: and the fruit of the womb is his reward.*
[164] William J. Federer, *America's God and Country Encyclopedia of Quotations*, "Lyman Beecher," (Coppell: FAME Publishing, Inc., 1994) 42-43 as citing from Lyman Beecher. 1831. *The Spirit of the Pilgrims.* Petty Miller, *The Life of the Mind in America from the Revolution to the Civil War-Books 1-3* (New York: Harcourt, Brace & World, 1966) 36; Peter Marshall and David Manuel, *The Glory of America* (Bloomington, MN: Garborg's Heart'N Home, Inc., 1991), 12:5.
[165] *Wikimedia Commons*, s.v. "Lyman Beecher - Brady-Handy.jpg," This work is in the public domain

President John Quincy Adams [166]

John Quincy Adams (1767-1848), son of Founding Father and signer of the *Declaration of Independence* John Adams, was a lawyer, diplomat, politician, and the sixth President of the United States of America. On July 4th, 1837, he gave a speech on the fiftieth anniversary of the *Declaration of Independence.* He interjected:

"Why is it that, next to the birthday of the Savior of the World, your most joyous and most venerated festival returns on this day?

Is it not that, in the chain of human events, the birthday of the nation is indissolubly linked with the birthday of the Savior? That it forms a leading event in the Progress of the Gospel dispensation?

Is it not that the Declaration of Independence first organized the social compact on the foundation of the Redeemer's mission upon earth?

That it laid the cornerstone of human government upon the first precepts of Christianity and gave to the world the first irrevocable pledge of the fulfilment of the prophecie announced directly from Heaven at the birth of the Saviour and predicted by the greatest of the Hebrew prophets 600 years before?" [167]

Daniel Webster (1782-1852) has been considered one of the greatest orators in American history. He was a lawyer and statesman who served as a U.S. Representative, a U.S. Senator, and as the Secretary of State for three different Presidents. On December 22, 1820, at the *Bicentennial Celebration* at Pilgrim's landing, Plymouth Rock there was conversation about plans for a national monument to be dedicated to our forefathers, the Pilgrims. Webster memorialized this most magnificent endeavor of the Kingdom jurisdiction on earth put forth in his speech…[168]

"Lastly, our ancestors established their system of government on morality and religious sentiment. Moral habits, they believed, cannot safely be trusted on any other foundation than religious principle, nor any government be secure which is not supported by moral habits…. Whatever makes men good Christians, makes them good citizens."

---

[166] *Wikimedia Commons*, s.v. "ADAMS, John Q-President (BEP engraved portrait).jpg," This work is in the public domain
[167] John Quincy Adams, *An oration delivered before the inhabitants of the town of Newburyport, at their request : on the sixty-first anniversary of the Declaration of Independence, July 4th, 1837,* (Newburyport, MA: Printed by Morss and Brewster, 1837) 67
[168] Daniel Webster, *An oration delivered before the inhabitants of the town of Newburyport, at their request : on the sixty-first anniversary of the Declaration of Independence, July 4th, 1837* (Newburyport, MA: Printed by Morss and Brewster, 1837) 67, 32-33, 73-74

"Cultivated mind was to act on uncultivated nature; and, more than all, <u>a government, and a country, were to commence, with the very first foundations laid under the divine light of the christian religion</u>. Happy auspices of a happy futurity! Who would wish that his country's existence had otherwise begun?"

"Finally, let us not forget the religious character of our origin. Our fathers were brought hither by their high veneration for the <u>Christian Religion</u>. They journeyed by its light, and laboured in its hope. <u>They sought to incorporate its principles with the elements of their society, and to diffuse its influence through all their institutions, civil, political, or literary.</u> Let us cherish these sentiments, and extend this influence still more widely; in full conviction, that that is the happiest society, which partakes in the highest degree of the mild and peaceful spirit of Christianity."[169] [Emphasis added]

Daniel Webster[170]

Daniel Webster expressed his Providential worldview when he said,

"History is God's providence in human affairs."[171]

In 1802, at the age of 20, Daniel Webster served as the headmaster of Fryeburg Academy in Fryeburg, Maine, where he delivered a *Fourth of July Oration*. His words of wisdom and exhortation still speak to the American people today as he exhorts them to hold onto the *Constitution* and to the Republic for which it stands. He warns that if the *Constitution* should fail, that there will be anarchy throughout the world.

"<u>If an angel should be winged from Heaven, on an errand of mercy to our country, the first accents that would glow on his lips would be, Beware! be cautious! you have everything to lose; you have nothing to gain.</u>

<u>We live under the only government that ever existed which was framed by the unrestrained and deliberate consultations of the people. Miracles do not cluster. That which has happened but once in six thousand years cannot be expected to happen often.</u>

<u>Such a government, once gone, might leave a void, to be filled, for ages, with revolution and tumult, riot and despotism.</u>"[172]

Now is the time to restore our heritage and birthright in a jurisdiction made possible by Christ and put forth by those who led the way on the path of Liberty. *"This is the way, walk ye in it."*[173]

---

[169] Daniel Webster, *The Works of Daniel Webster* (Boston: Little, Brown and Company, 1853), Vol. I, 22-44
[170] Library of Congress, "Daniel Webster," Published by E.C. Middleton & Co., Cincinnati, O. This work is in the public domain
[171] Wallbuilders.com, "God Missing in Action from American History," (December 31, 2016)
[172] Daniel Webster, *Fourth of July Oration 1802*, Fryeburg, Maine (Boston, Mass.: A. Williams & Co.; Fryeburg ME.; A.F. & C.W. Lewis, 1882) 13-14
[173] *Isaiah 30:21 ~ And thine ears shall hear a word behind thee, saying, This is the way, walk ye in it, when ye turn to the right hand, and when ye turn to the left.*

"The Gathering,"
by Brian Lee

Cover painting on *Re-inhabited: Republic for the United States of America*
Volume I: "America's Truthful History,"
by Jean Hallahan Hertler with David Carl Hertler

*Justice and judgment are the habitation of thy throne:
mercy and truth shall go before thy face.   ~ Psalm 89:14*

*Now it is in mine heart to make a covenant with the Lord God of Israel,
that his fierce wrath may turn away from us.   ~ 2 Chronicles 29:10*

*Ye children of Israel, turn again unto the Lord God of Abraham, Isaac,
and Israel, and he will return to the remnant of you…   ~ 2 Chronicles 30:6b*

Chapter Two

The Biblical View on the American Revolution with Nathaniel Whitaker, D.D. in 1777

Our history is our heritage. By studying history, we understand and see patterns that playout and repeat.[174] With a *Providential worldview*, along with knowledge and understanding of the *Scriptures*, we recognize the *Hand of Providence* on His people in the *Chain of Christianity* moving westward to America and are able to discern or predict the future because of knowing those established patterns. Wisdom would direct us to go back in time to our early fathers and seek their wisdom while also discerning the times.

This selection is a focused scope in review of a sermon preached in 1777 by Nathaniel Whitaker, D.D. (1732-1795), on a Biblical view of Creator God's position, as evidenced in the *Word of God*, in how His people are to view and respond to His enemies. It is a "living" sermon that speaks today, and for the *Body of Christ* today, to see and understand through the lenses of a revered Patriot Preacher of the *American Revolution* and the *War for Independence*. We will see how our current day drama parallels the conflict our Founding Fathers faced and gain perspective in the necessity and outlook of overcoming our enemies—both foreign and domestic—as we also come to see God's solution.

Reverend Nathaniel Whitaker, D.D.[175]
Courtesy of Hood Museum of Art,
Dartmouth College

We begin with the introduction written by Frank Moore (1828-1904), author of *The Patriot Preachers of the American Revolution: With Biographical Sketches*, published in 1862 [176]:

"*Nathaniel Whitaker, D.D.*"

"*Among preachers of the revolutionary period no one manifested a stronger dislike to the usurpations of the British crown than Doctor Whitaker. Possessed of great biblical learning and commanding powers of elocution [the art of rhetoric, the power of speaking], which he used upon every opportunity for the service of his suffering country, he exercised a wide influence among the people, and was looked upon as a 'great political counsellor.'*

---

[174] *Ecclesiastes 1:9 ~ The thing that hath been, it is that which shall be; and that which is done is that which shall be done: and there is no new thing under the sun.*
[175] Hood Museum of Art, Dartmouth College, "Reverend Nathaniel Whitaker (1730-1795), Class of 1780H," accessed April 2, 2021, https://hoodmuseum.dartmouth.edu/objects/p.866.1
[176] Frank Moore, *The Patriot Preachers of the American Revolution: With Biographical Sketches; Nathaniel Whitaker, D.D., "An Antidote against Toryism, or the Curse of Meroz,* (New York: Charles T. Evans, 1862) 186-231

He was a native of Long Island, New York, and was born on the twenty-second day of February, 1732. At the age of twenty, having passed his college life with marked attention to his studies and the cultivation of letters, he graduated at Princeton, and soon after was engaged in the ministry at Norwich, Connecticut. On the twenty-eighth of July, 1769, having agreed with the Third Church in Salem, Massachusetts, 'that he would become their minister without public instalment, and that they should be under Presbyterian order, until they saw cause to alter,' he preached a sermon and entered upon the duties of that church. Here he continued to labor with increased reputation.

In the early part of 1775, his church was destroyed by fire, and his people were obliged to worship in a schoolhouse. A letter of Doctor Whitaker, written at this time mentions the separation of many of his congregation from his church. This circumstance arose from a preference on the part of the seceders for the congregational form of government, under which Doctor Whitaker refused to preach. This spirit of dissension continued to increase until 1783, when the Third Church expressed a desire to return to congregationalism, and Doctor Whitaker retired from the pulpit.

Soon after he visited Virginia, where he died. The records of his life are scanty, but enough remains in his printed sermons to entitle him to the name he has received, 'an uncompromising man, pious, learned and charitable.' His sermon 'An Antidote against Toryism,' was delivered at Salem, Massachusetts, and printed in 1777, with an extended dedication to General Washington."

The British Burned Churches[177]

---

[177] The British Burned Churches, Screen grab from YouTube/helgargead, "The Patriot- Burn the Church" https://youtu.be/2Py2LZNb79Q

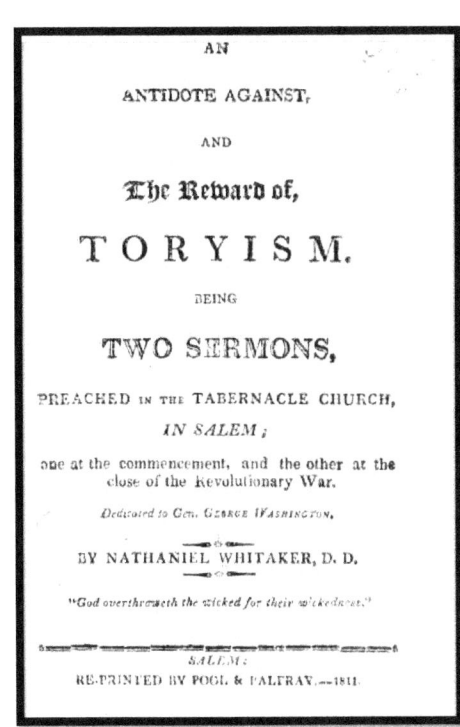

Title page of "An Antidote Against, and The Reward of, Toryism, Being Two Sermons"
Preached in the Tabernacle Church, in Salem:
One at the commencement,
and the other at the close of the Revolutionary War.
Dedicated to Gen. George Washington
By Nathaniel Whitaker, D.D.
"God overthroweth the wicked for their wickedness."
Salem: Re-printed by Pool & Palfray – 1811.

ANTIDOTE AGAINST TORYISM.

"Curse ye Moroz, said the angel of the Lord, curse ye bitterly the inhabitants thereof, because they came not to the help of the Lord against the mighty. – Judges, 5:23"

"The sum of the law of nature, as well as of the written law, is love. Love to God and man, properly exercised in tender feelings of the heart, and beneficent actions of life, constitutes perfect holiness."

The Declaration of Independence[178]

What preacher Whitaker was referencing was a phrase in the preamble to the *Declaration of Independence*, "the laws of nature and of nature's God." This phrase describes what God created and of His written word. The Founding Fathers made no laws repugnant to *the Laws of Nature and of Nature's God*. In 1766, this phrase was found in *Blackstone's Commentaries* of which the nation's Founders studied in law school and was also clearly expressed by Thomas Jefferson in 1776 as he penned the *Declaration of Independence*. Carefully consider as Whitaker goes on to say…

"The gospel breathes the same spirit, and acknowledges none as the disciples of Christ but those who love not their friends only, but even their enemies. Bless and curse not, is one of the laws of his kingdom. Yet the aversion of men to this good and benevolent law prompts them to frequent violations of it, which is the source of all the evils we feel or fear. And so lost are many to all the tender feelings required in this law, as to discover their enmity to their Creator, by opposing the happiness of his creatures, and spreading misery and ruin among them."

Remember this – the cause of happiness is the cause of God!

---

[178] *Wikimedia Commons* s.v. "United States Declaration of Independence," This work is in the public domain

> *"When such characters as these present themselves to our view, if we are possessed with the spirit of love required in the law and gospel, we must feel a holy abhorrence [repugnance or hatred] of them."*
>
> [Emphasis added]

Preacher Whitaker continues by saying…

> *"Love itself implies hatred to malevolence [ill-will or an evil disposition towards another], and the man who feels no abhorrence [repugnance] of it, may be assured he is destitute [spiritually bankrupt] of a benevolent temper, and ranks with the enemies of God and man. For, as God himself hates sin with a perfect hatred from the essential holiness of his nature, and sinners cannot stand in his sight, so the greater our conformity to him [Christ] is, the greater will be our abhorrence of those persons and actions which are opposite to the divine law.*
>
> *[Old Testament] David mentions this as an evidence of his love to God: Psalm 139, 'Do not I hate them, O Lord, that hate thee? and am I not grieved with them that rise up against thee? I hate them with a perfect hatred. I count them mine enemies. True benevolence [charity] is, therefore, exercised in opposing those who seek the hurt of society, and none are to be condemned as acting against the law of love, because they hate and oppose such as are injurious to happiness.'"* [Emphasis added]

Remember this—even God's hatred of sin, and the punishment He inflicts on the wicked, arises from His love of happiness, from the benevolence of His nature.

> *"But the weakness and corruption of nature, in the best, is such, that God hath not intrusted to men at large the exercise of the resentment due to such characters, nor allowed them to inflict those punishments which their crimes call for, even in this world…"*

Remember this—if we exercise resentment toward the people that carry misery, we can take on roots of bitterness toward them and find ourselves in bondage and locked in our own prison. Resentment must be released to our Father in heaven. So, God has strictly prohibited all of His subjects from taking vengeance for private or personal injuries in a private and personal manner, and requires that if *"one smite us on the one cheek, we turn to him the other also."*[179] And, in the language of love, exhorts us, *"Dearly beloved, avenge not yourselves."*[180]

Before continuing with Nathaniel Whitaker's sermon that he preached to the Third Church in Salem, Massachusetts in the autumn of 1777, let's go back in time 114 years earlier to a story about a man whose name was John Eliot (1604-1690).

> *"For one hundred and fifty years from the time of the first settlements <u>the American Colonists had learned government from **the Bible.**</u> Educated primarily by their ministers, as we shall see, the colonists learned the nature of man and the necessity of the Word of God for His government—as individuals and as colonists. They learned that without the Bible, society was not safe.* ***It was the source of all liberty—internal and external—the Textbook of Liberty for all men.***

---

[179] *Matthew 5:39 ~ But I say unto you, That ye resist not evil: but whosoever shall smite thee on thy right cheek, turn to him the other also.*
[180] *Romans 12:19 ~ Dearly beloved, avenge not yourselves, but rather give place unto wrath: for it is written, Vengeance is mine; I will repay, saith the Lord.*

With this conviction, it is not surprising that the first American Bible was an Indian Bible, published in 1663 in Massachusetts with funds collected by the Society for the Propagation of the Gospel in England. The moving force behind this unique Bible was John Eliot, pastor of the church in Roxbury. Before beginning the arduous work of translating the whole Bible, Reverend Eliot had to produce an Indian Grammar in the Algonquin language." [181] [Emphasis added]

John Eliot, 17th century[182]
Puritan missionary to the American Indians who some called "the apostle to the Indians"

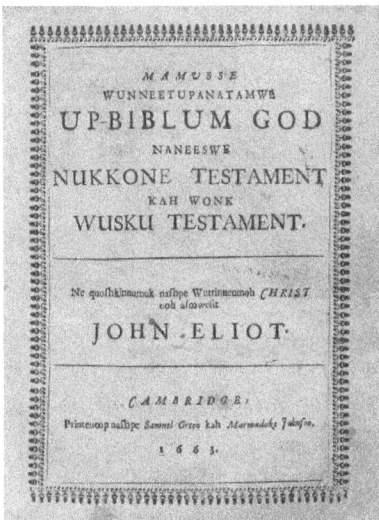

*Title page of
"Mamusse wunneetupanatamwe Up-Biblum God naneeswe Nukkone Testament kah wonk Wusku Testament,"
by John Eliot,
Cambridge, Massachusetts: 1663* [183]

The Eliot Indian Bible is the first Bible printed in America, translated into the Massachusett language by John Eliot.

"John Eliot's purpose as Apostle to the Massachusetts Indians in the seventeenth century was to prepare them to receive the character for Christian self-government. With the help of his Indian converts and the Massachusetts legislature, he set up fourteen Praying Towns. In these towns the Indians learned to be both self-governing and self-supporting.

The development of a Christian Constitutional character was difficult for the American Indian. But the Gospel changed hearts, minds and even tribal customs of character. John Eliot believed in the propagation of Christianity by the Indians themselves and sought to instruct them in the establishing of their own churches and towns. His work in the preparation of an Indian Bible was a great encouragement to this ministry. With his associate, Daniel Gookin, military commander of the Colony, the first historian of the Christian Indians, John Eliot spent many years preparing the Massachusetts Indians to assume the responsibility for Christian self-government. Despite the devastation of King Philip's War in 1675 [King Philip was chief of the

---

[181] Verna Hall, Rosalie Slater, *The Bible and the Constitution of the United States of America,* (Chesapeake: The Foundation of American Christian Education, 2nd ed. 2012) 17
[182] *Wikimedia Commons* s.v. "John Eliot (missionary)," This work is in the public domain
[183] *Wikimedia Commons* s.v. "File:Houghton AC6 E£452 663m - John Eliot, 1663, title.jpg," This work is in the public domain

Wampanoag Indians], John Eliot had demonstrated the ability of the American Indians to govern and support themselves."[184] [Emphasis added]

"*In 1659, John Eliot wrote 'The Christian Commonwealth: or The Civil Policy or The Rising Kingdom of Jesus Christ,' wherein he says:*

'It is the Commandment of the Lord, that a people should enter into Covenant with the Lord to become his people, even in their Civil Society, as well as in their Church-Society (a) Whereby they submit themselves to be ruled by the Lord in all things, receiving from him, both the platform of their Government, and all their Laws; which they do, then Christ reigneth over them in all things, they being ruled by his Will, and by the Word of his Mouth. Is. 33:22 The Lord is our <u>Judge</u>, the Lord is our <u>Law-giver</u>, the Lord is our <u>King</u>, he shall save us.'"[185]

[Emphasis added]

John Eliot Preaching to the Indians[186]
Courtesy of the Presbyterian Historical Society

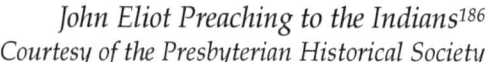

Now, having learned the story of John Eliot who taught *Christian Commonwealth and self-government*, it is essential to know and comprehend the foundation of self-government. It is based on,

Matthew 22:36-40 ~ ³⁶Master, which is the great commandment in the Law? ³⁷ Jesus said unto him, Thou shalt love the Lord thy God, with all thy heart, and with all thy soul, and with all thy mind. ³⁸ This is the first and great commandment. ³⁹ And the second is like unto it, Thou shalt love thy neighbor as thyself. ⁴⁰On these two commandments hang all the law and the prophets.

It was in the year 1620 when the Pilgrims brought the *Mayflower Compact* **to Plymouth Rock and along with it they established "***Civil and Religious Liberty.***" The Pilgrims lived with "***self-government and union***" as they established their commonwealth. Living a lifestyle of virtue, while also declaring the Gospel, created a strong Christian culture in the** *New World* **on the North American continent. Virtue was exercised in their homes, in their church fellowship, and in their civil society. As a result, they truly experienced** *Civil and Religious Liberty.*

---

[184] Verna Hall, Rosalie Slater, *The Bible and the Constitution of the United States of America*, (Chesapeake: The Foundation of American Christian Education, 2nd ed. 2012) 17-18

[185] John Eliot, *The Christian Commonwealth, or The Civil Policy of the Rising Kingdom of Jesus Christ*, (London, 1659. Reprinted by Arno Press, New Yor, 1972, pp. 1-2 as cited in Verna Hall, Rosalie Slater, *The Bible and the Constitution of the United States of America*, (Chesapeake: The Foundation of American Christian Education, 2nd ed. 2012) 17-18

[186] Pcusa.org, "Early American Bibles: Presbyterian Historical Society documents early scripture printing in U.S." Dec 19, 2017, https://www.pcusa.org/news/2017/12/19/early-american-bibles/

America hasn't experienced the preaching of *"the whole counsel of God"*[187] from the pulpit for scores of years. *Civil Liberty* is no longer talked about in our society or in our churches. Modern-day America doesn't know what true Liberty is!

Passengers of the Mayflower signing the "Mayflower Compact" including Carver, Winston, Alden, Myles Standish, Howland, Bradford, Allerton, and Fuller.

Postcard published by The Foundation Press, Inc., 1932. Reproduction of oil painting from series: The Pageant of a Nation. [188]

Dr. Whitaker started his sermon with these words, *"The sum of the law of nature, as well as of the written law, is love."* We emphasize again that Dr. Whitaker, "the great political counsellor," was referring to that specific phrase stated in the preamble of the *Declaration of Independence*, *"the Laws of Nature and of Nature's God."*

There are five derivative principles of *the Laws of Nature and of Nature's God*. They are <u>first</u>, that people are all created by God, and that by virtue of this circumstance are therefore entitled to be treated equally before the law. <u>Second</u>, all people are endowed by God with certain unalienable rights. <u>Third</u>, the people are also endowed with the right to govern themselves according to their written consent. <u>Fourth</u>, the people retain the right to alter or abolish an unlawful form of government as an exercise of self-government. <u>Fifth</u>, the people are free to organize the civil government's powers in such a way as to secure their happiness.[189]

Remember — the cause of happiness is the cause of God!

Dr. Whitaker continues…

> *"…Yet there are cases in which he requires us, as his servants, to take vengeance on his enemies. And it deserves our particular notice, that all these cases respect crimes which tend to destroy human happiness.*
>
> *…So God requires us to execute vengeance on the murderer, the thief, the adulterer, reviler [one who uses contemptuous language], and the like; all which sins strike at the peace and happiness of human society. God's heart is so much set upon diffusing happiness among his creatures, by which He most displays his glory, that he perfectly abhors whatever tends to frustrate this end; and has threatened the least opposition to it with everlasting death in the world to come. But some (through the*

---

[187] *Acts 20:27 (NKJV) ~ For I have not shunned to declare to you the whole counsel of God.*
[188] Library of Congress, "The Mayflower Compact 1620," Digital ID: cph 3g07155   This work is in the public domain
[189] Kerry L. Morgan, "The Laws of Nature and of Nature's God; The Cornerstone of Inalienable Rights," accessed April 2, 2021, https://lonang.com/commentaries/conlaw/organizing/cornerstone-of-inalienable-rights/

corruption of nature by sin) have not faith in a future state of rewards and punishments sufficient to influence them to their duty, or deter [discourage] them from opposing God's gracious purpose, therefore, to strike our senses with full conviction of his anger against such as counteract his benevolent designs, he has commanded every society of men, to inflict punishment on them in this world, and has specified the crimes, the punishments, and the officers who are to inflict them.

Every punishment involves in it a curse, and presupposes some crime; and the curse or punishment is by God exactly proportioned to the nature, heinousness, and circumstances of the crime. Therefore, when a grievous punishment is inflicted, we justly infer the aggravation of the offence. To inflict punishment, is actively to curse, and when we pronounce a curse, we do, as far as we can, consign over the object to some punishment. But when God commands us to curse any person or people, we are bound by his authority actually to punish them.

These observations may lead us to some apprehension of the aggravated nature of the sin of Meroz, whom Israel are commanded to curse bitterly for their conduct in an affair of a public nature." [Emphasis added]

Whitaker continues…

"The text [Judges 5:23] I have chosen as the theme of my discourse, is part of a song uttered by Deborah and Barak, in holy triumph and praise for a signal victory obtained over Jabin, king of Canaan, and Sisera, the captain of his host. This powerful prince, who had nine hundred chariots of iron, and a mighty army, had brought Israel into subjection, and grievously oppressed them for twenty years. [Judges chapter four.] This cruel and galling yoke awakened them to a sense of their sin against God, and to cry to him for deliverance. No sooner are they made sensible of their sin against, and dependence on him, and to repent and seek his favor and protection, than he appears for their help, and raises up and inspires Deborah and Barak with courage, and faith in his power and grace, to oppose the tyrant, and shake off his yoke. A few men of Zebulon and Naphtali, viz. [that is to say, namely], ten thousand, were designed by God to have the honor of conquering this potent king; for ten other tribes mustered and were ready for the war, yet it seems Zebulon and Naphtali only, were the people that jeoparded [put in danger] their lives to the death, in the high place of the field. And the little army – raised from two tribes only out of twelve – of Deborah and Barak march out and wage war against their oppressor, for the recovery of their [Liberty]." [Emphasis added]

Whitaker continues…

"Jabin, it seems, had no knowledge or thought that Israel was arming against him. The first intelligence brought him was, that Barak was gone up to Mount Tabor, that he had already marched, and was on his way to invade his country. Some traitors, who pretended friendship to Israel, carried him the news, hoping, doubtless, to ingratiate [to commend one's self to another's good will, confidence or kindness in seeking favor] themselves with Jabin, by giving him the earliest notice possible of this revolt." [Emphasis added]

On a side note, we find it of interest concerning women whose strength and confidence is in Almighty God:

Judges 4:8-9 ~ ⁸ And Barak said unto her, If thou wilt go with me, then I will go: but if thou wilt not go with me, then I will not go. ⁹ And she said, I will surely go with thee: notwithstanding the journey that thou takest shall not be for thine honour; for the Lord shall sell Sisera into the hand of a woman. And Deborah arose, and went with Barak to Kedesh.

Deborah and Barak[190]
Courtesy of AssociationCovenantPeople.org

Preacher Whitaker continues…

> *"No doubt, both Jabin and Sisera despised this small body of undisciplined, unarmed troops, and were confident they should carry all before them, and quickly reduce those rebels (as he, doubtless, termed them) to their former obedience."*

Again, a needed break from the sermon. It's important to demonstrate from recorded history in the *Scriptures* that when God's people stand in faith against His enemies, calling upon Him for assistance, Divine intervention takes place. Let's visit *Joshua 5:13-15* ~

"¹³And it came to pass, when Joshua was by Jericho, that he lifted up his eyes and looked, and, behold, there stood a man over against him with his sword drawn in his hand: and Joshua went unto him, and said unto him, Art thou for us, or for our adversaries? ¹⁴And he said, Nay; but as captain of the host of the Lord am I now come. And Joshua fell on his face to the earth, and did worship, and said unto him, what saith my Lord unto his servant? ¹⁵And the captain of the Lord's host said unto Joshua, Loose thy shoe from off thy foot; for the place where on thou standest is holy. And Joshua did so."

"Captain of the host of the Lord am I."
from The Art Bible (1896)
depicting Joshua 5:13–15[191]

---

[190] AssociationCovenantPeople.org, "Deborah and Barak," as displayed in "Deborah and Barak," by Jackie Edwards accessed February 5, 2024
[191] Free.messianicbible.com, "Is It a Man, Angel, or God?: Angels can watch or patrol the earth and fight with demonic beings; God is the Captain of the Host of Armies," https://free.messianicbible.com/feature/is-it-a-man-angel-or-god/

Deborah the judge[192]
Courtesy of Discover.hubpages.com
Pioneer Women

Now let's visit *Judges 4:14 and 15*…

> ¹⁴*And Deborah said unto Barak. Up; for this is the day in which the Lord hath delivered Sisera into thine hand: is not the Lord gone out before thee? So Barak went down from Mount Tabor, and ten thousand men after him.* ¹⁵*And the Lord discomfited or defeated Sisera, and all his chariots, and all his host, with the edge of the sword before Barak; so that Sisera lighted down off his chariot, and fled away on his feet.*

Now returning to Whitaker's sermon…

> "But God, who disposes all events, not only gave the victory to Israel, but utterly destroyed the whole host of Jabin, that not one escaped, except Sisera the captain-general, and him God delivered to be slain by the hand of a woman. Women have sometimes been deliverers of their country, and can, when God inspires them with courage, face the proudest foe. Oh, how easy is it with God to save from the greatest danger, and, by the weakest instruments, conquer the most powerful enemies!

> Deborah and Barak, deeply impressed with a sense of God's mercy in this deliverance, sang this song [Judges chapter 5] as an expression of their joy and gratitude, from which, would time allow, many instructive lessons might be deduced. But the words of my text lead us more directly to consider some things most worthy our attention this day, and therefore I have chosen them as the theme of the following discourse, and in them we may observe:

> **One**. The crime for which this bitter curse is denounced on the inhabitants of Meroz. Probably this was some town or state in Israel, who, being called to furnish their quota of men and money for the war, through fear of bad success and, in that case, of a heavier burden; or from a secret lurch [an awkward, swaying or staggering motion or gait] to the enemy, arising from hope of court preferment, or favors already bestowed on some of their leading men; or from some other sinister motive, thought best to lie still, and not meddle in the quarrel. So much is certain, they did not go with Barak to the war. The crime they are charged with, is not their aiding, assisting, or furnishing the enemy, or holding a secret correspondence with, or taking up arms to help them; they are not charged as laying plots to circumvent [bypass, avoid, evade or escape] the rest, or striving to discourage their neighbors from going to the war, or as terrifying others with description of the irresistible power of Jabin's nine hundred chariots of iron and the like." [Emphasis added]

---

[192] Discover.hubpages.com, "Deborah the judge," Pioneer Women - Part 1 - Deborah the Judge, https://discover.hubpages.com/religion-philosophy/Pioneer-Woman-Part-1-Deborah-the-Judge

Again, breaking away from the sermon. It would seem that the threat of losing their God-given Liberty was not the main focus or concern of all the people of Meroz. In drawing a parallel to the era of the *American Revolution*, it is historical fact that only three-to-four percent of the entire population of three million American colonists fought for independence from tyranny. The realization of the indifference and negligence of the people toward preserving their God-given Liberty is staggering.

Consider an excerpt from the great *"Give Me Liberty or Give Me Death"* speech that Patrick Henry, an American Revolutionary leader and five-time governor of Virginia, delivered before the *Second Virginia Convention* on March 23, 1775, that went like this:

> *"...and which we have pledged ourselves never to abandon until the glorious object of our contest shall be obtained we must fight! I repeat it, sir, we must fight! An appeal to arms and to the God of hosts is all that is left us! They tell us, sir, that we are weak, unable to cope with so formidable an adversary. But when shall we be stronger? Will it be the next week, or the next year? Will it be when we are totally disarmed, and when a British guard shall be stationed in every house? Shall we gather strength by irresolution and inaction? Shall we acquire the means of effectual resistance by lying supinely [with the face upward] on our backs and hugging the delusive phantom of hope, until our enemies shall have bound us hand and foot?"*[193] [Emphasis added]

Patrick Henry before the Virginia House of Burgesses
A painting of Patrick Henry's
speech against the Stamp Act of 1765,
"If this be treason, make the most of it!" [194]

As we consider the rational and valid point made by Patrick Henry in his speech, we are reminded that faith in God is more powerful than a thousand armies. As we realize that Almighty God was directing the war against Jabin and his nine-hundred chariots of iron, we also come to the realization in questioning how could the army of Israel lose? It furthers the realization that God also directed the American colonies to go to war against the British. That is how and why America gained her Independence!

Continuing forward with Preacher Whitaker…

> *"No, the inhabitants of Meroz were innocent people compared to these; they were only negatively wicked; they only failed in their duty;* **they did not arm to recover their liberties when wrested from them by the hand of tyranny.** *This is all the fault charged on them,* **yet for this they incurred the fearful curse** *in my text. Now, if for mere negligence they deserved this curse, what must they have deserved who aided and assisted the enemy? Surely a sevenfold bitterer curse.*

---

[193] Patrick Henry, *Give Me Liberty Or Give Me Death, Patrick Henry, March 23, 1775,* speech before the Virginia House of Burgesses at St. John's Church, https://avalon.law.yale.edu/18th_century/patrick.asp
[194] *Wikimedia Commons,* s.v. "Patrick Henry Rothermel.jpg," This work is in the public domain

Two. Observe the curse pronounced: 'Curse ye Moroz, curse ye bitterly the inhabitants thereof.' Their conduct, on that occasion, was such as deserved a severe punishment from the other states, who are commanded to separate them unto evil, as a just reward of their neglect.

Three. We observe by whom this curse was to be pronounced and inflicted. Not by Deborah and Barak alone, in a fit of anger, as profane persons in a rage curse their neighbors, and undertake to punish them; such often pronounce curses without cause, but the curse causeless shall not come. This curse was to be pronounced and inflicted <u>by all the people</u>, who are here <u>required to be of one heart</u>, and engage seriously, religiously, and determinately in cursing them, and as God's ministers to execute his wrath upon them. We may not suppose that this work was left to the people at large, or to a mob; but the rulers are first to proceed against them (this is evident from the order of government God established in Israel), and all the people to support and assist them in this work; and so <u>all were to join, as one man, to curse them, and that bitterly</u>, i.e. [for example], they were fully and without hesitation to condemn them to severe punishment, <u>and inflict it on them</u>. They were not to deal gingerly [cautiously or carefully] with them, nor palliate [gloss over, cover-up, lessen or soften] their offence. They are allowed to make no excuses for them, nor to plead 'that they were of a different opinion; that they thought it their duty not to take up arms against their king that ruled over them, but to submit to the higher powers; that liberty of conscience ought to be allowed to every one, and that it would be hard to punish them for acting their own judgments.'

Liberty of conscience is often pleaded as an excuse for the worst of crimes. In matters of mere conscience the plea is valid, but nothing else. Those are matters of mere conscience in which none are concerned but God and the person acting, as in matters of faith and worship. <u>But when actions disrespect society, and become injurious to the civil rights of men, they are proper subjects of civil laws, and may be punished, notwithstanding the plea for liberty of conscience</u>." [Emphasis added]

Whitaker continues…

"No such pleas might be made for them, nor one word spoken in their favor, their sin being against the great law of love and light of nature [the Laws of Nature and of Nature's God — Declaration of Independence]; but all, with full purpose of heart, were to curse those cowardly, selfish, cringing, lukewarm, half-way, two-faced people, and to treat them as outcasts, and unworthy the common protection or society of others.

Four. Observe by <u>whose command</u> they were required to curse Meroz. It was not by the command of Deborah and Barak, but of <u>God himself; yea by the command of Jesus Christ</u>, the meek and compassionate Saviour of men. Curse ye Meroz, said the angel of the Lord<u>. This was the angel of God's presence, who then fought for Israel, and who was so offended with the people of Meroz for their selfishness and indifference in this important cause, that he not only cursed them himself, but commands all the people to curse them, and inflict his wrath on them in this world</u>.

Five. Observe the circumstances which aggravated their crime, viz. [namely]: the enemy that enslaved them was mighty. Had the foe been weak and contemptible [abhorrent, disgusting or even hateful], there had been less need of their help. But when a powerful tyrant oppressed them, <u>and they were called upon to unite with their suffering brethren in shaking off his yoke, and all their strength little enough to oppose him, then to excuse themselves, was highly criminal, and in effect to join with the tyrant to rivet slavery and misery on the whole nation</u>. This was highly provoking to God, whose great end is, to diffuse happiness [by which the Lord is most *glorified], and not misery, among his creatures, and who never punishes but when his subjects oppose this design.*

This was the crisis when their all lay at stake. They well knew that their brethren (however they themselves might be distinguished with court favors by the tyrant) were groaning under cruel bondage. But as selfishness renders people callous and unfeeling to the distresses of others, so they were easy and satisfied to see their brethren tortured by the unrelenting hand of oppression, if so be they might sleep in a whole skin. They were contented that others should go forth and endure the hardships of war, but refused to engage in the work, or bear any part of the burden with them, though all was hazarded through their neglect. How base was this conduct, while they knew the strength of the enemy? This consideration was enough to have engaged every one, not lost to all the feelings of humanity, to the firmest union, and the most vigorous exertions [action or attempts]. But these servile [bootlicking, despicable] wretches would rather bear the yoke, and see the whole land involved in slavery, than enter the field and share the glory of regaining their [Liberty] from a powerful foe. They preferred their present ease, or some court favor, with chains and slavery, to the glorious freedom they were born to enjoy.

From this view of the text and context, we may deduce the following doctrinal observations:

<u>One</u>. *That the cause of liberty is the cause of God and truth.*

<u>Two</u>. *That to take arms and repel force by force, when our liberties are invaded, is well-pleasing to God.*

<u>Three</u>. *That it is lawful to levy war against those who oppress us, even when they are not in arms against us.*

<u>Four</u>. *That indolence [procrastination] and backwardness in taking arms, and exerting ourselves in the service of our country, when called thereto by the public voice, in order to recover and secure our freedom, is an heinous sin in the sight of God.*

<u>Five</u>. *That God requires a people, struggling for their liberties, to treat such of the community who will not join them, as open enemies, and to reject them as unworthy the privileges which others enjoy.*

<u>One</u>. ***The cause of [liberty] is the cause of God."***   [Emphasis added]

We pause to emphasize and remember — the cause of life, liberty, and happiness is the cause of God.

Whitaker continues…

"…*To open this, I will inquire:*

<u>First</u>. *What we are to understand by liberty, or freedom? And then,*"

Consider visiting <u>WhyLibertyMatters.com</u> and learn the depth and definition of Liberty:

> *"Having the opportunity to make a choice, assume responsibility, and accept the consequences."*[195]

Liberty Bell[196]
Courtesy of William Zhang

Whitaker continues…

> **Second**. *Prove that this is the cause of God.*
>
> **One**. *What [we are to understand] by liberty…?*
>
> *It is sufficient to my present purpose to distinguish liberty into moral, natural and civil.*
>
> *Moral liberty lies in an ability, or opportunity, to act or conduct as the agent pleases.*
>
> *He that is not hindered by any external force from acting as he chooses or wills to act, is perfectly free in a moral sense; and so far as he possesses this freedom, so far, and no farther, is he a moral, accountable creature, and his actions worthy of praise or blame.*
>
> *By natural liberty, I mean that freedom of action and conduct which all men have a right to, antecedent [or prior] to their being members of society. This Mr. Locke*[197] *defines to be 'that state or condition in which all men naturally are to order all their actions, and dispose of themselves and possessions as they think fit, within the bounds of the law of nature, without asking leave, or depending on the will of any man.'"*

Then Pastor Whitaker continues…

> *"In this state all men are equal, and no one hath a right to govern or control another. And the law of nature or the eternal reason and fitness of things, is to be the only rule of his conduct; of the meaning of which every one is to be his own judge.*
>
> *But since the corruption of nature by sin, the lusts and passions of men so blind their minds, and harden their hearts, that this perfect law of love is little considered, and less practised; so that a state of nature, which would have been a state of perfect freedom and happiness had man continued in his first rectitude [uprightness, honesty, integrity and righteousness], in a state of war, rapine [violent force, seizure] and murder. <u>Hence arises an absolute necessity that societies should form themselves into politic bodies, in order to enact laws for</u>*

---

[195] Dr. Marlene McMillan, *The Five Pillars of Liberty*, (Fort Worth: Liberty View Media, 2011) 17
[196] *Wikimedia Commons* s.v. "File:Liberty Bell 2017a.jpg," William Zhang, This file is licensed under the Creative Commons Attribution 2.0 Generic license.
[197] WallBuilders.com, "*John Locke—A Philosophical Founder of America*: *John Locke (1632-1704) is one of the most important, but largely unknown names in American history today. A celebrated English philosopher, educator, government official, and theologian, it is not an exaggeration to say that without his substantial influence on American thinking, there might well be no United States of America today – or at the very least, America certainly would not exist with the same level of rights, stability of government, and quality of life that we have enjoyed for well over two centuries.*"

the public safety, and appoint some to put them in execution, that the good may be encouraged, and the vicious deterred from evil practices; and these laws should always be founded on the law of nature."

So civil liberty is the freedom exercised by "bodies politic," the whole body of people united under one government, founded on *the Laws of Nature and of Nature's God*. It is to be the power of a civil society or state (body politic) to govern itself by its own discretion, or by laws of its own making, in order to enact laws for public safety without being subject to any foreign direction or the impositions, the laying on of something as a burden or obligation, of any extraneous power.

> *"Hence it appears, that perfect civil liberty differs from natural only in this, that in a natural state our actions, persons and possessions, are under the direction, judgment and control of none but ourselves; but in a civil state, under the direction of others, according to the laws of that state in which we live; which, by the supposition, are perfectly agreeable to the law of nature. [So], in the first case, private judgment; in the second, the public judgment of the sense of the law of nature, is to be the rule of conduct. When this is the case, civil liberty is perfect, and every one enjoys all that freedom which God designed for his rational creatures in a social state. All liberty beyond this is mere licentiousness – a liberty to sin, which is the worst of slavery. But when any laws are enacted which cross the law of nature, there civil liberty is invaded and God and man justly offended.* [Emphasis added]

Break! Think of the U.S. Supreme Court case, *Roe vs. Wade* concerning abortion. Think of taking prayer out of schools, also Bible curriculum. Think of the government prying itself into places of worship with corporate 501c3 status (the "Johnson gag order"[198]). These things terribly weakened the *Body of Christ* because the public effect was in violation of "*the Laws of Nature and of Nature's God*" and has resulted in bringing offense to both God and man.

Whitaker continues...

> *"Therefore, when those appointed to enact and execute laws, invade this liberty, they violate their trust, and oppress their subjects, and their constituents may lawfully depose them by force of arms, if they refuse to reform.*
>
> *Now, if it be unlawful for magistrates [public civil officers] in a state, to bind their subjects by laws contrary to the law of nature, and if in this case it is lawful for their subjects to depose [examine on oath] them, it follows, a fortiori [denoting or based on a conclusion for which there is strong evidence than for a previously accepted one], that should the rulers of one state assume a power to bind the people of another state who never intrusted them with a legislative power, by such unrighteous laws, those oppressed people would be under no kind of obligation to submit to them, but ought, if in their power, to oppose them and recover their liberty."*
>
> [Emphasis added]

---

[198] Ed. Gary Cass, *Gag Order,* (Fairfax: Xulon Press, 2005) p. 26
*In 1954, then-Senator Lyndon B. Johnson of Texas introduced "The Johnson Amendment" of which by enactment of Congress has come to affect the U.S. tax code resulting in the prohibiting of all 501(c)(3) non-profit organizations from endorsing or opposing political candidates. A quick summary: the IRS was given the power to "muzzle" free speech in churches.

Break! Let's take a look at the *Declaration of Independence*.[199]

"Let facts be submitted to a candid world:

~ He has kept among us, in times of peace, standing armies without the consent of our legislatures.
~ For quartering large bodies of armed troops among us.
~ For protecting them by a mock trial from punishment for any murders which they should commit to the inhabitants of these states.
~ For culling off our trade with all parts of the world.
~ For imploring taxes on us without our consent.
~ For depriving us in many cases of the benefit of trial by jury.
~ For transporting us beyond seas to be tried for pretended offenses.
~ For taking away our charters, abolishing our most valuable laws and altering fundamentally the forms of our government.
~ For suspending our own legislatures and declaring themselves invested with power to legislate for us in all cases whatsoever.
~ He has abdicated government here, by declaring us out of his protection and waging war against us.
~ He has plundered our seas, ravaged our coast, burned our towns, and destroyed the lives of our people."

Take note that there are sixteen more facts which were included that not only stated the specific reasons why the American people were under no obligation to submit to unrighteous laws, they also expressed the necessity in opposing them and recovering their Liberty. The Continental Congress, in the *Declaration of Independence*, proclaimed these reasons as notice "to a candid world."

Declaration of Independence
July 4th, 1776 [200]
painted by John Trumbull (1756-1843)
engraved by W.L. Ormsby (1834-1908)

---

[199] The U.S. National Archives & Records Administration, *The Declaration of Independence: A Transcription*, In Congress, July 4, 1776, https://dev.republicoftheunitedstates.org/wp-content/uploads/2014/03/NARA-The-Declaration-of-Independence-A-Transcription.pdf
[200] Library of Congress, "Declaration of Independence, July 4th, 1776," item 96521535 No known restrictions

Preacher Whitaker…

"Therefore the freedom of a society or state [body politic] consists in acting according to their own choice, within the bounds of the law of nature, in governing themselves independent of all other states. This is the liberty wherewith God hath made every state free, and which no power on earth may lawfully abridge, but by their own consent; nor can they lawfully consent to have it abridged, but where it appears for the greater good of society in general: and when this end cannot be attained, they have a right to resume their former freedom, if in their power.

<u>Two</u>. I proceed to prove that the cause of civil liberty is the cause of God. This follows from what hath now been said. For if the law of nature [and of nature's God] is the law of God, and if God hath given every society or state [body politic] liberty independent of all other states, to act according to their own choice in governing themselves [to secure their happiness] within the bounds of the law of nature, then it follows that this [liberty] is of God, and he that is an advocate [backer, promoter or supporter] for it espouses the cause of God, and he that opposes it opposes God himself. This liberty hath God not only given, but entailed [brought about] on all men, so that they cannot resign it to any creature without sin. Therefore, should any state [body politic], through fear, resign this [liberty] to any other power, it would be offensive to God. Thus, had America submitted to, and acquiesced in the declaration of the British Parliament, 'that they have a right to bind us in all cases whatsoever,' we should have greatly provoked God by granting that prerogative [an exclusive or peculiar privilege] to men, which belongs to God only; nor could we have reason to hope for pardon and the divine favor on our land, without unfeigned repentance; but, as repentance implies a change of conduct, as well as of mind, so we must have exerted ourselves to undo what we had done, and by every method in our power to cast off the chains and resume our liberty. But, to leave the dim light of reason, let us hear what divine revelation says in my text and context.

Israel were a free, independent commonwealth, planted by God in Canaan, in much the same manner that he planted us in America. The nations around always viewed them with an envious and jealous eye, as well they might, since they drove out seven nations more powerful than themselves, and possessed their land. But when, by their grievous sins they provoked God, he often permitted those neighboring nations to invade their rights [right arm of God's discipline], that they might be brought to a sense of their sin and duty.

Jabin, the king of Canaan, one of those states, was God's rod to humble them. **He invaded Israel, robbed them of their rights, and held them in slavery twenty years; in all which he acted the part of a cruel tyrant, and provoked God, to his own destruction. Jabin had long ruled over Israel; but this gave him no right. His dominion was still mere usurpation, as he robbed them of the liberty God had given them; and with a single view to recover this and punish the invader, God commanded them to wage war on the tyrant, and shake off his yoke.** *They obey the divine mandate, assemble their forces, call on the various states to join them in the glorious conflict; and God himself curses those who would not assist to punish this oppressor.*

No doubt, Jabin called this rebellion, and made proclamation that all who were found in arms, or any way aiding the revolt, should be deemed and treated as rebels, and their estates confiscated; but that all would make their submissions, should enjoy all their privileges, as before, at his sovereign disposal. A glorious offer! How worthy the joyful and thoughtful acceptance of men born to freedom! Rather where's the wretch so sordid as not to feel this as an insult to human nature? Or where's the Christian that does not view it as a reproach of his God? And who will not, with good Hezekiah, spread before the Lord, in humble prayer, the words of this Rabshekah ["chief of the princes"], published to reproach our God, as unable to defend us, though engaged in his cause? Or where is the man, so lost to all noble and generous feelings, that would not choose to die in the field of martial glory, rather than accept such insulting terms of peace, or rather of misery; to live and see himself, his friends, his wife, children and country, subjugated to the arbitrary will and disposal of a merciless tyrant?

But doubtless these inviting, gracious terms of peace, had great influence on some. The inhabitants of Meroz seem to have been such dastardly [cowardly, vile], low-spirited, court sycophants [bootlickers, doormats]; and also many in the tribe of Reuban, for whose divisions there were great searchings of heart. These probably trembled at the power of Jabin, and thought him invincible, though opposing God himself, whose cause they were called to espouse [adopt, embrace or maintain]. Some might call the war rebellion, and others, by open or secret practices, discourage and weaken the cause.

This is very applicable to our present case. We are declared rebels by the king of England. His servants offer pardon to all who will lay themselves at his feet to dispose of as he shall see fit, and 'to bind them, their children and estates, at his pleasure, in all cases whatsoever.' What gracious terms of peace! Must not this yoke sit with peculiar ease and pleasure on the necks of freeborn Americans! Yet, with horror be it spoken, there are freeborn sons of America so lost to all sense of honor, liberty, and every noble feeling, as to join the cry, and press for submission. O tell it not in Gath, publish it not in the streets of Ashkelon. **We have some, but blessed be God, that we have no more of the inhabitants of Meroz scattered among us; some whose endeavors to divide us, cause great searchings of heart. But be it known to them, and to all men, that they, as Meroz, are fighting against God. This assertion is confirmed by the curse denounced on Meroz by God's command; for had they not opposed him, he would not have cursed them. They, then, were the rebels, in the judgment of God, and not those who took up arms to recover their liberties: rebels against the God of Heaven; and therefore fell under his and his people's curse; as well as those shall, who oppose or neglect to promote the like glorious cause.**

King George III in 1765 [201]
"The king was completely blind with cataracts, increasingly deaf, and mad with mental illness." [202]

---

[201] *Wikimedia Commons, s.v.* "King George III in coronation robes, " by artist Allan Ramsay, Public domain
[202] Jean Hallahan Hertler with David Carl Hertler, *Re-inhabited: Republic for the United States of America,* Vol. I, "America's Truthful History," (Valley Assets Publishing, 2016) 21

From what hath been said, the truth of the second observation appears, viz. [namely]:

<u>*Two*</u>*. That to take arms, and repel force by force, when our liberties are invaded, is well pleasing to God.*

This is a natural consequence from what is said above, and from the text itself. Deborah and Barak, in taking arms against Jabin, acted agreeably to the law of nature [and of nature's God], which is the law of love; were also particularly excited, directed, and commanded thereto by God himself [Judges 4:6-7]. They did not, by this war, aim at dominion over others, nor seek to deprive any of their natural rights; ***but only to recover and secure the liberties and rights which had been wrested from them, that they might thereby spread peace and happiness through all the tribes of Israel; while the real happiness of others would not thereby be diminished.****"* [Emphasis added]

Remember — the cause of happiness is the cause of God. The cause of life and liberty is the cause of God.

"This, by the law of nature, was sufficient to justify them."

Remember, God's jurisdiction is *"the Laws of Nature and of Nature's God."* That includes the laws concerning what He has created (the immutable laws of the sciences), as well as His written Word.

"If, then they conformed to the law of love in taking up arms, and if God required them to make war on Jabin, then it was undeniably pleasing to him. But, if God approved their conduct in this case, he certainly will approve the like conduct in all similar cases. ***Therefore, when one country or state [body politic] invades the liberties of another, it is lawful, and well pleasing to God, for the oppressed to defend their rights by force of arms****."* [Emphasis added]

Make no mistake about it! The primary reason these men were willing to fight and some of them die, was **they believed that they were standing against tyranny, and they knew that if tyranny was not resisted in the *American Revolution* and *War for Independence*, tyranny would ultimately place its sites on the Church, and in the end the Gospel. The colonists were defending their right to preach and teach and live out their beliefs from *Scripture* as they believed God dictated to them.** The ministers of the *Revolution* were bold and fearless in the cause of their country. No class of men contributed more to carry forward the *Revolution* and to achieve independence than did the ministers.

*Reverend Peter Muhlenberg on January 21, 1776
at the close of a patriotic sermon,
threw aside his clerical robe and
revealed the uniform of a Continental colonel*

"There's a time to pray and a time to fight"

Courtesy of revolutionary-war-and-beyond.com

Preacher Whitaker...

> *"Yea, to neglect this, when there is a rational prospect of success, is a sin — a sin against God, and discovers a want of that benevolence, and desire of the* **happiness** *of our fellow-creatures, which* **is the highest glory of the saints***.*
>
> *I need not spend time to prove that our struggle with Great Britain is very similar to that of Israel and Jabin.* <u>*As they had, so have we been long oppressed by a power that never had any equitable right to our land, or to rule over us, but by our own consent, and agreeably to a solemn compact. When they violated this, all their right ceased, and they could have no better claim to dominion than Jabin had over Israel*</u>*. A power, indeed, has been usurped by Great Britain, 'to bind us in all cases whatsoever;' which claim that already produced many most unrighteous and oppressive laws, which they have attempted to enforce by their fleets and armies; in all which they can be no more justified than Jabin in his tyranny over Israel.* **Therefore, if it was their duty to fight for the recovery of their freedom, it must likewise be ours. And to neglect this, when called to it by the public voice, will expose us to the curse of Meroz. Yea;"** [Emphasis added]

The *Body of Christ* **in the 21st century is in the same position. It is time to break away from 501c3 corporate government status and repent and take up a war with the** *Money Changers* **and their Freemason progressive evil people in the "Deep State" who worship Satan. It is time for the "Body of Christ" in America to stand up and restore the** *Republic for the United States of America* **while also breaking away from the deceptive, tyrannical Corporate Democracy, which is Satan's government. The American Republic is God's government! This is part of God's solution for America!**

Whitaker continues...

> *"***Three***.* <u>*It is lawful, yea duty*</u>*, to levy war against those who oppress us, even when they are not in arms against us; if there be a rational probability of success.*
>
> *I say, if there be a rational probability of success. For the law of love or nature will not justify opposition to the greatest oppression, when such opposition must be attended with greater evils than submission. Therefore, the primitive Christians, and many of later ages, did not oppose their cruel persecutors; as it would, without a miracle, have brought on them inevitable destruction. But where there is a rational probability of success, any people may lawfully,* <u>*and it is their duty to, levy war on those who rob them of their rights, whether they be*</u>

rulers in the state [body politic] they live in, or any more distant powers, even before war is waged against them.

The truth of this appears from the instance before us. **Jabin at this time was not at war with Israel; no, they had been conquered and under his government twenty years; and nothing was heard, but the groans and cries of the oppressed. How then, it may be asked, can they be justified in commencing a war? Doubtless they had often petitioned for redress of grievances, as we have done, and to as little purpose. What more could they do in a peaceable way? They were reduced to the dreadful alternative, either tamely to submit themselves and children after them, to the galling yoke of merciless tyranny, or wage war on the tyrant. The last was the measure God approved, and therefore, by a special command, enjoined it on them.** *This we are sure he would not have done, had it been offensive to him. He did not require Israel to wait till Jabin had invaded their country and struck the first blow (as we did in respect to our British oppressors), but while all was peace in his kingdom, for aught we find, God commands Israel to raise an army, and invade the tyrant's dominions.*

The moral reason of this is obvious. **For usurpation or oppression, is offensive war, already levied. Any state [body politic] which usurps a power over another state, or rulers who, by a wanton use of their power, oppress their subjects, do thereby break the peace, and commence an offensive war. In such a case opposition is mere self-defence, and is no more criminal, yea, as really our duty as to defend ourselves against a murder, or highway robber. Self-preservation is an instinct by God implanted in our nature. Therefore we sin against God and nature, when we tamely resign our rights to tyrants, or quietly submit to public oppressors, if it be in our power to defend ourselves.**

A rebel, indeed, is a monster in nature, an enemy not only to his country, but to all mankind; he is destitute of that benevolence which is the highest honor and glory of the rational nature. **But what is a rebel? — what those actions, for which a man or people deserve this opprobrious [abusive, hateful or damaging] charge? Those only are rebels who are enemies to good government, and oppose such as duly execute it. A state of nature is a state of war. Civil government, which is founded in the consent of society to be governed by certain laws framed for the general good, and duly executed by some appointed thereto, puts an end to this state [condition], and secures peace and safety. He, therefore, who transgresses this compact, even he opposes good government, and is a rebel, rebellat — he raises war again.**

Deborah and Barak defeated Sisera and Jabin by Kishon River, Judges chapter 4
Courtesy of godswarplan.com[203]

---

[203] GodsWarPlan.com, "Deborah and Barak defeated Sisera and Jabin by Kishon River; Judges 4," as displayed at "Bible Battles | KISHON RIVER| Judges 4;" accessed April 1, 2021

In this, it matters not whether the person be a king or a subject; he is the rebel that breaks the compact, he renews the war, and is the aggressor; and <u>every member of the body politic is bound, by the eternal law of benevolence, to set himself against him, and if he persists, the whole must unite to root him from the earth, whether he be high or low, rich or poor, a king or a subject</u>. The latter, indeed, less deserves it, by how much less mischief he is capable of doing. But when a king or ruler turns rebel (which is vastly more frequent, in proportion to their numbers), being armed with power, he ever spreads desolation and misery around his dominions before he can be regularly and properly punished, and therefore is proportionably higher in guilt. Witness Pharaoh, Saul, Manasseh, Antiochus, Julian, Charles I., of blessed memory, and George III., who vies [competes] with the chief in this black catalogue [referring to the list of aforementioned names], in spreading misery and ruin round the world.

The ruler who invades the civil or religious rights of his subjects, levies war on them, puts them out of his protection, and dissolves all their allegiance to him; for allegiance and protection are reciprocal, and where one is denied the other must cease.

If these observations are true (and they cannot be denied with modesty), then it is as lawful, and as strongly our duty, to prosecute a war against the king of England for invading our rights and liberties as to bring an obstinate rebel to justice, or take arms against some foreign power that might invade us. Oppression alone, if persisted in, justifies the oppressed in making war on the oppressors; whether they be rulers or private persons, in our own or a foreign state. The reason is, because oppressors are enemies to the great law of nature, and to the happiness of mankind. For this, God commanded Israel to commence a war against Jabin, that, being free from his power, happiness and peace might be restored.

The Battle of Lexington[204]
1910 oil on canvas, National Army Museum

The Battles of Lexington and Concord on April 19, 1775 were the first military engagements of the American Revolutionary War. "The shot heard around the world," refers to the opening shot fired that began the War for Independence.

In our contest with the tyrant of Great Britain, we did not, indeed, commence the war. No. But though under a load of almost insupportable insult, abuse and reproach, we raised our humble and earnest petitions, and prayed only for peace, liberty and safety, the natural rights of all men. But, be astonished, O heavens! And tremble, O England! While our dutiful supplications ascended before the throne, the monster was meditating the blow; [King George III threatened to hang all of the members of the Continental Congress] and ere we rose from our knees, he fixed his dagger in our heart! If this is to be a father, where can be the monster? If this be

---

[204] *Wikimedia Commons,* s.v. "File:The Battle of Lexington.jpg," This work is in the public domain

the exercise of lenity [softness or tenderness] and mercy, as he vainly boasts what must be his acts of justice? O, merciful God, look down and behold our distress, and avenge us of our cruel foe.

Can we reflect on those scenes of slaughter and desolation which he hath spread before our eyes, and doubt of our duty? Is it any longer a scruple [a doubt] whether God calls us to war? If such insults and abuse will not justify us, no abuses ever can. Yea, had George withheld his hand from shedding our blood, the grievous oppressions we groaned under before, and the contempt and insult with which he treated our petitions, were fully sufficient to justify us in the sight of God, and all wise men, had we begun the war, and expelled his troops from our country by fire and sword. **Is it possible that Jabin could treat Israel with greater insult or more unjustly invade their rights? But for this, God commanded Israel to make war on him, and pronounces a heavy curse on those who refused to join in carrying it on.**

This leads me to show,

<u>*Four*</u>. *That those who are indolent [lazy], and backward to take up arms and exert themselves in the service of their country, in order to recover and secure their freedom, when called thereto by the public voice, are highly criminal in the sight of God and man.*

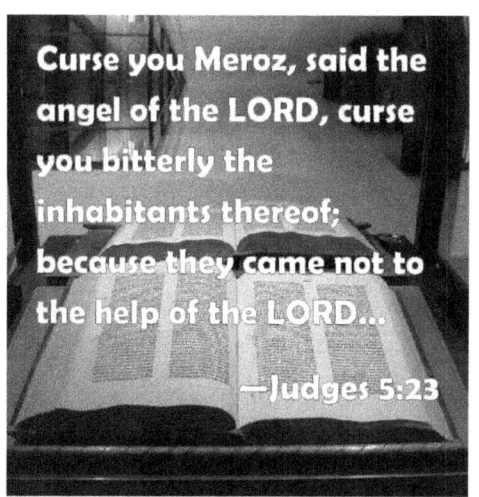

This doctrine is wrapt up in the very bowels of my text. **'Curse ye Meroz, said the angel of the Lord, curse ye bitterly the inhabitants thereof, because they came not to the help of the Lord, to the help of the Lord against the mighty.'** *The curse of God falls on none but for sin; for he delights in blessing, not in cursing. And he never permits any of his subjects to execute his curses on their fellow-subjects, but where the crime is highly aggravated; much less does he allow them to curse them bitterly, unless their guilt is exceeding great. Now, since God commands Israel to curse Meroz bitterly, we fairly infer, that their sin was of a crimson dye, and most provoking to him and his people. And whoever is guilty of the like conduct in our contest with Great Britain, incurs the like guilt."* [Emphasis added]

Is the *Body of Christ* in America guilty in the course of these 20th and 21st centuries? Is the *Body of Christ* too crippled to take down the *Money Changers* and their Progressive Freemasons (the Deep State) who worship Satan? The *Body of Christ* needs a new jurisdiction! It needs to stand-up and restore the lawfully re-inhabited *Republic for the United States of America*!

Preacher Whitaker continues and then we conclude with a summary conclusion…

"This needs no further proof; for if it be allowed that the state of the case between Great Britain and America, is, in its main parts, parallel with that between Jabin and Israel, as hath been shown, then the crime of negligence is as heinous in this struggle as in that. **And as Israel were required to curse bitterly those cowardly, selfish, half-way people, so are we to curse the like characters at this day.** *And as those people, for their neglect, exposed themselves to the loss of all the privileges and blessings of a free state [body politic] in this world, and to the eternal vengeance of God in the next; so it highly*

concerns all to take heed that they do not fall under the same condemnation. That we may avoid the rock on which they were lost, I will,

    1. Give their character.
    2. Mention some aggravations of their sin.
    3. I will hint at some things which discover people to be like the inhabitants of Meroz.

Few, I fear, are perfectly clear in this matter. Alas, there is too great negligence among people in general. Private interests and selfish considerations, engross the thoughts and cares of many, who wish well the cause of liberty, and divert their attention and exertions from the main things which calls for our first and chief regard, viz. [namely], the defence of our country from tyranny and securing our civil and religious freedom. It is mournful to see most men eagerly pursuing worldly gain, and heaping up unrighteous mammon by cruel oppression and grinding the faces of the poor, while our country lies bleeding of her wounds, and so few engaged to bind them up. Let such consider that they are guilty of the sin of Meroz, and, though they may not feel the curse of men in this world, they shall not, without sincere repentance, escape the wrath and curse of God in the world to come. Every one is called, at this day, to come to the help of the Lord against the mighty; either to go out to war, or in some way vigorously exert himself for the public good.

There are various things necessary for the defence of our country besides bearing arms, though this is the chief; and all may, one way or other, put to a helping hand. There are various arts and manufactures essential to the support of the inhabitants and army, without which we must soon be overcome. In one or other of these, men and women, youth, and even children, may be employed, and as essentially help in the deliverance of their country as those who go out to war. All are now called to have more than ordinary frugality and diligence in their respective callings; and those of ability should be liberal and forward to encourage manufactures for the public good. But alas, that so few make the interest and welfare of the public the main object of their pursuit. Yet there are some, and I hope many, who with truth can say, they have done their best, according to their circumstances, for the defence and safety of their country. Such, however the contest may arise, will enjoy the approbation [approval] of God, their own consciences, and of all the friends of mankind.

But not to make our case appear better than it really is, I fear there are many among us, in one disguise or other, who, when stript of their vizards [masks], will appear to be of the inhabitants of Meroz; and who, if their characters were justly drawn, would secretly, if not openly, say, as the Pharisees in another case, In saying this, thou reproachest us also. But as birds which are hit, show it by their fluttering, and it may serve to bring such contemptible characters to view, and expose them to the curse they deserve, and on the other hand, may convince some real friends to freedom of their sinful negligence in the common cause; I will venture to point out a few.

King Jabin of Hazor[205]
Courtesy of godswarplan.com

Among these characters I do not include such as aid, or in the words or actions defend, or openly declare for the enemy, and plead the right of Great Britain 'to bind us in all things whatsoever.' Of such there are not many among us, owing, probably, to their fear of a vast majority, which is on the side of freedom; and therefore they put on the guise of friendship, while they endeavor secretly to work destruction to the cause. These may be known by the following marks:

1. Observe the man who will neither go himself, nor contribute of his substance (if able) to encourage others to go into the war. Such do what in them lies to break up the army. **These incur the curse of Meroz.**

2. Others will express wishes for our success, but will be sure to back them with doubts of the event, and fears of a heavier yoke. You may hear them frequently magnifying the power of the enemy, and telling of the nine hundred chariots of iron, the dreadful train of artillery, and the good discipline of the British troops…

3. There are other pretended friends whose countenance betrays them. When things go ill with our army, they appear with a cheerful countenance, and assume airs of importance, and you'll see them holding conferences in one corner or another. The joy of their hearts, on such occasions, will break through all disguises, and discover their real sentiments…

4. Others, who talk much for liberty, you will find ever opposing the measures of defence proposed; making objections to them, and showing their inconsistency, while they offer none in their stead…

5. Some are discovered by the company they keep. You may find them often with those who have given too much reason to suspect their enmity [opposition] to our cause, and rarely with the zealous friends of liberty, except by accident…

6. There are others who in heart wish well to our cause; but, through fear of the power of our enemies, they are backward to join vigorously to support it. They really wish we might succeed; but they dread the hardships of a campaign, and choose so to conduct, that, on whatever side victory may declare, they may be safe.

7. Others wish well to the public cause, but have a much greater value for their own private and personal interest. They are high sons of liberty, till her cause crosses their private views…

Second. *To mention some aggravations of this sin.*

1. <u>This conduct is a violation of the law of nature</u>, which requires all to exert themselves to promote happiness among mankind….

---

[205] GodsWarPlan.com, "King Jabin of Hazor," as displayed at "Bible Battles | KISHON RIVER | Judges 4; Deborah and Barak; Sisera; King Jabin of Hazor; tent peg," accessed April 1, 2021

2. This sin is against posterity; our children after us must reap the fruit of our present conduct. If we nobly resist the oppressor, we shall, under God, deliver them from his galling yoke; at least shall avoid the guilt of riveting it on them....

3. Let us, for a moment, glance an eye on the next and succeeding generations. What a scene opens to view! Behold these delightful and stately mansions for which we labored, possessed by the minions of power; see yonder spacious fields, subdued to fruitfulness by the sweat and toil of our fathers or ourselves, yielding their increase to clothe, pamper, and enrich the tyrant's favorites, who are base enough to assist him in his cursed plots to enslave us. Does this rouse your resentment?...

4. This is a sin against our forefathers. They left us a fair inheritance; they forsook their native land, the land of tyranny and the furnace of iron; and, by their blood, treasure, and toil, procured this sweet, this peaceful retreat, subdued the soil when covered with eternal woods, raised for us the stately domes which afford us shelter from the storms, and safe repose, and were exceedingly careful to instruct us in the things which concern our temporal and eternal liberty and peace....

5. This is a sin against contemporaries. How provoking in the sight of God and man is it to see some, quite unconcerned for the good of the public, rolling in ease, amassing wealth to themselves, and slyly plotting to assist our enemies in their murderous designs, while others endure the fatigues of war, and hazard all that's dear to secure the peace, liberty, and safety of the whole! Surely, every benevolent heart must rise with indignation, and curse these enemies to God and nature.

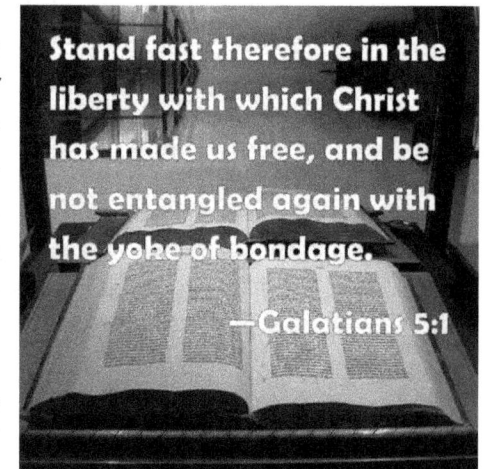

6. This is a sin against the express command of God. He commands us to stand fast in the liberty wherewith he hath made us free, and not to bow to any tyrant on earth, when it is in our power to oppose him."

In summary, it was with the *Peace Treaty of Paris* in 1783 when America officially won the *War for Independence*. In 1789, with George Washington as President of the United States of America, the American Republic, was governed by the Founding Fathers and came to be the greatest nation in the world, brighter than "a city on a hill."[206] There demonstrates that Almighty God was with America as she aligned and covenanted with Him and His laws.

Knowledge of our history clearly depicts the patterns in history that are playing out before us once again. It's like a tumbleweed through time rolling with a prophetic breeze across the continent that beckons this nation of people to stand to attention and to unite together in the cause of Liberty, which is the cause of God. In this rational prospect is also a want and a desire for the happiness of our fellow creatures, which is the highest glory of the saints, the people of faith. Therein is testimony to the superintending presence of Creator God and His lovingkindness toward what is good and right and true.

---

[206] *Matthew 5:14 ~ Ye are the light of the world. A city that is set on an hill cannot be hid.*

Chapter Three

American Republic vs. Corporate Democracy
The Counterfeit Begins

The National Monument to the Forefathers[208]
Plymouth, Massachusetts

vs.

Statue of Liberty[207]
Liberty Island,
New York City, NY

Liberty – Civil & Religious   **vs.**   *Man's "Enlightenment"*

"Advance ye the gospel of the kingdom"   **vs.**   *Globalism, world dominion by domination*

▶ Who is America's enemy? In answer, we will look at the history of secret societies and that which has been kept hidden while we also discover the reason why.

▶ Who made us "U.S. Citizens" and slaves?

▶ Who gave us the Federal Reserve?

▶ Who gave us a Corporate Democracy?

▶ Who gave us Freemason Progressive Presidents?

Statue of Liberty
Freemason Plaque

"At this site on August 5, 1884, the cornerstone of the pedestal of the Statue of Liberty Enlightening the World was laid with ceremony by William A. Brodie, Grandmaster of the Masons of the State of New York, Grand Lodge members, representatives of the United States, and French governments, Army and Navy officers, members of foreign legations, and distinguished citizens were present. This plaque is dedicated by the Masons in New York in commemoration of the 100th anniversary of the historic event."

---

[207] *Wikimedia Commons* s.v., "File:Lady Liberty under a blue sky (cropped).jpg" This work is in the public domain
[208] T.S. Custadio, aka ToddC4176, Wikimedia Commons s.v. "File:Monument to the Forefathers 1.jpg," Permission granted

▶Who pushed aside our *Declaration of Independence* along with our *Constitution* with the original and missing *Thirteenth Article of Amendment*?

▶Who gave us State governments as well as our national government that are run by the Satanic illuminists?

There are many more questions to be asked. Know this—you were all born in a matrix where the world was pulled down over your eyes to blind you of the truth! You were born in bondage. You were born in a prison you can't taste, that you can't smell, that you can't see; a prison for your mind. Let's take a look!

Dedication Panel[209]
National Monument to the Forefathers
(formerly known as the Pilgrim Monument)
Plymouth, Massachusetts
Courtesy of Wikimedia Commons/Dsdugan

"National Monument to the Forefathers
erected by a grateful people
in remembrance of their
labors, sacrifices and sufferings
for the cause of Civil and Religious Liberty."

Recorded history points to the East as the cradle of secret societies of which emanated from the lands where the first recorded acts of the great human drama were played out--Egypt, Babylon, Syria, and Persia. For whatever purpose they may have been employed, these mysterious associations have played an important and significant part behind the scenes in world history. These associations have a pattern of shrouding themselves in secrecy for the pursuit of esoteric [210] [211] knowledge while also using mystery and secrecy as an ulterior motive in political endeavors.[212]

In the case of Freemasonry, of which its birthplace was in England, several masonic manuscripts that are important in the study of the emergence of Freemasonry that predate the formation of Grand Lodges point to perhaps the 10th century and are assumed to be of Scottish origin. The Society began simply with individuals who were masons by trade who formed a social club, though in 1648 it was opened to others of

---

[209] *Wikimedia Commons* s.v., "File:15 23 0519 monument.jpg," Courtesy of Dsdugan
[210] Esoteric refers to philosophical doctrine kept secret or confidential and intended to be revealed only to the initiates of a group.
[211] *Noah Webster's First Edition of An American Dictionary of the English Language,* 1828:
  Esoteric: [Gr. Interior, from within.] Private; an epithet applied to the private instructions and doctrines of Phythagoras; opposed to exoteric, or public.
[212] Nesta Webster, *Secret Societies and Subversive Movements,* (London: Boswell Printing & Publishing Co., Ltd, 1924) 3

different trades and professions. As lodges opened on the continent in Europe, they strayed from the English Mason principles.[213]

Pope Clement XIV, portrait 1773 [214]

We move forward on the timeline to 1773, when Pope Clement XIV (papacy 1769-1774) disbanded and suppressed the Jesuit *Order of Loyola*, a Roman Catholic order of priests founded in 1540 by St. Ignatius Loyola, because they had become too politically powerful throughout Europe while also gaining economic control of countries. In survival mode, the Jesuits took refuge in non-Catholic nations, particularly in Prussia (Germany). The Jesuits pursued infiltration of Freemason Lodges and influenced them in the occult practices of *Illuminism* along with a combination of gnostic[215] teaching, Jewish mysticism of the Cabala (Kabbalah), and added some pretense of Christianity (of which they despised) while also falsifying the founding principles and history of Freemasonry. The German Lodges transformed into a society that excessively indulged their freedoms in immoral behavior and licentious, unrestrained practices.[216]

Portrait of Adam Weishaupt (1748-1830)[217]

Secrecy was employed in the Lodges of European countries while men were emboldened to teach subversive, immoral doctrines under the pretext of "enlightening the world" by the torch of philosophy in matters of civil and religious matters. Gradually, an "association" was formed for the express purpose of rooting out all religious establishments and civil institutions existing in Europe. This association, the **Order of Illuminati** (*Illuminati,* plural of Latin *illuminatus*, "enlightened"), was founded in 1775 by Dr. Adam Weishaupt, a Jesuit-trained university professor of canon law in Bavaria (today part of Germany).[218]

---

[213] John Robison, A.M., *Proofs of a Conspiracy Against All the Religions and Governments of Europe, Carried on in the Secret Meetings of Free Masons, Illuminati, and Reading Societies, Collected from Good Authorities*, (New-York: 1798) Introduction
[214] *Wikimedia Commons*, s.v. "Clement XIV," This work is in the public domain
[215] *Noah Webster's First Edition of An American Dictionary of the English Language,* 1828:
  Gnostic: [Gr. To know.] The Gnostics were a sect of philosophers that arose in the first ages of Christianity, who pretended they were the only men who had a true knowledge of the Christian religion. They formed for themselves a system of theology, agreeable to the philosophy of Pythagoras and Plato, to which they accommodated their interpretations of scripture. They held that all natures, intelligible, intellectual and material, are derived by successive emanations from the infinite fountain of deity. ...These doctrines were derived from the oriental philosophy.
[216] Robison, *Proofs of a Conspiracy,* Intro, 25
[217] *Wikimedia Commons* s.v., "File: Johann Adam Weishaupt.jpg" This work is in the public domain
[218] Robison, *Proofs of a Conspiracy,* Intro, 38, 76

Weishaupt was embittered when he lost his job at Ingolstadt University at the time the Jesuits were disbanded in 1773. A group of self-serving Jewish bankers (namely Moses Mendelssohn) financed Weishaupt's *Order of Illuminati* believing he would be useful in their cause against the Roman church.[219] [220] It was in 1782 when representatives of all Masonicsecret societies gathered at the *Congress of Willhemsbad* (Germany), and *"the alliance between Illuminism and Freemasonry was finally sealed."*[221] [222]

King George III, who ruled England 1760-1820, secretly preserved the political and financial power of the Jesuit *Order of Loyola* during the years of its suppression until 1814 when the *Jesuit Company* was formally restored by Pope Pius VII (papacy 1800-1823).[223] That timeframe is of great significance to our truthful early American history, as well as that of the world.[224]

King George III in 1765 [225]

Pope Pius VII
(born Barnaba Niccolò Maria Luigi Chiaramonti; 1742–1823)
was head of the Catholic Church and ruler of the Papal States
from 14 March 1800 to his death in August 1823.

The association of the *Order of Illuminati* operated systematically and through secrecy. European Freemason leaders had come to be unprincipled and immoral men who publicly projected a falsehood of their association as they lied and taught false doctrines with <u>an overall objective to abolish all religion, overturn every government, and create chaos in the world</u>. Their *"express purpose of breaking all the bands of society [is] that the leaders might rule the world with uncontrollable power [in] a plan so big with mischief, disgraceful to its underlying adherents and so uncertain in its issue,"* of which is their calculated end and ultimate result.[226]

---

[219] Dr. Stephen Jones, *Studies in the Book of Revelation*, chapter 3, "The Beast from the Earth" (God's Kingdom Ministries, 2016)
[220] Dr. Stphen Jones, *Studies in the Book of Revelation*, "The Beast from the Earth, part 1," (God's Kingdom Ministries, 2016) as citing William Guy Carr, *Pawns in the Game,"* (Willowdale, Ontario: Federation of Christian Layment, 1958 3rd ed.) 50
[221] Dr. Stephen Jones, "Chapter 3: The Beast from the Earth" as citing Nesta H. Webster, *World Revolution: The Plot Against Civilization,* (Boston: Small, Maynard & Company Publishers, 1921) 31
[222] Carr, *Pawns in the Game,* Intro
[223] Eric Jon Phelps, *Vatican Assassins,* (Eric Jon Phelps, PO Box 306, Newmanstown, PA 17073) (2001) 66
[224] Jean Hallahan Hertler and David Carl Hertler, *Re-inhabited: Republic for the United States of America,* Vol. I, "America's Truthful History," (Valley Assets Publishing, 2016) 6
[225] *Wikimedia Commons, s.v.* "King George III in coronation robes, " by artist Allan Ramsay, This work is in the public domain
[226] Robison, *Proofs of a Conspiracy,* Intro, 39, 78

To accomplish this world domination, the *Illuminati* needed to eliminate all opposition. Recognizing that the Roman church had the most power, they focused upon destroying the papacy. Once they accomplished this goal (1798-1800) through the *Jesuit Order of Illuminati*, they were then able to control and use the church, having infiltrated it as they had done previously with Freemason lodges. [227] [228]

A "holy alliance" between Masonic kings and popes made room for Freemasons within Catholicism and their Congresses (i.e., Vienna-1814, Verona-1822, Chieri-1825) with a *Counter-Reformation* agenda to destroy Protestantism (the religion of Liberty), to suppress popular government in the American Republic under the color of and disguise of religion, and to restore the temporal power of the papacy globally while promoting and establishing the religion of Luciferianism.[229]

It is an important matter in our truthful history[230] that is documented with evidence in being aware that American Freemason Lodges were not infused with the Illuminized Luciferian religion[231] until around 1801 when Isaac Long brought a statue of Baphomet (Satan) and the skull of the Templar Grand Master Jacques de Molay from Paris to Charleston, South Carolina, when at that time he helped establish the *Ancient and Accepted Scottish Rite*. Charleston had been selected because it was geographically located on the 33rd parallel of latitude, which is of significance to Satanists. [232] [233]

Hyman Isaac Long was a physician in New York City, having immigrated from the British colony of Jamaica in the West Indies. Dr. Long is listed in the first New York City directory of 1786. Long returned to Jamaica for some Freemason events and rites, where the organization was more developed. After returning to the United States, he continued to work on developing membership in the Freemason lodges and is known for his leadership in developing Freemason organizations in New York, Virginia, and South Carolina. Isaac Long was succeeded in Freemason leadership by Albert Pike (pictured later is in this chapter).[234]

The culture in America from her inception with the Pilgrims and Puritans going forward through the 1800s, was one where children were raised with the Holy Bible as their main textbook throughout life. Biblical character traits like virtues (trustworthiness, uprightness, prudence, respectability, worth, honor, integrity, moral excellence, goodness, Godly character, faith in God, kindness, love, purity, righteousness, merit,

---

[227] Dr. Stephen Jones, *Studies in the Book of Revelation*, chapter 1, "The Beast from the Sea" (God's Kingdom Ministries, 2016)
[228] Modern History Project Staff, "Satan: Prince of This World," in citing William Guy Carr, *Satan, Prince of this World,* (1959) 63
[229] Hertler, *Re-inhabited* Vol. I, 7, 49; Vol. II, 19
[230] Hertler, *Re-inhabited* Vol. I, 155
[231] "To George Washington from G. W. Snyder, 22 August 1798," Founders Online, National Archives, https://founders.archives.gov/documents/Washington/06-02-02-0435. [Original source: The Papers of George Washington, Retirement Series, vol. 2, 2 January 1798 – 15 September 1798, ed. W. W. Abbot. Charlottesville: University Press of Virginia, 1998, pp. 554–557.]
[232] Dr Stephen Jones, *Foundation for Intercession Newsletter*, "The Book of Revelation – Part 28 The Sixth Vial," (God's Kingdom Ministries, Feb 2005) https://godskingdom.org/studies/ffi-newsletter/2005/the-book-of-revelation-part-28-the-sixth-vial/
[233] "History of the Temple," The Scottish Rite of Freemasonry Supreme Council, 33° Southern Jurisdiction, U.S.A, accessed Nov. 1, 2014, http://scottishrite.org/headquarters/history_of_the-temple/
[234] Baynard, Samuel Harrison, Jr. *History of the Supreme Council, 33°, Ancient Accepted Scottish Rite of Freemasonry, Northern Masonic Jurisdiction of the U.S.A. and its Antecedents,* 2 vols. (1938) vol. I, pg. 77. Boston, Massachusetts: Supreme Council, N.M.J.; Jackson, A.C.F. (1980). *Rose Croix: A History of the Ancient and Accepted Rite for England and Wales* (rev. ed. 1987) pp. 66-68. London: Lewis Masonic Publ., as cited by *Wikipedia*, "Hyman Isaac Long," https://en.wikipedia.org/wiki/Hyman_Isaac_Long and *Wikipedia,* "Scottish Rite," https://en.wikipedia.org/wiki/Scottish_Rite

charity, faithfulness, justice, innocence, temperance, and morality) were instilled in those generations along with a good understanding of *self-government and union.*

Charles Finney (1792-1875) was the minister and leader of the *Second Great Awakening* in America. He has been called "*The Father of Modern Revivalism*" in that he led spiritual revival and renewal in the *Body of Christ* throughout America throughout much of the 19th century.[235] Finney was a young lawyer in 1821 when after reading through Blackstone's *Law Commentaries* several times and seeing so many references to Bible verses that he bought a Bible and soon after incurred a living faith experience and giving his life to Christ. He immediately began to preach, presenting the Gospel with the manner of a convincing lawyer's argument.[236]

His impact for Christianity and advancing the Gospel is profound. Those who came to salvation under his preaching went on to make impacts in American society inspiring the inception of the YMCA – Young Men's Christian Association (1844), The Salvation Army (1865), the *Benevolent Empire* (1834) to aid the poor and aged with healthcare and social needs, which had a budget that rivaled the Federal Government. Back then there were no government run welfare programs. It was churches, ministries, and volunteer organizations that took care of the sick.[237]

Finney served as the President of Oberlin College (1851-1866) during which time the school served as a station on the *Underground Railroad,* smuggling slaves to freedom. His preaching fueled the abolitionist movement. Under Finney's leadership, Oberlin College granted the first college degree in the United States to a black woman, Mary Jane Patterson. This man of God left a legacy to the American People today because of his published works. He had the holy boldness as a visionary and never flinched at calling out and exposing evil.[238]

 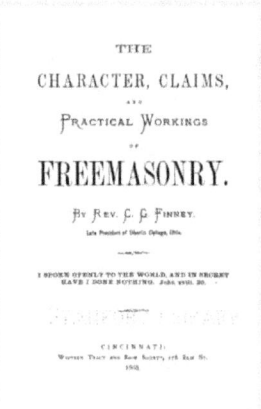

Rev. Charles Finney[239] *and the title page of his 1869 book,*
The Character, Claims and Practical Workings of Freemasonry [240]

---

[235] Hertler, *Re-inhabited:* Vol. I, "America's Truthful History," 197
[236] Bill Federer, American Minute blog post American Minute with Bill Federer, "Blackstone's Commentaries of Laws of England, Charles Finney's Gospel Revival, & 'another gospel'—Liberation Theology Social Justice," published Aug 21, 2023
[237] Ibid.
[238] Ibid.
[239] *Wikimedia Commons* s.v., "File:Charles Grandison Finney, Father of American Revivalism (cropped).jpg," This work is in the public domain
[240] Finney, *Character, Claims,* Title page This work is in the public domain

It was in 1869 when Charles Finney published his book, *The Character, Claims and Practical Workings of Freemasonry.*"[241] Finney tells the story of the great revival, of which he was a significant leader of, that occurred in America 40 years earlier during the period 1826-1835 and how it began, particularly in upstate New York and Manhattan. As the story unfolds, seen is an incredible scandal with the Freemason-orchestrated murder of a defecting Mason and obstruction of justice that stained the moral fabric of this nation. In reviewing this history, it becomes magnificently clear to the understanding of how this tremendous revival and renewal came about. This Divine interaction was in response to the public repentance of most of the members of this secret society after the scandal's exposure in the murder of William Morgan, a former Freemason who announced his intentions of publishing a book that exposed the oaths of the first few degrees of Freemasonry.

Capt. William Morgan [242]

As Finney concludes telling the story of the murder of William Morgan— yes, the Freemasons assassinated him — and recounting the great scandal while also exposing Freemasonry as an immoral secret society, he reminisces on the public reaction. Specifically, pertaining to the various denominations of the churches in the Northern States in renouncing and denouncing the evil institution—and what resulted. Finney said,

> *"God set the seal of His approbation [approval, admiration] upon the action taken by those churches at that time, by pouring out His Spirit upon them. Great revivals immediately followed over that whole region. The discussion of the subject and the action of the churches took place in 1827-'8 and '9, and in 1830 the greatest revival spread over this region that had ever been known in this or any other country."*[243] [Emphasis added]

What Finney was referring to is what is known today as the *Second Great Awakening*. Now 40 years later, Finney published the story explaining that at the time of William Morgan's murder in 1826, the facts were well-known to the public. Finney stated that subsequently through the years Freemasons had gone to great lengths to destroy any writing that related to the murder and exposure of the oaths. Finney said,

> *"...much pains have been taken by Freemasons to rid the world of the books and pamphlets, and every vestige of writing relating to that subject, by far the larger number of young people seem to be entirely ignorant that such facts ever occurred."*[244]

By publishing the story, Finney intended to make known to that current society in 1869, and particularly the younger generations, the truth concerning the dangers of Freemasonry. Finney's book includes critical insights that help to understand the stance of the *Radical Republicans* of the U.S. Congress in that era of a nation that was torn in two sections because of the *War Between the States* and heated debates on *Reconstruction*. The *Radical Republicans* were members of the Republican Party who were committed to emancipation of the slaves, both during and after the *Civil War*, and later to the equal treatment and

---

[241] Rev. C. G. Finney, Late President of Oberlin College, Ohio, *The Character, Claims and Practical Workings of Freemasonry*, (Cincinnati: Western Tract and Book Society, 1869)
[242] *Wikimedia Commons*, s.v. "William Morgan (anti-Mason).jpg," This work is in the public domain
[243] Finney, *Character, Claims,* 266
[244] Ibid. 9

enfranchisement of the freed blacks. The *Radical Republicans* were a vocal and powerful faction in the U.S. Congress who also insisted on harsh penalties for the *Slave Power* of the Southern States following the war, during the period of *Reconstruction*.

In chapter two of Finney's book, entitled "Scrap of History," he tells the story of what led up to the *Second Great Awakening*. Finney informs the reader of vital facts that occurred in the nation 40 years earlier. It was at that time when the details and secrets of Freemasonry were well-exposed to the American People. Now, a generation later, Finney expressed concern because the dangers of the institution were alarmingly no longer general knowledge for most Americans.

Reader — what is the danger of this secret society institution today??

Finney interjected that the elder generation, especially in the Northern States, would universally remember the Freemason murder of William Morgan along with facts and circumstances connected with the great scandal and tragedy. The elder generation had experiential knowledge of the dangers in what Freemason infiltration and controls over government present, and that being a horrific danger in the potential of ending our institutions of *Liberty — Civil and Religious*.[245]

Since that time, great effort was made by Freemasons to destroy books, pamphlets, and every bit of writing relating to the subject. He asserted that this coverup was the reason why the younger generation was now entirely ignorant of the exceedingly dangerous scandal as well as the obstruction of justice that had occurred in the nation in 1826.[246]

In laying out the foundation of facts in history pertaining to the scandal of Freemasonry 40 years earlier, Finney points out that this good man, William Morgan, who lived in Batavia, New York, defected from Freemasonry. After much reflection, Morgan decided that it was his duty to publish the aspects of Freemasonry so the world would know of its immorality. Morgan regarded Freemasonry as highly injurious to the cause of Christ and as eminently dangerous to the American *republican form of government* (not the Republican Party) and institutions of Liberty.[247]

Finney interjected that Masons held all the civil offices in the country and were also completely in control of the press (newspapers). Masons were even boastful in the fact that all the civil officers in the country were in their control. It is thought-provoking to consider how many offices across this great country are in their control today![248]

Finney recounted that where he resided as a young man, and while being a Mason, that all the civil offices in the country were in their control. He couldn't recall a magistrate, constable, or sheriff in his county that was not a Freemason.[249]

David C. Miller was a publisher who also lived in Batavia, New York and agreed to publish Morgan's book. Freemasons learned of Morgan and Miller's intention and then conspired to destroy both of them. Their

---

[245] Ibid.
[246] Ibid.
[247] Ibid. 10
[248] Ibid.
[249] Ibid.

Freemason oaths bound them to destroy that defecting brother mason Morgan and his publisher for betraying the secrets of the society.[250]

A group of selected Freemasons kidnapped Morgan and held him hostage in the magazine (building that stores arms and ammunition) at a federal fort on the Niagara River where it empties into Lake Ontario, until they could arrange the assassination. Great efforts were made by citizens in Morgan's community to find and save him. When the Masons learned that they were suspected of holding William Morgan at Fort Niagara, they moved quickly to dispose of him. It was years later, upon their deathbed, that two or three involved in Morgan's murder confessed their part—they drowned him in the Niagara River.[251]

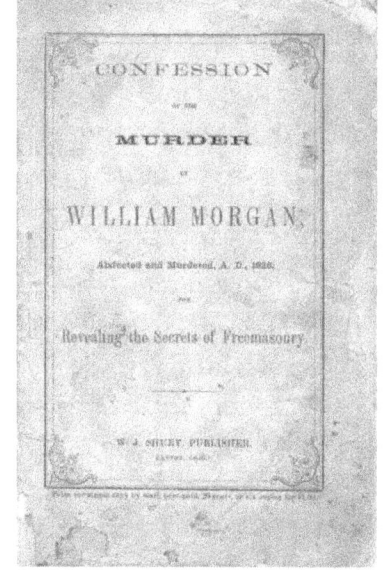

Confession of the Murder of William Morgan,
Abducted and Murdered, A.D., 1826,
for Revealing the Secrets of Freemasonry.
As taken down by Dr. John L. Emery,
of Racine County, Wisconsin
In the summer of 1848,
and now (1849) first given to the public
Title Page
By John L. Emery, M.D.[252]

In his book, Reverend Finney referred to the deathbed confession of one of the murderers of which had been published in a book entitled, *Stearns on Masonry* by John G. Stearns, who was also an elder of a Baptist church. The confession was by Henry L. Valance, the man who pushed Morgan out of the boat into the Niagara River. The confession was also printed in a pamphlet entitled, "*Confession of the Murder of William Morgan as taken down by Dr. John L. Emery, of Racine County, Wisconsin, in the summer of 1848, and now (1849) first given to the public.*"[253]

The deathbed confession was made to Valance's physicians, who wrote it down and published it after his death. Henry Valance confessed that he was one of the three who were selected to assassinate Morgan. Valance lived with a tremendous burden of guilt for the rest of his life. Valance said he viewed himself much like the *Old Testament* character, Cain, who was marked for life as "*a fugitive and a vagabond.*"[254]

> "*Go where I would, or do what I would, it was impossible for me to throw off the consciousness of crime. If the mark of Cain was not upon me, the curse of the first murderer was – the blood-stain was upon my hands and could not be washed out.*"[255]

Valance's confession,

---

[250] Ibid.
[251] Ibid. 10-11
[252] John L. Emery, M.D., *Confession of the Murder of William Morgan, Abducted and Murdered, A.D., 1826, for Revealing the Secrets of Freemasonry.*, (Dayton, Ohio: W. J. Shuey, Publisher, 1869) Ownership rights
[253] Finney, *Character, Claims,* 12
[254] Ibid.
[255] Ibid.

"My last hour is approaching; and as the things of this world fade from my mental sight, I feel the necessity of making, as far as in my power lies, that atonement which every violator of the great law of right owes to his fellow men."[256]

In this violation of law, he says,

"I allude to the abduction and murder of the ill-fated William Morgan..."[257]

Valance confessed the details of what he and his fellow Freemasons had done with Morgan, including incarcerating him at the magazine at Fort Niagara. Valance said many discussions were held and proposals made about what to do with Morgan. Finally, these Freemasons knew they had to act, or they would be caught, so a council of eight decided on Morgan being...

"...consigned to a 'confinement from where there is no possibility of escape: THE GRAVE.' Three of their number were to be selected by ballot to execute the deed. 'Eight pieces of paper were procured, five of which were to remain blank, while the letter D was written on the others. These pieces of paper were placed in a large box, from which each man was to draw one at the same moment. After drawing we were all to separate, without looking at the paper that each held in his hand. So soon as we had arrived at certain distances from the place of rendezvous, the tickets were to be examined, and those who held blanks were to return instantly to their homes; and those who should hold the marked tickets were to proceed to the fort at midnight, and there put Morgan to death, in such a manner as should seem to themselves most fitting."[258]

Valance was one of the three who drew the ballots with the letter "D." Valance returned to the fort, where he was joined by the other two who had also drawn the death tickets. Immediate arrangements were made for executing the sentence passed upon their prisoner, which was to sink him in the river with weights; in hope, *"that he and our crime alike would thus be buried beneath the waves."*[259]

Valance's part was to go to the magazine where Morgan was confined and tell him his fate. The other two were to procure a boat and weights with which to assist in drowning Morgan. When informed of their intentions, Morgan demanded by what authority they had condemned him, and who were his judges.

"He commenced wringing his hands, and talking of his wife and children, the recollections of whom, in that awful hour terribly affected him. His wife, he said, was young and inexperienced, and his children were but infants; what would become of them were he cut off, and they even ignorant of his fate?"[260]

---

[256] Ibid.
[257] Ibid. 13
[258] Ibid. 13-14
[259] Ibid. 14
[260] Ibid.

Publication in Paris, France, 1886
Français : Une des gravures du document de Léo Taxil, Les Mystères de la Franc-Maçonnerie, Paris, 1886.[261]
Assassination of William Morgan
13 September 1826

Valance's accomplices returned and advised that everything was ready to go. Morgan was told that it wouldn't do any good to protest as he had to die that night. He continued to plead for his life on behalf of his family to no avail. The Masons gave him a half-hour to prepare himself for his inevitable fate and left; Valance said that Morgan was quiet in the magazine for that time.[262]

When they returned for Morgan, they bound his hands behind him, placed a gag in his mouth, and led him to the boat. Morgan was placed in the bow with Valance, while the other two rowed the boat out into the river. The night was pitch-dark to where they could hardly see ahead. Once they reached a distance from the shore, the weights were all secured together by a strong cord, with another length of cord connected to it. Valance said he fastened the cord securely above Morgan's hips and told him to stand up. Valance and another lifted the weights from the bottom to the side of the boat and then pushed Morgan into the river. As Morgan fell forward, the weights went with him, and the waters closed over him.[263]

The three assassins remained quiet for a couple of minutes, and then rowed the boat back to shore. While all of this was going on, there were other Freemasons who kidnapped David Miller the publisher, however, citizens of Batavia learned about it and were able to rescue him.[264]

Records evidenced in fact were established by those seeking justice that the conspiracy was so widespread among Masons that courts of justice were unable to perform due process of law. There was such an obstruction of justice that nothing could be done with the courts, with the sheriffs, with the witnesses, or with the jurors, and all their efforts were entirely impotent for a time. Justice was never served in the ability to prove the murder of Morgan, or to prosecute those involved. Though, William Morgan's book was published which exposed to the world the immorality and dangers of Freemasonry.[265]

Tremendous effort was made by this band of evil brotherhood of *the Craft* to cover up the murder. As much as possible, they also attempted to deceive the public about the truth of Freemasonry that Morgan had published. Finney stated that it was affirmed by the very best authority that this masonic society published two bogus editions of Morgan's book, which were designed to deceive Masons who had never seen Morgan's edition and in order to discredit the integrity of Morgan. The false editions were circulated as if they were the true edition. Because Morgan's book was published and released to the public, along with

---

[261] *Wikimedia Commons*, s.v. "File:Léo Taxil-Mystères de la Franc-Maçonnerie-gravure 79.jpg," This work is in the public domain
[262] Ibid. 15
[263] Ibid.
[264] Ibid. 16-17
[265] Ibid. 17-18

knowledge about the kidnapping and murder, great numbers of Masons were led to reconsider Freemasonry.[266]

The conscientious among them almost universally renounced Masonry altogether with about 2,000 lodges coming to be suspended. The ex-president of a Western college, who was a Freemason, also published important information on the subject, even though he justified Masonry. He reported that of 50,000 Masons in the United States at that time, 45,000 left Freemasonry (at that time the U.S. population was about 9.6 million).[267]

William Morgan Pillar[268]
Batavia Cemetery
April 2011

Conventions were held in various locations of the country for Masons who desired to renounce Freemasonry. At the conventions, held at Le Roy, New York on July 4 and 5, 1828, public confession was made about their relationship to Freemasonry while at the same time renouncing the institution. At one of the large conventions, a committee was appointed to oversee publishing and disclosing all the oaths for degrees of Masonry. The committee was composed of men of integrity who were also generally known to the public. David Bernard, a Baptist elder in good standing, was on one of the committees that obtained an accurate version of 48 degrees. The proceedings of those conventions were published and disclosed to the public in his 1829 book, *Light on Masonry*.[269] [270]

Light on Masonry
Title page, (1829) [271]
by Elder David Bernard

---

[266] Ibid. 17-18
[267] Ibid. 18
[268] *Wikimedia Commons*, s.v. "File:WIlliam Morgan Pillar Apr 11.JPG," This work is in the public domain
[269] Finney, *Character, Claims*, 19
[270] John Quincy Adams, Charles Francis Adams, *Letters and Addresses on Freemasonry*, (Dayton: United Brethren Publishing House, 1875) 279
[271] Elder David Bernard, *Light on Masonry*, (Utica: William Williams, Printer, 1829) Title page, This work is in the public domain

> *"Light on Masonry: a collection of all the most important documents on the subject of Speculative Free Masonry: embracing the Reports of the Western Committees in relation to the abduction of William Morgan, Proceedings of Conventions, Orations, Essays, &c. &c [etc. etc.] with all the degrees of the order conferred in a Master's Lodge. As written by Captain William Morgan; all the degrees conferred in the Royal Arch Chapter and Grand Encampment of Knights Templars, with the appendant orders, as published by the Convention of Seceding Masons, held at Le Roy, July 4 and 5, 1828. Also, a revelation of all the degrees conferred in the Lodge of Perfection, and fifteen degrees of a still higher order, with seven French degrees: making forty-eight degrees of Free Masonry with Notes and Critical Remarks."*[272]

Great effort was made by courts of justice to investigate the matter. Several speeches were made by prominent men in New York state so that a correct view of Freemasonry was revealed and then also published in *Light on Masonry*.[273]

Reverend Finney included in his book the sources where to purchase other books he referenced so the public, especially the Church, would more fully examine this lawless and hideous institution. He proclaimed that he had no interest in the sale of the books, not even his own book, so that Freemasons would not have grounds to accuse him of self-interest in exposing their institution.

In the Northern or non-slaveholding States, Masonry was almost universally renounced at that time. It was discovered that Freemasonry had developed such deep roots in all of New England that newspapers refused to report the death of William Morgan, or the circumstances connected with it.[274] Even throughout the North, independent or alternative newspapers had to be established for the purpose of making disclosures about the truth of Freemasonry. Now 40 years later, Finney advised that the same thing was occurring to where independent newspapers had to be established to get the truth out. Even still, those independent newspapers were being intercepted before they could be delivered.[275]

Masonry so completely baffled the courts of law and obstructed the course of justice, that it became a political matter. The anti-masonic sentiment of the Northern States carried it into politics. The result was that almost all Masons became ashamed, discontinued their affiliation with it, and publicly renounced Freemasonry. If they didn't publicly renounce their affiliation with Freemasonry, they did suspend their lodges, having nothing more to do with them and made no pretense about it.[276]

Finney stated that 40 years earlier these things were so infamous and universally known and confessed, that there was held a general consensus that Masonry would never again have any public respect. Now in the period of time known as the *Reconstruction Era* (1863-1877), Finney satirically stated that he would have expected slavery to be re-established in the country and become more popular than ever before than to ever

---

[272] Finney, *Character, Claims* 18
[273] Ibid.
[274] John Quincy Adams, "Address to the People of the Commonwealth of Massachusetts," Autumn, 1833 as included in John Quincy Adams, *Letters and Addresses on Freemasonry*, (Dayton, United Brethren Publishing House, 1875) 269-325
[275] Finney, *Character, Claims*, 20
[276] Ibid. 21

expect that Freemasonry would revive (another way of saying he didn't think it possible). It was astounding for Finney to realize that Freemasonry had again taken control of the government and of all civil offices while also having grown bold, impudent, and defiant.[277]

Finney reported feeling astonished, grieved, and indignant when "Christian Freemasons"* of the churches in his town of Oberlin, Ohio discussed and denied that Morgan and others had in fact revealed the true secrets of Freemasonry. *(*Note: one cannot be a Christian and a Freemason, it is oxymoron, as one follows Christ and the other Lucifer.)* Finney stated that just a few years earlier such denial would have ruined the character of any intelligent man, and much more a professed Christian.[278]

Freemasons exerted themselves in an extensive marketing campaign of literature in effort to present Freemasonry in a favorable light. It is an intriguing realization that Masons never attempted to discount how it was revealed and reported in *Light on Masonry.*"[279] Nor did Masons reply to any arguments or attacks that were successfully made upon it, neither did they pretend to reveal its secret. Instead, Masons eulogized it in a way that was revolting to those that understood what Freemasonry really is.[280]

With Masonic literature circulating among the young, thousands of young men were led into Masonry who otherwise would never have thought of engaging in such a thing.[281]

Capt. William Morgan [282]

Whose stand for righteousness led to his murder that led to the formation of the political Anti-Masonic Party and Second Great Awakening

Chapter three of *The Character, Claims and Practical Workings of Freemasonry,* "How Known" presents Charles Finney's firsthand account of our truthful American history. Finney has addressed the critical importance and need of the American People to know the truth on what Freemasonry really is and what it aspires. Included here is a summary of his key points.

First, from a negative aspect.

One. The truth of what Masonry is, cannot be known by perusing books written by adhering Masons because they are under oath to not reveal the secrets of Masonry, and it is their secrets that the American People must concern themselves in knowing. Finney, a lawyer before becoming a minister of the Gospel,

---

[277] Ibid.
[278] Ibid.
[279] (Elder) David Bernard, *Light on Masonry,* (Utica: William Williams, 1829) http://tinyurl.com/Bernard-on-Freemasonry
[280] Finney, *Character, Claims,* 22
[281] Ibid.
[282] "Wm. Morgan" as included in Elder David Bernard's 1829 book *Light on Masonry,* (Utica:William Williams, Printer, 1829) Front matter pages http://economictheology.com/Downloads/Special/Light_on_Masonry-by_David_Bernard.pdf This work is in the public domain

stated that in examining Masonic books, they were found to be meaningless and nonsense. In reviewing their books, Finney stated that the published orations and sermons in support of Masonry are false, full of long-windedness and pretentious boasting. They are written by men who are ignorant or dishonest. Adhering Masons do not profess to publish their secrets.[283]

Americans and the *Body of Christ* must obtain an understanding of what Masons never disclose, one being their oaths. Therefore, what they write is false because of being under oath.[284]

Two. The truth of what Masonry is, cannot be known by what adhering Masons verbalize. Every one of them is under oath to conceal and in no way reveal the secrets of the order. Freemasons don't deny this. So if asked if their books are true, they will either evade the question or else they will lie, and are under the binding obligation of their oaths to do so. When asked if the books that reveal the true accounts of Masonry are true, they consider themselves under an obligation to deny it, if they will say anything about it. Additionally, they know that in refusing to say anything of substance is a virtual acknowledgment that those revealing books are true, and would therefore be an indirect revelation of Masonry. They will almost universally deny that those revealing books are true. Some of them are ashamed to say anything more than that there is some truth and a lot of falsehood in them.[285]

Three. Because of being under oath to conceal the secrets of Masonry, their testimony regarding those revealing books holds no value. It is unsound to receive testimony of men who place themselves under horrid oaths; oaths sustained by horrific penalties in concealing their secrets. It matters not who they are. Masons have no right to expect an intelligent person to believe them. Nor have they a right to complain if we reject their testimony. We cannot ignore the testimony of thousands who risked their lives in conscientiously renouncing those oaths, many of them under the sanction of judicial oaths lawfully administered, and declared together in one accord that Morgan, Bernard and others truly revealed the secrets and a correct exposition of Freemasonry as it was and is.[286]

From a positive aspect - how the American People can know the truth about Masonry…

One. We can know what Masonry is from the published and oral testimony of those who have taken Freemason degrees and afterward, from conscientious motives, confessed their error, and have publicly renounced Masonry. If an argument is made that these defecting Masons are perjured men, and not trustworthy, this very accusation is an admission that they have published the truth. For unless they've truthfully published the secrets of Masonry, they've violated no Masonic oath. So, when Masons accuse them of being perjured, the very objection is an acknowledgment that the published secrets are true. If revealing the secrets of Masonry is perjury, then it stands to reason that to accuse the revealers of Masonry of perjury, is itself perjury because their accusation is softly or faintly admitting that is a true revelation of Masonry and therefore their accusation is a violation of their oath of secrecy. The very objection and accusation is an acknowledgment that the witnesses are entirely credible. In making an objection, they commit perjury themselves, if it be perjury to reveal their secrets because in accusing the witnesses of

---

[283] Finney, *Character, Claims*, 23
[284] Ibid.
[285] Ibid. 24-25
[286] Ibid. 25-26

perjury, they add their testimony to the fact that these witnesses have published Masonry as it is. So, by their own testimony in bringing a charge of perjury, they themselves add to the number of witnesses in the truthfulness of these revelations.[287]

Two. Renouncing Masons who are the best possible witnesses by whom to prove what Masonry really is and are competent witnesses. They testify from their own personal knowledge of what it is. They are in the highest degree credible witnesses. First, because they testify against themselves in their own wrong in having taken those oaths, and in having had any part in sustaining the institution. Secondly, their testimony is given with the certainty of incurring a most unrelenting persecution. Adhering Freemasons are under oath to persecute them, to destroy their characters and to seek to bring them to "fitting" punishment. Adhering Masons still persecute those that reveal their secrets. They are in the highest degree intolerant and every Mason knows this.[288]

Finney pointed out that Freemason leaders admonished their members to not patronize and support the businesses of those who oppose them. Those who renounce Masonry are well aware of their danger, however, are conscientiously compelled, by the fear and love of God, and by regard to the interests of their country, to renounce and expose it. Witnesses that testify under these circumstances are entitled to credit, especially in light of the fact that they have had no conceivable motive in deceiving the public. Their testimony was compelled by conscience.[289]

Also pointed out is that the authors of the books that Finney referenced in revealing the truth about Freemasonry were sustained by the testimony of 45,000 who publicly renounced Masonry out of the 50,000 Freemasons that existed in the United States. It is thought-provoking to contemplate that of the 5,000 who remained in Freemasonry for the most part, belonged to the slaveholding States and had "peculiar" reasons for still adhering to the institution of Masonry. Because they adhered to Masonry, their testimony was null, as they still regarded themselves as under oath to not reveal their secrets. Consequently, they would, of course, deny that these testimonial books had truly revealed Masonry.[290]

---

[287] Ibid. 26-27
[288] Ibid. 28-29
[289] Ibid.
[290] Ibid. 29

In 1912, Pastor Martin L. Wagner of St. Johns English Evangelical Lutheran Church in Dayton, Ohio published his book, *Freemasonry: An Interpretation.*[291] Wagner points out that John Quincy Adams, who was President of the United States at the time of the William Morgan murder, spoke against Freemasonry. Because of the excitement produced by the heinous murder and out of patriotic motives, President John Quincy Adams was led to make an impartial examination and investigation of Freemasonry. Also, compelling were the facts that surfaced in court testimony of witnesses, as well as the investigative action taken by the New York Legislature that brought exposure. With the opposing stand of defense for Freemasonry by the *Grand Lodge of Rhode Island*, it was obvious that something was seriously wrong.

President John Quincy Adams (1825-1829)[292]

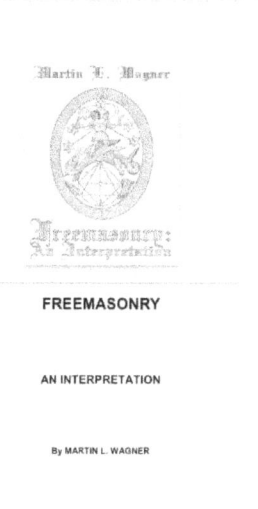

Freemasonry: An Interpretation
Title Page, (1912)[293]
by Pastor Martin L. Wagner
St. Johns English Evangelical Lutheran Church

Wagner included an excerpt of President Adams' views as expressed in his *Address to the People of Massachusetts* as well as a comment:

"I saw a code of Masonic legislation adapted to prostrate every principle of equal justice and to corrupt every sentiment of virtuous feeling in the soul of him who bound his allegiance to it. I saw the practice of common honesty, the kindness of Christian benevolence, even the abstinence of atrocious crimes, limited exclusively be lawless oaths and barbarous penalties, to the social relations between the brotherhood and the craft. I saw slander organize into a secret, widespread and affiliated agency, fixing its invisible fangs into the hearts of its victims, sheltered by the darkness of the lodge room, and armed with the never ceasing penalties of death.

I saw self-invoked imprecations of throats cut from ear to ear, of hearts and vitals torn out and cast off and hung on spires. I saw wine drank from a human skull with solemn invocation of all the sins of its owner upon the head of him who drank it. I saw a wretched mortal man dooming himself to eternal punishment, when the

---

[291] Martin L. Wagner, *Freemasonry: An Interpretation*, (Chicago: Ezra A. Cook, 1912; reprinted Seminar Tapes and Books of Grosse Pointe, MI) , accessed November 29, 2014, http://www.mindserpent.com/American_History/organization/mason/freemasonry/freemasonry.html#p_163
[292] *Wikimedia Commons*, s.v. "File:John Quincy Adams by GPA Healy, 1858.jpg," This work is in the public domain
[293] Ibid. This work is in the public domain

last trump shall sound, as a guarantee for idle and ridiculous promises. Such are the laws of Masonry; such are their indelible character, and with that character perfectly corresponds the history of Masonic lodges, chapters, encampments, and consistories, from that day to the present. A conspiracy of the few against the equal rights of the many; anti-republican in its sap from the first blushing of the summit of the plant to the deepest fiber of its root.

Notwithstanding these horrid oaths and penalties of which a common cannibal would be ashamed, the General Grand Royal Arch Chapter of the U.S. forbade their abandonment. That Masonry sanctions these barbarities, is therefore proven beyond a question." [294]

Moving forward on the historic timeline, there have been several others who have defected from Freemasonry and published books about their knowledge and experience.

In 1983, Jack Harris, former Freemason "Worshipful Master" published his book, *Freemasonry: The Invisible Cult In Our Midst*.[295]

A "Worshipful Master" is the senior officer of a Masonic Lodge who chairs all the business of his lodge. He is vested with considerable powers that include presiding over ritual and ceremonies. The office of *Worshipful Master* is the highest honor to which a lodge may appoint any of its members. Just the name of the title finds discrepancy with the *Word of God*, as Jesus forbade His disciples from calling anyone "Master." Mr. Harris reveals Freemasonry as an anti-Christian cult with damnable heresies in its teachings and doctrines.[296]

Matthew 23:8-10 ~ 8 But be not ye called Rabbi: for one is your Master, even Christ; and all ye are brethren. 9 And call no man your father upon the earth: for one is your Father, which is in heaven. 10 Neither be ye called masters: for one is your Master, even Christ.

Jack Harris stated,

> "A cult is defined as any group that embraces, teaches, or practices religious doctrine contrary to the accepted and established truth of biblical Christianity."[297]

Harris also stated his belief that the humanistic teachings of Freemasonry in all its branches will be a primary catalyst allowing the antichrist and one-world apostate church to come to power during the *Tribulation* period in the *End Times* of the *Latter Days*.[298]

---

[294] Ibid. 555-556, as cited in John Quincy Adams, *Letters and Addresses on Freemasonry*, "Address to the People of Massachusetts," (Dayton, Ohion: United Brethren Publishing House, 1875) 282, 283, 296, 107
[295] Jack Harris, *Freemasonry: The Invisible Cult In Our Midst*, (New Kensington, Whitaker House, 1983)
[296] Ibid., Preface
[297] Ibid. Preface, 11
[298] Ibid., 10

Freemasonry: The Invisible Cult In Our Midst[299]
A Biblical Expose' of Freemasonry
Written by a formerformer Worshipful Master…
Jack Harris
Cover (1983)

Providing insight on the basics of Freemasonry, Harris quoted the most well-known and important of Masonic authorities such as, Albert Mackey, Albert Pike, J.S.M. Ward, and Frank C. Higgins, who by their own words and doctrine agree that Masonry is indeed a religion. Harris pointed out that Masonry categorizes as a false religion.

A few of the vital practices and duties as a member of Freemasonry include:

<u>One</u>. Never to mention God's name.

<u>Two</u>. Prayers may not be closed in the name of the Lord Jesus Christ because it would offend Lodge brothers of other religions.

<u>Three</u>. Any book of law, not the Holy Bible, must be on their altar. This practice allows Freemasonry to initiate men from nearly all religions because <u>every religion has a book of "law."</u>

<u>Four</u>. The bible as spoken of in Freemasonry is not the same as that of Biblical Christian New Testament theology as based on Jesus Christ, the Son of Almighty God. In Freemasonry, holy writ refers to whichever religion is being discussed. Where many Christian Masons (an oxymoron-type phrase) believe they are worshipping Almighty God in the Lodge because of Biblical terminology being used, they are in fact worshipping the god of Masonry, Satan. Albert Pike, Freemasonry's revered leader whose bones are entombed at their world headquarters in Washington, DC, declared Lucifer (Satan) as the god of their religion.

<u>Five</u>. The men meet in the Lodge on one common level. In the Church of Christ members are gathered in the name of the Lord Jesus Christ. It is not possible to meet in Jesus' name in the Masonic Lodge.

<u>Six</u>. Although there are Bible verses and Christian symbols displayed in the Lodge room, most Christian symbols are limited as in relation to the Knights Templar. In the third degree, many Bible verses are presented to point out the fact of and in explaining eternal life and immortality, however, not once is Jesus Christ projected as the Person of eternal life or as *the Resurrection and the Life*. Each degree of Masonry uses Bible verses to support the ritual, however, is not used in a manner or for the purpose that the Author of the Bible gave it. For instance, Hosea 11:4a states, *"I drew them with cords of a man, with bands of love…"* The Masonic bible references this scripture as a cable tow, a six-foot blue cord wrapped around the candidate's neck as he is led blindfolded into the Lodge room. The length of the cable tow relates to the measurement of distance that Freemasonry will bury the mutilated body of someone who reveals its secrets.

---

[299] Jack Harris, *Freemasonry: The Invisible Cult In Our Midst,* (Springdale, PA: Whitaker House, 1983,) https://archive.org/details/freemasonry00jack_0 This work is in the public domain

2 John 7 ~ For many deceivers are entered into the world, who confess not that Jesus Christ is come in the flesh. This is a deceiver and an antichrist.

2 John 9-10 ~ Whosoever transgresseth, and abideth not in the doctrine of Christ, hath not God. He that abideth in the doctrine of Christ, he hath both the father and the Son. If there come any unto you, and bring not this doctrine, receive him not into your house, neither bid him God speed:

Freemasonry: A Grand Chaplain Speaks Out[300]
Cover (1984)
by Harmon R. Taylor

On November 25, 1984, Reverend Harmon R. Taylor, former Grand Chaplain of a New York Freemason Lodge published a letter entitled, "*Freemasonry: A Grand Chaplain Speaks Out.*"[301] Reverend Taylor addresses those who love the Lord and may be struggling with the same situation he experienced. Taylor stated that he sent the facts contained in this subject letter to all Masonic bodies of which he had been a member. Taylor makes an invitation to prayerfully read his letter that explains why he was resigning as the Grand Chaplain of the *Grand Lodge of Free and Accepted Masons of the State of New York* as well as from all bodies of the Masonic fraternity.

Harmon Taylor stated that many had asked him if Freemasonry is a religion and that he always responded, "*no,*" though others had told him that it *is* a religion. <u>Study has concluded the fact that learned writers in the fraternity say that Masonry is indeed a religion</u>.[302] Taylor interjects from *Matthew 18:16* that the Lord Jesus Christ said, *"In the mouth of two or three witnesses, every word is established,"* and then quoted four Masonic authorities who proclaim that Masonry is a religion.[303]

---

[300] Harmon R. Taylor, "Freemasonry: A Grand Chaplain Speaks Out," Cover, Ownership rights
[301] Harmon R. Taylor, "Freemasonry: A Grand Chaplain Speaks Out" as cited in Lt. Col. Gordon "Jack" Mohr, *The Hidden Power Behind Freemasonry*, (Burnsville: Weisman Publications, 1993 2d ed.) 5
[302] Taylor, *Freemasonry*, 5
[303] Ibid.

Albert Mackey (1807-1881) is considered the leading historian and scholar of Freemasonry, and one of the most well-known Masonic authorities. Mackey wrote in his 1860 book, *A Lexicon of Freemasonry*,

"*The religion, then, masonry, is pure theism...*"[304]

Mackey also declared that, "*The religion of Freemasonry is not Christianity.*"[305]

Albert Mackey about 1870[306]

Albert Pike [307]

Pike's Freemason regalia depicts the number "33" as in Freemason degrees. The double-headed eagle is a common symbol in the Scottish Rite and associated with the 32nd degree. Albert Pike associates this bird with the Egyptian god Mendes.[308] *Also regarded as the Phoenix Rising, it is an occult and witchcraft doctrine for reincarnation and immortality. The two heads on the bird pointing in opposite directions represent the Masonic doctrine of the necessity of both good and evil, light and darkness,*[309] *which is dualism — a dogma contrary to the Holy Bible.* [310] [311]

Albert Pike (1809-1891), called the "Plato of Freemasonry," was the former "*Sovereign Grand Commander of the Supreme Council of Grand Sovereign Inspectors General of the Thirty-third Degree.*" His remains are entombed at the Freemason Temple world headquarters in Washington, DC and is reverenced by Masons as the most important of all American Masonic authorities. Pike stated in his 1871 book, *Morals and Dogma*,

---

[304] Albert Mackey, *A LEXICON OF FREEMASONRY* (Pg. 402) as cited in Harmon R. Taylor, "Freemasonry: A Grand Chaplain Speaks Out," November 25, 1984
[305] Albert Mackey, *Mackey's Revised Encyclopedia of Freemasonry,* (Richmond, VA: Macoy Publishing, 1966) 618
[306] *Wikimedia Commons*, s.v. "File:Albert mackey.jpg" This work is in the public domain
[307] Library of Congress, "Albert Pike," Control Number brh2003002446/PP, http://www.loc.gov/item/brh2003002446/PP/ No known restrictions on publication.
[308] Albert Pike, *Morals and dogma,* (Charleston, 1871), 291
[309] Ibid. 792
[310] Dualism is the belief in two equal but opposite forces in the universe, good and evil. Contrary to what is commonly taught, the devil is not the opposite of Creator God because that would mean that Satan and God are equals. They are not. Creator God is so far above Satan in power that it cannot be comprehended. Lucifer was a creation of YHWH and is known in his fallen state as Satan. Creation is not greater or equal to the Creator.
[311] Modern History Project Staff, "Satan Prince of this World," as citing William Guy Carr, *Satan, Prince of This World,* (1959) 81

> *"Every Masonic lodge is a temple of religion, and its teachings are instructions in religion…this is true religion revealed to the ancient patriarchs; which masonry has taught for many centuries, and which it will continue to teach as long as time endures."*[312]

> *"It is the universal, eternal, immutable religion…"*[313]

J.S.M. (John Sebastian Marlow) Ward (1885-1949), a Masonic authority, English author, and psychic medium who made many contributions to the history of Freemasonry, wrote in his book, *Freemasonry: Its Aims and Ideals*…

> *"I consider freemasonry is a significantly organized school of mysticism to be entitled to be called a religion. …Freemasonry…taught that each man can by himself, work out his own conception of god and thereby achieve salvation."*[314]

Ward asserts that there are many paths that lead to the throne of the all-loving father which all start from a common source. According to Ward, Freemasonry believes…

> *"…that through these paths appear to branch off in various directions, yet they all reach the same ultimate goal, and that to some men, one path is better and to other, another."*[315]

Frank C. Higgins, a high-level Mason, stated in his 1923 book, *Ancient Freemasonry: An Introduction to Masonic Archeology*,

> *"It is true that Freemasonry is the parent of all religion."*[316]

These Masonic witnesses all agree with their doctrine that Masonry is, indeed, a religion and is not Christianity.

In his letter, Harmon Taylor explained how to ascertain whether Masonry is a true religion or a false religion and presented an article published in the November/December 1974 issue of *Faith for the Family*, which is entitled, "*How to Recognize a False Religion.*" A prominent Christian leader wrote:

> *"All false religions, have some things in common. Here are three simple tests by which any religion should be judged; FIRST: What is its attitude toward the Bible? SECOND, Any religious teaching should be tested by*

---

[312] Albert Pike, *Morals and dogma of the ancient and accepted Scottish Rite of Freemasonry,* Entered according to the Act of Congress, in the year 1871, by Albert Pike, (Charleston), 213-214 as cited in Harmon R. Taylor, "Freemasonry: A Grand Chaplain Speaks Out"
[313] Albert Pike, *Morals and dogma*, (Charleston, 1871), 219
[314] J.S.M. Ward, *Freemasonry: Its Aims and Ideals*, (Philadelphia: David McKay, 1925) 185,187
[315] Ibid.
[316] Frank C. Higgins, *Ancient Freemasonry: An Introduction to Masonic Archeology*, (Pyramid Book Company, 1923) 10

this question; What is its attitude toward Jesus Christ? THIRD, In judging a religious system, we should ask, What is its attitude toward the blood of Jesus Christ!"[317]

According to these three tests in judging a religion, Masonry is indeed a false religion that manifests a satanic attitude toward the Holy Bible, the Deity of Jesus Christ, and the blood atonement of Jesus Christ. Taylor affirmed this charge as he tells the reader to be mindful that in the *Word of God*, it is recorded that Jesus said,

"In the mouth of two or three witnesses every word shall be established."[318]

In referring to the testimony of Masonic authorities that reveal Masonry's satanic attitude toward the Holy Bible, the Deity of Jesus Christ and the vicarious atonement for the sins of mankind by the shedding of Christ's blood on the cross, his point is made.

Joseph Fort Newton, D.D. (1880-1950), a Freemason and famous authority and writer, stated in an article entitled, *"The Bible in Masonry,"*

"[T]he Bible, so rich in symbolism, is itself a symbol... Thus, by the very honour which Masonry pays the Bible, it teaches us to revere every book of faith in which men find help for to-day and hope for the morrow, joining hands with the man of Islam as he takes his oath on the Koran, with the Hindu as he makes covenant with God upon the book that he loves best."[319]

Joseph Fort Newton, D.D., around 1916[320]

Albert Pike, in *Morals and Dogma*, stated,

"Masonry propagates no creed except its own most and Simple sublime One; that universal religion, taught by Nature and Reason."[321]

"That rite raises the corner of the veil...for there it declares that Masonry is a worship.[322]

Harmon Taylor points out in his letter that a truly born-again Christian has ability to see from Pike's statement that Masonry totally rejects the doctrine of an infallible, God-breathed, inerrant Holy Bible.

According to the Second Test, Masonry is a false religion because it totally rejects the crucial doctrine of the Deity of the Lord Jesus Christ.

---

[317] *Faith for the Family*, "How to Recognize a False Religion," November/December 1974 as cited in Taylor, Freemasonry: A Grand Chaplain Speak Out,
[318] Matthew 18:16 ~ *But if he will not hear thee, then take with thee one or two more, that in the mouth of two or three witnesses every word may be established.*
[319] R.W. and Rev. Joseph Fort Newton, *The Bible in Masonry*, accessed April 9, 2021 http://www.phoenixmasonry.org/bible.htm
[320] *Wikimedia Commons*, s.v. "File:Joseph Fort Newton.jpg" This work is in the public domain
[321] Pike, *Morals and dogma*, p 718 as cited in Harmon R. Taylor, "Freemasonry: A Grand Chaplain Speaks Out"
[322] Ibid. 718

According to the Third Test, Masonry is a false religion because Masonry dogmatically rejects the doctrine of salvation from the penalty of sin by faith in the vicarious (substituted in the place of another) atonement of Christ's shed blood on the cross.

In 1917, another Masonic author, Thomas Milton Stewart, published, *Symbolic Teaching on Masonry and its Message*, which ascribed support in his doctrine by quoting an apostate Episcopal minister,

"Did Jesus count Himself, conceive of Himself as a proprietary sacrifice, and of His work as an expiation? The only answer possible is, clearly, He did not… He does not call Himself the world's priest, or the world's victim."[323]

Symbolic Teaching on Masonry and its Message
Title page (1917)[324]
by Thomas Milton Steward

Reverend Taylor interjects that salvation by faith in the vicarious atonement is not *"ignorant perversions of the original doctrines"* as Masonry teaches. Salvation by faith is pivotal in the message of the glorious Gospel of Christ because the Gospel is the power of God unto salvation to everyone who believes.[325] Therefore, Masonry fails all three tests. It manifests a satanic attitude toward the Holy Bible, the Deity of Christ, and the vicarious atonement. In addition to failing these core tests, there is much more proof that Masonry is indeed a false religion.

Henry Clausen[326]

Henry C. Clausen (1905-1992), 33° former *Sovereign Grand Commander of the Supreme Council 33° mother council of the world*, in the November 1970 issue of *NEW AGE Magazine*, wrote regarding masonry,

"It is dedicated to bringing about the Fatherhood of God, the Brotherhood of Man, and making better men in a better world."[327]

---

[323] Ibid. 177, as cited in Harmon R. Taylor, "Freemasonry: A Grand Chaplain Speaks Out"
[324] Thomas Milton Steward, *Symbolic Teaching on Masonry and its Message,* (Cincinnati: Stewart & Kidd Company, 1914) Title page, This work is in the public domain
[325] *Romans 1:16 ~ For I am not ashamed of the gospel of Christ: for it is the power of God unto salvation to every one that believeth; to the Jew first, and also to the Greek.*
[326] Henry Clausen, Scottish Rite Freemason, https://youtu.be/V6ScOMV1h7s , Youtube/Bunte of World Knete, screengrab, Fair use
[327] Henry C. Clausen, *NEW AGE Magazine,* November 1970, p4

Clausen was also a former Assistant United States Attorney from San Francisco as well as a Special Investigator for the Secretary of War Henry L. Stimson, carrying out an investigation ordered by (*de facto*) Congress.[328]

Reverend Taylor points out in his letter that the doctrine of the Fatherhood of God and the Brotherhood of Man is not found in the Holy Bible. It is a doctrine taught consistently by apostates. Also, the Holy Bible makes it crystal clear that no organization, Masonry included, can make better men. Only Almighty God can make better men.

Taylor also points out that according to a creed found in the *Masonic Bible*, masonry teaches that *"character determines destiny."* The teaching that character determines destiny is a false doctrine of the *Arch Deceiver of Souls*. The Holy Bible says, *"There is none that doeth good,"*[329] and *"for by Grace are you saved through faith, and that not of yourselves; it is a gift of God, not of works, lest any man should boast."*[330]

Freemasonry: Its Aims and Ideals[331]
By J.S.M. Ward
1925

Reverend Taylor continues by stating that Masonry is anti-Christian in its teachings. He again references J.S.M. Ward in *Freemasonry: Its Aims and Ideals* as stated,

"[I] boldly aver that Freemasonry is a religion… yet it no way conflicts with any other religion, unless that religion holds that no one outside its portals can be saved."[332] [Emphasis added]

In his statement, Ward reveals the fact that Masonry has no conflict with any apostate religion on the face of the earth, and that Masonry is in conflict with Christianity. The Holy Bible says,

"Neither is there salvation in any other, for there is none other name under heaven given among men whereby we MUST be saved." Acts 4:12 [Emphasis added]

Jesus said,

"No man cometh unto the father but by Me." John 14:6

---

[328] *Wikipedia*, "Henry Clausen," (last edited 17 May 2023) https://en.wikipedia.org/wiki/Henry_Clausen
[329] *Romans 3:12 ~ They are all gone out of the way, they are together become unprofitable; there is none that doeth good, no, not one.*
[330] *Ephesians 2:8-9 ~ For by grace are ye saved through faith; and that not of yourselves: it is the gift of God: 9Not of works, lest any man should boast.*
[331] J.S.M. Ward, *Freemasonry: Its Aims and Ideals*, (Philadelphia: David McKay Co., 1925) Title page, This work is in the public domain
[332] J.S.M. Ward, *Freemasonry: Its Aim and Ideals*, (Philadelphia: David McKay Co., 1925) 187-188 as cited in Harmon R. Taylor, "Freemasonry: A Grand Chaplain Speaks Out"

The Holy Bible clearly teaches that there is only one way to heaven and that is through faith in Christ.

Reverend Taylor includes the documented statement of what a prominent college president stated pertaining to Masonry,

> *"It is a luciferian religion. We are fully aware of its diabolical origin and purpose. I believe that any born-again Christian, when the facts from the lips of Masonic writers themselves are presented showing that Masonry is a religion and is the worship of Satan, will immediately withdraw."*[333]

Harmon responded…

> *"To this I must add my hearty agreement! The God and Father of the Lord Jesus Christ, the only True and Living God, has clearly commanded Christians, 'Be ye not unequally yoked together with unbelievers,[334] and 'swear not at all,'[335] and 'have no fellowship with the unfruitful works of darkness, but rather reprove them.'"* [336][337]

As previously stated, it was in the 1820s and 1830s, when the renowned evangelist, Charles Finney, was mightily used of Almighty God as an evangelist and leader in a major revival in America. He stated,

> *"Surely, if Masons really understood what Masonry is, as it is delineated in these books, no Christian Mason would think himself at liberty to remain another day a member of the fraternity. The fact is, a great many nominal [existing in name only] Masons are not so in reality. It is as plain as possible that a man knowing what it is, and embracing it in his heart, cannot be a Christian man. To say he can is to belie [or contradict] the very nature of Christianity."*[338] [Emphasis added]

Charles Finney, 1850 [339]

---

[333] Harmon R. Taylor, "Freemasonry: A Grand Chaplain Speaks Out"
[334] *2 Corinthians 6:14 ~ Be ye not unequally yoked together with unbelievers: for what fellowship hath righteousness with unrighteousness? and what communion hath light with darkness?*
[335] *Matthew 5:34-37 ~ But I say unto you, Swear not at all; neither by heaven; for it is God's throne: Nor by the earth; for it is his footstool: neither by Jerusalem; for it is the city of the great King. Neither shalt thou swear by thy head, because thou canst not make one hair white or black. But let your communication be, Yea, yea; Nay, nay: for whatsoever is more than these cometh of evil.*
[336] *Ephesians 5:11 ~ And have no fellowship with the unfruitful works of darkness, but rather reprove them.*
[337] Harmon R. Taylor, "Freemasonry: A Grand Chaplain Speaks Out"
[338] Rev. C. G. Finney, Late President of Oberlin College, Ohio, *The Character, Claims and Practical Workings of Freemasonry*, (1869) 115
[339] *Wikimedia Commons*, s.v. "File:Finney.gif" This work is in the public domain

In his 1984 letter, Harmon Taylor points out that we are now living in the *Last Days* at the *End of the Age* by comparing the signs of the time with prophetic Scripture. Certainly, knowing that his time is short, Satan is hard at work to hinder believers' spiritual growth, while also trying to keep the unsaved from entering the *Kingdom of God*.[340] Taylor admonishes that Freemasonry is one of Satan's master deceptions. He testifies to the fact that many ministers, elders, deacons, trustees, and Sunday school teachers belong to this cult.

Taylor closes his letter telling what he would now do with his life while emphasizing the critical need in exposing evil. Having come to a new life in Christ, Taylor began a new ministry in Biblical Christianity. He points out that there is a tremendous need to scrutinize the occult nature of Freemasonry because of the massive infiltration of its effects on the working body of the Christian Church. Exposing Freemasonry in the true Light of Jesus Christ is necessary in depicting its inherent evil.

> *3 John 11 ~ Beloved, follow not that which is evil, but that which is good. He that doeth good is of God: but he that doeth evil hath not seen [known] God.*

President John Quincy Adams [341]

President John Quincy Adams was not only the son of Founding Father, John Adams, and the sixth President of the United States, he also served in office as a former U.S. Ambassador, as U.S. Secretary of State, and as a U.S. Representative.

As Secretary of State, John Quincy Adams was chief in the writing and formulating of the 1823 *Monroe Doctrine,* a critically important response to the secret treaty of the *Congress of Verona (Holy Alliance* of Jesuit-Freemason associations*)* in their plan to suppress and destroy the popular government in the American Republic, as well as Protestantism, the Christian religion of Liberty.

In 1830, John Quincy Adams was elected to the U.S. House of Representatives on the *Anti-Mason Party* ticket of which he was instrumental in establishing. He was President of the United States in 1826, at the time of William Morgan's murder, and spoke out against Freemasonry. Because of the overwhelming excitement that occurred in the country, along with phenomenal obstruction of justice at every level of government, Adams conducted his own investigation.

President Adams was so convinced of the unethical, unscriptural, and unholy secret society that he carried on an active and heated literary and speaking campaign against Freemasonry. His book, *Letters on Freemasonry*, contains critically important correspondence that he had written on the controversial subject. Originally published in 1833, copies amazingly (or maybe not so amazingly) disappeared, until recent years.

---

[340] *Revelation 12:12 ~ Therefore rejoice, ye heavens, and ye that dwell in them. Woe to the inhabiters of the earth and of the sea! for the devil is come down unto you, having great wrath, because he knoweth that he hath but a short time.*
[341] *Wikimedia Commons,* s.v. "File:John Quincy Adams by GPA Healy, 1858.jpg," This work is in the public domain

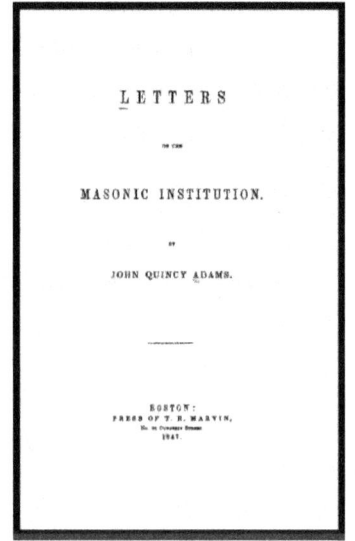 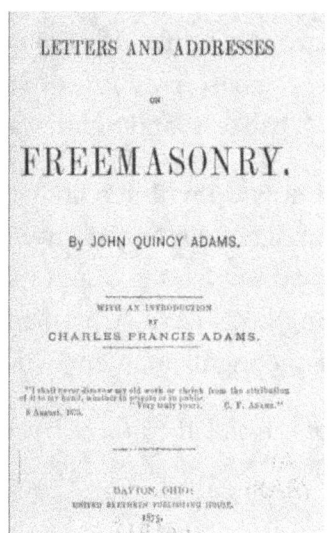

Left: Title page of
Letters on the Masonic Institution
by John Quincy Adams [342]
Published in 1847
(originally published in 1833)

Right: Title page of
Letters and Addresses on Freemasonry
Published in 1875 [343]
with an Introduction by his son,
Charles Frances Adams

Because there was a "revival" of Freemasonry after the Civil War, Charles Adams brought his father's book back into print.

Included in Adams' writing is an important fact. Where effort was made in defending the society during public outrage, a particular Mason made a false public claim that Adams, as well as his illustrious father, were Masons. The matter was addressed with response and clearly established that neither had ever been initiated in the Order, nor had knowledge of the Masonic secrets, oaths, and penalties.

In his book, Adams refers to Thomas Jefferson's writings pertaining to George Washington that make it clear that these two Founding Fathers were also vehemently opposed to the society of Freemasonry.[344]

Adams was known to be a devout Christian. There is no doubt that it was his sense of duty as a Christian which compelled him to fiercely battle against injustice and prejudice, and to support freedom, liberty, and human rights. He never quit fighting for the abolition of slavery. He held an intense desire to expose the Masonic Lodge and left a legacy to the American people through his writings while directing that *"they must ever remain as a standing testimony."*[345]

Adams' son, Charles, followed his father's and grandfather's legacy by also serving his career in government. Because of a stir of revival that was occurring in Freemasonry, in 1875, Charles Francis Adams, Sr. (1807-1886), republished his father's book. It was Charles' conviction to be certain that this invaluable work and evidence on the matter be available to the American people.[346]

---

[342] John Quincy Adams, *Letters on the Masonic Institution*, (Boston: Press of T. R. Marvin, 1847) Title page, This work is in the public domain
[343] John Quincy Adams, Charles Frances Adams, *Letters and Addresses on Freemasonry*, (Dayton: United Brethren Publishing House, 1875) Title page, This work is in the public domain
[344] Ibid., 52-54, 49
[345] Ibid., Introduction
[346] Ibid., Introduction 1-41

Charles wrote the Introduction in the 1875 reprinted edition of his father's book. Laying out a summary of the William Morgan murder and the obstructions of justice incurred because of Freemasons, he points out that the *republican form of government* in the American Republic cannot co-exist with the secret society of Freemasonry.

"The pride of freeman—living under a system of equal laws, with guaranties of the rights of each individual—should be to sustain the junction of innocence with liberty, the union of an open, honest heart with an efficient and liberal hand. Such a state can not co-exist with secret obligations."[347]

Charles Francis Adams[348]

Here you have it. Presented with documented evidence is America's greatest of enemies. Freemasonry and the *Illuminist* Jesuits, are Satan's evangelists and workers of *the Craft*. Together with their rulers, the *Illuminati* with their *Committee of 300, Council of 33* and *Supreme Council of 13* are the *High Priests of the Luciferian Creed* who control the *Synagogue of Satan* and direct Lucifer's secret *One World Government-New World Order*. Members of this dark society include those of the *Black Nobility* and are of the highest ranks and degrees of all branches of witchcraft.[349] They are enemies of our Founding Fathers' American Republic that was established based on the *"Laws of Nature and of Natures God,"* Creator God's Law. Moral Law. These sons and daughters of Satan are enemies to the Church/*ekklesia* of Jesus Christ as well as any institution established in Liberty.

Fritz Springmeier wrote about these families in 1995, saying,

> *"Evil powerful groups of men organized themselves to perpetuate their powerful bloodlines. This organization was known as the Brotherhood (or the Brotherhood of the Snake). The goal of the Brotherhood was to unite the world by any means and bring it under Satanic rule. The Brotherhood and its network of organizations began working throughout history to bring about this Satanic dictatorship."*[350]

As Creator God has believers around the world who fellowship and worship in various Biblical Christian denominations or organizations, so does His archenemy and master counterfeiter, Satan, have members of various rites and covens of witchcraft around the globe. The Freemason Lodge is a part of a huge network of world-wide witchcraft organizations. It could be viewed that Freemasonry is the world's largest coven of witches. Espoused as a mystery religion, it is a pagan religion in which secret doctrines are kept from the

---

[347] John Quincy Adams, Charles Frances Adams, *Letters and Addresses on Freemasonry*, (Dayton: United Brethren Publishing House, 1875) 40
[348] *Wikimedia Commons*, s.v. "File:C. F. Adams - Warren. LCCN2013651550 (cropped)" This work is in the public domain

public and known only to its initiated worshipers by secret rites and rituals. The great mystery of the mystery religions is the worship of the sexual reproductive function in all aspects of perception.

We continue in reasoning together…

What makes people think like they do? What makes them form words and talk like they do? Why is there so much confusion in America? Why is there so much evil and corruption in our societies?

Let's look at and consider ideology. Think, "frame of reference," or a perspective; it's like a lens. It's a set of preconceived ideas through which one sees the world. The more accurate one's frame of reference, the more accurately one will see the world. Premises, or first propositions (suggesting something to be considered), are the basis on which rest one's subsequent reasonings. A premise is the first thought that leads to a later thought or idea. A premise is a proposition that supports or helps to support, a conclusion. Every idea has a premise, and every belief system has an underlying philosophy (the rational investigation of the truths and principles of being knowledge or conduct). The philosophy, or thought process, is the lens through which that belief-system filters and that comes from some underlying philosophy. The most important realization is the fact that every philosophy or belief system has a religious premise.[351]

So, we reflect and calculate — what schools we attended, what churches we went to, what television programs we watched, and most importantly, what newscast we took-in almost daily. Who were in our circle of friends? What did our parents teach us? Who or what shaped and molded us to be who we are? What or who do we believe in when it comes to religion? Are we *Secular Humanist*? Catholic, Lutheran, Congregationalists, Baptist, Hindu, Mormon, Muslim, etc.? Who or what do we believe in spiritually? This is the foundation of our frame of reference. What kind of wisdom and understanding do we have?

When we visit the *New Testament* at *James 3:13-18* this is what is revealed:

> *[13]Who is a wise man endued with knowledge among you? Let him show out of a good conversation his works with meekness of wisdom. [14]But if ye have bitter envying and strife in your hearts, glory not and lie not against the truth. [15]This wisdom descendeth not from above, but is earthly, sensual, devilish. [16] For where envying and strife is, there is confusion and every evil work.*
>
> *[17]But the wisdom that is from above is first pure, then peaceable, gentle, and easy to be entreated, full of mercy and good fruits, without partiality and without hypocrisy. [18]And the fruit of righteousness is sown in peace of them that make peace.*

So, people talk and act the way they do because they carry with them their own frame of reference and wisdom that is either earthly or heavenly. This foundation distinguishes how we think, our ideology.

Let us go a step farther. Why are there such differences of opinion in the U.S. House of Representatives and in the U.S. Senate, as well as in our State Assemblies?

Let's look at the *Old Testament* in the book of *Daniel*. Daniel told King Nebuchadnezzar what his dream was and interpreted it for him. Daniel said to the King:

---

[351] Dr Marlene McMillian, *Five Pillars of Liberty*, (Fort Worth: Liberty View Media, 2011) 43-45

> ⁴¹*And whereas thou sawest the feet and toes, part of potters clay and part of iron, the kingdom shall be divided; but there shall be in it of the strength of the iron, forasmuch as thou sawest the iron mixed with miry clay.* ⁴²*And as the toes of the feet were part of iron and part of clay, so the Kingdom shall be partly strong and party broken.* ⁴³*And whereas thou sawest iron mixed, with miry clay, they shall mingle themselves with the seed of men: but they shall not cleave one to another, even as iron is NOT missed with clay. Daniel 2:41-43*
>
> [Emphasis added]

So, the feet and toes are part iron and part clay, but the clay doesn't get any strength by mixing itself with the iron. The iron doesn't get any strength from the clay. Neither adheres to one another. It's the same with oil mixed with water—they don't work together.

Man will not mix with one another with two separate ideologies, with two separate wisdoms (one from below and one from above). They have two different frames of reference!

This is why we need people in our County, State, and Federal Government with a *Biblical worldview* in their frame of reference—people who have *wisdom from above*. This s why we need the *Republic for the United States of America*. "Republic: A state in which sovereign power is lodged in representatives elected by the people."[352] We need God-fearing people in our governments. We need a civil society practicing Almighty God's virtue, and *Christian self-government and union* so that righteousness will exalt our nation.[353] When achieved, America will be the greatest nation in the world.

Before George Washington became America's first President under the *Constitution for the United States*, before there was established a functioning Republic that became "a city on a hill," it was necessary to ratify (to approve and sanction) the newly written *Constitution*.

---

[352] *Noah Webster's First Edition of An American Dictionary of the English Language,* 1828:
"REPUB'LK;, n. [L. respublica; res and publica ; public affairs.]
    1. A commonwealth ; a state in which the exercise of the sovereign power is lodged in representatives elected by the people. In modern usage, it differs from a democracy or democratic stale, in which the people exercise the powers of sovereignty in person. Vet the democracies of Greece are often called republics.
    2. Common interest ; the public. [Not in use.] B. Jonson.
    Republic of letters, the collective body of learned men."
[353] *Proverbs 14:34 ~ Righteousness exalteth a nation: but sin is a reproach to any people.*

Samuel Langdon, D.D.[354]

Samuel Langdon (1723-1797) graduated from Harvard with Founding Father, Samuel Adams. On June 5, 1788, Reverend Langdon gave a speech in New Hampshire. The speech was delivered with an intention of persuading the people of New Hampshire to support the ratification of the *Constitution*, being the ninth State that would qualify a quorum to ratify, so that the *Constitution* would be a working instrument, the nation's Operating Document. This speech describes where America is today! We need our Republic restored! We need a functioning *Declaration of Independence* and our Founding Fathers' *Constitution* with the original and missing *Thirteenth Article of Amendment* acknowledged in its proper and lawful place.[355]

Dr. Langdon's speech is for today! Following is Reverend Langdon's speech – read it very carefully.

"Preserve your government with the utmost attention and solicitude, for it is the remarkable gift of heaven. From year to year be careful in the choice of your representatives and all the higher powers of government.

Fix your eyes upon men of good understanding and known honest; men of knowledge, improved by experience. Men who fear God and hate covetousness, who love truth and righteousness, and sincerely wish the public welfare.

Beware of such as are cunning rather than wise, who prefer their own interest to everything whose judgment is partial or fickle and whom you ould not willingly trust with your own private interest.

When meetings are called for the choice of your ruler, do not carelessly neglect them or give your votes with indifference but act with serious deliberation and judgment as in a most important matter, and let the faithful of the land serve you.

Let not men openly-irreligious and immoral become your legislators, for how can you expect good laws to be made by men who have no fear of God...and who boldly trample on the authority of his commands? If the legislative body are corrupt, you will soon have bad men for counsellors, corrupt judges, unqualified justices, and officers in every department who will dishonor their stations.

Therefore, be always on your guard against parties and the methods of unworthy men, and let distinguished merit always determine your vote. And when all places in government are filled with the best men you can find, behave yourselves as good subjects, obey the laws, be cheerfully subject to such taxation as the necessities

---

[354] American Minute with Bill Federer, "We have rebelled against God. We have lost the true spirit of Christianity... Harvard President Samuel Langdon, 1775..." May 31, 2015, This work is in the public domain, Fair use

[355] Thirteenth Article of Amendment, *"If any citizen of the United States shall accept, claim, receive, or retain any title of nobility or honour, or shall without the consent of Congress, accept and retain any present, pension, office, or emolument of any kind whatever, from any Emperor, King, Prince, or foreign Power, such person shall cease to be a citizen of the United States, and shall be incapable of holding any office of trust or profit under them, or either of them."*

of the public call for. Give tribute to whom tribute is due, custom to whom custom, fear to whom fear, and honor to whom honor is due as the gospel commands you.

Never give countenance to the turbulent men, who wish to distinguish themselves and rise to power by forming combinations and exciting insurrections against government for this can never be the right way to redress real grievances.

I call upon you also, to support in all your towns that the rising generation may not grow up in ignorance…It is a debt you owe to your children and that God to whom they belong…I call upon you to preserve the knowledge of God in the land, and attend to the revelation written to us from heaven. If you neglect or renounce that religion taught and commanded in holy scriptures, think no more of freedom, peace, and happiness.

May the general government of these United States, when established appear to be the best which the nations have yet known, and be exalted by uncorrupted religion and morals! And may the everlasting gospel diffuse its Heavenly light and spread Righteousness, Liberty, and Peace through the whole world.

Avoid all the vices and corruption of the world; the judgments of heaven will pursue you. There will be a resurrection of the dead, both of the just and the unjust, and a day of solemn judgment when all mankind must give an account of their conduct in this world.

Will you permit me now to pray in behalf of the people, that all the departments of government may be constantly filled with the wisest and best [people]. [356] [Emphasis added]

The Portsmouth Daily Evening Times[357]
January 1, 1891
Acknowledged Rev. Samuel Langdon's Influence
in the ratification of the Constitution for the united States
"by his voice and example he contributed more perhaps, than any other man to the favorable action of that body."

---

[356] Frank Moore, *The Patriot Preachers of the American Revolution: With Biographical Sketches*; Samuel Langdon, D.D., "Government corrupted by Vice; a Sermon preached before the Honorable Congress of the Colony of Massachusetts Bay, on the 31st of May, 1775," (New York: Charles T. Evans, 1862) 49-73

[357] American Minute with Bill Federer, "Was America established a CHRISTIAN NATION on STATE LEVEL? Read these original State Constitutions to find out…," as cited by Pastor Dewey Moede, June 22, 2016, https://www.fggam.org/2016/06/was-america-established-as-a-christian-nation/ This work is in the public domain

We must heed the words of *wisdom from above* exhorted in this sermon in order for righteousness to exalt our nation, restoring God's government on earth and for America to be the greatest country in the world, to be "a city upon a hill." America was the greatest nation in all the world from 1789, when the *Constitution* was established until 1861, when the Civil War began. The actual beginning of its downfall occurred after the assassination of Lincoln on *Good Friday,* April 14, 1865.

This is an example of a true American Pastor, one who did not shy away from exercising his civic duty to the *Body of Christ.*

So, who took down and set aside the American Republic?

Shortly after Abraham Lincoln was inaugurated into the office of President of the United States, on March 27, 1861, there was a call to do some business in Congress. It was discovered, with the number of Representatives and Senators from the South having abandoned their seats as members of Congress, the Federal Government did not have enough members of Congress for a quorum to do business. President Lincoln knew that an "*interim Executive Congress*" had to be exercised during the *War Between the States* for the government to continue throughout the conflict. After the Civil War ended, before President Lincoln was able to restore the operations of government through his presidential *Reconstruction Plan,* he was assassinated.[358]

The *Radical Republicans* in Congress endured conflict in the government that was also exacerbated (irritated, to inflame angry passions) by the scandals of the secret society of Freemasonry. They fully understood that Congress was lacking the Representatives of the vacant seats for the Southern States, but to fill them and the Halls of Congress, would very likely be filling them with the ex-Confederate/*Slave-Power*/Freemasons who would forever seek to gain the legislative balance of power and institute slavery again.[359]

Radical Republican Leaders

Sen. Charles Sumner [360]   *Sen. Benjamin Wade* [361]

---

[358] Jean Hallahan Hertler with David Carl Hertler, *Re-inhabited: Republic for the United States of America,* Vol. I, "America's Truthful History," (ValleyAssetsPublishing.com, 2016) 123, 135, 172
[359] Ibid., 180, 211
[360] *Wikimedia Commons,* s.v. "Charles Sumner steel engraving c1860.jpg," This work is in the public domain
[361] Library of Congress, "Benjamin F Wade - Brady-Handy.jpg," No known restrictions on publication.

Rep. George Washington Julian [362]

Rep. Thaddeus Stevens [363]

What these men of principle, the *Radical Republicans,* did not realize is that the "cunning, ambitious, and unprincipled men,"[364] as President George Washington had referred to them, would end up making slaves of ALL Americans — black and white — and do it through the *14th Amendment* which would federalize citizens into a different type of citizenship. These cunning, ambitious, and unprincipled Luciferians would then craft an illusion once they had fully infiltrated the Federal Government (and State and local governments just like a cancer), and trick the American People into their jurisdiction of *MYSTERY BABYLON*[365] – the Corporate UNITED STATES, also known as THE UNITED STATES OF AMERICA, INC.[366] — a very different type of government from the American Republic. It was an easier task now that the Union was no longer a Christian republic but had changed law forms and became a Corporate democracy beginning with the *14th Amendment.*[367]

---

[362] Library of Congress, "Hon. Geo. Washington of Indiana," No known restrictions on publication.
[363] Library of Congress, "Hon. Thaddeus Stevens of Penn.," No known restrictions on publication.
[364] President George Washington, in his *Farewell Address* to the People of the United States, 1796:
"...**cunning, ambitious, and unprincipled men** will be enabled to subvert the power of the people, and to usurp for themselves the reins of government; destroying afterwards the very engines which have lifted them to unjust dominion... The spirit of encroachment tends to consolidate the powers of all the departments in one, and thus to create, whatever the form of government, a real despotism..."   [Emphasis added]
[368] *Revelation 17:1-6 ~ And there came one of the seven angels which had the seven vials, and talked with me, saying unto me, Come hither; I will shew unto thee the judgment of the great whore that sitteth upon many waters: ² With whom the kings of the earth have committed fornication, and the inhabitants of the earth have been made drunk with the wine of her fornication. ³ So he carried me away in the spirit into the wilderness: and I saw a woman sit upon a scarlet coloured beast, full of names of blasphemy, having seven heads and ten horns. ⁴ And the woman was arrayed in purple and scarlet colour, and decked with gold and precious stones and pearls, having a golden cup in her hand full of abominations and filthiness of her fornication: ⁵ And upon her forehead was a name written, <u>Mystery, Babylon The Great, The Mother Of Harlots And Abominations Of The Earth</u>.
⁶And I saw the woman drunken with the blood of the saints, and with the blood of the martyrs of Jesus: and when I saw her, I wondered with great admiration.*
[366] Delaware Department of State, Division of Corporations, File Number 4525682, THE UNITED STATES OF AMERICA, INC., in Filing History as "Incorp Delaware Stock Co.", <u>https://delecorp.delaware.gov/tin/controller</u>
[367] Hertler, *Re-inhabited, Volume I,* 211

The Congressional Reconstruction Plan.

In early to mid-1867, Republicans passed three laws of *Congressional Reconstruction* over the vetoes of Lincoln's successor as President, Andrew Johnson. The Acts stipulated the new terms in which Southern State governments were required to apply for readmission to the Union, essentially starting all over again after President Johnson astoundingly made attempts by Presidential Proclamation saying that the *Reconstruction* process was completed (*Presidential Proclamations* dated June 13, 1865, April 2, 1866, and August 20, 1866). The insurrection and domestic violence along with blatant executive moves obvious as federal abandonment were to such a degree that historians refer to this Era as "*The Second Civil War.*"[368]

President Andrew Johnson in the Masonic Order of Knights Templar Commandery Regalia, 1869, his final year in Presidential Office [369]
"Sir Knight" Johnson was also a Royal Arch Mason and Scottish Rite Mason[370]
The Knights Templar Degree is also known as the "Commandery Degree" and is considered the highest degree in York Rite Freemasonry.[371]
Knights Templar is the equivalent of the 32nd degree in Scottish Rite Masonry

After the Civil War, Albert Pike was found guilty of treason and jailed, only to be pardoned by fellow Freemason President Andrew Johnson on April 22, 1866, who met with him the next day at the White House. On June 20, 1867, Scottish Rite officials conferred upon President Johnson the 4th to 32nd Freemasonry degrees, and Johnson later went to Boston to dedicate a Masonic Temple.[372] *We note that Freemason revivalist and leader of Freemasonry in the western hemisphere, Albert Pike, was President Andrew Johnson's occult Masonic master and White House advisor.*[373]

The *Radical Republicans* were vigorously and vehemently opposed by the Democrat Party and were often opposed by moderate and liberal Republicans as well. *Radical Republican* leaders Representative Thaddeus Stevens and Senator Charles Sumner led the campaign for full voting rights for all black Americans. In a speech Stevens gave before the House of Representatives on January 3, 1867, in support of the *Congressional*

---

[368] American Experience, *Reconstruction The Second Civil War,* accessed November 29, 2014, http://www.pbs.org/wgbh/amex/reconstruction/filmmore/pt.html
[369] Photographer Carl Casper Giers (1828-1877), "President Andrew Johnson in Masonic Regalia, 1869," Shades of Gray and Blue, as sourced from Tennessee State Museum, http://www.civilwarshades.org/andrew-johnson-in-masonic-regalia/ No known restrictions on publication.
[370] Grand Commandery Knights Templar of Tennessee, @TNCommandery, The official Twitter of Tennessee's Grand Commander Knights Templar, 5/6/2021, https://twitter.com/tncommandery/status/1390335730304667653?s=46
[371] Brick Masons, "Knights Templar Regalia, accessed 9/30/202, https://bricksmasons.com/pages/knights-templar-regalia-1
[372] Three World Wars Staff, "Who Was Albert Pike?," https://www.threeworldwars.com/albert-pike.htm
[373] Eric Jon Phelps, *Vatican Assassins*, (Eric Jon Phelps, PO Box 306, Newmanstown, PA 17073) (2001), 391

Reconstruction bill then being debated, he issued a response to those who said his stance was radical and inflammatory.

> *"I am for negro suffrage [a vote; a voice given in deciding a controverted question] in every rebel State. If it be just, it should not be denied; if it be necessary, it should be adopted; if it be a punishment to traitors, they deserve it."*[374]

Since becoming a Senator in 1851, Senator Charles Sumner's position on slavery had been clear. As one of the founders of the Republican Party, Senator Sumner declared,

> *"Familiarity with that great story of redemption, when God raised up the slave-born Moses to deliver His chosen people from bondage, and with that sublime story where our Savior died a cruel death that all men, without distinction of race, might be saved, makes slavery impossible… [Because Christians are in the minority,] there is no reason for renouncing Christianity, or for surrendering to the false religions; nor do I doubt that Christianity will yet prevail over the earth as the waters cover the sea."*[375] [Emphasis added]

The *Radical Republicans* were assertive to a point of being aggressive in legislation to ensure at every turn that their *Congressional Reconstruction* program would prevail.

Pay close attention to every sentence in this next section and then proclaim this information to as many people as you can.

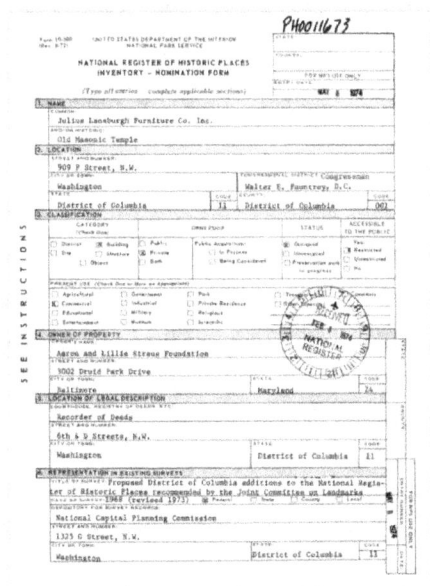

Construction of a New Masonic Temple in the Nation's Capital.

Today it's known as "the old Masonic Temple" in Washington City as recorded at the *U.S. Department of the Interior National Park Service* in the *National Register of Historic Places*. The *Inventory-Nomination Form* of the *National Register of Historic Places* for the "old Masonic Temple" in Washington, DC, was prepared by an architectural historian in October 1973.[376]

National Register of Historic Places Inventory –
Nomination Form [377]
For the "Old Masonic Temple"
in Washington, District of Columbia
Prepared by an architectural historian October 1973

---

[374] Thaddeus Stevens, Speech in favor of black suffrage, House of Representatives, January 3, 1867, *Congressional Globe,* 39th Cong., 2nd sess., Jan. 3, 1867, pp 250-253
[375] American Minute with Bill Federer, "Democrat Rep. Brooks beat anti-slavery Republican Senator with his gutta-percha cane till it broke…"
[376] NPS.gov, United States Department of the Interior National Park Service, *National Register of Historic Places Inventory – Nomination Form* as recorded, accessed October 18, 2014, http://pdfhost.focus.nps.gov/docs/NRHP/Text/74002164.pdf
[377] Ibid.

Ground was broken in the fall of 1867 and the cornerstone was laid on May 20, 1868, in a public ceremony. This government document states that President Andrew Johnson issued an *Executive Order* directing that Masons employed by the government were to be released from work to participate in the cornerstone-laying ceremony. Also stated on the document,

> *"President Andrew Johnson, in his character as a Master Mason, marched the entire length of the route, as did the architects and master-builders."*

It is of significance that at the same time the cornerstone-laying ceremony took place, an impeachment trial of President Johnson was going forth. President Johnson had a defense team and was not required to attend the trial. Instead, he celebrated the building that would be noted as Freemasonry's world headquarters. It would be the place where all Masonic bodies in the world would be under one head. In the ultimate sense, the head would be Lucifer. Albert Pike would be Lucifer's human regent from the *New World* in the western hemisphere, and Giuseppi Mazzini (1805-1872), the creator of the Masonic Mafia in Sicily (and successor of Adam Weishaupt, founder of the *Jesuit Order of the Illuminati*), would be Lucifer's human regent from the *Old World* in the eastern hemisphere.[378][379]

Pike was the Grand Master of the "Order of the Palladium," or "Sovereign Council of Wisdom," which had been founded in Paris in 1737. Having originated in Egypt, Palladism was a Satanic cult that was introduced to the inner circle of the Masonic lodges.[380] It was aligned with the "Palladium of the Templars."

It was in 1870 when Albert Pike and the *Freemason Supreme Council* moved from Charleston, South Carolina to the newly built Temple in Washington, DC. This Masonic Temple would become headquarters for an international alliance of key Masons and form Pike's *New and Reformed Palladian Rite* as the pinnacle of the devil's pyramid of power. It was a dark spiritual revolution and transformation of America from the American Republic to the Corporate Democracy done under the cover of secrecy and to exist for the next four generations of where we are today.

On the *National Register of Historic Places Inventory-Nomination Form* it is states:

> *"…On December 17, 1868, the Grand Lodge first met in the completed Temple. The building was dedicated and permanently occupied on May 20, 1870. Even before the dedication the Masonic Hall, located in one of the most fashionable areas of the city, was becoming a popular place for concerts and balls. By 1876 it was known as 'the scene of some of the most brilliant balls and State sociable given at the capital.' Some of the more notable occasions included a banquet given by the British Minister for the Prince of Wales, a memorable ball and supper given by the Illinois Association and attended by President Grant, and a debutante party given by silver magnate Sen. Wm. Stewart. At the latter, attended by 500 persons, 'the dressing was the most*

---

[378] Dr Stephen Jones, *Foundation for Intercession Newsletter*, "The Book of Revelation – Part 28 The Sixth Vial," (God's Kingdom Ministries, Feb 2005) https://godskingdom.org/studies/ffi-newsletter/2005/the-book-of-revelation-part-28-the-sixth-vial/
[379] Dr Stephen Jones, "Sliding toward World War 3 and what you need to know," 10/30/2023, https://godskingdom.org/blog/2023/10/sliding-toward-world-war-3-and-what-you-need-to-know/
[380] "Palladism," Ancient and Primitive Right of Memphis Misraim.

gorgeous and extravagant ever seen in this city…A magnificent supper was spread; the music was the best that could be afforded; so much nakedness was probably never revealed in Washington.'" [381]

Thought-provoking is the behind-the-scenes plans for strategically moving this secret society's world headquarters for the *"Mother Supreme Council of all Masonic Lodges of the World,"* **from Charleston, South Carolina to the nations' capital city amid the** *Reconstruction Era* **while the country was war-torn!**

Historic American Buildings Survey Old Photograph Note Dated, Courtesy of Library of Congress[382]

LOOKING ALONG F STREET – The Masonic Temple is the 4-story building to the right

F & Ninth Streets Northwest, Washington, District of Columbia, DC

Circa Late 1800ss

Was the new construction of the soon-to-be world headquarters of *The Scottish Rite of Freemasonry Supreme Council, 33° Southern Jurisdiction, U.S.A.*, moved from Charleston, South Carolina, to the nation's capital right after the Civil War somewhat of an announcement of a type of victory?

A parallel of this blatant action in our current day is the insensitive plan for the construction of a Muslim community center and mosque to be built three blocks from Ground Zero, the site of the September 11, 2001, attacks of which the *de facto* Federal Government claims was done by Islamic terrorists.

The initial master plan for the layout of the nation's capital city, Washington, was made in 1791 by Freemason architect, Pierre Charles L'Enfant, who was employed (and fired) in the task by President Washington. Apparently, L'Enfant had conceived the capital as the seat of a "vast empire," designing it as an enormous grid of streets crisscrossed by wide diagonal avenues.[383] The 1791 L'Enfant Plan includes an

---

[381] NPS.gov, United States Department of the Interior National Park Service, *National Register of Historic Places Inventory – Nomination Form* as recorded, accessed October 18, 2014, http://pdfhost.focus.nps.gov/docs/NRHP/Text/74002164.pdf
[382] Library of Congress, Prints & Photographs Division, HABS, Reproduction number HABS DC,WASH,175-4
Library of Congress Prints and Photographs Division Washington, D.C. 20540 USA http://hdl.loc.gov/loc.pnp/pp.print, "4. Historic American Buildings Survey Old Photograph Note Dated, Courtesy of Library of Congress LOOKING ALONG F STREET - Masonic Temple, F & Ninth Streets Northwest, Washington, District of Columbia, DC, HABS DC,WASH,175—4, No known restrictions
[383] Jon A. Peterson, "DESIGNING THE NATION'S CAPITAL: The 1901 Plan for Washington, D.C.

equestrian (on horseback) statue of George Washington in the location where the *Washington Monument* currently stands.[384] The *Washington Monument*, completed in 1884, is an obelisk, which is regarded in the occult as a phallic symbol (an image of the male reproductive organ).[385]

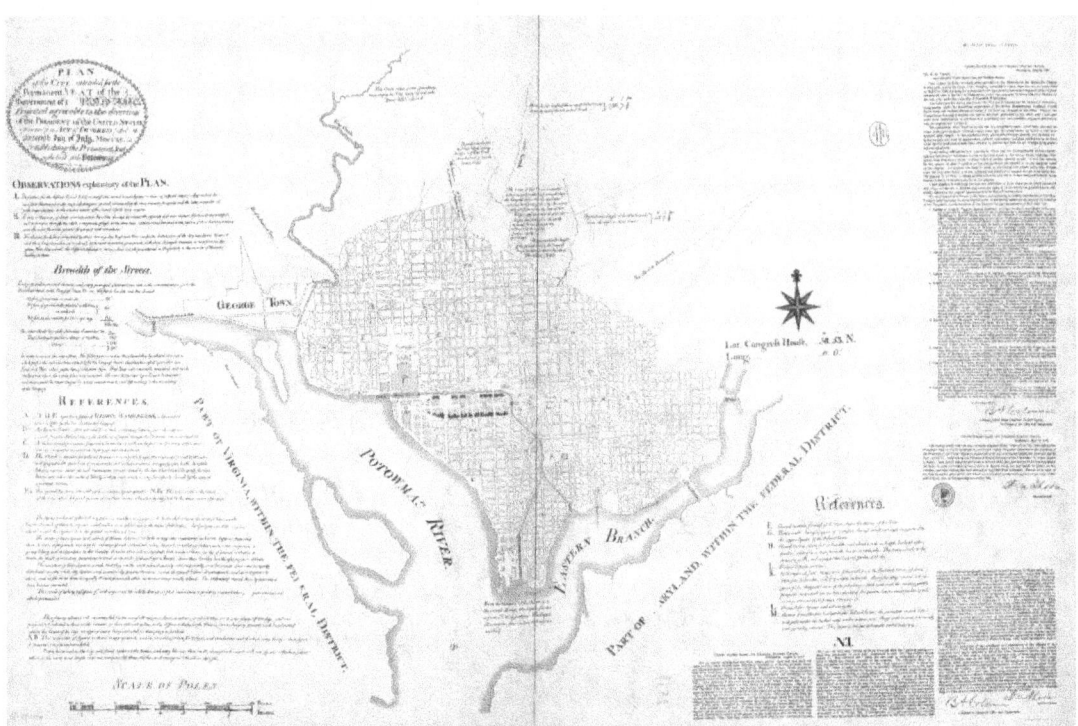

The 1791 L'Enfant Plan[386]
"Plan of the City, for the Permanent Seat of the Government of the United States.
Projected agreeable to the direction of the President of the United States
in pursuance of an Act of Congress ratified the sixteenth day of July MDCCXC2 (1792)
'establishing the Permanent Seat on the bank of the Potomac.'"

The Senate Park Commission Plan for Washington, D.C.: A NEW VISION FOR THE CAPITAL AND THE NATION, accessed April 5, 2021, https://www.nps.gov/parkhistory/online_books/ncr/designing-capital/sec1.html#11

[384] National Mall Coalition, "Historic Plans," accessed July 23, 2021, https://www.nationalmallcoalition.org/resources/historic-plans/

[385] Christian-restoration.com, "The Washington Monument: History," accessed April 6, 2021, https://www.christian-restoration.com/fmasonry/obelisks.htm

[386] National Mall Coalition. "Historic Plans," source: *Library of Congress,* https://www.nationalmallcoalition.org/resources/historic-plans/ This work is in the public domain

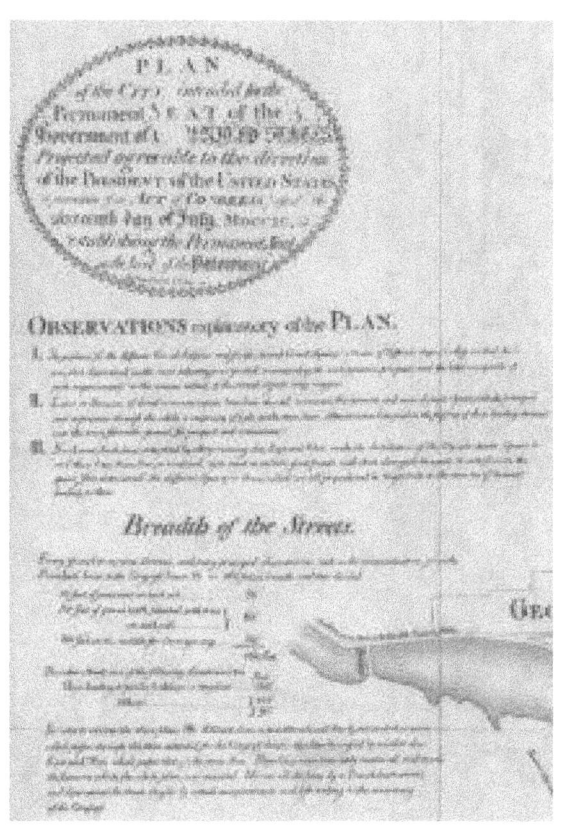

Inset of the 1791 L'Enfant Plan "Observations"[387]

"Plan of the City,
for the Permanent Seat of the
Government of the United States.
Projected agreeable to the direction of the
President of the United States
in pursuance of an Act of Congress ratified the
sixteenth day of July MDCCXC2 (1792)
'establishing the Permanent Seat on the bank of the Potomac.'"

*Note that OBSERVATIONS explanatory of the PLAN is not legible nor is there clarifying text made available at the source, Library of Congress.

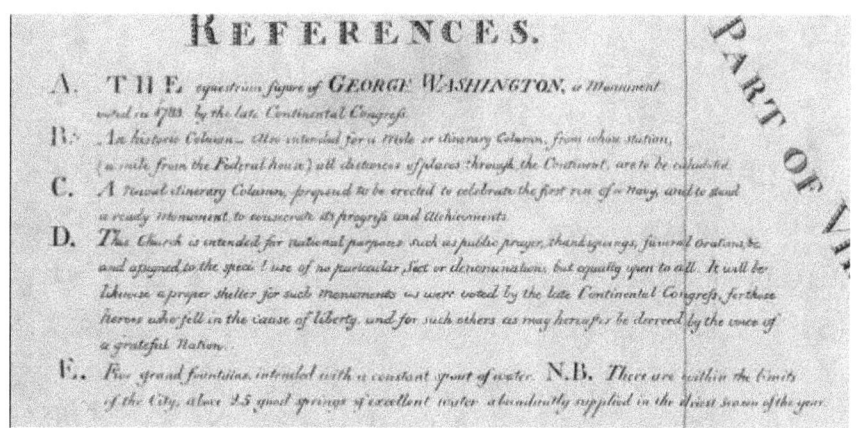

Inset of the 1791 L'Enfant Plan "References"

Reference A.
"THE equestrian [on horseback] figure of
GEORGE WASHINGTON,
a Monument voted in 1783
by the late Continental Congress."

---

[387] Ibid.

George Washington in Military Service[388]

Battle of Trenton, December 26, 1776
"Washington receiving a salute on the field of Trenton"

*This depiction of President Washington on his horse is perhaps the idea for the Washington Monument planned for Washington City and passed by Continental Congress in 1792.

During the *Reconstruction Era,* in 1874, city plans were made for extending the U.S. Capitol grounds. Architect John Fraser created the master plan for the U.S. Capitol grounds. It is of interest that Fraser also served on the Commission (1879-1884) to complete the *Washington Monument* (with a Freemason endeavor).

General Plan for the Extension of the U.S. Capitol Grounds. John Fraser, Architect, 1874[389]

In this Plan layout created in 1874, we will come to identify an image within the design that relates to occult symbolism of an owl.

---

[388] Library of Congress, "George Washington," http://www.loc.gov/item/98501986/ This work is in the public domain
[389] Library of Congress Geography and Map Division, "General plan for the extension of the U.S. Capitol grounds," Item 88690772, This work is in the public domain

In 1901, comprehensive planning went forward in the nation's capital city by the *Senate Park Commission*, also known as the *McMillan Commission,* to develop the monumental core and entire park system in and around the city while discreetly incorporating Freemason symbolism throughout the layout. The plan "redefined" the National Mall and surrounding area.

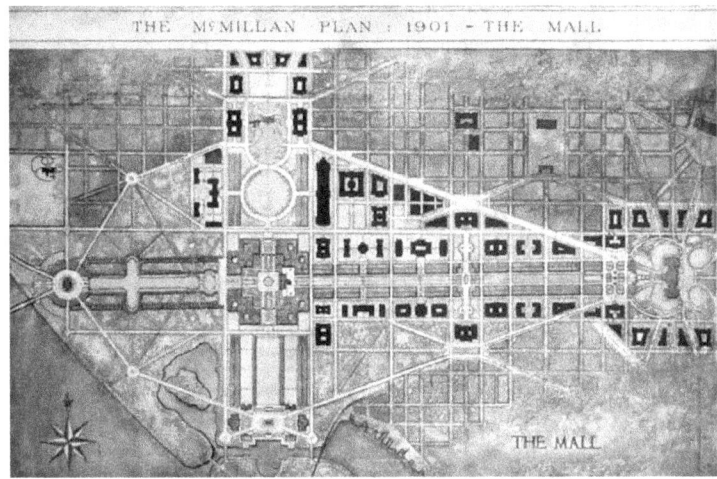

The McMillan Plan of 1901[390]

The Mall

The *McMillan Plan* (1901-1902) was implemented piecemeal in the decades after its release inclusive of demolishing strategic areas and then building large city and federal office buildings.

In view of the architect's *General Plan for the Extension of the U.S. Capitol Grounds* dated 1874, and then aerial pictures of the grounds layout that reflect enhancements and ground extensions that were planned by the 1901 *McMillan Commission,* observation is made of what forms the image of an owl. The owl is a significant character in occult symbolism with specific meaning to those in secret societies as the place where "masters of the trade nest." It is typical in the occult-brotherhood to keep their secret society symbolism "hidden in plain sight" while also having an awareness of a sense of dominion because of their luciferian craft.

---

[390] *Wikimedia Commons,* s.v., "File:McMillan Plan.jpg," source: National Capital Planning Commission, Washington, DC., This work is in the public domain

Note the positioning of the Capitol building, the seat of Congress, is prominently center-focused in the owl, and perhaps has been the "nest" of many "masters of the trade" through the years of the Freemason Corporate Democracy.

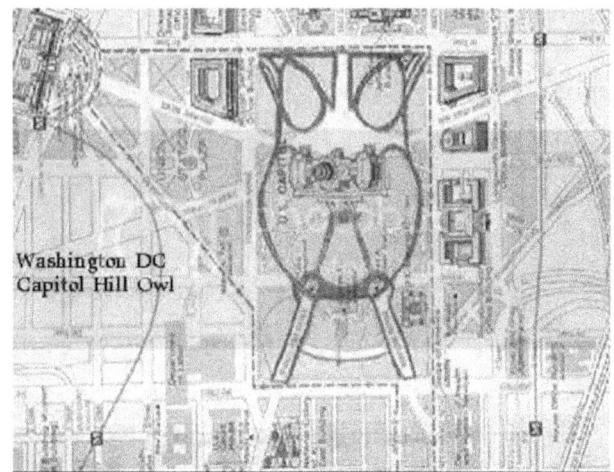 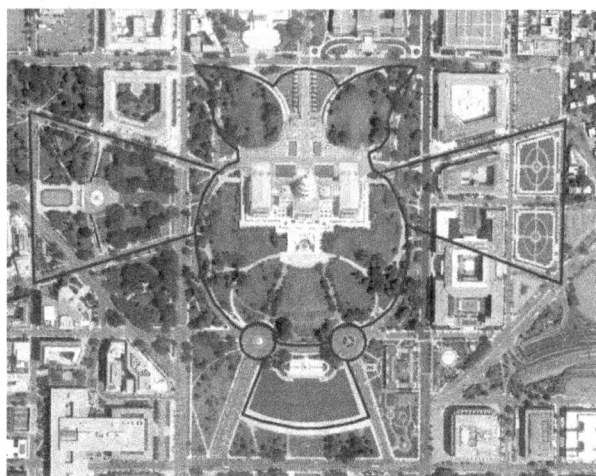

Pictured are two aerial views of the layout of the park system in Washington, D.C. where the Capitol building is positioned in the National Mall.

Government records indicate that it was <u>after 1874</u> when changes were made to street patterns and Freemason symbolism added in the layout. It was in the early 1900s when significant construction of large buildings went forward as well as relocation of two railroads and construction of a new railroad passenger terminal! We keep in mind from the writings of President Washington in 1798 that the Freemason lodges in America were not yet contaminated with occult doctrines.[391] The occult "illumination" was not brought into the American lodges until after 1801[392] and then further expanded upon by Albert Pike just after the *War Between the States*.

An aerial view depicts the design and the layout of the streets of the city to project an inverted Pentagram. In witchcraft, the Pentagram is an inverted, five-pointed star and the symbol for Baphomet (Lucifer), the god of Freemasonry. The pentagram is regarded as a very powerful magical device and probably the most well-known symbol of witchcraft.

---

[391] "To George Washington from G. W. Snyder, 22 August 1798," Founders Online, National Archives, https://founders.archives.gov/documents/Washington/06-02-02-0435. [Original source: The Papers of George Washington, Retirement Series, vol. 2, 2 January 1798 – 15 September 1798, ed. W. W. Abbot. Charlottesville: University Press of Virginia, 1998, pp. 554–557.]

[392] Lt. Col. Gordon "Jack" Mohr, "The Hidden Power Behind Freemasonry, Freemasonry: Satan's Door to America," http://www.themasonictrowel.com/books/the_hidden_powe_behind_freemasonry/files/chapter_06.htm as taken from J. Edward Decker, www.saintsalive.com *Freemasonry – Is it Satan's Door to America?*, January 20, 2017 https://www.raptureforums.com/forums/threads/freemasonry-is-it-satans-door-to-america.124338/

Layout of the streets of Washington, DC[393]

Baphomet Pentagram and Masonic Compass

There is a great deal of Freemason witchcraft symbolism in the layout and positioning location of buildings as well as symbolic meaning in particular memorials in our nation's capital that is not commonly known.

Baphomet[394]

Head of Baphomet in an inverted pentagram[395]

Its significance in design is the projection that Baphomet is the ruler of Washington D.C., with the White House positioned at the "mouth" of Baphomet, at the bottom point of the Pentagram. Plans were in place to make the President the mouthpiece of Baphomet.[396] The Freemason world headquarters Temple, located between the two upper points of the Pentagram, in symbolism equates to the flame of a candle, or "enlightenment" or "intellect." The related position is the brains of Baphomet in the inverted Pentagram.

The *Square and Compass* is a well-known symbol that identifies Freemasonry. Masonry exalts sexuality to the level of deity/worship though disguised in allegorical type fashion. The *Square and Compass* symbolize

---

[393] Frank Joseph, "America's Arcane Origins," March 15, 2014, http://thegipster.blogspot.com/2014/03/americas-arcane-origins-frank-joseph.html with graphic sourced from http://worldtruth.tv/wp-content/uploads/2014/03/star.jpg

[394] *Wikimedia Commons, s.v.* "Baphomet.png," from Eliphas Levi's "Dogme et Rituel de la Haute Magic", 1854, This work is in the public domain

[395] pumpkinhead90, "Baphomet," http://pumpkinhead90.deviantart.com/art/Baphomet-32136295 No known restriction on publication.

[396] Dr. Stephen E. Jones, *Wars of the Lord,* Chapter 38, "2004: The Fifth Bowl,"(Fridley: Gods Kingdom Ministries, 2009), http://gods-kingdom-ministries.net/teachings/books/wars-of-the-lord/chapter-38-2004-the-fifth-bowl/

the human reproductive organs, locked in coitus when displayed together. When worn in jewelry or displayed on personal property it's thought to have magical or protective powers as a talisman. In the design projected on the layout of streets and buildings of Washington, D.C., this symbol leaves much to the imagination of Satanic identification and belief related to the Corporate UNITED STATES government and their god, Lucifer as its head.

Portrait of Andrew Jackson (1767-1845)[397]
painted by D.M. Carter ; engraved by A.H. Ritchie c1860

When the moneyed power and their secret society henchmen encountered anyone that could not be bought or corrupted into supporting their banking and economic agenda, they would simply eliminate the individual. There was an assassination attempt on President Andrew Jackson in 1835 after he vetoed the bill to recharter the Second Bank of the United States inspite of the fact that the bankers threatened to ruin the business of the country if he did. Jackson returned the bill to Congress unsigned, along with a message in which he announced his veto, declaring that the Bank was *"…unauthorized by the Constitution, subversive to the rights of States, and dangerous to the liberties of the people."*[398]

Fortunately the assassin's gun misfired and a second gun also misfired. President Jackson reacted in beating his would-be assassin with his hickory cane as the shooter was apprehended and subdued. Amazingly, an investigation found the pistols to be in perfect working order. The odds of both guns misfiring were found to be 125,000 to 1.[399]

Two more U.S. Presidents who stood against such corruption are William Henry Harrison (1773-1841, in office March 4, 1841 – April 4, 1841) and Zachary Taylor (1784-1850, in office March 4, 1849 – July 9, 1850), both were victims of *Illuminati* doctors supervising their potential recovery from the effects of poisoning.
[400] [401]

---

[397] *Wikimedia Commons,* s.v. "File:Andrew Jackson Portrait.jpg," This work is in the public domain
[398] President Andrew Jackson's speech Transcript, "July 10, 1832: Bank Veto," https://millercenter.org/the-presidency/presidential-speeches/july-10-1832-bank-veto
[399] Christopher Klein, "10 Things You May Not Know About Andrew Jackson, March 15, 2017," https://www.history.com/news/10-things-you-may-not-know-about-andrew-jackson
[400] Mimi L. Eustis, "New Orleans Mardi Gras Mystick Crewe of Comus Secrets Revealed," Feb 18, 2010, http://whale.to/c/mardi_gras.html
[401] Henry Makow PhD, "Rothschilds Murdered at least Seven US Presidents," March 9, 2017, https://www.henrymakow.com/002009.html

William Henry Harrison, 1841 [402]   *Zachary Taylor, 1848* [403]

At this point on the historic timeline, we acknowledge the honorable President James A. Garfield (1831-1881) who held his office a brief six months from March 4, 1881, to September 19, 1881, before he was assassinated. In what is known as the *Bankers' Rebellion of 1881,* the *Money Barons* made threats to Congress of their intention in ruining the business interests of the country if Congress did not make legislation in favor of the bankers' interests. Contrary to the bankers' demands, President Garfield went ahead and converted national bonds into small interest-bearing bonds payable at the government's option.

President Garfield understood the *Babylonian Black Money-Magick*[404] of the *Money Changers* and their powerful domination by usury and monopolizing industry and commerce.[405] He said,

"Whoever controls the volume of money in any country is absolute master of all industry and commerce."[406]

And, *"He who controls the money of a nation, controls the nation."*[407]

President James Garfield in 1881 [408]

During the Civil War, Garfield fought for the Union and rose to the rank of Major General. Garfield went on to represent his home state of Ohio in

---

[402] *Wikimedia Commons,* s.v. "William Henry Harrison daguerreotype edit.jpg," This work is in the public domain
[403] *Wikimedia Commons,* s.v. "Zachary Taylor by Joseph Henry Bush, c1848.jpg," This media file is in the public domain
[404] Preston James, Mike Harris, "Hidden History of the Incredibly Evil Khazarian Mafia," March 11, 2015, https://geopolitics.co/2015/03/11/hidden-history-of-the-incredibly-evil-khazarian-mafia/
[405] Butler, Search, *Lincoln Money Martyred,* 152
[406] Ibid. 151
[407] Ibid. 148
[408] Library of Congress, "Pres. James Garfield," http://www.loc.gov/pictures/item/brh2003000342/PP/ No known restrictions on publication.

the U.S. House of Representatives as a Republican, where he served from 1863 to 1881 before elected to the office of President where he served for just over six months before his death.

The "official" story or narrative held is that on July 2, 1881, a disgruntled constituent shot President Garfield pointblank at a train station while on his way to meet his family for a vacation when he was struck by two shots; one glanced off his arm while the other pierced his back, shattering a rib and embedding itself in his abdomen. It is also known that he would have survived his wounds had his medical doctor not probed his wound with unsterilized fingers and instruments. He died less than three months later.

By 1911, plans were in place to begin new construction of the Freemason *"House of the Temple"* modeled after one of the *Seven Wonders of the Ancient World* and in viewing the layout of Washington, DC, is located between the two upper points of the Pentagram which positions as the brains of Baphomet in the inverted pentagram and signifying or equating to the flame of a candle, or "enlightenment" or "intellect."[409]

It was in the *Progressive Era*, in the early 1900s, when plans went forth that included Freemason occult symbolism in the layout and architecture of Washington City; specifically, 1901 with the *McMillan Commission*. We are not taken by surprise that it was the year that President McKinley was assassinated! It was orchestrated by the *Illuminist* Jesuits with the help of their Freemasons of which they control that murdered both President Garfield and McKinley.[410]

William McKinley (1843-1901) [411]
25th President of the United States, 1897-1901

---

[409] Jones, *Wars of the Lord, Chapter 38: 2004: The Fifth Bowl*
[410] Burke McCary, *The Suppressed Truth About the Assassination of Abraham Lincoln,* Merrimac, Massachusetts: Destiny Publishers, 1973; originally published in 1924) p. 166 as cited in Eric Jon Phelps, *Vatican Assassins*, (Eric Jon Phelps, PO Box 306, Newmanstown, PA 17073) (2001), 377, 418, 599
[411] *Wikimedia Commons*, s.v. "Mckinley.jpg," This media file is in the public domain

Theodore Roosevelt, the Master Mason [412]

In Satanism and ceremonial magick, aprons are the symbols of the priesthood of Lucifer.[413]

Vice President Theodore Roosevelt, a passionate Freemason, became U.S. President on September 14, 1901, upon the assassination of President William McKinley. Shortly thereafter it was Roosevelt who erected the statue of the devil-worshipping Albert Pike in Washington, DC and when the enemies of Christ would have absolute control of the White House.[414]

It is obvious from the documented evidence presented that the national government was being re-instituted and positioned as an evil government that was infiltrated with men who worship Satan.

Continuing on with the *Reconstruction Era* (1863-1877) …

Congress commences presidential impeachment trial.

There were high suspicions that Andrew Johnson, Vice President to Abraham Lincoln, was an *accessory before the fact* of Lincoln's assassination due to unusual behaviors the night of the assassination as well as an alleged association with the assassin John Wilkes Booth, in Johnson' home State of Tennessee. Also, witnesses had linked Booth's stopping by the Kirkwood house in Washington City where Johnson stayed, hours before Lincoln was shot, leaving a note for Johnson. [415]

One of the Congressional members of the *Johnson Impeachment Committee* made mention of a similar third-party claim in his 1886 book *The Great Conspiracy: Its Origin and History*.[416] John Alexander Logan of southern Illinois served in both the Illinois legislature and the U.S. House of Representatives and then went on to serve as a General in the Union Army, later elected to the U.S. Senate. He had been a staunch Democrat

---

[412] Library of Congress, "Theodore Roosevelt, the master mason," Digital Id ppmsca 35829, http://www.loc.gov/item/2010645452/ No known restrictions on publication. No renewal in Copyright office.
[413] William Schnoebelen, *Masonry Beyond the Light*, 1991, p.123
[414] Eric Jon Phelps, *Vatican Assassins*, (Eric Jon Phelps, PO Box 306, Newmanstown, PA 17073) (2001), 388
[415] Hamilton Gay Howard, *Civil War Echoes: Character Sketches and State Secrets*, (Washington, D.C.: Howard Publishing Co., 1907) Ch 2, 70-109
[416] John A. Logan, *The Great Conspiracy: Its Origin and History*, (New York: A. R. Har, Col, 1886) Ch XXXI

throughout his career though after watching the nation divide in a bloodbath of war and seeing the potential of losing the Republic government and Union, flipped to the Republican Party.

John Alexander Logan[417]
c1886

Logan makes clear his obvious sense of disdain for Johnson because he was responsible for letting *"the Rebel chiefs, who had been captured and imprisoned … go Scott-free, without even the semblance of a trial for their Treason."*[418]

Likewise, Mr. Logan leaves a stained impression of Johnson because of *"the devious ways and subtle methods through and by <u>which the Rebel leaders succeeded in flattering the vanity, and worming themselves into the confidence and control of Andrew Johnson</u> — by pretending to believe that his occupation of the Presidential Office had now, at last, brought him to their 'aristocratic' altitude, and to a hearty recognition by them of his 'social equality;' or to follow, either in or out of Congress, <u>the great political conflict</u>, between their unsuspecting <u>Presidential dupe</u> and the Congress, which led to the impeachment trial of President Andrew Johnson, for high crimes and misdemeanors in office…"*[419] [Emphasis added]

In early 1868 the U.S. House of Representatives sought to restrain presidential opposition to their *Congressional Reconstruction Plan* by commencing an impeachment trial against President Johnson. Before this time, no president had before been impeached. The House resolved to impeach Andrew Johnson, the 17th president of the United States, for "high crimes and misdemeanors." The alleged high crimes and misdemeanors were afterwards specified in eleven articles of impeachment adopted by the House about a week later. The primary charge against Johnson was that as Chief Executive, he violated the provisions of the 1867 *Tenure of Office Act* which required the consent of the Senate in the firing of any officials who had required Senate confirmation in the first place. While the Senate was not in session, Johnson had removed and replaced Secretary of War Edwin Stanton, a staunch supporter of the *Radical Republicans.*

Of eleven articles of impeachment, two of them accused Johnson of violating his oath of office by <u>bringing into disgrace the Congress of the United States *"through ridicule, hatred, contempt, and reproach"* in his public speeches.</u> Article eleven charges that Johnson publicly claimed that the <u>*Thirty-ninth Congress of the United States* was not authorized by the *Constitution* to exercise legislative power because it was a Congress of only part of the States without representation of the Southern States, and therefore denied them constitutional power of any legislation, including proposing amendments to the *Constitution*</u>. Johnson claimed it was not valid or obligatory upon him as President to acknowledge any Acts of Congress unless he saw fit to approve them.[420] [421]

---

[417] *Wikimedia Commons* s.v., "File: John Alexander Logan crop," This work is in the public domain
[418] Ibid.
[419] Ibid.
[420] *Wikipedia,* s.v. "Impeachment of Andrew Johnson," last modified 2 July 2023, https://en.wikipedia.org/wiki/Impeachment_of_Andrew_Johnson
[421] *Wikipedia,* s.v. "Articles of impeachment adopted against Andrew Johnson," last modified 9 September 2023, https://en.wikipedia.org/wiki/Articles_of_impeachment_adopted_against_Andrew_Johnson

The impeachment hearings were held by the Senate from March to May, 1868, and the result was one vote short of the required two-thirds needed for conviction on the first three articles of impeachment. After this, the trial was adjourned *sine die* without votes being held on the remaining eight articles of impeachment. Adjourning without day, or *sine die* (pronounced "sie-na die-ee,"[422] meaning without a day fixed), is a parliamentary practice that formally ends the duties for the current session of that legislative body. [423]

Aides carried a very ill Representative Thaddeus Stevens in an armchair to attend the impeachment hearing. As he was being carried out, Stevens was furious in the failure to impeach President Johnson. Stevens responded to an inquiry in the crowd as to what the result of the hearing was…

"The country is going to the Devil!"[424]

Mr. Thaddeus Stevens Being Conveyed to the House of Representatives by His Assistants, Joseph Reese and John Chauncey.[425]
Frank Leslie's Illustrated Newspaper, March 26, 1868

Stevens obviously well understood the Freemason agenda, their man Johnson; and that Andrew Johnson remaining in office was a victory for the sons of Satan and the *Kingdom of Darkness*.

At the same time as the impeachment trial was going forth, President Johnson was leading a fanfare cornerstone-laying ceremony of a new Masonic Temple, a 4-story, prestigious building of French Renaissance-style architecture with a dining hall on the second story that could seat a thousand persons, the largest in Washington City at the time of its construction. In view of historic government records, it appears that President Johnson was more interested in construction of the devil's temple than he was in *Reconstruction* of the Southern States.

Stevens had only a few weeks to live and used them to write legislation and work on plans for free schools. After Stevens' death, his body lay in state in the Capitol building. Only Abraham Lincoln had ever received more tribute.

---

[422] *TheFreeDictionary.com*, s.v. "sine die," accessed November 1, 2014, http://www.thefreedictionary.com/sine+die
[423] *Wikipedia*, s.v. "Adjournment sine die," last modified August 26, 2014, http://en.wikipedia.org/wiki/Adjournment_sine_die
[424] Erick Trickey, "'Kill the beast': The empeachment trial that nearly took down a president 150 years ago," May 16, 2018, *The Washington Post*
[425] United States Senate Art & Artifacts, Mr. Thaddeus Stevens Being Conveyed to the House of Representatives by His Assistants, Joseph Reese and John Chauncey, This work is in the public domain

Thaddeus Stevens lying in state in the U.S. Capitol rotunda in August 1868.[426]

Members of the Butler Zouaves, an African American company of the District of Columbia, served as honor guards. It is reported that 25 guards were on duty, commanded by Captain Hawkins. The body was brought to the Capitol near mid-day on August 13 and remained on display the rest of the day and through the night. Harper's Weekly reported that five or six thousand people, both white and black, viewed the body. Funeral services were held the morning of August 14th at the Capitol.

Representative Stevens directed that he be buried in a cemetery that was not restrictive based on race, as were other cemeteries at the time. He composed his own tombstone epitaph, which reads:

> "I repose in this quiet and secluded spot, not for any natural preference for solitude. But finding other cemeteries limited as to race by charter rules, I have chosen this that I might illustrate in my death the principles which I advocated through a long life, equality of man before his creator."

A desperate *interim Executive Congress.*

The desperation of this congressional body is understandable; however, we review the American Republic's history in the light of constitutional law. Technically and lawfully, the rump (lacking a quorum) *interim Executive Congress* was not a lawful deliberative body under the *Constitution* and passed laws while the Southern States did not have representation in Congress as guaranteed by *Article IV, Section 4* of the *Constitution*. The Southern States did not cease to be States because secession from the Union of States is not lawful or possible. Therefore, the citizens of those States did not cease to be citizens of the Union.

Article IV, Section 4 of the *Constitution*:

> "The United States shall guarantee to every State in this Union a Republican Form of Government, and shall protect each of them against Invasion; and on Application of the Legislature, or of the Executive (when the Legislature cannot be convened) against domestic Violence."[427]

The foundational government of the United States had established precedence in the universal and fundamental *Law of Perpetuity*. Any attempt to secede from the Union of States would be lawfully void. The *Constitution for the United States* will always be "the law of the land" and was very thoughtfully written to sufficiently provide for managing various situations.

---

[426] *Wikimedia Commons*, s.v., "File:Remains of Thadeus Steven lying in state - NARA - 530043.tif," This work is in the public domain

[427] "Article 4, Section 4," The Founders Constitution, accessed November 1, 2014, http://press-pubs.uchicago.edu/founders/tocs/a4_4.html

The *interim Executive Congress* passed the *Reconstruction Acts of 1867* that divided the Confederate States (except for Tennessee, which had been readmitted to the Union) into five military districts. The *interim executive Congressional Reconstruction Plan* included the appointment of military Generals over each military district that were then responsible for appointing State officers such as Governor and other various officials.

Each of those Southern States was forced to accept the (non-original and unlawful) 13th and (unlawful) 14th *Amendments* to the *Constitution*, which was thought to have achieved freedom and political rights for black Americans.

While the *Emancipation Proclamation* signed by President Lincoln on January 1, 1863, did free the slaves in the Southern States, it was the (non-original) *13th Amendment* passed on December 6, 1865 that outlawed slavery throughout the United States.[428] The *13th Amendment, Section 1* states:

> "Neither slavery nor involuntary servitude, except as a punishment for crime whereof the party shall have been duly convicted, shall exist within the United States, or any place subject to their jurisdiction."

It is significant to point out that the aforementioned *13th Amendment* unconstitutionally replaced the original and missing *Thirteenth Article of Amendment* that had been ratified on March 12, 1819, and which reads,

> "If any citizen of the United States shall accept, claim, receive, or retain any <u>title of nobility or honour</u> or shall without the consent of Congress accept and retain any present, pension, office or emolument of any kind whatever, from any emperor, king, prince, or foreign power. <u>Such person shall cease to be a citizen of the United States</u>, and <u>shall be incapable of holding any office of trust or profit under them, or either of them</u>."[429] [Emphasis added]

Because of a long history of abuses and excesses against the rights of man during colonial times, our Founding Fathers held an intense disdain and distrust regarding a privileged "Black Nobility," ancient aristocratic wealthy family lines who were enmeshed in secret occult societies and prideful ambitions. Our Founding Fathers knew the immoral, unethical, deceitful means of this wealthy elite and their *modus operandi* of infiltration in governments by their agents with a goal of destruction and overturning the will of the people. For that reason, they established as law in the *Constitution for the United States* two injunctions against the use of recognition of "titles of nobility or honor" and acceptance of any emoluments whatever from external sources. The first pertains to the Federal Government, *Article I, Section 9*, and the second pertains to the individual States, *Article I, Section 10*.

In relation to the original and missing *Thirteenth Article of Amendment's* language and historical context, the principal intent of this *Amendment* was to prohibit "Esquires," or *British Accredited Registry BAR attorneys,* from serving in government. The meaning of the *Amendment* is seen in its intent to prohibit persons having

---

[428] GeneologyToday, "When were African Americans granted citizenship?," (accessed March 19, 2017), http://www.genealogytoday.com/genealogy/answers/When_were_African_Americans_granted_citizenship.html
[429] Barefoot Bob Hardison, *The Real Thirteenth Article of Amendment to the Constitution of the United States – Titles of Nobility and Honour,* "Amendment Article XIII" accessed September 2, 2014, http://www.barefootsworld.net/real13th.html [Recovered through the Internet Archive Wayback Machine Website
https://web.archive.org/web/20130412200422/http://www.barefootsworld.net/real13th.html]

titles of nobility and loyalties to foreign government, foreign bankers, and with secret societies from voting, holding public office, or using their skills to subvert the government.[430]

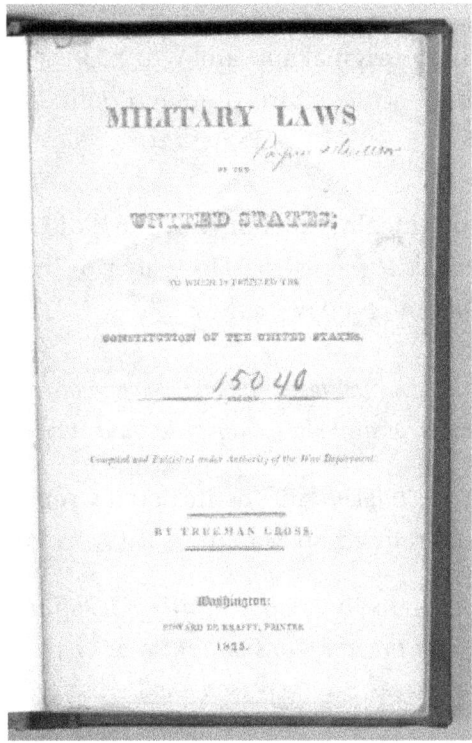 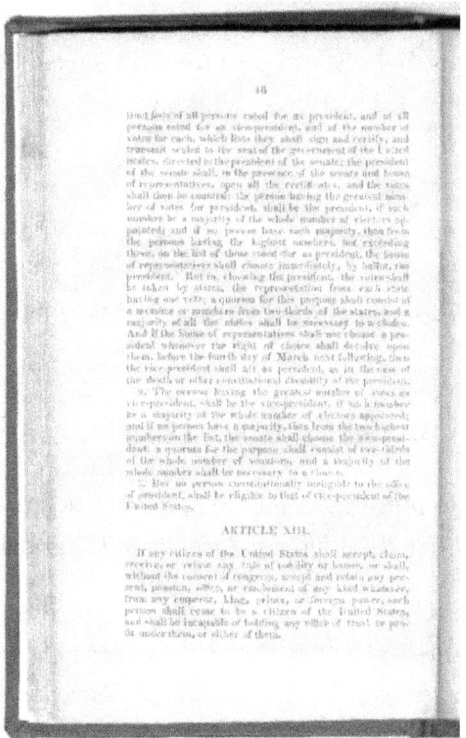

*<u>1825 book</u>, Military Laws of the United States;
to Which is Prefixed the Constitution of the United States
- Compiled and Published under Authority of the War Department* [431]
By Major Trueman Cross (Deputy Quarter-Master-General of the Army)

Left: Title page;
Right: page displaying <u>the original</u> Thirteenth Article of Amendment in its proper place.

---

[430] David Dodge, Researcher, Alfred Adask, Editor, "The Missing 13th Amendment "TITLES OF NOBILITY" AND "HONOR", as reprinted by *The Millennium Report*, "The True Back Story Of The Missing 13th Amendment," April 11, 2016, https://themillenniumreport.com/2016/04/the-true-back-story-of-the-missing-13th-amendment/

[431] Trueman Cross, *Military Laws of the United States; to Which is Prefixed the Constitution of the United States Compiled and Published under Authority of the War Department* (Washington, Edward De Krafft Printers, 1825) as displayed at Amendment-13.org, *The Original Thirteenth Article of Amendment To The Constitution For The United States,* last updated September 9, 2002, http://www.amendment-13.org/publications.html [Recovered through the Internet Archive Wayback Machine, https://archive.org/web/web.php]
By Major Trueman Cross (Deputy Quarter-Master-General of the Army)

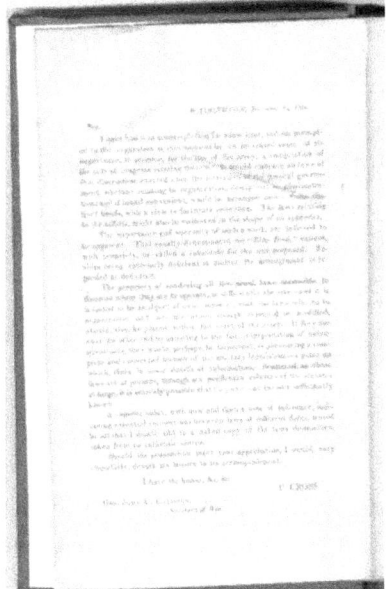 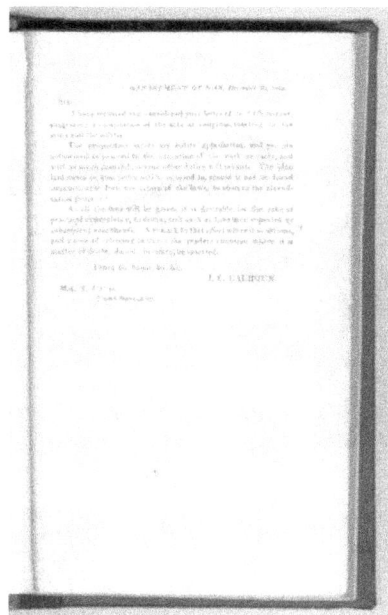

Left: Page displaying Major T. Cross' letter of request to the Secretary of War for authorization
Right: Page displaying authorization by Secretary of War John C. Calhoun

Courtesy of the TONA Research Committee, a group that describes themselves as "ordinary, concerned American citizens who happened to stumble on a bit of interesting historical data, and as time has gone on, have banded together with an indefatigable sense of curiosity and duty, have expended a very great amount of time and no little amount of personal funds to ferret out the history of the 13th Titles of Nobility and Honour Article of Amendment to the Constitution For The United States."[432]

President Lincoln desired for (what came to be numbered as the non-original) 13*th Amendment* to be ratified by the States as he needed it for his plan of reconstructing the Rebel States into Loyal ones. He understood there was a quorum of States issue that would be *"questionable and sure to be persistently questioned"* in law. He understood the need to keep the State of Louisiana's vote to achieve a quorum of States ratifying the Amendment. The State of Louisiana had just recently formed a new and loyal government with its state Legislature having already voted to ratify this constitutional amendment that had been passed by Congress to abolish slavery throughout the Nation; he could not risk losing Louisiana's vote. If his presidential *Reconstruction Plan* failed, then they would lose Louisiana's vote in favor of the proposed Amendment which was needed to validly ratify it.

---

[432] Amendment-13.org, "The TONA Research Committee," (last updated October 15, 2002), http://www.amendment-13.org/trc.html [Recovered through the Internet Archive Wayback Machine, https://web.archive.org/web/20161025000116/http://amendment-13.org/publications.html]

President Lincoln is quoted:

"If we reject Louisiana, we also reject one vote in favor of the proposed Amendment to the National Constitution. To meet this proposition it has been <u>argued</u> that no more than three-fourths <u>of those States which have not attempted Secession are necessary to validly ratify the Amendment</u>. I do not commit myself against this further than to say <u>that such a ratification would be questionable, and sure to be persistently questioned</u>; whilst a ratification by three-fourths of <u>all</u> the States would be <u>unquestioned and unquestionable</u>."[433] [Emphasis added]

President Abraham Lincoln, 1863 [434]

With regard to the (unlawful) *14th Amendment* (1868), we must understand the significance of this Amendment in that it made "federal" citizens, which is very different from citizenship that was originally of both the State (first) <u>and</u> the United States of America (second); now citizenship was reversed, federalized, broadened, and constituents then came to be referred to as *"U.S. Citizens"* where they had been "citizens of the United States."[435]

Because President Lincoln was clear in his *Reconstruction Plan* that he wanted the Southern States to re-enter the Union the same way in which they had left, we can safely surmise that had he been alive and fulfilling his second term as President, he would <u>never</u> have supported the *14th Amendment* which made a new citizenship and a new government.[436]

Amendment 14. Rights of Citizens (1868)

> *Section 1. Citizenship defined. All persons born or naturalized in the United States and subject to the jurisdiction therof, are citizens of the United Sttes and of the state wherein they reside. No state shall make or enforce any law which shall abridge the privileges or immunities of citizens of the United States; nor shall any state deprive any person of life, liberty, or property, without due process of law, nor deny to any person within its jurisdiction the equal protection of the laws.*

This Section of the *14th Amendment* contains a number of important "provisions." By the definition of citizenship here, black Americans were granted citizenship. It also forbids States to abridge the privileges and immunities, or the rights, of citizens. In other words, the States could not interfere in the right of black Americans and other citizens to live a peaceful, useful life, or to travel. This Amendment, like the <u>5th Amendment</u> denies to Congress and <u>Amendment 14 denies to the States</u> the power to deprive any person of

---

[433] John A. Logan, *The Great Conspiracy: Its Origin and History,* (New York: A. R. Har, Col, 1886) Ch XXXI
[434] *Wikimedia Commons,* s.v. "Abraham Lincoln November 1863.jpg," This work is in the public domain
[435] Jean Hallahan Hertler with David Carl Hertler, *Re-inhabited: Republic for the United States of America,* Vol. I, "America's Truthful History," (ValleyAssetsPublishing.com, 2016) 145 as citing John S. Wise, *A Treatise on American Citizenship,* (Northport: Edward Thompson Co., 1906) 10-12
[436] Abraham Lincoln: "Proclamation 93 - Declaring the Objectives of the War Including Emancipation of Slaves in Rebellious States on January 1, 1863," September 22, 1862. Online by Gerhard Peters and John T. Woolley, The American Presidency Project., accessed October 15, 2014, http://www.presidency.ucsb.edu/ws/?pid=69782

life, liberty, or property without "due process of law." It was originally intended to protect the black freedmen's citizenship. Three years later in passing the *1871 Federal Dictionary Act*, the definition of the word "person" was changed to include artificial or unnatural persons, such as corporations, to have the same equal rights as a natural person or a living man or woman. This is nothing short of an abomination before Creator God and has been used and manipulated by the *Money Changers* for their corporate moneyed interests and control in the court system by broad interpretation of this Amendment at every point in turn.[437]

> SEC. 2. *And be it further enacted,* That in all acts hereafter passed words importing the singular number may extend and be applied to several persons or things; words importing the plural number may include the singular; words importing the masculine gender may be applied to females; the words "insane person" and "lunatic" shall include every idiot, non-compos, lunatic, and insane person; and the word "person" may extend and be applied to bodies politic and corporate, and the reference to any officer shall include any person authorized by law to perform the duties of such office, unless the context shows that such words were intended to be used in a more limited sense; and the word "oath" shall include "affirmation" in cases where by law an affirmation may be substituted for an oath, and in like cases the word "sworn" shall include the word "affirmed."
>
> Rules of construction; singular and plural words; masculine and feminine; "insane person" and "lunatic." "Person" to include corporation. "Oath" and "sworn" to include "affirmation" and "affirmed."

The Statutes at Large and Proclamations of the United States of America,
from December 1869 to March 1871, Vol. XVI, page 431
CHAP. LXXI – *An Act prescribing the Form of the enacting and resolving Clauses of Acts and Resolutions of Congress, and Rules for the Construction thereof. Feb. 25, 1871*

We reason that the God-given liberties as stated in the *Declaration of Independence* such as life, liberty, and the pursuit of happiness, and all men as created equal should not have needed provision as an *Amendment* to the *Constitution* as "civil" liberties." The law form is specified in the *Declaration* as *the Laws of Nature and of Natures God*. Liberty comes from the Great Liberator and keeping His Laws. Our liberty does not come from civil government or from the States.

There are five Sections in the *14th Amendment*. We abbreviate this topic in stating that the *Radical Republicans* sought to preserve the Union by exterminating the Luciferian Freemason agenda which led them to operate outside of the *Constitution*. The *Radical Republicans* also disregarded President Lincoln's intention of quickly restoring the loyal Southern States (ex-Confederates excluded from holding office) into the Union. Their actions resulted in forcing this (unlawful) *14th Amendment* to the *Constitution* which federalized ALL Americans as *U.S. Citizens* creating a different type of jurisdiction, and of which initiated the beginnings of a democracy. The Founding Fathers absolutely hated democracy and viewed this law form as "the devil's own government."[438] [439]

---

[437] For example, the federal regulatory agency, the Interstate Commerce Commission, can fix railroad rates only after giving the railroad corporations an opportunity to present their side of the case.
[438] Dr. Benjamin Rush, quote *"A simple democracy, or an unbalanced republic, is one of the greatest of evils. I think with Dr. Zubly that 'a democracy (with only one branch) is the Devil's own government.'"* The Founders' Constitution, Volume 1, Chapter 4, Document 30, http://press-pubs.uchicago.edu/founders/documents/v1ch4s30.html, The University of Chicago Press;
Letters of Benjamin Rush. Edited by L. H. Butterfield. 2 vols. Memoirs of the American Philosophical Society, vol. 30, parts 1 and 2. Princeton: Princeton University Press, for the American Philosophical Society, 1951.
[439] David Barton, "Republic v. Democracy," WallBuilders, January, 2001, http://www.wallbuilders.com/libissuesarticles.asp?id=111

The *Constitution for the United States* contains an oath of office only for the President. For other members, including members of Congress, the *Constitution* specifies only that they *"shall be bound by Oath or Affirmation to support this constitution."*[440] In 1789, the *First Congress* reworked this requirement into a simple fourteen-word oath, *"I do solemnly swear (or affirm) that I will support the Constitution of the United States."*[441]

In July 1862, the *interim Executive Congress* passed a resolution adopting a new oath, the *"Ironclad Test Oath."* It was originally devised by Congress at that time for ALL federal employees, lawyers, and federal elected officials. In comparing the original oath as specified in the *Constitution for the United States* to the *Ironclad Test Oath*, we find that a significant positional change had been made. By this resolution, the *interim Executive Congress* made members of Congress to now be classified as civil officers/officials rather than representatives of the American People as originally designed.

This new oath also contributed to a **change of law form**. Members of Congress and legislators of the free-States were by constitutional design to be the direct representation of the American People, sent in their place to "support the Constitution." They were intended to be members and to hold seats in Congress and the State legislatures, not to be civil officers. This Act is repugnant to the *Constitution for the United States* and significantly contributed to the **transition from a Republic to a Democracy**. It deprived the American people of suffrage (the right to vote) as well as representation as guaranteed and specified in the *Constitution*.

The (unlawful) *14th Amendment* affirmed the *Ironclad Oath* while it also gave all pardoning power to Congress rather than to the President. The *Constitution* specifies in *Article II, Section 2* that the President *"shall have Power to grant Reprieves and Pardons for Offences against the United States, except in Cases of Impeachment."* Congress always had the right to judge their own membership, though what they did was to make a blanket statement of expulsion from government offices at all levels of those who had engaged in the insurrection and gave themselves the power (not the President) the ability to remove (pardon) that disability (not able to hold any office). Bear in mind that the President never had the ability to remove anyone from office at any level (except for when the State was still a Territory). The President never had the power to expel anyone from Congress, only Congress had that power per the *Constitution*. The offence or "disability" was created by the *14th Amendment*, itself, otherwise there was no "disability" to hold office.

14th Amendment, Section 3:

> "No person shall be a Senator or Representative in Congress, or elector of President and Vice President, or hold any office, civil or military, under the United States, or under any state, who, having previously taken an oath, as a member of Congress, or as an officer of the United States, or as a member of any state legislature, or as an executive or judicial officer of any state, to support the Constitution of the United States, shall have

---

[440] *Constitution of the United States, Article VI*

[441] Clarification of **"of"** and **"for"** in referencing our *Constitution* correctly and considering the Corporate UNITED STATES' version of the name used for its constitution: In review of the use of the words by our Founding Fathers in the Founding Documents, it was concluded that the two are the same. Reasoning – the *Constitution **for** the United States* became the *Constitution **of** the United States* upon adoption by the several States. In other words, it was put up **"for"** adoption, but once it was adopted became ours, **"of."** In further, the First Congress of the *Republic for the United States of America* claimed ownership of all forms of our nation's name – both "of" and "for" in the re-inhabiting document, *Declaration of Sovereign Intent (c2010)*. In effort to dispel confusion and to aid the reader the word "for" is used throughout this work. Where original *de jure* documents use the word "of" and are quoted in this work, the original citing is quoted as lawfully recorded in government archives.

engaged in insurrection or rebellion against the same, or given aid or comfort to the enemies thereof. But Congress may by a vote of two-thirds of each House, remove such disability."

"Cunning, ambitious, and unprincipled men"[442] would come to take advantage of this legislated change in law form by infiltrating the "interim Executive" government and secretly crafting a jurisdiction for ALL of their intended chattel "slaves." All the while they manipulated money and the workforce under their control, while creating an illusion that the American People would think they were free.

The logic of the *Radical Republican Congress* was steeped in their desperation to ensure that once the Southern States were reconciled back into the Union with congressional representation, the *Slave Power* in the Southern State legislatures would not have the ability to rebel and amend their State constitutions to reinstall slavery.

The *Radical Republicans* also calculated that in giving black males the right to vote, it would disable the white-supremacist Democrat Party while preventing the loss of Republican congressional control. Although the *interim Executive Congress* made way through the *14th Amendment* for black Americans to have voting rights, the *Slave Power* would enforce "Black Codes" and other forms of oppression and entrapment of the freedmen in an economic form of slavery. Understanding the position of the freedmen in most owning no land, having no education, and living in poverty, working to bring Liberty to black Americans in the midst of a prejudiced, corrupt, moneyed wealth of a people who believed in immoral entitlement was indeed a desperate task.

In the years following the *War Between the States,* the main concern of the Federal Government was the restoration of the Union. Providing aid to the war-ravaged South and to needy Southerners took second place. The *Freedmen's Bureau* was authorized to administer the new laws and help black Americans attain their economic, civil, educational, and political rights. The newly created State governments were generally republican in character and were governed by political coalitions of black Americans, Northerners who had migrated to the South, called "carpetbaggers" by Southern Democrats, and Southerners who allied with the black Americans and carpetbaggers, referred to as "scalawags" by their opponents. This uneasy coalition of black and white Republicans passed significant civil rights legislation in many States. Courts were reorganized, judicial procedures improved, and public-school systems established. Segregation existed but was somewhat flexible.

---

[442] President George Washington, in his *Farewell Address* to the People of the United States, 1796:
"…**cunning, ambitious, and unprincipled men** will be enabled to subvert the power of the people, and to usurp for themselves the reins of government; destroying afterwards the very engines which have lifted them to unjust dominion… The spirit of encroachment tends to consolidate the powers of all the departments in one, and thus to create, whatever the form of government, a real despotism…" [Emphasis added]

*Glimpses at the Freedmen's Bureau:
Issuing rations to the old and sick* [443]

As black Americans slowly progressed, white Southerners resented their achievements and their empowerment, even though they were in a political minority in every State but South Carolina. A greater number of the white populace rallied around the Democrat Party which sought to maintain the preexisting social order of white supremacy in the South and regain control of their State governments. They were related to the *White Knights of the Ku Klux Klan* which was cofounded by Confederate General Albert Pike who was "Grand Dragon" of the "Realm" of the *KKK*.[444] [445] [446] When bribery failed the *KKK* members, which were led by merchants, Democrat politicians, and plantation owners, the *KKK* used violent coercion to eliminate their competitors, white and black.

Visit of the Ku-Klux [447]

Black American woman cooking, man seated alongside, and three children, with man from Ku Klux Klan aiming rifle in doorway.

---

[443] Library of Congress, "Glimpses at the Freedmen's Bureau. Issuing rations to the old and sick / from a sketch by our special artist, Jas. E. Taylor.," No known restrictions on publication.
[444] Dr Stephen Jones, *Foundation for Intercession Newsletter*, "The Book of Revelation – Part 28 The Sixth Vial," (God's Kingdom Ministries, Feb 2005) https://godskingdom.org/studies/ffi-newsletter/2005/the-book-of-revelation-part-28-the-sixth-vial/
[445] William Guy Carr, *Satan, Prince of this World*, (1959) 302-303
[446] Mimi L. Eustis, "New Orleans Mardi Gras Mystick Crewe of Comus Secrets Revealed," Feb 18, 2010, http://whale.to/c/mardi_gras.html
[447] Library of Congress, "Visit of the Ku-Klux," No known restrictions on publication.

Secret Societies and Terrorism a Deterrent in Restoring the American Republic.

Between 1868 and 1871 terrorist organizations, especially the *Ku Klux Klan*, murdered blacks (as well as supportive whites) who tried to exercise their right to vote or to receive an education. Their objective was to undermine *Reconstruction* so that the *"Great American Experiment"*[448] would fail and that blacks would never again receive such an opportunity. Ironically, the *Klan* contributed to prolonging the *Reconstruction Era* when <u>the KKK was in fact formed with an objective of defeating reconstruction</u>.

In response to the plea for assistance by the Southern States who were working toward reconstruction, the *interim Executive Congress* passed three *Enforcement Acts* in 1870 and 1871 to combat attacks on black Americans from State officials or violent secret societies like the *Ku Klux Klan*. By early 1871, if States failed to prosecute anyone who conspired to deprive citizens of the right to serve on juries, hold office, enjoy equal protection under the law, or vote, the federal district attorneys could now prosecute them. In passing this legislation, the Federal Government furthered its path in the unchartered territory of a democracy – and even began to resemble a democracy, of which our Founding Fathers loathed.

Very apparently, the white South did not hold a monopoly on widespread racist sentiments. The North was the birthplace of segregation, particularly in its urban areas. Blacks were separated from whites in Northern modes of public transportation like horse-drawn buses, stagecoaches, railway cars, and steamboats – or they were excluded altogether. They were not permitted to sit next to whites in theaters or lecture halls, and they could only enter restaurants or hotels as servants. The North rather emulated the South during *Reconstruction* and yet demanded that the white South recognize the fact of emancipation.

Example of Racial Segregation:
Separate water fountains for
"White Men" and "Colored Men" [449]

---

[448] In 1787, when the Founding Fathers had completed framing the U.S. Constitution in Independence Hall in Philadelphia, Benjamin Franklin told an inquiring woman what the gathering of the delegates of the states had produced, "*A republic, madam, if you can keep it.*" In all of recorded history such a republican form of government based on God's Laws, also known as "the Laws of Nature and of Nature's God," had never before been done. Our Founding Fathers referred to it as "The American Experiment."

[449] Library of Congress, Lee, Russell, 1903-1986, photographer, "Negro drinking at "Colored" water cooler in streetcar terminal, Oklahoma City, Oklahoma," No known restrictions.

Reconstruction **ended for various reasons.**

The Federal Government changed its original cause in emancipation. Where it made provision for the freedmen by distributing the treasonous Confederate plantation owners' land to these former slaves, they now abandoned the cause and left the freedmen with no land or means of survival. This change of heart was long remembered as a betrayal with gloomy repercussions, though this was not the reason for ending *Reconstruction*. It was the Southern white terrorism and violence propelled by secret societies that branched off Freemasonry that had intentions of destroying black leadership and coercing black labor, that was primarily the cause of the collapse and subsequent takeover by the so-called Southern *"Redeemers."*

By the early 1870s most Southern States had been "redeemed," as referred to by many white Southerners, from *Republican Radical* rule. It was because of Freemason influence on President Johnson by his masters that this counterrevolution was permitted through the lack of federal presence in the South due to continual demobilization of military troops, and because the *Freedmen's Bureau* was understaffed. It was like hell on earth for the blacks as well as the Southern whites. Northerners' interest in the cause of the freedmen faded as the *Reconstruction Era* extended for well over a decade.

Division continued throughout the nation through racial prejudice, segregation, terrorism, deception, and transformation to a democracy. Division is a chief tool of the *Illuminati* in its objective to keep power and control toward its goal of a *One World Government-New World Order*.[450] As the brotherhood of the secret society craft and its white persuasion regained power over the South by 1877 and throughout the century that followed, whites from both North and South branded the *Reconstruction Era* as a disaster. They placed blame on the blacks by claiming and insisting that the blacks were responsible because they were in charge. They claimed that blacks were unfit to rule, unprepared for the rights, responsibilities, and freedoms granted to them.

In the century that followed, there was gross exaggeration among historians about the *Era* — including some of the nation's considered foremost scholars having written exaggerated, irate histories that portray the period of supposed deplorable treatment of white Southerners along with twisted blatant racist tales about the *"ignorance and savage lust"* of black officeholders.

During the late 19th century, while ignoring the fate of the black population, the two sides of the Civil War reunited basing their reunited culture on the concept of white supremacy in aspects such as education and society. In reality it was black success in ambition, confidence, and aptitude that appeared to threaten the society of the former Confederacy in their power structure, institutions, labor system, and society more than black corruption or ignorance ever could. By discrediting the era in which blacks were most active politically, historians, filmmakers, politicians, and writers from across the country astoundingly, yet effectively, cleared as guiltless the white South of depriving blacks of their legal rights. This is the power of the media — and of the *Money Changers* who own and control it. They permitted racial segregation and

---

[450] William Guy Carr, *Pawns in the Game*, Intro

discrimination, even endorsing it and fueling it in the media, indoctrinating its viewers in a false belief system — for over a century.[451]

In a democracy, rights are granted with permission through the State. In the American Republic, rights are acknowledged in the *Declaration of Independence* as God-given. <u>Our Founding Fathers had intention to honor ALL men as equal though forces of evil and the sons of Satan used every excuse and glitch to prevent it.</u>

Radical Reconstruction ended at different times in different States throughout the next decade of the 1870s. Ultimately, all three branches of the Federal Government had turned away when blacks needed them most. In retrospect, the *Radicals* in Congress certainly tested the limits of federal commitment and power. In the end, the country was simply unprepared to commit itself to a vision of racial equality that most white citizens did not believe in — and apparently not even the Northerners who preached abolition. Again, it was black success in overcoming the adversity through education and pushing forward in their God-given rights that brought them forward as dignified Americans.

By the time the last federal troops had been withdrawn in 1877, *Reconstruction* was all but over, and the Freemason white supremacist Democrat Party controlled the destiny of the South — as well as the North. Few *Radicals* were still alive in the *Gilded Age* (1877-1896) when the Republican Party had assumed the role of ally to the *Big Business* interests who were rapidly accumulating power and capital while turning the country into the world's leading industrial power by the turn of the century. Again, any legislation passed by the *"interim executive Congress"* — that exchanged jurisdictions into the new law form of Corporate democracy where they are not members of Congress that represent the American People but are civil officers more like a board of directors for their owners of the USA, INC. — is not lawful.

In the American Republic the whole sovereignty rests with the American People and is exercised through their representatives in Congress assembled. For laws to be binding, they must have the consent of the American People through their representatives as *Article IV, Section 4* of the *Constitution* guarantees to EVERY State in the Union a representative form of governance.

Additionally, the *Ironclad Oath* taken by ALL federal employees and elected officials contributed to a change of law form that is contrary to a *republican form of governance*. Any legislation passed in this period of time, and thereafter, is by law repugnant to the *Constitution for the United States* and therefore null and void.[452]

The re-inhabited American Republic, the Republic for the United States of America, has correctly established re-inhabitation in its pick-up point from December 20, 1860, preceding the loss of congressional quorum in both houses, as well as the period of executive authority under Martial Law and suspension of the *Writ of*

---

[451] Buter, Search, *Money Martyred*, 73, 96, 111

[452] Wikipedia s.v., Marbury v. Madison, 5 U.S. (1 Cranch) 137 (1803), was a landmark U.S. Supreme Court case that established the principle of judicial review in the United States, meaning that American courts have the power to strike down laws and statutes that they find to violate the Constitution of the United States. Decided in 1803, Marbury is regarded as the single most important decision in American constitutional law. The Court's landmark decision established that the U.S. Constitution is actual law, not just a statement of political principles and ideals, and helped define the boundary between the constitutionally separate executive and judicial branches of the federal government. <u>"A law repugnant to the Constitution is void."</u>

Habeas Corpus. President Lincoln referred to this *color of law* interim government as *"the Executive Government"* in his September 22, 1862, *Presidential Proclamation* described as *"Declaring the Objectives of the War Including Emancipation of Slaves in Rebellious States on January 1, 1863."*

He also twice referred to *"the Executive Government"* in his January 1, 1863, *Presidential Proclamation* known as *"The Emancipation Proclamation."* For this reason, we now refer to the congressional body with the Southern seats refilled as "the *de facto* Congress" (*de facto* means, "in practice but not necessarily ordained by law," color of law).

We point out that on December 1, 1865 President Andrew Johnson made his last Presidential Proclamation before leaving office and proclaimed that December 25, 1868 would be a day of *"Granting Full Pardon and Amnesty for the Offense of Treason Against the United States During the Late Civil War."*[453] It appears to be quite the Christmas gift in looking out for his Freemason brethren of *the Craft* and in-line with his Freemason oath…

Accelerating forward, it is a dark mark in history when in 1871 the District of Columbia was craftily re-incorporated and setup for a new jurisdiction without the knowledge or consent of the American People. The *de facto* Congress passed the *District of Columbia Organic Act of 1871*, which created a <u>private corporation</u> with a trademark name of the all-capital-letter, *THE UNITED STATES OF AMERICA, INC.*,[454] (hereinafter *"Corporate UNITED STATES"*) for the ten-mile square region of the City of Washington, in the District of Columbia.

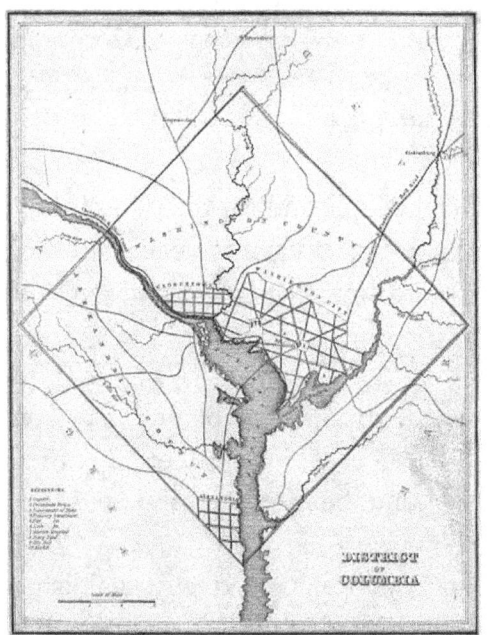

This regional area, of which in 1801 had constitutionally been designated for carrying out the business needs of the Federal Government, had now experienced a <u>private</u> incorporation and given a business name which was unlawfully and strategically manipulated at every opportunity under the circumstances of change in law form, and with it — a change of jurisdiction unknown to We the People.

1835 Map of the District of Columbia [455]

---

[453] Andrew Johnson: "Proclamation 179 - Granting Full Pardon and Amnesty for the Offense of Treason Against the United States During the Late Civil War," December 25, 1868. Online by Gerhard Peters and John T. Woolley, The American Presidency Project., accessed November 29, 2014, http://www.presidency.ucsb.edu/ws/?pid=72360

[454] Delaware Department of State, Division of Corporations, File Number 4525682, THE UNITED STATES OF AMERICA, INC., in Filing History as "Incorp Delaware Stock Co.", https://delecorp.delaware.gov/tin/controller

[455] *Wikimedia Commons*, "Map of the District of Columbia, 1835.jpg," This work is in the public domain

> CHAP. LXII.—*An Act to provide a Government for the District of Columbia.* Feb. 21, 1871.
>
> Vol. xvii. p. 16.
>
> *Be it enacted by the Senate and House of Representatives of the United States of America in Congress assembled,* That all that part of the territory of the United States included within the limits of the District of Columbia be, and the same is hereby, created into a government by the name of the District of Columbia, by which name it is hereby constituted a body corporate for municipal purposes, and may contract and be contracted with, sue and be sued, plead and be impleaded, have a seal, and exercise all other powers of a municipal corporation not inconsistent with the Constitution and laws of the United States and the provisions of this act.
>
> District of Columbia constituted a body corporate for municipal purposes.
>
> Powers, &c.

The Statutes at Large and Proclamations of the United States of America, from December 1869 to March 1871, Vol. XVI, page 419
CHAP. LXII – An Act to provide a Government for the District of Columbia – Feb. 21, 1871

In summation, we've brought forward evidence of the infiltration and insurgency of the *Illuminati* along with their *Money Changers* and secret occult society religion of Luciferian Freemasonry in America. The evidence as recorded in historical records may be viewed as demonstration, particularly now in the light of understanding the American Republic's foundational principles and insight along with an accurate historical outlook on its founding and objective.

This Corporate Democracy that masquerades as the American Republic has a different law form. Understanding that all governments spring from religion, we recognize that the American Republic sprang from Biblical Christianity, the religion of Liberty. The Corporate Democracy sprang forth because of manipulation by the *Illuminati* along with the *Money Changers* and their secret societies which are steeped in witchcraft and whose tenets are shrouded in secrecy and crafted with illusion, the religion of bondage, death, and destruction. Its law form is commercial for-profit for the benefit of the Luciferian *Illuminati* rulers of evil, who are at the top of Lucifer's chain-of-command at the expense of the American People in economic slavery and control. There is no longer Liberty either Civil or Religious; only an illusion of freedom in both—and even those limited freedoms are quickly being usurped.

Next, we will witness the monstrous destruction done to America and her once beautiful institutions as well as the demoralizing and degrading of the American people, all of which affect the whole world. Once comprehended and understanding is gained, we will see the bigger picture from cause-to-effect and determine the necessary course of action in reversing the curse as God's solution for America. In that solution is also her National Purpose and Prophetic Destiny which foreshadows the redemption of the nations of the world as they too heed and follow the light that goes forward once again as "a city upon a hill." This is a spiritual revolution!

Iniquitous Reprobates
The Black Nobility
Courtesy of One World of Nations[456]

"The Illuminati, Jesuits, Freemasons, Bilderbergs, Club of Rome, etc, actually are all predated by a powerful family dynasty known as the Black Nobility that arose to prominence during the 9th century (at least 400-500 years earlier). The Black Nobility were called such, not because of skin color, but because of the inhumane and dirty methods they used to accomplish great wealth and influence. This included terrorism, rape, murder, assassinations and fraud. [They also infiltrated in position of] control of the Papacy and ignorant masses… [as well as of intelligence agencies such as] the CIA. The Black Nobility expanded from Venice [Italy] into Europe and eventually founded the Bank of England and the Bank of Amsterdam."

---

[456] One World of Nations, "Iniquitous Reprobates, The Black Nobility, Report #1, Reach for truth and fact," 13 June 2015, www.oneworldofnations.com/2015/06/ir-the-black-nobility-report-1.html

Illuminati Government Structure[457]

Lucifer/Satan
World Monarch/ "The Pindar"
Crown Council of 13
Council of 33
Committee of 300

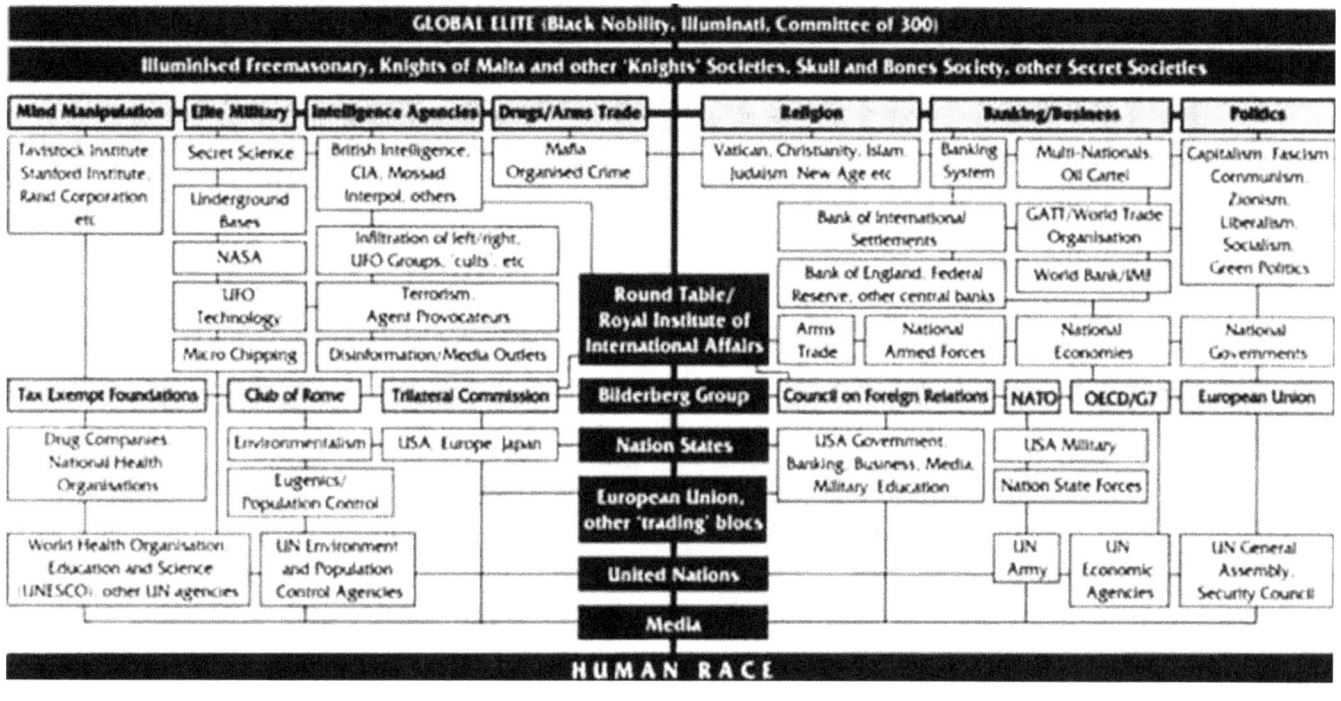

---

[457] HAF, he 'Committee of 300': Complete List of Members," Sept 30, 2020, https://humansbefree.com/2020/09/committee-of-300-complete-list-of-members.html Fair use

Chapter Four
Worshipers of Satan Setup Their Corporate Democracy

Worshipers of Satan setup their corporate Democracy to rule America with Freemason *Progressive* presidents—who were selected and not elected.[458] The Freemasons, with their *Iron Clad Oath*[459] sought to fill Congress with as many worshipers of Satan as they could.

Franklin D. Roosevelt about 1932
"Presidents are selected, not elected."[460]

The *Progressive* movement in America dawned with the 20th century. The *Progressive Era* (1896-1917) was a period of widespread social activism and political reform which dominated the intellectual climate across America from the 1890s. This movement was animated by a common dedication to statism—the practice or doctrine of giving a centralized government extensive control over economic planning and policy and was influenced by the evolution ideas of the *Illuminati's* Charles Darwin.[461]

Charles Darwin (1809-1882) became famous for his 1859 book, *On the Origin of Species by Means of Natural Selection, or the Preservation of Favoured Races in the Struggle for Life*. His view of evolution also included a posture in the natural white supremacy of white people over black. He believed in improving the world through selective breeding of humans. A consequence of his theory of evolution in the scientific world *"was the notable increase of radical propositions justifying racism veiled in the language of science."* It should come as no surprise that the Southern *Slave Power* Freemason white supremacists readily took to Darwin's writings as a vindication of their position in defending their beliefs and religious doctrines regarding slavery.[462]

Charles Darwin[463]
Photograph for the Literary and Scientific Portrait Club (1855)

---

[458] New World Order Today Staff, "Franklin D. Roosevelt, 32th President of the United States, from 1933 to 1945," accessed March 2, 2021, http://www.nwotoday.com/the-socialist-review-american-politicians/franklin-d-roosevelt [Recovered through the Internet Archive Wayback Machine, http://web.archive.org/web/20230326032615/http://www.nwotoday.com/the-socialist-review-american-politicians/franklin-d-roosevelt]

[459] Iron Clad Oath. In 1862, *de facto* U.S. Congress mandated that civil servants and military personnel take an Ironclad Test Oath that they had never voluntarily aided the Confederacy. As Reconstruction evolved, the Ironclad Oath emerged as the strictest of several possible standards for the readmission of Southerners into the political life of the Union. With the Second Reconstruction Act (1867) it made the oath a condition for holding federal office. This unconstitutional oath has been used in the Counter-Reformation objective through infiltration and insurgency ever since.

[460] New World Order Today Staff, "Franklin D. Roosevelt"

[461] Carr, *Pawns in the Game,* Ch 3, Ch 16

[462] WallBuilders Staff, "Darwin and Race," January 10, 2018, https://wallbuilders.com/darwin-and-race/

[463] *Wikimedia Commons* s.v., "File:Charles Darwin by Maull and Polyblank, 1855-crop.png," This work is in the public domain

The *Progressive* objective included the push of *Relativism*, the belief that concepts such as right and wrong, goodness and badness, or truth and falsehood are not absolute but change from culture to culture and situation to situation—and *Relativism* became the prominent ideology over *Absolutes*. This pagan ideology is contrary to the Holy Bible where Truth is permanent and enduring for all people and all ages.

Self-identified *Progressives* believed that the problems associated with the urban and industrial revolutions required government to assume a more active and powerful role in the lives of citizens. They believe that the principles and institutions of government must change and "evolve" over time and in-sync with social and scientific changes. The *Progressive* movement was embraced by those who did not acknowledge or desire to live in covenant with the *Supreme Judge of the world*,[464] or the *Great Governor of the world*.[465]

Some of the main *Progressive Era* presidents were Theodore Roosevelt, William Howard Taft, and Woodrow Wilson. Their administrations espoused intense social and political change in American society. President Woodrow Wilson echoed these sentiments declaring,

"All that Progressives ask or desire is…to interpret the Constitution according to the Darwinian principle; all they ask is recognition of the fact that a nation is a living thing and not a machine."[466]

de facto Corporate UNITED STATES Presidents
Theodore Roosevelt[467], *1901-1909 (left), William Howard Taft,* [468] *1909-1913 (center),*
and Woodrow Wilson,[469] *1913-1921 (right)*

---

[464] *Declaration of Independence, In Congress, July 4, 1776, closing paragraph:* We, therefore, the Representatives of the united States of America, in General Congress, Assembled, appealing to the <u>Supreme Judge of the world</u> for the rectitude of our intentions, do, in the Name, and by Authority of the good People of these Colonies, solemnly publish and declare, That these United Colonies are, and of Right ought to be Free and Independent States;…

[465] *Articles of Confederation,* August 8, 1778 closing paragraph: "And whereas it has pleased the <u>Great Governor of the world</u> to incline the hearts of the legislatures we respectfully represent in Congress, to approve of, and to authorize us to ratify the said articles of confederation and perpetual union."

[466] Prof. Paul Moreno, Hillsdale College Online Courses, "Progressivism," *History 102: American Heritage—From Colonial Settlement to the Reagan Revolution*

[467] *Wikimedia Commons*, s.v. "President Theodore Roosevelt, 1904.jpg," This work is in the public domain

[468] *Wikimedia Commons*, s.v. "William Howard Taft, Bain bw photo portrait, 1908.jpg," William Howard Taft, Bain bw photo portrait, 1908.jpg This work is in the public domain

[469] *Wikimedia Commons*, s.v. "Thomas Woodrow Wilson, Harris & Ewing bw photo portrait, 1919.jpg, This work is in the public domain

Rejecting the timeless principles of the *Declaration of Independence, Progressives* believed that the *Constitution's* arrangement of government based upon the separation of powers, checks and balances, and federalism,[470] only impeded (hindered, obstructed) effective government. *Progressives* argued that a truly just and democratic government in the business of politics, namely, elections—should be separated from the administration of government. They projected that government would be overseen by nonpartisan (not supporting or controlled by a political party) and therefore be politically neutral experts. They purported that the president should be the only nationally elected public official as they claimed that he best embodies the will of the whole people. Therefore, the president <u>has a legislative mandate</u> to create administrative agencies and government and programs to improve the lives of citizens.[471]

Consider the following while determining whether the *Progressive* stance is right or wrong. We have come to understand the fact that every government springs from a religion. [472][473] These *Progressives* worship Satan, therefore, their government system has no place for God-given Biblical principles or *Absolutes*, the basis of a jurisdiction in Liberty. The *Progressive* religion of Satanism is one of bondage, the basis of a jurisdiction in tyranny and despotism.

The meaning of "politics" is *"that part of ethics for the regulation and government of a nation or state, for the preservation of its peace, safety and security and prosperity."*[474] When the American Republic was birthed forth by our Founding Fathers, that government was based on Biblical Christianity with the cornerstone being Jesus Christ. The American Republic had a Biblical Christian government that acknowledged that Biblical Christianity is the only true religion that brings liberty, virtue, truth, life, happiness, and the Creator's unalienable rights. In addition, Creator God's Republic provided the authority and framework based on the right to have government limited to those powers delegated to it by the People.

Understand that the "separation of powers" instilled in the *Constitution for the United States* is based on God's Law (*Absolutes*). If the power to make the law, administer the law, and interpret the law all rest in the same hands, it describes the definition of tyranny or a dictatorship.[475] Our Founding Fathers separated government into three branches in order to guarantee our Liberty.

---

[470] *Noah Webster's First Edition of An American Dictionary of the English Language,* 1828: "<u>Federal</u>: 1. Pertaining to a league or contract; derived from an agreement or covenant between parties, particularly between nations. ... 2. Consisting in a compact between parties, particularly and chiefly between states or nations; founded on alliance by contract or mutual agreement; as a federal government, such as that of the United States. 3. Friendly to the constitution of the United States."
[471] Prof. Paul Moreno, "Progressivism," *History 102: American Heritage—From Colonial Settlement to the Reagan Revolution*
[472] S. D. Baldwin, *Armageddon: or, The Overthrow of Romanism and Monarchy; The Existence of the United States Foretold in the Bible, Its Future Greatness; Invasion by Allied Europe; Annihilation of Monarchy; Expansion into the Millennial Republic, and its Dominion Over the Whole World,* (Cincinnati: Applegate & Co., Publishers, 1864) 20
[473] Verna M. Hall, *The Christian History of the Constitution of the United States of America: Christian Self-Government,* (San Francisco: Foundation for American Christian Education, 1960 rev 1975) Preface III
[474] *Noah Webster's First Edition of An American Dictionary of the English Language,* 1828: "<u>Politics</u>."
[475] *Noah Webster's First Edition of An American Dictionary of the English Language,* 1828: "<u>Tyranny</u>: 1. Arbitrary or despotic exercise of power; the exercise of power over subjects and others with a rigor not authorized by law or justice, or not requisite for the purposes of government. Hence tyranny is often synonymous with cruelty and oppression. 2. Cruel government or discipline; as the tyranny of a master. 3. Unresisted and cruel power. 4. Absolute monarchy cruelly administered. 5. Severity; rigor; inclemency."

Isaiah 33:22 ~ For the Lord is our judge [Judicial], the Lord is our lawgiver [Legislative], the Lord is our king [Executive]; he will save us. [Emphasis added]

"No king but King Jesus!" [476]

Justice by reparation (apology, atonement, redress, or restitution) is based on God's Law. It requires that he who hurts shall be hurt or must apologize and make reparation to his victim. [477][478]

Just before the *Money Changers* and their Luciferian Freemason *Progressive Era* dawned, U.S. Supreme Court Justice David Josiah Brewer (1837-1910) had given the court's opinion in the 1892 case of *Church of the Holy Trinity vs. United States*.[479] In opening he stated,

"Our laws and our institution must necessarily be based upon and embody the teachings of the Redeemer of mankind. It is impossible that it should be otherwise; and in this sense and to this extent our civilization and our institutions are emphatically Christian...This is historically true. From the discovery of this continent to the present hour, there is a single voice making this affirmation."[480]

David Josiah Brewer [481]
Associate Justice of the U.S. Supreme Court (1889-1910)

---

[476] Committees of Correspondence, 1774
[477] *Numbers 5:7* ~ "Then they shall confess their sin which they have done: <u>and he shall recompense his trespass with the principal thereof</u>, and add unto it the fifth part thereof, and give it unto him against whom he hath trespassed."
[478] *Luke 19:1-10* ¹*And Jesus entered and passed through Jericho.* ²*And, behold, there was a man named Zacchaeus, which was the chief among the publicans, and he was rich.* ³*And he sought to see Jesus who he was; and could not for the press, because he was little of stature.* ⁴*And he ran before, and climbed up into a sycamore tree to see him: for he was to pass that way.* ⁵*And when Jesus came to the place, he looked up, and saw him, and said unto him, Zacchaeus, make haste, and come down; for to day I must abide at thy house.* ⁶*And he made haste, and came down, and received him joyfully.* ⁷*And when they saw it, they all murmured, saying, That he was gone to be guest with a man that is a sinner.* ⁸<u>*And Zacchaeus stood, and said unto the LORD: Behold, LORD, the half of my goods I give to the poor; and if I have taken any thing from any man by false accusation, I restore him fourfold.*</u> ⁹*And Jesus said unto him, This day is salvation come to this house, forsomuch as he also is a son of Abraham.* ¹⁰*For the Son of man is come to seek and to save that which was lost.*
[479] Church of the Holy Trinity v. United States, 143 U.S. 457 (1892)
[480] William J. Federer, *America's God and Country Encyclopedia of Quotations*, "David Josiah Brewer," (Coppell: FAME Publishing, Inc., 1994) 70
[481] Library of Congress, "David Josiah Brewer, 1837-1910," No known restrictions on reproduction.

Noah Webster (1758-1843), known as the *"Schoolmaster of America,"* who provided us the wonderful 1828 *American Dictionary of the English Language,* said it this way,

> *"The moral principles and precepts contained in the scriptures ought to form the basis of all our civil constitutions and laws."* [482]

Noah Webster [483]
The Schoolmaster of the Republic

These Freemason *Progressives, "cunning, ambitious, and unprincipled men"*[484] in their progressive quest, managed to secret their luciferian *Counter-Reformation New World Order* agenda into the nation, by means of disguising the *de facto* (color-of-law) Corporate UNITED STATES while masquerading as the American Republic.

The undeniable fact that two governments exist in America is made clear by U.S. Supreme Court Justice Marshall Harlan (1833-1911) in his dissenting opinion in *Downes v. Bidwell,* 182 U.S. 244, (1901). Justice Harlan said,

> *"The idea prevails with some--indeed, it found expression in arguments at the bar — that <u>we have in this country substantially or practically two national governments</u>; <u>one</u> to be maintained under the Constitution [de jure], with all its restrictions; <u>the other</u> to be maintained by Congress [de facto], outside and independently of that instrument by exercising such powers as other nations of the earth are accustomed to exercise."* [Emphasis added]

John Marshall Harlan [485]
Associate Justice of the U.S. Supreme Court (1877-1911)

---

[482] Federer, *America's Quotations,* "Noah Webster,"678 as citing Noah Webster, *The History of the United States,* (New Haven: Durrie & Peck, 1832) 309, paragraph 53
[483] *Wikimedia Commons,* s.v. "Noah Webster The Schoolmaster of the Republic.jpg," print by Root & Tinker. Courtesy of the Library of Congress, Division of Prints and Photographs Online,
[484] President George Washington, in his *Farewell Address* to the People of the United States, 1796:
"...**cunning, ambitious, and unprincipled men** will be enabled to subvert the power of the people, and to usurp for themselves the reins of government; destroying afterwards the very engines which have lifted them to unjust dominion... <u>The spirit of encroachment tends to consolidate the powers of all the departments in one, and thus to create, whatever the form of government, a real despotism...</u>" [Emphasis added]
[485] *Wikimedia Commons, s.v. "JudgeJMHarlan.jpg,"* No known copyright restrictions on the use of this work.

Education Reforms

As the 20th century began in this *Progressive Era,* many classrooms started each day with the *Pledge of Allegiance,* a prayer, and a reading from the Holy Bible. Many churches turned their schools over to a State-run educational system. For a time, State-run schools continued to teach moral values using the *McGuffy Reader* with its Bible verses.[486] America had one of the best school systems in the world. That began to change with the *Progressive* movement.

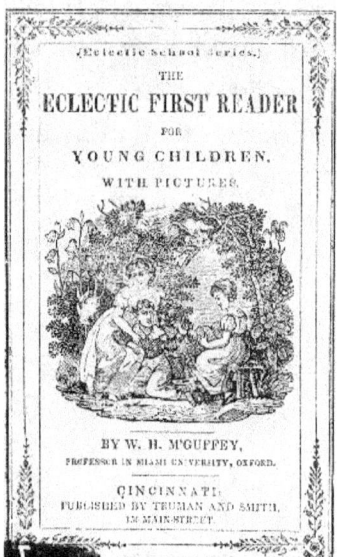

McGuffey's First Eclectic Reader, 1841 [487]

The *American Civil Liberties Union* (ACLU) was founded in 1920 by individuals who were Communists and Socialists with 80-percent of its National Committee members having communist connections. Despite the clever name of the organization, "civil liberties," in reality it is a movement in the United States that advocates force and violence to overthrow the government. They are a finger organization of the *Illuminati* and are most noted for their cases involving separation of church and state. [488] [489] [490]

In 1930, the U.S. House of Representatives formed a *Special Committee* to investigate Communist activities in the United States. On January 17, 1931, the Committee reported:

> *"The American Civil Liberties Union is closely affiliated with the communist movement in the United States, and fully 90 percent of its efforts are on behalf of communists who have come into conflict with the law. It claims to stand for free speech, free press, and free assembly, but it is quite apparent that the main function of the ACLU is to attempt to protect the communists in their advocacy of force and violence to overthrow the Government, replacing the American flag by a red flag and erecting a Soviet Government in place of the republican form of government guaranteed to each state by the Federal Constitution."*[491]

In 1925, the *American Civil Liberties Union* (ACLU) offered to defend any teacher prosecuted under law for teaching the theory of evolution. A young Tennessee science teacher agreed to stand as a defendant to challenge the Tennessee State law. *Biblical Creation* had always been taught throughout America. Teaching the *theory of evolution* was a violation of Tennessee State law. While the ACLU lost the case, it set in motion

---

[486] *The McGuffy Readers*, accessed December 1, 2014, http://www.mcguffeyreaders.com/1836_original.htm
[487] *Wikimedia Commons,* s.v. "Cover of McGuffey's First Eclectic Reader.jpeg," This work is in the public domain
[488] David Allen Rivera, "Final Warning: A History of the New World Order Illuminism and the master plan for World domination," 1994, source darivera.com as cited by https://modernhistoryproject.org/mhp?Article=FinalWarning&C=7.7
[489] Historyhalf Staff, "The Real History of the ACLU," Sept 19, 2010, https://historyhalf.com/the-real-history-of-the-aclu/
[490] Discover the Networks Staff, "Roger Balwin: Founder of the American Civil Liberties Union: Enthusiastic proponent of Communism: Died in 1981," https://www.discoverthenetworks.org/individuals/roger-baldwin/
[491] David Allen Rivera, "Final Warning: A History of the New World Order Illuminism and the master plan for World domination," 1994, source darivera.com as cited by https://modernhistoryproject.org/mhp?Article=FinalWarning&C=7.7

a re-evaluation in the teaching of science. Amazingly, within four decades the laws were reversed so that teaching *Creation* is now outlawed, while teaching *Evolution* is mandatory.[492]

By 1947, the ACLU was influential in using the court system to change school policy. In the 1947 case, *Everson v. Board of Education,* the U.S. Supreme Court stated, *"The First Amendment has erected a wall of separation between church and state. That wall must remain high and impregnable."*[493] These *Progressives* in government seats wanted the American People to believe that those words were actually included in the *First Amendment*.

The *Mainstream News Media* "fakenews" repeated that U.S. Supreme Court phrase for fifteen years. The *First Amendment* clearly reads, *"Congress shall make no law respecting an establishment of religion, [Christian denomination], or prohibiting the free exercise thereof; or abridging the freedom of speech, or of the press; or the right of the people peaceably to assemble, and to petition the government for a redress of grievances."* [Emphasis added]

So, the seed was planted and the inertia that was propelled in cause-to-effect was manifested in what occurred in 1962 with the removal of prayer from public schools.

Banking and Finance Reforms

In this same era of the Freemason *Progressive* movement, the Corporate UNITED STATES began to generate debts via bonds *etc.*, which came due in 1912. With banking and finance monopolized by a consortium (partnership) of eight very wealthy families of *Black Nobility*, only four of which resided in the U.S., these families strategically bought-up and owned the bonds tied to the U.S. national debt.[494]

The *Venetian Black Nobility* are some of the wealthiest and oldest European families whose lineage extends for centuries. They are dubbed as the "Black Nobility" for their nefarious deeds and occult worship. These families, that came to include the wealthy ruling elitist U.S. families, are high-up in Lucifer's triangular chain-of-command as part of the *Committee of 300*, also self-identifying as the "Olympians."[495]

President Woodrow Wilson said,

> *"Since I entered politics, I have chiefly had men's views confided to me privately. Some of the biggest men in the United States, in the field of commerce and manufacture, are afraid of somebody, are afraid of something. They know that there is a power somewhere so organized, so subtle, so watchful, so interlocked, so complete, so pervasive that they had better not speak above their breath when they speak in condemnation of it."*[496]

---

[492] "State of Tennessee v. Scopes," ACLU.org, accessed Dec 1, 2014, https://www.aclu.org/religion-belief/state-tennessee-v-scopes
[493] Everson v. Board of Education, 330 U.S. 1 (1947)
[494] Barefoot Bob Hardison, *"Who Is Running America"* Dec. 9, 1996, http://barefootsworld.net/usfraud.html [Recovered through the Internet Archive Wayback Machine Website https://web.archive.org/web/20080915215033/http://www.barefootsworld.net/usfraud.html
[495] Coleman, *Conspirators Hierarchy, 6, 22, 100*
[496] Ibid.; *Woodrow Wilson, The New Freedom: A Call for the Emancipation of the Generous Energies of A People,* (Englewood Cliffs, NJ: Prentice-Hall, Inc., 1961) 24

The "power" Wilson was talking about is the *Committee of 300* and Wilson knew he dare not mention it by name..

These devil-worshipping families are upper-level in Lucifer's secret government, servants of the *One World Government-New World Order* agenda. They are aligned with the *Illuminati,* Freemasonry, and other secret occult societies. They also oversee their "Think Tanks" known as the Round Table along with the Trilateral Commission, Council on Foreign Relations, the United Nations, the Bilderberg Group, the Club of Rome, and the Royal Institute of International Affairs. Their objective has been to overthrow the U.S. Constitution (even the Corporation's constitution), and to merge this country, which was chosen by Creator God as His country with His government and law form *the Laws of Nature and of Nature's God,* with an evil *One World Government-New World Order* which entails chaos, death, and destruction of the most heinous designs.[497]

"Money is power." Knowing the Corporate UNITED STATES was unable to make payment on the debt, these cunning families made demands of payment. These families include the Goldman Sachs, Rockefellers, Lehmans, and Kuhn Loebs of New York; the Rothschilds of Paris and London; the Warburgs of Hamburg; the Lazards of Paris; and the Israel Moses Seifs of Rome. These *Black Nobility* families are of the highest ranks and degrees of all branches of witchcraft.[498] These families settled the debt by receiving payment of <u>all</u> of the UNITED STATES assets — and — for <u>all</u> of the assets of the Treasury of the United States. [499] [500] [501]

In 1913, the Corporate UNITED STATES had no funds to carry out the necessary business needs of the government and went to these same families, asked to borrow money, and were declined. Of particular interest is that the families foresaw this situation and, in the previous year, strategically finalized the creation of a private corporation by the name, "*Federal Reserve Bank.*"

The Corporate UNITED STATES then formed a relationship with the *Federal Reserve Bank* whereby they could transact their business via note rather than with money. On December 23, 1913, the *Federal Reserve Act*[502] was passed by the *de facto* Congress and signed into law by Jesuit coadjutor President Woodrow Wilson.[503] Astoundingly, only five senators passed this Act while the rest were home for the Christmas holiday. There was no quorum in representation of the American People in this major decision that has made economic slaves of every American. President Wilson did not even read this "routine banking bill" and later admitted that it was the greatest mistake of his career.

---

[497] Dr. John Coleman, *Conspirators Hierarchy: The Story of the Committee of 300,* (1992) 4
https://www.cia.gov/library/abbottabad-compound/4A/4A92FD2FB4DAE3F773DB0B7742CF0F65_Coleman.-.CONSPIRATORS.HIERARCHY.-.THE.STORY.OF.THE.COMMITTEE.OF.300.R.pdf
[498] Fritz Springmeier, *Bloodlines of the Illuminati,* (Spring Arbor Distributors, 1998)
[499] Dean Henderson, "The Federal Reserve Cartel: the Eight Families," *Global Research,* Dec 1, 2011, http://www.globalresearch.ca/the-federal-reserve-cartel-the-eight-families/25080
[500] Ethan White, "Dr. John Coleman's Final Warning: The Black Nobility, the WEF-UN Partnership, and the chilling Resurgence of Eugenics and Transhumanism!" May 9, 2023 https://gazetteller.com/dr-john-colemans-final-warning-the-black-nobility-the-wef-un-partnership-and-the-chilling-resurgence-of-eugenics-and-transhumanism/
[501] Coleman, *Conspirators Hierarchy*, 5
[502] The short title of the Act of December 23, 1913, ch. 6, 38 Stat. 251, shall be the "Federal Reserve Act," Cornell University Law School, Legal Information Institute, accessed Dec 4, 2015, https://www.law.cornell.edu/uscode/text/12/226
[503] Alan Lamont, "The Jesuit Vatican New World Order: THIS IS WORLD HISTORY," April 6, 2012, http://vaticannewworldorder.blogspot.com/2012/04/fidel-castro-of-cuba-profile-of.html

After signing the *Federal Reserve Act* into law, *de facto* President Wilson said,

> "I am a most unhappy man. I have unwittingly ruined my country. A great industrial nation is controlled by its system of credit. Our system of credit is concentrated. The growth of the nation, therefore, and all our activities are in the hands of a few men. We have come to be one of the worst ruled, one of the most completely controlled and dominated governments in the civilized world no longer a government by free opinion, no longer a government by conviction and the vote of the majority, but a government by the opinion and duress of a small group of dominant men."[504]

Signing of the Federal Reserve Act[505]
Courtesy of Woodrow Wilson Presidential Library
Painting by Wilbur G. Kurtz

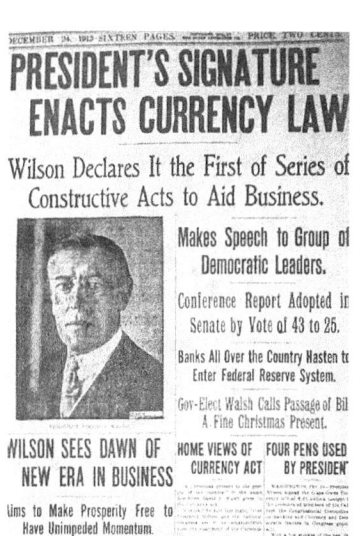

U.S. Newspaper, Dec. 24, 1913 [506]
Woodrow Wilson signs
creation of the Federal Reserve

Shadow workers of the *de facto* Federal Government included Jesuit "Colonel" Edward Mandell House (1858-1938) who was a powerful American diplomat, politician, and presidential advisor to Woodrow Wilson, commonly known as "Colonel" House though he had no military experience.[507] He was a highly influential back-state politician in Texas before becoming a key supporter of the presidential bid of Woodrow Wilson in 1912. Woodrow Wilson offered Mr. House any presidential cabinet position he wanted except Secretary of State; however, House declined as he preferred to work in the shadows as the president's most trusted advisor.[508]

---

[504] TheMoneyMasters.com, "Famous Quotes on Banking: President Woodrow Wilson," accessed Dec 1, 2014
[505] Federal Reserve History, "Signing of the Federal Reserve Act, Courtesy of Woodrow Wilson Presidential Library; Painting by Wilbur G. Kurtz," http://www.federalreservehistory.org/Events/DetailView/10 This work is in the public domain
[506] *Wikimedia Commons,* s.v. "Fed Reserve.JPG," This work is in the public domain
[507] Alan Lamont, "The Jesuit Vatican New World Order: World War One" April 18, 2012, http://vaticannewworldorder.blogspot.com/2012/04/unseen-titanic-photos-from-jesuit.html
[508] Robert Higgs, PhD, "Who Was Edward M. House?," August 13, 2008, http://www.independent.org/newsroom/article.asp?id=2294

It was a peculiar role that President Wilson delegated upon his intimate friend, Col. Edward Mandell House. Wilson once went so far as to say, "*Mr. House is my second personality. His thoughts and mine are one.*"[509]

President Wilson never read the *Federal Reserve Act* before he signed it because of his trust in Colonel House.[510]

Col. Edward Mandel House [511]

In a private meeting with President Wilson, Edward Mandell House is accredited in giving a very detailed outline of the plans to be implemented to enslave the American people:

"Very soon, every American will be required to register their biological property [that's you and your children] in a national system designed to keep track of the people and that will operate under the ancient system of pledging. By such methodology, we can compel people to submit to our agenda, which will affect our security as a charge back for our fiat paper currency.

Every American will be forced to register or suffer being able to work and earn a living. They will be our chattels [properties] and we will hold the security interest over them forever, by operation of the law merchant [judges in the de facto court system] under the scheme of secured transactions. Americans, by unknowingly or unwittingly delivering the bills of lading [birth certificates] to us will be rendered bankrupt and insolvent, secured by their pledges.

They will be stripped of their rights and given a commercial value designed to make us a profit and they will be none the wiser, for not one man in a million could ever figure our plans and, if by accident one or two should figure it out, we have in our arsenal plausible deniability. After all, this is the only logical way to fund government, by floating liens and debts for the registrants in the form of benefits and privileges. This will inevitably reap us huge profits beyond our wildest expectations and leave every American a contributor to this fraud, which we will call 'Social Insurance.' Without realizing it, every American will unknowingly be our servant, however begrudgingly. The people will become helpless and without any hope for their redemption and we will employ the high office [presidency] of our dummy corporation [Corporate UNITED STATES] to foment this plot against America." [512] [513]

[Emphasis added]

The relationship between the Corporate UNITED STATES and the *Federal Reserve Bank* was one actually made between two private corporations and did not involve government. In the 1943 case of *Clearfield Trust*

---

[509] Professor Ralph Raico, "FDR: The Man, the Leader, the Legacy," *Independent Institute,* April 1, 2001, http://www.independent.org/publications/article.asp?id=1468
[510] The Public Ownership League of America, *Proceedings Public Ownership Conference, Bulletin No. 11*, (Chicago, 1919), 165-171
[511] Library of Congress, "Edward Mandell House, 1858-1938," This work is in the public domain
[512] Mary Elizabeth: Croft, *How I Clobbered Every Bureaucratic Cash-Confiscatory Agency Known to Man,* (2008), 21, accessed June 4, 2014, http://www.spiritualeconomicsnow.net/solutions/How_I_08.pdf
[513] 1215.org Staff, "A Quote To Remember, Edward Mandel House, He said in a letter to President Woodrow Wilson [1913-1921]," accessed Sept 18, 2023, https://www.1215.org/lawnotes/lawnotes/house.htm

Co. v. United States, the *de facto* Supreme Court of the United States held that federal negotiable instruments were governed by federal law.[514] The *Clearfield Doctrine* states,

> "Governments descend to the level of a mere private corporation, and take on the characteristics of a mere private citizen [before Freemasonry was infiltrated by the Illuminati, Americans were a virtuous, self-governing people] where private corporate commercial paper [Federal Reserve Notes] and securities [checks] is concerned…for purpose of suit, such corporations and individuals are regarded as entities entirely separate from <u>government</u>."[515] [Emphasis added]

What the *Clearfield Doctrine* conveys is that when private commercial paper is used by corporate government, then government loses its sovereignty status and becomes no different than a mere private corporation with a business name like, for example, the UNITED STATES, INC.

The *16th Amendment* of the Corporate UNITED STATES' constitution was passed by the *de facto* Congress on July 2, 1909, and ratified by the States on February 3, 1913. It states, *"The Congress shall have power to lay and collect taxes on incomes, from whatever source derived, without apportionment among the several states, and without regard to any census or enumeration."*

This was the first amendment that gained ratification in more than 40 years. The *16th Amendment* in effect altered *Article I, Section 9, Clause 4* of the *Constitution for the United States*: "No capitation, or other direct, tax shall be laid, unless in proportion to the census or enumeration herein before directed to be taken." [516]

It was in 1933 when *de facto* President Franklin D. Roosevelt became the 32nd U.S. President. F.D.R. was a 32nd degree Freemason, member of the *Skull and Bones* secret society, as well as a member of the *Council on Foreign Relations*. President Roosevelt is known as having achieved the greatest progress for Socialism in his administration (1933-1945), particularly with his *New Deal* program. Noteworthy is that there was a general consensus among Americans that a vast underground horde of communists were working to overthrow the government through subversive means. Following *World War II*, Socialism was equated with Communism. Outside of modern history no president has been so criticized as a Socialist, Communist, and traitor to the American system than Franklin Delanore Roosevelt. [517] [518]

Today these same programs are among the nation's worst widely accepted and popular, such as Social Security, mandatory bank deposit insurance, and regulation of securities sales. F.D.R. made two powerful

---

[514] Clearfield Trust Co. v. United States, 318 U.S. 363
[515] "Governments Have Descended to the Level of Mere Private Corporations: Supreme Court Annotated Statute, Clearfield Trust Co. v. United States, 318 U.S. 363-371 (1943)," AntiCorruption Society, accessed Dec 4, 2015, https://anticorruptionsociety.files.wordpress.com/2014/05/clearfield-doctrine.pdf
[516] Shmoop Editorial Team, "16th Amendment" *Shmoop* University, Inc. 11 November 2008. http://www.shmoop.com/constitution/16th-amendment.html
[517] New World Order Today Staff, "Franklin D. Roosevelt," accessed Dec 1, 2014, http://www.nwotoday.com/the-new-world-orders-history/the-socialist-review-american-politicians/franklin-d-roosevelt [Recovered through the Internet Archive Wayback Machine, https://web.archive.org/web/20191008162051/http://www.nwotoday.com/the-socialist-review-american-politicians/franklin-d-roosevelt]
[518] Steven Sora, *Secret Societies of America's Elite: From the Knights Templar to Skull and Bones*, (Rochester, Destiny Books, 2003), 270

statements when he said, *"Presidents are <u>selected, not elected</u>"* — and — *"In politics, nothing happens by accident. If it happens, you can bet it was planned that way."*[519] [520]

In 1933, after the Corporate UNITED STATES was declared as bankrupt, the governors of the then 48 States pledged the *"full faith and credit"* of their States, <u>including their citizenry</u>, as collateral for loans of credit from the *Federal Reserve System*. On April 5, 1933, President Franklin D. Roosevelt signed Executive Order 6102, *"Forbidding the hoarding of gold coin, gold bullion, and gold certificates within the continental United States."* [521]
"If it happens, you can bet it was planned that way."[522]

Gold Confiscation Poster[523]
Signed by the U.S. Secretary of the Treasury
On the reverse side is the text of
FDR's Executive Order 6102 dated April 5, 1933
On the top of the Poster is a note by the Postmaster General
To the Postmaster with a directive to post in a Conspicuous Place

Also, on June 5, 1933, the *de facto* Congress passed *House Joint Resolution (HJR) 192*.[524] Upon being passed, *HJR 192* was immediately implemented to suspend the gold standard and abrogate (repeal) the gold clause in the *de facto* Corporate UNITED STATES' constitution. Since that time, Americans have not had the ability to lawfully pay a debt or lawfully own anything. The only legal provision and ability provided is to tender in transfer of debts, with the debt being perpetual. The suspension of the gold standard and prohibition against paying debts removed the substance for constitutional law to operate while creating a void in law. This substance was replaced with a *"public national credit system"* where debt is *"legal tender"* money.[525]

The day after President Roosevelt signed *HJR 192* into law and soon after the U.S. Treasury offered the public new government securities (dollars), without the traditional *"payable in gold"* clause. Since the *de facto* Corporate UNITED STATES went bankrupt in 1933, all new money has been borrowed into existence.[526] All *de facto* States began issuing serial-numbered "warehouse receipt" certificates for births and marriages in order to pledge the American People as collateral against those loans and municipal bonds created in

---

[519] New World Order Today Staff, "Franklin D. Roosevelt."
[520] New World Order Today Staff, "Franklin D. Roosevelt."
[521] The American Presidency Project, Franklin D. Roosevelt, *34 - Executive Order 6102 - Requiring Gold Coin, Gold Bullion and Gold Certificates to Be Delivered to the Government.*
[522] New World Order Today Staff, "Franklin D. Roosevelt."
[523] Source from https://www.monetarygold.com/wp-content/uploads/2021/04/Gold-Confiscation.pdf This work is in the public domain
[524] *House Joint Resolution 192*, 73d Congress, Sess. I, Ch. 48, June 5, 1933 (Public Law No. 10); Approved, June 5, 1933, 4:40 p.m. 31 U.S.C.A. 462, 463
[525] Education Center 2000 Admin, "House Joint Resolution – 192," accessed 11/12/2023, http://www.educationcenter2000.com/legal/HJR_192_73rdCongress.html
[526] Federal Reserve Bank of Chicago, *Modern Money Mechanics, (Chicago: 1975),* accessed April 14, 2014, http://lisgi1.engr.ccny.cuny.edu/~makse/Modern_Money_Mechanics.pdf

conjunction with the *Federal Reserve Bank*. The *"full faith and credit"* of the American people is that which backs the nation's debt. This is slavery! [527] [528] [529]

It was President Franklin D. Roosevelt that ordered the all-seeing eye to be placed upon all new dollar bills along with the motto, *Novus Ordo Seclorum*. This is Latin for "A New Order of the Ages." FDR served his masters well in their goal of a *One World Government-New World Order*.[530]

President Lyndon B. Johnson, 1964 [531]

In 1954, *de facto* Congress approved an *Amendment* proposed by then high-level Freemason Senator Lyndon B. Johnson in changing the U.S. tax code in order to prohibit tax exempt organizations from endorsing or opposing political candidates.[532] [533] Essentially the result was a "gag order" on the pulpit in not bringing "politics" before the people while preaching on sin and immorality.[534] For over 300 years American preachers taught government *"the science of politics"* from "the *Great Political Textbook*," the Holy Bible. No longer would this *whole counsel of Creator God*[535] be taught from the Pulpit. This censuring would also ensure that there would be no repeat in history of a *"Black Robe Regiment,"* patriot preachers of the Revolutionary Era.[536]

Church organizations are now set-up in law as corporations with fiscal reporting responsibilities to the government.[537] Ministers of the *Word of God* are required by law to become licensed (asking permission of the government) to marry people before God. People used to simply record their nuptials in their family Bible; the *de facto* government now requires a license (permission or privilege) be granted and obtained in order to be allowed to marry.

---

[527] "The Sheppard-Towner Maternity and Infancy Act," United States House of Representatives, History, Art & Archives, accessed Dec 1, 2014, http://history.house.gov/HistoricalHighlight/Detail/36084?ret=True

[528] *USLegal.com Definitions,* s.v. "Sheppard-Towner Act Law & Legal Definition," accessed December 1, 2014, http://definitions.uslegal.com/s/sheppard-towner-act/

[529] Mary Elizabeth: Croft, *How I Clobbered Every Bureaucratic Cash-Confiscatory Agency Known to Man,* (2008), 21, accessed June 4, 2014, http://www.spiritualeconomicsnow.net/solutions/How_I_08.pdf

[530] Andrew Hitchcock, "The History of the House of Rothschild," 10-31-2009, https://rense.com/general88/hist.htm

[531] *Wikimedia Commons,* s.v. "37 Lyndon Johnson 3x4.jpg," This work is in the public domain

[532] "Charities, Churches and Politics," Internal Revenue Service, Updated July 12, 2007 http://www.irs.gov/uac/Charities,-Churches-and-Politics

[533] New World Order Today Staff, "Lyndon B. Johnson," accessed Nov 2, 2014, http://www.nwotoday.com/the-new-world-orders-history/the-socialist-review-american-politicians/lyndon-b-johnson [Recovered through the Internet Archive Wayback Machine, http://web.archive.org/web/20160426110811/http://www.nwotoday.com/the-new-world-orders-history/the-socialist-review-american-politicians/lyndon-b-johnson/]

[534] Ed. Gary Cass, *Gag Order,* (Fairfax: Xulon Press, 2005), 26

[535] *Acts 20:27 (NKJV) ~ For I have not shunned to declare to you the whole counsel of God.*

[536] David Barton, "The Black Robed Regiment," August 30, 2011, WallBuilders.com, http://www.wallbuilders.com/libissuesarticles.asp?id=105213

[537] "Churches & Religious Organizations: Filing Requirements," Internal Revenue Service, page last updated November 18, 2015, http://www.irs.gov/Charities-&-Non-Profits/Churches-&-Religious-Organizations/Filing-Requirements

When an organization such as a church files a *501c3* application, it is giving its consent to be governed by all applicable statutes and *501c3* rules pertaining to *Title 26* of the *U.S. Internal Revenue Code*. A church organization which has filed a *501c3* application has <u>agreed to relinquish its constitutional right</u> to practice religion without government interference. In effect, the church disestablishes its religious nature (with Jesus Christ as its Head) and instead becomes a secular agency of government policy. One of the implications directs an inability to speak or preach *the whole counsel of God* while also consenting to government dictates by silence. The *501c3* church organization can only operate under the "color of religion" — a very serious Biblical matter of Divine condemnation.[538]

The *Word of God* already establishes that His ministries are tax exempt:

> *Ezra 7:24 ~ You are also to know you have no authority to impose taxes, tribute or duty on any of the priests, Levites, musicians, gatekeepers, temple, servants or other workers at this house of God.*

The *de facto* U.S. Supreme Court's lie to the American People concerning *"the separation of church and state."*

Let it be known and understood that for 170 years from the time of instituting the *Constitution for the United States* along with the *Bill of Rights*, up until June 25, 1962, the meaning of church by the government, was *"any federally established denomination."*

The *First Article of Amendment* of the *Constitution for the United States* (Establishment of religion) ~ *"Congress shall make no law respecting an establishment of religion, or prohibiting the free exercise thereof; or abridging the freedom of speech, or of the press; or the right of the people peaceably to assemble, and to petition the government for a redress of grievances."*

Joseph Story [539]
Associate Justice of the U.S. Supreme Court (1812-1845)

Joseph Story (1779-1845), a Supreme Court justice appointed by President James Madison, said this about the *First Amendment*:

"The real object of the First Amendment was not to countenance [approve or support] much less to advance Mohammedanism or Judaism or infidelity [disbelief of the inspiration of the Holy Scriptures] by prostrating Christianity, <u>but to exclude all rivalry among Christian sects or denominations, and to prevent any national ecclesiastical patronage of the national governments</u>."[540] [Emphasis added]

---

[538] "Churches & Religious Organizations: Filing Requirements," Internal Revenue Service
[539] *Wikimedia Commons*, s.v. "Daguerreotype of Joseph Story, 1844 (edit).jpg," This work is in the public domain
[540] William J. Federer, *America's God and Country Encyclopedia of Quotations*, "Joseph Story," (Coppell: FAME Publishing, Inc., 1994) 575 as citing Judge Brevard Hand, in *Jaffree v. Board of School Commissioners of Mobile County*, 544 F. Supp. 1104 (S. D. Ala. 1983)

Portrait of Thomas Jefferson, 1800 [541]

After hearing a rumor that the Congregational Church was going to take over the Connecticut State government, on October 7, 1801, the Danbury Baptist Association wrote a letter to then President Thomas Jefferson. The original intent of Founding Father Thomas Jefferson in his letter written January 1, 1802, in response to that committee of the Danbury Baptist Association was to calm their fears that Congress was not in the process of choosing any one single Christian denomination to be the "State" denomination as was the case with the Anglican Church in England. [542]

In his letter to the Danbury Baptists, who had experienced harsh persecution for their faith, Jefferson borrowed phraseology from the famous Puritan minister Roger Williams founder of the First Baptist Church of Providence, who said, *"the hedge or wall of separation between the garden of the church and the wilderness of the world, God hath ever broke down the wall…"* [543]

Jefferson's letter included,

> *"Believing with you that religion is a matter which lies solely between man & his God, that he owes account to none other for faith or his worship, that the legitimate powers of government reach actions only, & not opinions, I contemplate with sovereign reverence that act of the whole American people which declared that their legislature should 'make no law respecting an establishment of religion [Jefferson meant an establishment of a denomination], or prohibiting the free exercise thereof,' thus building a wall of separation between Church & State [between a particular denomination and State government]."* [544] [Emphasis added]

Statue of Roger Williams (1603-1683) [545]

This personal letter reassured the Baptists that the government's hands were tied from interfering with, or in any way controlling, the affairs or decisions of the churches in America. Jefferson also made it clear that the government was never granted the authority to establish as State run religion, such as was instituted by the *501c3* legislation.

---

[541] *Wikimedia Commons,* S.V. "File:Thomas Jefferson by Rembrandt Peale, 1800.jpg," This work is in the public domain
[542] WallBuilders.com, "Letters Between the Danbury Baptists and Thomas Jefferson," accessed Nov 2, 2014, http://www.wallbuilders.com/libissuesarticles.asp?id=65
[543] David Barton, *The Myth of Separation* (Aledo, TX: WallBuilder Press, 1991), 42
[544] Ibid. as citing Thomas Jefferson. January 1, 1802, in a personal letter to Nehemiah Dodge, Ephraim Robbines, and Stephen Nelson of the Danbury Baptist Association, Danbury, Connecticut. *Reymolds v. U.S., 98 U.S. 164 (1878). A.A. Lipscomb and Albert Bergh, eds.,* The Writings of Thomas Jefferson, 20 vols. (Washington, D.C.: The Thomas Jefferson Memorial Association, 1903-1904).
[545] *Wikimedia Commons,* s.v. "File:Roger Williams statue by Franklin Simmons.jpg," This work is in the public domain

The misguided and misinterpreted 1947 *de facto* U.S. Supreme Court ruling set the tone in cause-to-effect for what came later in 1962. The seed of Satan was indeed sewn when that Supreme Court said, *"The First Amendment has erected a clause of separation between church and state. That wall must remain high and impregnable."*

Next, on June 25, 1962, the *de facto* U.S. Supreme Court changed the meaning of "church" as they struck down voluntary school prayer. Prior to 1962, prayer in school was common in school districts throughout America. Some teachers led in spontaneous prayer, simply expressing their thoughts and desires while others implemented structured prayers, such as the Lord's Prayer or others approved by local school boards. New York students prayed each day: *"Almighty God, we acknowledge our dependence on Thee and beg Thy blessing over us, our parents, our teachers, and our nation."* It was this simple prayer which came under fire and ended in lawsuit before the *de facto* U.S. Supreme Court with the landmark decision in *Engel v. Vitale*.[546]

Next, on June 17, 1963, in the case *Abington School District v. Schempp*,[547] the *de facto* U.S. Supreme Court declared that school-sponsored Bible reading in public schools was unconstitutional. For over 300 years the Holy Bible had been the main text in schools and from which American children learned to read. Noah Webster, the *"Schoolmaster of America,"* said,

> *"Education is useless without the Bible."*[548]

He also said,

> *"God's word contained in the Bible has furnished all necessary rules to direct our conduct."*[549]

It is important to understand our foundational history on the critical nature of this topic.

In 1787 the *Constitutional Convention* was taking place at the very same juncture in time that Thomas Jefferson worked with Congress on a plan of government for the western territory northwest of the Ohio River, the *Ordinance of 1787*. The *Northwest Ordinance* of July 13, 1787, which had become codified into law by the First Congress as *1 Statute 50* on August 7, 1789, declared the *Articles of Confederation* which were adopted on April 23, 1784, as null and void. The *Constitution of the United States* replaced the *Articles of Confederation*.

This same Founding Father that drafted the *Declaration of Independence* which acknowledges Creator God four times — including the government law form being *the Laws of Nature and of Natures God* — felt so strongly about a *Biblical Worldview* in education in the public schools that it is addressed in *Article 3* of the *Northwest Ordinance*, one of our nation's four Founding Documents. Territories that desired to become States were lawfully required to follow this law before statehood could be achieved.

---

[546] *Engel v. Vitale*, 370 U.S. 421 (1962)
[547] *Abington School District v. Schempp*, 374 U.S. 203 (1963)
[548] Federer, *America's Quotations*, Noah Webster, 676 as citing "Our Christian Heritage," *Letter from Plymouth Rock* (Marlborough, NH: The Plymouth Rock Foundation) 5
[549] Ibid. as citing Verna M. Hall and Rosalie J. Slater, *The Bible and the Constitution of the United States* (San Francisco: Foundation for American Christian Education, 1983), 27

Article 3 of the Northwest Ordinance; July 13, 1787, *An Ordinance for the government of the Territory of the United States northwest of the River Ohio*:

> *"Religion, morality, and knowledge, being necessary to good government and the happiness of mankind, schools and the means of education shall forever be encouraged.* The utmost good faith shall always be observed towards the Indians; their lands and property shall never be taken from them without their consent; and, in their property, rights, and liberty, they shall never be invaded or disturbed, unless in just and lawful wars authorized by Congress; but laws founded in justice and humanity, shall from time to time be made for preventing wrongs being done to them, and for preserving peace and friendship with them."[550]

Additionally, the apostle Paul said, *"all the treasures of wisdom and knowledge,"* are hid in Christ Jesus.[551] Education without Christ, who is the *Word of God*,[552] will be void of the wealth of wisdom and knowledge that comes only from our Creator. Reading moral precepts of the Holy Bible that says *thou shalt not kill*,[553] *thou shalt not steal*,[554] and *love your neighbor as yourself*,[555] astoundingly became outlawed in America.

Statistical evidence indicates that what has happened in our country since these landmark *de facto* U.S. Supreme Court rulings is what began this separation of religious (Christian Biblical governmental) principles from our education system, government, and public affairs. The downward slide away from moral behavior started around the time of these rulings. The decision to remove prayer and Bible reading from the school system was an outright effort to steal the birthright of the American People in their covenant with Almighty God as well as removing the pillars of our country's foundation—*Religion and Morality*—that our first president under the *Constitution for the United States* and *"Father of his country,"* George Washington, had emphasized were pillars of America's foundation.[556]

There was an aggressive Freemason *Progressive* Luciferian effort to replace America's founding values and Christian *Biblical worldview* in the classrooms with Darwinian materials on the "theory" of evolution along with the religion of *Secular Humanism* of which has overtaken the mindset of society through school administrators, teachers, professors, legislators, and judges throughout the country.

In 1961 the U.S. Supreme Court acknowledged that *Secular Humanism* is a religion.[557] *Secular Humanism* is a religion that subscribes to the belief that there are no absolute moral standards. Paul Kurtz (1925-2012) was

---

[550] "Northwest Ordinance; July 13, 1787," accessed at *The Avalon Project*, Lillian Goldman Law Library, Yale Law School, accessed November 2, 2014, http://avalon.law.yale.edu/18th_century/nworder.asp

[551] *Colossians 2:2-3 ~ ² That their hearts might be comforted, being knit together in love, and unto all riches of the full assurance of understanding, to the acknowledgement of the mystery of God, and of the Father, and of Christ ;³ In whom are hid all the treasures of wisdom and knowledge.*

[552] *Revelation 19:13 ~ And he was clothed with a vesture dipped in blood: and his name is called The Word of God.*
John 1:1-3 ~ ¹ In the beginning was the Word, and the Word was with God, and the Word was God. ²The same was in the beginning with God. ³All things were made by him; and without him was not any thing made that was made.

[553] *Exodus 20:13 ~ Thou shalt not kill.*

[554] *Exodus 20:15 ~ Thou shalt not steal.*

[555] *Leviticus 19:18; Matthew 19:19, 22:39; Mark 12:31; Luke 10:27; Romans 13:9*

[556] President George Washington, in his *Farewell Address* to the People of the United States, 1796:
"Of all the dispositions and habits which lead to political prosperity, religion and morality are indispensable supports."

[557] Torcaso v. Watkins, 367 U.S. 488 (1961),

a *Secular Humanist* philosopher who advocated that behavior should be guided by science and reason over religion. His stance of *"reason ahead of faith"* helped define *Secular Humanism* and gained him notoriety as *"the Father of Secular Humanism."*[558] Kurtz stated,

> *"Humanists have confidence in human beings, and they believe that the only bases for morality are human experiences and human needs"*[559]

Everyone has a philosophy or belief system with a religious premise — even if they are atheist/agnostic. [560]

As demonstrated throughout this presentation, the ideology and mindset of *Secular Humanism* is the State religion of the Corporate UNITED STATES. It is a religion that violates the Founding Documents of this country. We recall that all governments spring from a particular religion. Where the American Republic sprang from Biblical Christianity, the religion of Liberty, likewise, the Corporate UNITED STATES sprang from Satanism/*Secular Humanism*, the religion of death and destruction.

1871 Editorial Cartoon: "A Venerable Orang-outang," a caricature of Charles Darwin as an ape (1871) published in The Hornet, a satirical magazine [561]

A message was sent to the American People by the *de facto* U.S. Supreme Court that landmark day in 1963 that it was not only okay to remove Creator God from His rightful place in American institutions, they also mandated it to be so. What was not communicated was the consequence of opening the door and jeopardizing the American People in the curses that come from not teaching our posterity to obey God and

---

"11 <u>Among religions in this country</u> which do not teach what would generally be considered a belief in the existence of God are Buddhism, Taoism, Ethical Culture, <u>Secular Humanism</u> and others. See Washington Ethical Society v. District of Columbia, 101 U.S.App.D.C. 371, 249 F.2d 127; Fellowship of Humanity v. County of Alameda, 153 Cal.App.2d 673, 315 P.2d 394; II Encyclopaedia of the Social Sciences 293; 4 Encyclopaedia Britannica (1957 ed.) 325 327; 21 id., at 797; Archer, Faiths Men Live By (2d ed. revised by Purinton), 120—138, 254—313; 1961 World Almanac 695, 712; Year Book of American Churches for 1961, at 29, 47." https://www.law.cornell.edu/supremecourt/text/367/488

[558] *Wikipedia* s.v., Paul Kurtz," last modified 11 August 2023

[559] Dr. Justin Imel, Sr., "Why Should I Worry about Secular Humanism," as citing Paul Kurtz, In Defense of Secular Humanism (Buffalo, NY: Prometheus Books, 1983), 33

[560] Dr Marlene McMillian, *Five Pillars of Liberty*, (Fort Worth: Liberty View Media 2011) 44-45

[561] *Wikimedia Commons*, s.v. "Editorial cartoon depicting Charles Darwin as an ape (1871).jpg, This work is in the public domain

keep Him forefront in their lives.[562] In removing our Christian heritage of truthful American history and the presuppositional *Biblical worldview* from schools, *"We hold these truths to be self evident"* (*Declaration of Independence*), that sacred knowledge is no longer evident and the American People are at great risk in perishing.[563]

There can be no denying that this was a very dark victory for the principalities and powers, rulers of darkness[564] as a spiritually bankrupt group of carnally-minded[565] men that love money more than truth.[566] In the same way that *Old Testament* Balaam counseled Balaak in how to cause the people of God to bring a curse upon themselves.[567] The effect is seen in the deterioration and demoralization of the cornerstone of our society, the very fabric of our nation — the family.

With no conscious fear (reverential awe) of God, there was no longer any conscious reason to respect marriage vows as sacred, or to bring up God-fearing children. From there America spiraled quickly into demise in all other immoral circumstances that we find ourselves in today; teen pregnancies, violent crime, suicide, illegal drug use and alcohol abuse which are the very logical fruits that are reaped in a society that has forgotten the curses that come from disobedience to the *Word of God.*[568]

The Holy Bible is the Creator's manual that instructs how to live an abundant life while also warning of the consequences of foolish and sinful choices in not heeding the safety of the loving boundaries set for His creation, *"the Laws of Nature and of Nature's God."* The elimination of the fear of God (reverential awe), symbolized by the *de facto* U.S. Supreme Court's action in the matter of school prayer, led to a dramatic increase in crime, sexually transmitted diseases, premarital sex, illiteracy, suicide, chemical dependency, public corruption, and other social ills.

Evidence has been documented[569] through research that has been professionally compiled and tabulated using government data made available by agencies such as:

> The Department of Health and Human Services
> The Center for Disease Control
> Statistical Abstracts of the United States

---

[562] *Deuteronomy 28:15-68* (the curses for disobedience to the Word of God)
[563] *Hosea 4:6 ~ My people are destroyed for lack of knowledge: because thou hast rejected knowledge, I will also reject thee, that thou shalt be no priest to me: seeing thou hast forgotten the law of thy God, I will also forget thy children.*
[564] *Ephesians 6: 12 ~ For we wrestle not against flesh and blood, but against principalities, against powers, against the rulers of the darkness of this world, against spiritual wickedness in high places.*
[565] *Romans 8:6-8 ~ ⁶ For to be carnally minded is death; but to be spiritually minded is life and peace. ⁷ Because the carnal mind is enmity against God: for it is not subject to the law of God, neither indeed can be. ⁸ So then they that are in the flesh cannot please God.*
[566] *2 Peter 2:14-15 ~ ¹⁴ Having eyes full of adultery, and that cannot cease from sin; beguiling unstable souls: an heart they have exercised with covetous practices; cursed children: ¹⁵ Which have forsaken the right way, and are gone astray, following the way of Balaam the son of Bosor, who loved the wages of unrighteousness;*
[567] *Numbers 22-25* (the story of Balaak and Balaam);
Revelation 2:4 ~ Nevertheless I have somewhat against thee, because thou hast left thy first love.
[568] *Deuteronomy 28:15-68* (the curses for disobedience to the Word of God)
[569] The Forerunner Editorial Staff, "What Happened When the Praying Stopped," *The Forerunner*, April 6, 2008, http://www.forerunner.com/forerunner/X0124_When_America_stopped.html

Vital Statistics of the United States
The U.S. Department of Commerce
And the Bureau of Labor Statistics

The deterioration and demoralization of our society is documented in a report that includes graphs[570] and statistical analysis, entitled *"America, To Pray Or Not To Pray?: A Statistical Look at What Happened When Religious Principles Were Separated From Public Affairs,"*[571] by *Specialty Research Associates* under the direction of David Barton of *WallBuilders*. Following are a few examples of the reported results:

Young People:
    * For 15 years before 1963, pregnancies in girls ages 15 through 19 years of age had been no more than 15 per thousand. After 1963, pregnancies increased **187%** in the next 15 years.
    *For younger girls, ages 10 to 14 years, pregnancies since 1963 are up **553%**.
    *Before 1963, sexually transmitted diseases among students were 400 per 100,000. Since 1963, they were up **226%** in the next 12 years.

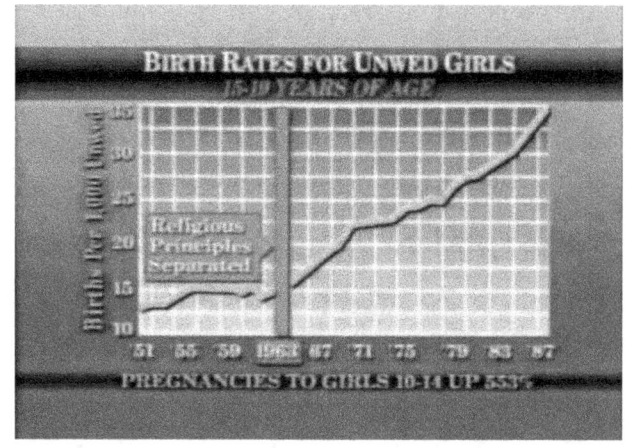

The Family:
    *Before 1963, divorce rates had been declining for 15 years. After 1963 divorces increased **300%** each year for the next 15 years.
    *Since 1963 unmarried people living together is up **353%**.
    *Since 1963, single parent families are up **140%**.
    *Since 1963, single parent families with children are up **160%**.

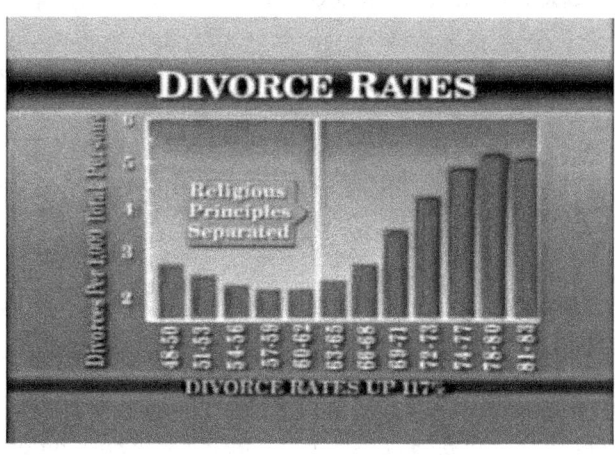

---

[570] ▪ Linda Clements, What You Know Might Not Be So, graphs as sourced from David Barton, "America to Pray or not to Pray" http://www.whatyouknowmightnotbeso.com/graphs.html
    ▪ The graphs included in this chapter are screengrabs from YouTube/Philip C "The Devastating Effects When Prayer Was Removed From School in America in 1962-63 - David Barton," Sept 16, 2016 https://www.youtube.com/watch?v=1No--GpdqCY Fair use
[571] David Barton, "America, To Pray Or Not To Pray?: A Statistical Look at What Happened When Religious Principles Were Separated From Public Affairs," (Aledo: WallBuilders Press, 1991)

Education:
*The educational standard of measure has been the [Scholastic Aptitude Test] SAT scores. SAT scores had been steady for many years before 1963. From 1963 they rapidly declined for 18 consecutive years, even though the same test has been used since 1941.
*In 1974-75, the rate of decline of the SAT scores decreased, even though the scores continued to decline. That was when there was an explosion of private religious schools. There were only 1,000 Christian schools in 1965. Between 1974 and 1984 Christian schools increased to 32,000.

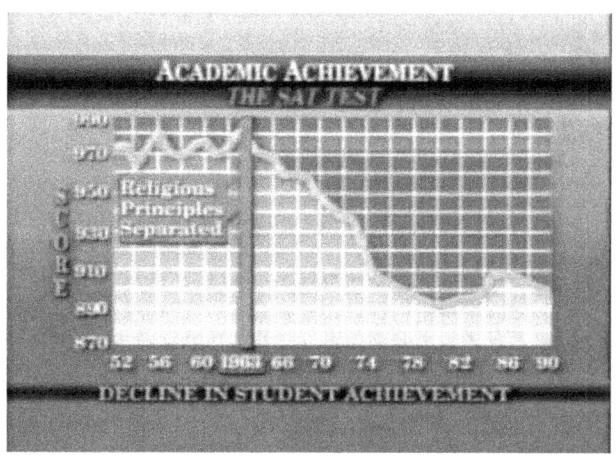

*That could have an impact if the private schools had higher SAT scores. In checking with the SAT Board, it was found that, indeed, the SAT scores for private schools were nearly 100 points higher than public schools.
*In fact, the scores were at the point where the public schools had been before their decline started in 1963 when prayer and Bible reading/instruction was removed from the schools.
*The scores in the public schools were still declining.
*Of the nation's top academic scholars, 3 times as many come from private religious schools, which operate on 1/3 the funds as do the public schools.

The Nation:
*Since 1963 violent crime has increased **544%**.
*Illegal drugs have become an enormous and uncontrollable problem.
*The nation has been deprived of an estimated 30 million citizens through legal abortions just since 1973.

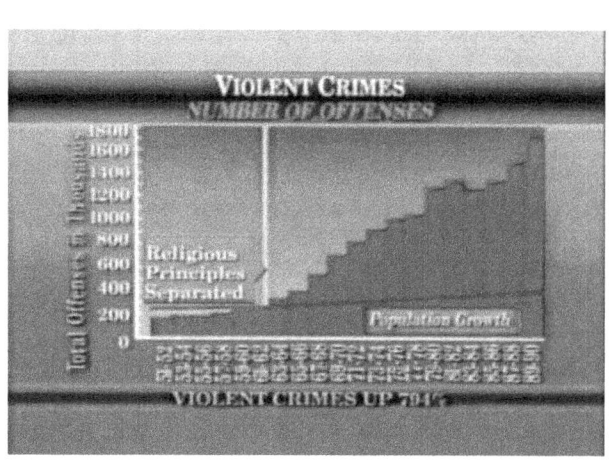

The results of this report, published in 1991, leave no room for doubt that it would shock the conscience, in those who have one, as to what the statistics would be in today's culture more than thirty years later.

It was a 1985 *de facto* U.S. Supreme Court case that decided whether a law that authorizes a period of silence in public schools for *"meditation or voluntary prayer"* is a violation of the First Amendment Establishment Clause.[572] Associate Justice William Rehnquist pointed out the error of the 1947 *de facto* Supreme Court ruling based on a misleading metaphor of the letter written in 1802 by Thomas Jefferson to the Danbury Baptist Association:

> *"It is impossible to build sound constitutional doctrine upon a mistaken understanding of constitutional history... The establishment clause had been expressly freighted with Jefferson's misleading metaphor for nearly forty years... There is simply no historical foundation for the proposition that the framers intended to build a wall of separation between church and state... The recent court decisions are in no way based on either the language or intent of the Framers."*[573]

William Rehnquist (1924-2005)[574]
Associate Justice of the U.S. Supreme Court (1972-1986)
Chief Justice (1986-2005)
Descendent of Pilgrim leader William Bradford[575]

The *de facto* U.S. Supreme Court decision was 6-3 in holding that a "moment of silence" law is unconstitutional when the explicit purpose and meaning of such a statute is to promote prayer. Remember this, and hold it with conviction in your heart, that the Founding Fathers built the commonwealth of the American Republic on Creator God's government with the *Laws of Nature and of Nature's God*, and the cornerstone being Jesus Christ.

The summary of the statistical analysis having to do with students (children) attending public school, parents of the students, teachers in the public schools, and the nation reflects a tremendous demoralization which took place. Cause-to-effect, the consciences of the people are now controlled by a wicked media, there has been a degenerating of American churches with a loss of interest in Biblical Christianity while a carnal mindset dominates society. The divorce rate became so high that many young children could not truly understand the dynamics of what a family is, or is meant to be, as established by our Creator.

---

[572] Wallace v. Jaffree, 472 U.S. 38 (1985)
[573] Federer, *America's Quotations*, "William Hubbs Rehnquist," 531-532 as citing William Hubbs Rehnquist. 1985, *Wallace v. Jafree*, 472 U.S. 38, 99. "Our Christian Heritage," *Letter from Plymouth Rock* (Marlborough, NH: The Plymouth Rock Foundation) 8
[574] *Wikimedia Commons* s.v., "File:William Rehnquist.jpg," This work is in the public domain
[575] History.com Editors, ' William Bradford," Oct 27, 2009, https://www.history.com/topics/colonial-america/william-bradford

Romans 8:6-8 ~ 6 For to be carnally minded is death; but to be spiritually minded is life and peace. 7 Because the carnal mind is enmity against God: for it is not subject to the law of God, neither indeed can be. 8 So then they that are in the flesh cannot please God.

Violent crimes have risen steadily ever since the early 1960s, and the overloaded prison system then became a thought-provoking for-profit *"Prison Industry"* in many facets. One shocking facet being the creation of bonds related to the convict and then <u>sold on the Stock Exchange</u>.[576]

Another for-profit aspect of the *Prison Industry* includes contracts that are made with private corporations that profit by charging exorbitant prices (much at taxpayer expense) for the food service, commissary items, phone calls, to name a few, at the numerous and growing prisons. The *"cunning, ambitious, and unprincipled"* individuals have gone so far as to have unconstitutionally incarcerated Americans of victimless crimes, who are now made victims of being "warehoused" for profit![577]

The President's Commission on Obscenity and Pornography

A 1969 *de facto* U.S. Supreme Court decision held that people could view whatever they wished in the privacy of their own homes.[578] This prompted the *de facto* U.S. Congress to fund the *President's Commission on Obscenity and Pornography*, which was set-up by *de facto* then President Lyndon Johnson to conduct a study on pornography. The Commission's report was published in 1970 recommending sex education, funding of research into the effects of pornography and restriction of children's access to pornography and recommended against any restrictions for adults. [579]

On balance, the report found that obscenity and pornography were not important social problems, that there was no evidence that exposure to such material was harmful to individuals, and that current legal and policy initiatives were more likely to create problems than solve them. The report was widely criticized and rejected by Congress. The Senate rejected the Commission's findings and recommendations by a 60-5 vote, with 34 (outrageously and immorally) abstaining from the vote, and in particular pointing out the absurdity of the following:

> There was "*no evidence to date that exposure to explicit sexual materials plays a significant role in the causation of delinquent or criminal behavior among youths or adults.*"
>
> That "*a majority of American adults believe that adults should be allowed to read or see any sexual materials they wish.*"

---

[576] Sham Gad, "Private Prisons Have Future Growth All Locked Up," October 17, 2009, http://www.investopedia.com/stock-analysis/2009/private-prisons-have-future-growth-all-locked-up-cxw-geo-crn1020.aspx

[577] *Revelation 18:11-13 ~ 11 And the merchants of the earth shall weep and mourn over her; for no man buyeth their merchandise any more: 12 <u>The merchandise</u> of gold, and silver, and precious stones, and of pearls, and fine linen, and purple, and silk, and scarlet, and all thyine wood, and all manner vessels of ivory, and all manner vessels of most precious wood, and of brass, and iron, and marble, 13 And cinnamon, and odours, and ointments, and frankincense, and wine, and oil, and fine flour, and wheat, and beasts, and sheep, and horses, and chariots, and slaves, and <u>souls of men</u>.*

[578] Stanley v. Georgia, 394 U.S. 557 (1969)

[579] *Wikipedia,* s.v. "President's Commission on Obscenity and Pornography," accessed Nov 2, 2014

That "*there is no reason to suppose that elimination of governmental prohibitions upon the sexual materials which may be made available to adults would adversely affect the availability to the public of other books, magazines, or films.*"

That there was no "*evidence that exposure to explicit sexual materials adversely affects character or moral attitudes regarding sex and sexual conduct.*"

That "*Federal, State, and Local legislation prohibiting the sale, exhibition, or distribution of sexual materials to consenting adults should be repealed.*"

Although 60 congressional members displayed moral sense in their votes, the Truth of America's essential pillars of civil society being *Religion and Morality* is plumb-lined in consideration of what the *Word of God* has to say — *Psalms 101:3a ~ I will set no wicked thing before mine eyes.*

Focus on the Family, a global Christian ministry dedicated to helping families thrive, reported on the effects of pornography and makes available the findings of extensive research by behavioral scientists and PhDs.

> "*Whether legally classified as obscene or indecent, <u>all pornography is harmful</u>. Pornography reduces human beings to sexual commodities that can be bought, sold, used and discarded. No one is immune to the mental, emotional, spiritual and even physical consequences of viewing pornographic material. These effects are not confined to the individuals viewing pornography; they extend to families and culture as well.*"[580]

Just before his execution on January 24, 1989, serial killer and rapist of at least 25 women and girls, Ted Bundy, granted an interview to psychologist Dr. James Dobson founder of *Focus on the Family*. In the interview, Bundy explained the progression into his compulsive pornography addiction and how it fueled the monstrous crimes he committed:

> "*I've lived in prison a long time now, and I've met a lot of men who were motivated to commit violence. Without exception, every one of them was deeply involved in pornography – deeply consumed by the addiction. The F.B.I.'s own study on serial homicide shows that the most common interest among serial killers is pornography.*"[581]

*Ted Bundy being interviewed by
Reverend Dr. James Dobson
for 'Focus on the Family,'
January 23, 1989*[582]

---

[580] Focus on the Family Issue Analysts, "Cause for Concern (Pornography), Whether legally classified as obscene or indecent, all pornography is harmful," 2008, http://www.focusonthefamily.com/socialissues/social-issues/pornography/cause-for-concern.aspx
[581] "Ted Bundy, Serial Killer and Rapist, Wanted to Tell the World about Pornography," EndAllDisease.com, accessed Nov 2, 2014, http://www.endalldisease.com/ted-bundy-serial-killer-and-rapist-wanted-to-tell-the-world-about-pornography/
[582] "Ted Bundy - Full Interview with Reverend James Dobson for 'Focus on the Family,' January 23, 1989," Screengrab from Youtube.com/Erin Banks, Published on Aug 17, 2022, https://youtu.be/7C-9eOb30L4?si=j93jzLo1r9aAy0pj

With utmost exhortation, do everything you can to protect your children and grandchildren from viewing pornography. It could easily ruin their lives.

The *National Education Association* (NEA), the largest labor union in the U.S. during the early 20th century, was among the leading *Progressive* advocates of establishing a U.S. Department of Education. By the 1970s, the NEA emerged as a factor in modern liberalism. While claiming to be non-partisan, it has proven to hold an exclusive favoritism in support of the Democratic Party and in nominating Democratic candidates.

The NEA has been telling public school teachers what to teach and helping students to give their allegiance to the State with an objective of making global citizens for the *New World Order*.

Dr. Marlene McMillan, an author and teacher with *Why Liberty Matters,* addresses the topic of better schools:

> *"To the progressive, better schools are laboratories of social engineering where children are conditioned to accept the New World Order and embrace social change. It is a place where traditional values are replaced by <u>transitional</u> values, followed by humanistic and socialistic values in order to implement a utopian society where humans are able to evolve to perfection. Then a new social order is able to be implemented that replaces the traditional family and has no mention of sin, and therefore no need of Jesus."*[583]

Dr. Marlene teaches people to think from principles,

> *"...because an issue cannot be passed down from one generation to the next, but you can pass a principle. You don't know what issues the next generation will face. Issues are always changing. Principles do not change, so when you teach people to think from principles, you end up with people who are empowered. They recognize that some new law may look like it will solve the issue today, but it actually puts our grandchildren in bankruptcy! Or it means that people in other parts of the country will be damaged by this law. And it makes you start thinking about the consequences of the choices you make, and the bills you support."*[584]

Dr. Marlene relays an accurate definition of Liberty:

> *"...having the opportunity to make a choice, to assume responsibility and accept the consequences."*[585]

Another trademark statement of Dr. Marlene:

> *"People who live in liberty think differently than people who live in bondage."*[586]

America must have Christian teachers lead our public schools in prayer and teach Holy Bible curriculum. A modest dress code is needed!

---

[583] Dr. Marlene McMillan, *Mountains of Deceit*, (Fort Worth: Liberty View Media, 2010) 15
[584] Dr. Marlene McMillan, *The Five Pillars of Liberty*, (Fort Worth: Liberty View Media, 2011) 17
[585] Ibid.
[586] Ibid. 126

We will recall that signer of the *Declaration of Independence*, John Witherspoon (1723-1794), is known as the "Father of fathers." Why? He was a teacher of renown at the College of New Jersey, now Princeton University, who taught his students a *Biblical worldview*.

John Witherspoon, circa 1790[587]

In the mix of his graduates are…
1 U.S. President,
1 U.S. Vice President,
3 Supreme Court justices,
10 cabinet members,
13 governors,
28 U.S. Senators,
49 U.S. Congressmen,
37 judges,
114 ministers,
12 members of the Continental Congress and
9 of the 55 writers of the U.S. Constitution including James Madison[588]

Witherspoon said,

> *"It is in the man of piety [reverence for God or devout fulfillment of religious obligations] and inward principle that we may expect to find the uncorrupted patriot, the useful citizen, and the invincible soldier. God grant that in America true religion and civil liberty may be inseparable and that the unjust attempts to destroy the one, may in the issue tend to the support and establishment of both."* [589] [Emphasis added]

---

[587] *Wikimedia Commons,* s.v. "File:Peale, Charles Willson, John Witherspoon (1723-1794), President (1768-94).jpg" This work is in the public domain
[588] Bill Federer, American Minute blog post American Minute with Bill Federer, "A Republic must either reserve its Virtue or lose its Liberty—Rev. John Witherspoon, Signer of Declaration of Independence," Nov 10, 2020
[589] Federer, *America's Quotations,* "John Witherspoon," (Coppell: FAME Publishing, Inc, 1994) 703 as citing John Witherspoon. 1768-1794. Martha Lou Lemmon Stohlman, *John Witherspoon: Politician, Patriot* (Philadelphia: Westminster Press, 1897) 172

Abigail Adams, the wife of Founding Father John Adams, wrote in a letter to her friend Mercy Warren, whose writing played a critical role in supporting and promoting the Patriot cause:

"A patriot without religion in my estimation is as great a paradox as an honest man without the fear of God. Is it possible that he whom no moral obligations bind, can have any real Good Will towards Men? Can he be a patriot who, by an openly vicious conduct, is undermining the very bonds of Society? ... The Scriptures tell us 'righteousness exalts a Nnation." [590]

Abigail Adams, 1766 [591]

In the war between good and evil, the war between the Kingdom of Heaven and the Domination of Hell, Christians and patriots in America have not only experienced a sobering concern while watching evil prevail throughout the decades but have come to the realization that they are considered and marked as the "enemy of the State" by this Luciferian government.

Under the Obama presidency, the Department of Homeland Security (DHS) along with the FBI's partner, the *Southern Poverty Law Center* (SPLC), Christians and patriots have been labeled as terrorists! [592] Beware!

President John F. Kennedy signs Executive Order 11110 [593]

On June 4, 1963, President John F. Kennedy signed *Executive Order No. 11110* of which returned to the (*de facto*) U.S. government the power to issue currency, without going through the *Federal Reserve*. President Kennedy's order gave the (*de facto*) U.S. Treasury the power *"to issue silver certificates against any silver bullion, silver, or standard silver dollars in the Treasury."* Kennedy brought nearly $4.3 billion in U.S. silver certificate notes into circulation.

---

[590] Ibid., "Abigail Adams," p. 3 as citing Abigail Adams. November 5, 1775 (circa), in a letter to her friend, Mercy Warren. *Warren-Adams Letters, 1743-1777* (Massachusetts Historical Society Collections), Vol. I, p. 72.

[591] *Wikimedia Commons*, s.v. "Abigail Adams.jpg," https://commons.wikimedia.org/wiki/File:Abigail_Adams.jpg This work is in the public domain

[592] "National Consortium for the Study of Terrorism and Responses to Terrorism, A Center of Excellence of the U.S. Department of Homeland Security Based at the University of Maryland, 'PROFILES OF PERPETRATORS OF TERRORISM- UNITED STATES (PPT-US)'," Last Update: January 30, 2012, https://info.publicintelligence.net/START-US-TerrorismProfiles.pdf

[593] Justice Network, "President John F. Kennedy issued Executive Order 11110," http://www.nosue.org/banking/united-states-note-vs-federal-reserve-note/ Fair use under United States copyright law

President Kennedy was on his way to putting the Federal Reserve Bank out-of-business. This was a bold step forward in cutting off the *Money Power* of those who control the *de facto* Corporate UNITED STATES and toward restoring the American Republic. President Kennedy was assassinated on November 22, 1963.

In presenting the gross corruption caused by infiltration of the Freemason Luciferians, we could easily continue pointing out topics of human trafficking; sex trafficking, Pizzagate, Agenda 21 and Agenda 30, and much more. It is now time to move forward with God's solution for America that will "reverse the curse" caused by violating the covenant of the *Declaration of Independence* and losing Dominion to the *Rulers of Evil*.

Reversing the curse begins with knowledge and education.

Hosea 4:6 ~ My people are destroyed for lack of knowledge: because thou hast rejected knowledge, I will also reject thee, that thou shalt be no priest to me: seeing thou hast forgotten the law of thy God, I will also forget thy children.

We take comfort in the prophetic *Holy Scriptures* as we realize the American Republic has a National Purpose and Prophetic Destiny.

Daniel 2:44 ~ And in the days [of the end times of the Last Days] of these kings [the Money Barons] shall the God of heaven set up a kingdom [with God's government], which shall never be destroyed: and the kingdom shall not be left to other people, but it shall break in pieces and consume all these kingdoms [of tyrannical democracy built by the Money Barons], and it shall stand for ever.

Daniel 7:18 ~ But the saints of the most High shall take the kingdom, and possess the kingdom for ever, even for ever and ever.

Daniel 7:22 ~ Until the Ancient of days came, and judgment was given to the saints of the most High; and the time came that the saints possessed the kingdom.

Chapter Five
God's Solution for America

Moses Receiving the *Law of the Covenant* [594]
from the *Creator of the universe*
for the people of Old Testament Israel
Lithograph published in 1877

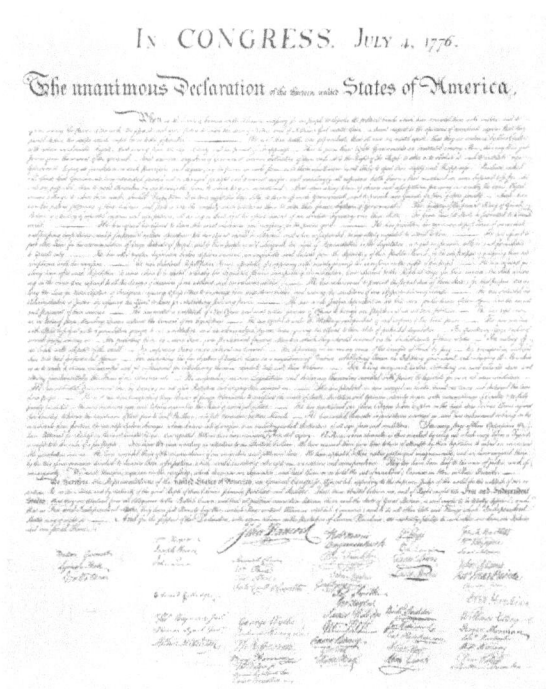

Declaration of Independence, the *Law of the Covenant*
made with the *Creator of the universe*
and the American people
1823 William Stone facsimile [595]

We are now apprised of our true history, of our nation's inception and founding as a unique republican commonwealth. Unique because it was created in covenant with Creator God to be governed by His Laws, the *Laws of Nature and of Natures God*. Because of this, America became a beacon of light in its jurisdiction of Liberty, a "city upon a hill,"[596] a light to the other nations with "a model government" of how they too

---

[594] Library of Congress, "Moses receiving the law," https://www.loc.gov/item/2007684725/ This work is in the public domain

[595] *Wikimedia Commons*, s.v. "United States Declaration of Independence.jpg,"
https://commons.wikimedia.org/wiki/File:United_States_Declaration_of_Independence.jpg This work is in the public domain

[596] The phrase "city on a hill that cannot be hid" is a metaphor used by Jesus (*Matthew 5:14 ~ Ye are the light of the world. A city that is set on an hill cannot be hid.*). It refers to a city positioned on top of a hill that is meant to be seen and found even in the darkness of night. The phrase is also used by Puritan leader John Winthrop in a sermon to warn his fellow Puritans that their new community would be "*as a city upon a hill, the eyes of all people are upon us.*" This means that if the Puritans failed to uphold their covenant with Creator God, then their sins and errors would be exposed for all the world to see.

can achieve a society and culture of Liberty and prosper with happy lives (happiness is the cause of God). This speaks of our mandate in dominion over all the earth[597] and the *Great Commission*.[598]

We understand that as Creator God's covenant people by faith in Christ individually and as a nation based on His rule of law that we have a right to be ruled by His Laws rather than be ruled by carnal men who uphold the doctrine of the *Divine Right of Kings* and who think they are gods. Men and women who hold a pagan idea of man and government and espouse a global agenda of domination which includes chaos, death, and destruction.

We have reviewed the story of our early fathers exercising wisdom from above as they discerned the times from a *Biblical and Providential worldview*. We saw their source of all Liberty — internal and external — to be the *Word of God,* the Holy Bible — the *Textbook of Liberty* for all men. We witnessed how they reasoned from Biblical stories and *Old Testament* characters of God's covenant people in following His ways and acting by faith in their right and duty to repel tyranny or tyrant that rebels against the Creator and causes harm to His covenant people. How our fathers reasoned from the counsel of God's Word that to <u>not</u> confront the rebels against the God of heaven to recover their God-given liberties would bring a curse or judgment of God upon themselves.

We have presented and reviewed our modern-day enemies, those who rebel against God as they practice witchcraft in their esoteric mystery religions done in secret settings. We understand their belief system and their god, Lucifer, along with their pursuit to maintain domination throughout the globe. Their strategy has been through infiltration of our country and that of the world while capturing all areas or spheres of influence inclusive of Religion/Church, Family, Government/Law, Education, Business/Economics, Media, and the Arts/Entertainment.[599]

Why was there judgment and a pronounced sentence on the American Republic by the *Supreme Judge of the world*? As we go forward in presentation our answer will be made clear. How did Satan gain a foothold in America but by the People violating the Covenant of the *Declaration of Independence*.

In recalling the first of the five derivative principles of the *Laws of Nature and of Nature's God,* the law form of the American Republic, "*that people are all created by God, and that by virtue of the circumstance are therefore entitled to be treated equally before the law,*"[600] our Founding Fathers <u>as a whole</u> were not successful in

---

[597] *Genesis 1:26* ~ And God said, Let us make man in our image, after our likeness: and <u>let them have dominion</u> over the fish of the sea, and over the fowl of the air, and over the cattle, and <u>over all the earth</u>, and over every creeping thing that creepeth upon the earth.

[598] *Matthew 28:18-20* ~ *¹⁸And Jesus came and spake unto them, saying, All power is given unto me in heaven and in earth. ¹⁹<u>Go ye therefore, and teach all nations</u>, baptizing them in the name of the Father, and of the Son, and of the Holy Ghost: ²⁰ <u>teaching them to observe all things whatsoever I have commanded you</u>: and, lo, I am with you always, even unto the end of the world. Amen.*

[599] Lance Walnau, "7 Mountain Strategy Explained," Lance Walnau YouTube; Os Hillman, "Impacting the 7 Mountains of Culture: A New Move of God," Feb 19, 2019, godtv.com; Ray Edwards, "The Seven Mountains," June 2, 2013, rayedwards.com; Curt Landry, "What are the 7 Mountains of Influence?," July 2, 2022, Curtlandry.com; GotQuestions Staff, "What is the seven mountain mandate, and is it biblical?," gotquestions.org

[600] There are five derivative principles of the Laws of Nature and of Nature's God. They are **first,** <u>that people are all created by God, and that by virtue of this circumstance are therefore entitled to be treated equally before the law</u>. **Second**, all people are endowed by God with certain unalienable rights. **Third**, the people are also endowed with the right to govern themselves according to their written consent. **Fourth,** the people retain the right to alter or abolish an unlawful form of government as an

recognizing the humanity and dignity of the Native American people as well as the Black slaves. Though the *slave trade* was ended in 1808, every effort extended to end the *institution of slavery* was not.

How did our Creator judge the sins of our fathers as He says in His Word, visiting their iniquity to the fourth generation[601] of which began with the scourge of civil war (1861-1865 — 4 generations forward x a 40 Biblical-year generation = 160 years, arriving at the *Baby Boomer* generation, born 1946-1964, being that fourth generation). As done in *Old Testament* times, God's people were put in slavery and ruled by a foreign people for a sentence of time until their rulers became cruel taskmasters and the people cried out to God in repentance. God would hear their cry and send a deliverer and then destroy the cruel taskmasters for their hardness of heart toward His people. As nothing is new under the sun, we can expect this Biblical pattern to repeat, however, it will be through the *Body of Christ,* His covenant people, taking back the Kingdom of Heaven on earth.

Ecclesiastes 1:9 ~ The thing that hath been, it is that which shall be; and that which is done is that which shall be done: and there is no new thing under the sun.

Matthew 11:12 ~ And from the days of John the Baptist until now the kingdom of heaven suffereth violence, and the violent take it by force.

We can be certain of Divine intervention and assistance as we go about our Father's business and work to restore the Kingdom. We can count on a harvest of souls to be added to the Kingdom. As we have a living hope to live to see the *Second Coming of Christ,* we must do our part in our callings until He returns.[602]

Matthew 13:30 ~ Let both grow together until the harvest: and in the time of harvest I will say to the reapers, Gather ye together first the tares, and bind them in bundles to burn them: but gather the wheat into my barn.

Revelation 14:15 ~ And another angel came out of the temple, crying with a loud voice to him that sat on the cloud, Thrust in thy sickle, and reap: for the time is come for thee to reap; for the harvest of the earth is ripe.

Acts 3:20-21 ~ [20]And he shall send Jesus Christ, which before was preached unto you: [21]Whom the heaven must receive until the times of restitution of all things, which God hath spoken by the mouth of all his holy prophets since the world began.

Luke 19:13 ~ And he called his ten servants, and delivered them ten pounds, and said unto them, Occupy till I come.

In regard to the areas of influence in culture and society, we have seen the effect of the damage done by the pagan infiltrators who hate Liberty and love bondage, contrived in their plan to destroy Liberty. To name a few:

---

exercise of self-government. **Fifth,** the people are free to organize the civil government's powers in such a way as to secure their happiness. Kerry L. Morgan, "The Laws of Nature and of Nature's God; The Cornerstone of Inalienable Rights," accessed April 2, 2021, https://lonang.com/commentaries/conlaw/organizing/cornerstone-of-inalienable-rights/

[601] *Numbers 14:18 ~ The Lord is longsuffering, and of great mercy, forgiving iniquity and transgression, and by no means clearing the guilty, <u>visiting the iniquity of the fathers upon the children unto the third and fourth generation</u>.*

[602] *Titus 2:13-14 ~ [13] Looking for that blessed hope, and the glorious appearing of the great God and our Saviour Jesus Christ; [14] Who gave himself for us, that he might redeem us from all iniquity, and purify unto himself a peculiar people, zealous of good works.*

One. Religion/Church — Government inserting itself in the church (through the deception of *501c3* incorporation originating because of the 1954 *Johnson Amendment*); the *whole counsel of God* not preached or taught.

Two. Family — its disintegration while morality and virtue are lost.

Three. Government/Law — Infiltration of foreign law — *Uniform Commercial Code* (UCC); corruption of the court system; diminishing the property rights of the people; manipulation of the monetary system — the *Federal Reserve Act* (1913-1914) which eventually became *debt money* that was turned into *legal tender*; government seeking to disarm the people while the government remains armed.

Four. Education — Biblical principles/Creation no longer taught and instead the pagan religion of *Secular Humanism* and the *theory of evolution* is now taught in our schools.

Five. Business/Economics — Business corporations have risen up and monopolized all industry extracting the wealth of the Middle Class while poisoning and perverting our food and products.

Six. Media — Lies, filth and propaganda are broadcast while brainwashing the masses.

Seven. Arts/Entertainment — There is virtually nothing wholesome or holy that is produced that can be set before our eyes.

We now recognize — by what has been revealed as th *Rulers of Evil's* plan of continued Domination to be a malignant and pernicious design under the guise of what's called "Sustainable Development"[603] of which is a false storyline that's been fabricated in order to control the masses and to keep the American People's true history and knowledge secreted away from them and their children. Our history is our heritage — and our birthright!

Hosea 4:6 ~ My people are destroyed for lack of knowledge: because thou hast rejected knowledge, I will also reject thee, that thou shalt be no priest to me: seeing thou hast forgotten the law of thy God, I will also forget thy children.

America has experienced foreign and domestic interference along with obstruction of justice as evidenced by the stolen *2020 Presidential Election* in which our domestic enemies claimed the victory. Could we possibly think that our nation would even have four years to survive this counterfeit jurisdiction and that America would recover if we do not heed the knowledge put before us now and act on it?!

It is necessary to again revert to and consider the wisdom of our nation's fathers while we reason together from their insight and experiential knowledge. We will "hear" the *wisdom from above* as we reason together with our early fathers such as Charles Finney, Frederick Douglass, Francis Grimké, Samuel Adams, Edmund Burke, Patrick Henry, John Adams, William Bradford, Daniel Webster, Joseph Story, Benjamin Rush, and Samuel Landon. Along with an introduction to their background, character, and position, a sound impression will in effect bring their words to life.

---

[603] "At the U.N. Earth Summit in Rio de Janeiro in 1992 a program of sustainable development known as U.N. Agenda 21 was introduced to an unsuspecting world. This far ranging U.N. program called for a complete transformation of society wherein private property, individual liberty, and God given (unalienable) rights would no longer exist and mankind would succumb to a totalitarian one world socialist/Marxist government that would control every aspect of our lives from cradle to grave." Dan Happel, "Private Property—cornerstone of freedom," June 15, 2021, www.danhappel.com

We recount the great evangelist, Charles Finney (1792-1875), who had been a Freemason as a young man while studying law in college at the time when he experienced a tremendous conversion to Christ and was compelled to defect from the secret society. Because of Finney's knowledge of law he well understood the enormous obstruction of justice that concerned the scandalous end of another defecting Freemason. William Morgan sought to expose the atrocious, immoral oaths of the secret society by publishing them in a book. We recall that it was in 1826 when "the brotherhood of the Craft" murdered William Morgan and the people of his hometown of Batavia, New York were prevented from seeing the prosecution of those involved because of the depth of obstruction of justice that occurred.

Reverend Finney recounted the story in his 1869 book, *The Character, Claims, and Practical Workings of Freemasonry*. Because of the national outcry of this scandal that occurred between 1826 and 1830, forty-five thousand Freemasons publicly renounced this luciferian religion. Finney pointed out that God responded by pouring out His Spirit in a profound way. Charles Finney led the charge and gained the reputation of being the prodigious leader of this *Second Great Awakening*.

In his story 40 years and a generation later in 1869, Finney sounded the alarm as he explained that the same thing was happening all over again with a revival of Freemasonry. The *Union of States* still recovering from having been divided in civil war and traumatized by the assassination of President Lincoln, Freemasons successfully infiltrated our national government and all of its institutions. Through orchestrated wickedness, "the brotherhood of the Craft" managed to gain control and have ruled our country as a *Deep State/Shadow Government* ever since.[604]

Reverend Charles Finney[605]
circa early 19th century

How did they pull off this great deception? Where was the Church? Who was responsible for not correcting this atrocity that stole our God-given Liberty — Civil and Religious — while demoralizing society, the citizenry? In 1873, Reverend Finney published an article, "The Decay of Conscience," in *The Independent*, and points to the pulpit…

> "Brethren, our preaching will bear its legitimate fruits. If immorality prevails in the land, the fault is ours in a great degree. If there is a decay of conscience, the pulpit is responsible for it. If the public press lacks moral discrimination, the pulpit is responsible for it. If the church is degenerate and worldly, the pulpit is responsible for it. If the world loses its interest in religion, the pulpit is responsible for it. If Satan rules in our halls of legislation, the pulpit is responsible for it. If our politics become so corrupt that the very foundations of our

---

[604] Rev. C. G. Finney, *The Character, Claims, and Practical Workings of Freemasonry*, (Cincinnati: Western Tract and Book Society, 1869) Chapter II: Scrap of History
[605] Charles Finney, ponderingprinciples.com, This work is in the public domain

government are ready to fall away, the pulpit is responsible for it. Let us not ignore this fact, my dear brethren; but let us lay it to heart, and be thoroughly awake to our responsibility in respect to the morals of this nation.[606]

It was in 1835, through his *Lectures on Revivals*, that Finney admonished the Church concerning their responsibility and duty in participating in politics:

"The church must take right ground in regard to politics. Do not suppose, now, that I am going to preach a political sermon, or that I wish to have you join and get up a Christian party in politics. No, I do not believe in that. But the time has come that Christians must vote for honest men, and take consistent ground in politics, or the Lord will curse them. They must be honest men themselves, and instead of voting for a man because he belongs to their party, Bank or Anti-Bank, Jackson, or Anti-Jackson, they must find out whether he is honest and upright, and fit to be trusted. They must let the world see that the church will uphold no man in office, who is known to be a knave [a dishonest man], or an adulterer, or a Sabbath-breaker, or a gambler. Such is the spread of intelligence and the facility of communication in our country, that every man can know for whom he gives his vote. And if he will give his vote only for honest men, the country will be obliged to have upright rulers… As on the subject of slavery and temperance, so on this subject, the church must act right or the country will be ruined. God cannot sustain this free and blessed country, which we love and pray for, unless the church will take right ground. Politics are a part of religion in such a country as this, and Christians must do their duty to the country as a part of their duty to God. It seems sometimes as if the foundations of the nation were becoming rotten, and Christians seem to act as if they thought God did not see what they do in politics. But I tell you, he does see it, and he will bless or curse this nation, according to the course they take."[607]

Charles Finney [608]
circa mid-19th century

*REMEMBER! ALL GOVERNMENT SPRINGS FROM RELIGION!

AMERICA WAS FOUNDED ON BIBLICAL CHRISTIANITY, THE RELIGION OF LIBERTY.

Were there any other voices that "cried out in the wilderness" while also pointing out the true direction? Let's look at a couple.

---

[606] Charles G. Finney, President, "The Decay of Conscience," *The Independent of New York,* December 4, 1873, as sourced as original by https://www.gospeltruth.net/1868_75Independent/731204_conscience.htm

[607] Charles Grandison Finney, *Lectures on Revivals of Religion*, ed. William G. McLoughlin, (Cambridge: The Belknap Press of Harvard University Press, 1960) pp. 9–12, 293–305, sourced as original by https://wwnorton.com/college/history/archive/resources/documents/ch13_02.htm

[608] *Wikimedia Commons,* s.v. "Charles g finney.jpg," version of *Christian History* vol VII, n.4, issue 20 This work is in the public domain

Reverend Frederick Douglass (1817-1895) was a former slave that became a commanding abolitionist and spokesman for all slaves. Thousands of people were affected and experienced a change in attitude toward the value of human life because of his powerful orations exposing the silent scream of the enslaved. Douglass became a great civil rights leader and pointed out,

> *"I have one great political idea... That idea is an old one. It is widely and generally assented to; nevertheless, it is very generally trampled upon and disregarded. The best expression of it, I have found in the Bible. It is in substance, 'Righteousness exalteth a nation; sin is a reproach to any people.' [Proverbs 14:34] This constitutes my politics...and the whole of my politics... I feel it my duty to do all in my power to infuse this idea into the public mind, that it may speedily be recognized and practiced upon by our people."[609]*

Reverend Frederick Douglass [610]

There is another voice of wisdom that articulated how America would lose her jurisdiction of Liberty, which is maintained only by keeping the Creator's laws and moral principles.

Reverend Francis Grimké (1850-1937) was a Presbyterian minister in Washington, DC, and a leading advocate of civil rights. A former slave, Grimké was born to a wealthy landowner and his slave mistress. For more than half a century, he was regarded as one of the leading African American clergy of his era as well as a fiery orator. In a sermon preached in 1909, Reverend Grimké warned,

> *"If the time ever comes when we shall go to pieces, it will ...be...from inward corruption, from the disregard of right principles... from losing sight of the fact that 'righteousness exalteth a nation, but that sin is a reproach to any people.' [Proverbs 14:34] ...The secession of the Southern States in 1860 was a small matter compared with the secession of the Union itself from the great principles enunciated in the Declaration of Independence, in the Golden Rule, in the Ten Commandments, in the Sermon on the Mount. Unless we hold, and hold firmly to these great fundamental principles of righteousness...our Union... will be "only a covenant with death and an agreement with hell." [611]*

Reverend Francis James Grimké, D.D.[612]

---

[609] Frederick Douglass, "The Frederick Douglass Papers," John Blassingame, editor (New Haven: Yale University Press, 1982), Vol. 2, p. 397, from a speech delivered at Ithaca, New York, October 14th, 1852.
[610] *Wikimedia Commons,* s.v. "File:Frederick Douglass ambrotype (1856).jpg," This work is in the public domain
[611] Rev. Francis J. Grimke, D.D., from "Equality of Right for All Citizens, Black and White, Alike," March 7, 1909, published in *Masterpieces of Negro Eloquence*, Alice Moore Dunbar, ed. (New York: The Bookery Publishing Company, 1914) 348-349
[612] *Wikimedia Commons* s.v., "Francis James Grimke," This work is in the public domain

Reverend Grimké also pointed to how the righteousness of a nation is measured:

> *"How is the righteousness of a nation measured? By its public policies, and by their conformity to God's standards."*[613]

From the late 1800s up until 1954 (when the government inserted itself in the churches via *501c3* State government incorporation), there were periodic and notable, profound outpourings of God's Spirit. In his book, *God's Generals: Why They Succeeded and Why Some Failed,* Roberts Liardon presents this question to the reader:

> *"Are you a leader? If you want to fight the good fight of faith for God, then you will want to start by studying the lives of God's Generals – men and women who were dynamically empowered by the Holy Spirit to bring a revival of God's miraculous presence, worldwide!"*[614]

Roberts Liardon presents fascinating biographies of the following:

> John Alexander Dowie, "The Healing Apostle."
> Maria Woodworth Etter, "Demonstrator of the Spirit"
> Evan Roberts, "Welsh Revivalist"
> Charles Parham, "The Father of Pentecost"
> William J. Seymour, "The Catalyst of Pentecost"
> John G. Lake, "A man of Healing"
> Aimee Semple McPherson, "A woman of Destiny"
> Smith Wigglesworth, "Apostle of Faith"
> Kathryn Kuhlman, "The Woman Who Believed in Miracles"

Since 1954, God's Generals are seemingly no more. This is not a coincidence! The *Old Testament* prophet Daniel knew this would occur and said it would occur because there would be a division.[615]

Based on the authority of God's Word, *Ezra 7:24*[616] was the only authority that was needed to clarify and establish tax exemption. Inserting government status on the church meeting house was crafted as "great deception" by Satan and his minions in order to prevent preaching *the whole counsel of God* including His government and thereby weakening the power of the *Body of Christ*. We now understand and perceive that the worship centers across America are essentially paralyzed, yoked to a government that sprang forth in deception and because of it has been blinded by deception.[617]

---

[613] Rev. Francis J. Grimke, D.D., from "Equality of Right for All Citizens, Black and White, Alike," March 7, 1909, published in *Masterpieces of Negro Eloquence*, Alice Moore Dunbar, ed. (New York: The Bookery Publishing Company, 1914) 348-349
[614] Roberts Liardon, *God's Generals: Why They Succeeded and Why Some Failed*, (New Kensington, Whitaker House, 1996)
[615] *Daniel 2:41* ~ And whereas thou sawest the feet and toes, part of potters' clay, and part of iron, the kingdom shall be divided; but there shall be in it of the strength of the iron, forasmuch as thou sawest the iron mixed with miry clay.
[616] *Ezra 7:24* ~ Also we certify you, that touching any of the priests and Levites, singers, porters, Nethinims, or ministers of this house of God, it shall not be lawful to impose toll, tribute, or custom, upon them.
[617] *2 Peter 1:3-11* ~ ³According as his divine power hath given unto us all things that pertain unto life and godliness, through the knowledge of him that hath called us to glory and virtue: ⁴Whereby are given unto us exceeding great and precious promises: that by these ye might be partakers of the divine nature, having escaped the corruption that is in the world through lust. ⁵And

Based on all of the above we are driven to ask the following questions:

> How does America get righteousness back to exalt this nation?
> How can America once again be "a city on a hill which cannot be hid?"
> How can America clean-up the TV programming and clean-up Smart phones?
> How can American schools have modest dress codes?
> How can our children have Christian public-school teachers that will lead their classes in prayer and teach Bible curriculum?
> How can sex-trafficking and slavery finally be eliminated?
> How can America do away with the Prison Industry?

Give serious heed to what is being asked and reason it out. The American People can continue to attend church on Saturday or Sunday like they have been for the past 150+ years since the Corporate Democracy was established, though these things will not change!

> How can the American People rid themselves from "fakenews?"
> How can the American People rid themselves from the proven harm of pornography?
> How can the American People rid themselves from adultery and fornication?
> How can the American People rid themselves from gambling?
> How can families be wholesome with great morals?

The American People can continue to go to church meetings in their buildings of worship every Wednesday night and these things will remain the same!

> How can the American People have a Biblical culture?
> How can the American People enjoy *Civil and Religious Liberty*?
> How can the American People practice Virtue and Biblical Christianity seven days a week?
> How can American students attend universities and colleges and graduate with a *Biblical worldview*? A *Providential worldview*?

Prayer meetings can continue to be held one night a week, as has been done for the last several years and—with all honesty in reasoning this through—will these things really change?

> How can the American people have sacred weddings and marriages?
> How can the American People experience a drastic decline in divorces and preserve the family unit?
> How can the People enjoy true happiness in America?

---

beside this, giving all diligence, add to your faith virtue; and to virtue knowledge; ⁶And to knowledge temperance; and to temperance patience; and to patience godliness; ⁷And to godliness brotherly kindness; and to brotherly kindness charity. ⁸For if these things be in you, and abound, they make you that ye shall neither be barren nor unfruitful in the knowledge of our Lord Jesus Christ. ⁹But he that lacketh these things is blind, and cannot see afar off, and hath forgotten that he was purged from his old sins. ¹⁰Wherefore the rather, brethren, give diligence to make your calling and election sure: for if ye do these things, ye shall never fall: ¹¹ For so an entrance shall be ministered unto you abundantly into the everlasting kingdom of our Lord and Saviour Jesus Christ.

AMERICA NEEDS "GOD'S SOLUTION FOR AMERICA!"

Righteousness must exalt this nation! There must be a nationwide cleansing from wickedness! How is that going to happen?

It is now revealed <u>who has been our enemy</u>. That enemy has made all of us slaves, stripped us of our God-given rights, and even made us into "unnatural persons," corporations that operate in commerce through our artificial "strawman."[618] That enemy took away the *Declaration of Independence* and our State and national constitutions. By passing the *Organic Act of 1871* into law, the newly formed government is in all actuality a Corporation with a business name, THE UNITED STATES OF AMERICA, INC.[619] That enemy changed our form of governance from a representative republic to a corporate democracy without the knowledge or consent of the American People and this corporate government is run by Freemasons who worship Satan and operate in witchcraft!

The fruit of unrighteousness sewn in deception and continuous lies have now brought us to the precipice of destruction in having been deceived and lied to for generations. God's government with a law form based on the *Laws of Nature and of Natures God*, the Republic commonwealth, must be raised up and restored by *We the People*. The American People must embrace the *Declaration of Independence* and our original national and State constitutions and recognize them as a covenant with Creator God just as our Founding Fathers did. That is what made America the greatest nation in the world.

REPENTANCE IS THE KEY AND IS NECESSARY!

When we as a nation of people put away the "Old Man" and embrace the "New Man" (in Christ), God gives us the gift of righteousness.[620]

> *Romans 6:19 ~ I speak after the manner of men because of the infirmity of your flesh: for as ye have yielded your members servants to uncleanness and to iniquity unto iniquity; <u>even so now yield your members servants to righteousness unto holiness</u>.*

> *Romans 6:22 ~ But now being made free from sin, and become <u>servants</u> to God, ye have your fruit unto holiness, and the end everlasting life.*

> *Romans 7:6 ~ But now we are delivered from the law, that being dead wherein we were held; that we should serve in newness of spirit, and not in the oldness of the letter.*

We are then to live according to *Romans* chapter eight.

---

[618] Freedom-school.com, Strawman: *"Your straw man (Strawman) is an artificial person created by law at the of your birth, the inscription of an ALL-CAPITAL LETTERS NAME on your birth certificate/document, which is a document of title and a negotiable instrument. Your lawful, Christian name of birthright was replaced with a legal, corporate name of deceit and fraud. Your name in upper and lower case letters (Jane Mary Doe) has been answering when the legal person, your name in ALL-CAPTIAL LETTERS (JANE MARY DOE), is addressed, and therefore the two have been recognized as being one and the same. When, you Jane Mary Doe, the lawful being distinguish yourself as another party than the legal person, the two will be separated."* https://freedom-school.com/aware/your-straw-man-is-an-artificial-person.html

[619] Delaware Department of State, Division of Corporations, File Number 4525682, THE UNITED STATES OF AMERICA, INC., in Filing History as "Incorp Delaware Stock Co.", https://delecorp.delaware.gov/tin/controller

[620] *Ephesians 4:24 ~ And that ye put on the new man, which after God is created in righteousness and true holiness.*

Romans 8:11 ~ But if the Spirit of him that raised up Jesus from the dead dwell in you, he that raised up Christ from the dead shall also quicken your mortal bodies by his Spirit that dwelleth in you.

Not only did Christ give us the gift of righteousness after repentance, not only did He give us the "New Man" (Christ is to live in our hearts), He also made us sons and daughters of God. He gave us a new identity! From then on, we are to live by faith and recognize that all the fullness of God is inside of us through an earnest, or deposit of His Holy Spirit.[621]

Having received our new identity in Christ, He has also given us His authority and, as led by His Spirit, so that His power can work through us.

2 Corinthians 4:7 ~ But we have this treasure in earthen vessels, that the excellency of the <u>power</u> may be of God, and not of us.

Ephesians 3:20 ~ Now unto him that is able to do exceeding abundantly above all that we ask or think, according to the <u>power</u> that worketh in us,

Colossians 1:10-11 ~ [10] That ye might walk worthy of the Lord unto all pleasing, being fruitful in every good work, and increasing in the knowledge of God; [11] <u>Strengthened with all might, according to his glorious power</u>, unto all patience and longsuffering with joyfulness;

REMEMBER: ALL GOVERNMENTS ARE DERIVED FROM A PARTICULAR RELIGION!

We understand and know that repentance is a gift and by faith in Christ we receive the gift of righteousness unto holiness. He gives us a new identity to become His sons and daughters. He gives us His authority and His power <u>to serve Him and to serve one another</u>.

We understand that the American Republic, a commonwealth, a state in which <u>the sovereign power</u> is lodged <u>in representatives</u> elected by the people, differs from democracy or a democratic state where the people exercise <u>the power</u> of sovereignty <u>in person</u>. We now proceed to the next heart of the matter.

It was those of the *Illuminati*, the *High Priests of the Luciferian Creed* who rule from the *Synogue of Satan*, who rule over the Freemasons and were behind introducing the "Darwinian Theory" to the American People when it was published as a book in 1859.[622] Later, it would be referred to by the 28th President of the UNITED STATES (Corporation), Woodrow Wilson, as the "Darwinian Principle." Next interjected was "the Big Bang Theory," and then (the religion of) *Secular Humanism*, along with the influence of "situational ethics." This great stealth and deception were introduced using the method of *Gradualism*, making small changes happen over time which have made a very large change overall with the goal of indoctrinating American children to not believe in God or the *Creator of the universe*.[623]

The enemies of mankind, the *Illuminists*, knew that if they could influence us and our posterity, the future generations, to believe in Darwin's *theory of evolution*, or another means in displacing the story of *Biblical*

---

[621] *2 Corinthians 1:21-22 ~ [21]Now it is God who establishes both us and you in Christ. He anointed us, [22]placed His seal on us, and put His Spirit in our hearts as a pledge of what is to come.*
[622] Carr, *Pawns in the Game,* Ch 3, Ch 16
[623] Prof. Paul Moreno, Hillsdale College Online Courses, "Progressivism," *History 102: American Heritage—From Colonial Settlement to the Reagan Revolution*

Creation, then they would achieve their goal of deceiving the people into belief that there is no Creator God and therefore no need for the *Ten Commandments* and no need for Divine law, in particular, the "*Laws of Nature and of Nature's God.*"

Following is the authority on why it is imperative for you and your family to embrace *Biblical Creation*:

> *Colossians 1:15-19* ~ *[15]Who is the image of the invisible God, the firstborn of every creature: [16] For by him were all things created, that are in heaven, and that are in earth, visible and invisible, whether they be thrones, or dominions, or principalities, or powers: all things were created by him, and for him: [17] And he is before all things, and by him all things consist. [18] And he is the head of the body, the church: who is the beginning, the firstborn from the dead; that in all things he might have the preeminence. [19] For it pleased the Father that in him should all fulness dwell;*

What is a *frame of reference* as it relates to a *perspective*? It's a lens through which one sees the world. It is a set of preconceived ideas through which an individual sees the world. The more accurate one's frame of reference, the more accurately they will see the world.[624]

A *premise* is the basis on which something is to be considered. A *premise* is the first proposition on which rest subsequent reasonings. It is the first thought that leads to a later thought. A *premise* is a proposition supporting, or helping to support, a conclusion. This is important to understand because every idea has a premise, and every belief system has an underlying philosophy.

A *philosophy* is the rational investigation of the truths and principles of being, knowledge, or conduct. The philosophy or thought process is "the lens" through which that belief system filters and comes from some underlying philosophy. What's important to grasp is that <u>every philosophy (or belief system) has a religious premise</u>.[625] There is cause to pause with the stunning realization that congressmen use a religious premise while voting on legislative matters.

When we have understanding, we also have ability to reason why people think like they do. Why they act like they do. Why they talk like they do. Let's take this subject a little farther to more fully comprehend the depth of it.

God's Divine reasoning, His perfect thinking for His people, is involved with His true laws. Adding up all of His Divine reasoning, along with His perfect laws, and His perfect teaching, equates to God's Divine wisdom. Christians that love God study His nature and His perfect Person by spending time reading His Word. Studying the *Word of God* leads to an understanding of God's heavenly reasoning as well as in taking on God's wisdom. Wisdom and understanding are pinnacle in the *Kingdom of God*.[626]

---

[624] Dr. Marlene McMillian, *Five Pillars of Liberty*, "Pillar One: Truth," (Fort Worth: Liberty View Media 2011) 31-49
[625] Ibid.
[626] *Proverbs 4:5-7* ~ *[5]Get wisdom, get understanding: forget it not; neither decline from the words of my mouth. [6] Forsake her not, and she shall preserve thee: love her, and she shall keep thee.[7] Wisdom is the principal thing; therefore get wisdom: and with all thy getting get understanding.*

In contrast, there is an earthly wisdom as well as an earthly reasoning. It is important to understand and also consider that there are two sources of wisdom. So, to build on the study of *frame of reference*, let's study wisdom.

> *James 3:13-16 ~ ¹³Who is a wise man and endued [equipped] with knowledge among you? let him shew out of a good conversation [by his good life] his works with meekness of wisdom. ¹⁴ But if ye have bitter envying and strife [quarreling] in your hearts, glory not [do not be proud], and lie not against the truth. ¹⁵ This wisdom descendeth not from above, but is earthly, sensual, devilish. ¹⁶ For where envying and strife is, there is confusion and every evil work.* [Emphasis added]

People who live in envy and strife have earthly wisdom and are functioning in their sin nature (the *Old Man*) and operating carnally in the flesh.[627] This is the opposite of "living in the Spirit."[628] These people have not had a living faith encounter with Jesus Christ, Yeshua HaMaschiah. According to *Galatians 5:16-21*[629] these people with earthly wisdom are very capable of practicing *"adultery, fornication, uncleanness, lasciviousness, idolatry, witchcraft, hatred, variance, emulations, wrath, strife, seditions, heresies, envyings, murders, drunkenness, revellings and such like."* These people shall not enter the Kingdom of God as they are not born again of the Spirit of God by a living faith in Christ Jesus. They are in need of a schoolmaster as they've been deprived of this knowledge because of a lack of exposure and teaching of the *Word of God* and His *Commandments*. These are people that have earthly wisdom.

> *Galatians 3:24 ~ Wherefore the law was our schoolmaster to bring us unto Christ, that we might be justified by faith.*

What was the schoolmaster that brought Israel, our fathers, to Christ? The *Ten Commandments*? Yes, for without the Torah (the first five books of the Hebrew Bible) leading the Jewish People (and in fact all mankind) to an understanding that we all have sinned and come short of God's expectations for each of us,[630] then we would not understand that we are in need of a Savior, the One Who can redeem us from our unrighteousness.[631]

---

[627] *Romans 8:5-8 ~ ⁵ For they that are after the flesh do mind the things of the flesh; but they that are after the Spirit the things of the Spirit. ⁶ For to be carnally minded is death; but to be spiritually minded is life and peace. ⁷ Because the carnal mind is enmity against God: for it is not subject to the law of God, neither indeed can be. ⁸ So then they that are in the flesh cannot please God.*

[628] See *Romans 8; Galatians 5:22-24 ~ ²² But the fruit of the Spirit is love, joy, peace, longsuffering, gentleness, goodness, faith, ²³ Meekness, temperance: against such there is no law. ²⁴ And they that are Christ's have crucified the flesh with the affections and lusts.*

[629] *Galatians 5:16-21 ~ ¹⁶ This I say then, Walk in the Spirit, and ye shall not fulfil the lust of the flesh. ¹⁷ For the flesh lusteth against the Spirit, and the Spirit against the flesh: and these are contrary the one to the other: so that ye cannot do the things that ye would. ¹⁸ But if ye be led of the Spirit, ye are not under the law. ¹⁹ Now the works of the flesh are manifest, which are these; Adultery, fornication, uncleanness, lasciviousness, ²⁰ Idolatry, witchcraft, hatred, variance, emulations, wrath, strife, seditions, heresies, ²¹ Envyings, murders, drunkenness, revellings, and such like: of the which I tell you before, as I have also told you in time past, that they which do such things shall not inherit the kingdom of God.*

[630] *Romans 3:23 ~ For all have sinned, and come short of the glory of God;*

[631] *Romans 3:24-26 ~ ²⁴ Being justified freely by his grace through the redemption that is in Christ Jesus: ²⁵ Whom God hath set forth to be a propitiation through faith in his blood, to declare his righteousness for the remission of sins that are past, through the forbearance of God; ²⁶ To declare, I say, at this time his righteousness: that he might be just, and the justifier of him which believeth in Jesus.*

This atonement for our sins was pictured by the ceremonial law of sacrifices. Every year the high priest went into the holy of holies with the blood of the lamb and he made atonement for the sins of the nation. And every time that atonement was made, it was a reminder of the need of the shedding of blood for the atonement of sin. When Christ came, the ceremonial law was no longer necessary, because He made the complete sacrifice so that we might be <u>justified by faith</u>. Man was never justified by <u>the deeds</u> of the Law.

That ceremonial law of the lamb performed each year by the high priest, for the sins of the people and that justified our fathers, had to be repeated every year. The day was to come when the type was to be fulfilled in the Antitype.[632] When Christ came, He offered himself as the perfect sacrifice for sin, and then with the *New Covenant* He made, His Word was to identify our sin,[633] and hence our need for the Messiah who forgives that sin. This is what Paul was saying in *Galatians 3:24* ~

> *Galatians 3:24 ~ Wherefore the law was our schoolmaster to bring us unto Christ, that we might be justified by faith.*

However, according to the Holy Bible, that isn't the only purpose of the *Word of God*. It also shows how to walk in righteousness once Christ has forgiven us of our sins. It also shows us how to love God with all of our heart, soul, mind and strength and our neighbor as ourself, as Jesus declared in *Mark 12:28-31*.[634] Love is also the fulfilling of the law, as Paul states in *Romans 13:8-10*.[635] The *Word of God* also shows us how to know God intimately (*1 John 2:3*)[636] and how to have the love of God in us (*1 John 2:5*)[637] and how to walk as Jesus walked (*1 John 2:6*).[638] The *Word of God* also shows us how to love Christ (*John 14:15*).[639] The *Word of God* also shows us how to be blessed physically in this lifetime (*Deuteronomy chapter 28*),[640] and will determine our level of spiritual rewards in the world to come (*Matthew 5:19*).[641]

---

[632] In the Bible, an antitype is a fulfillment or completion of an earlier truth revealed in the Bible. An antitype in the New Testament is foreshadowed by a type, its counterpart in the Old Testament.

[633] *1 John 3:4 ~ Whosoever committeth sin transgresseth also the law: for sin is the transgression of the law.*

[634] *Mark 12:28-31 ~ 28 And one of the scribes came, and having heard them reasoning together, and perceiving that he had answered them well, asked him, Which is the first commandment of all? 29 And Jesus answered him, The first of all the commandments is, Hear, O Israel; The Lord our God is one Lord: 30 And thou shalt love the Lord thy God with all thy heart, and with all thy soul, and with all thy mind, and with all thy strength: this is the first commandment. 31 And the second is like, namely this, Thou shalt love thy neighbour as thyself. There is none other commandment greater than these.*

[635] *Romans 13:8-10 ~ 8 Owe no man any thing, but to love one another: for he that loveth another hath fulfilled the law. 9 For this, Thou shalt not commit adultery, Thou shalt not kill, Thou shalt not steal, Thou shalt not bear false witness, Thou shalt not covet; and if there be any other commandment, it is briefly comprehended in this saying, namely, Thou shalt love thy neighbour as thyself. 10 Love worketh no ill to his neighbour: therefore love is the fulfilling of the law.*

[636] *1 John 2:3 ~ And hereby we do know that we know him, if we keep his commandments.*

[637] *1 John 2:5 ~ But whoso keepeth his word, in him verily is the love of God perfected: hereby know we that we are in him.*

[638] *1 John 2:6 ~ He that saith he abideth in him ought himself also so to walk, even as he walked.*

[639] *John 14:15 ~ If ye love me, keep my commandments.*

[640] See Deuteronomy chapter 28

[641] *Matthew 5:19 ~ Whosoever therefore shall break one of these least commandments, and shall teach men so, he shall be called the least in the kingdom of heaven: but whosoever shall do and teach them, the same shall be called great in the kingdom of heaven.*

Galatians 2:20-21 ~ 20 I am crucified with Christ: nevertheless I live; yet not I, but Christ liveth in me: and the life which I now live in the flesh I live by the faith of the Son of God, who loved me, and gave himself for me. 21 I do not frustrate the grace of God: for if righteousness come by the law, then Christ is dead in vain.

Philippians 3:9 ~ And be found in him, not having mine own righteousness, which is of the law, but that which is through the faith of Christ, the righteousness which is of God by faith:

Moving forward. There is a good chance that you have never in your lifetime heard the following from the pulpit or in the schools that you attended. Let's visit *2 Peter 1:3-11*.

2 Peter 1:3-4 ~ 3According as his divine power hath given unto us all things that pertain unto life and godliness, through the knowledge of him that hath <u>CALLED US TO GLORY AND VIRTUE</u>: 4 Whereby are given unto us exceeding great and precious promises: that by these ye might be partakers of the divine nature, having escaped the corruption that is in the world through lust. [Emphasis added]

Consider really pondering those six words written by the apostle Peter, "*called us to glory and virtue*." (*Remember, Peter walked on water!) Going on…

2 Peter 1:5 ~ And beside this, giving ALL DILIGENCE [a constant and earnest effort to accomplish], add to your faith virtue; and to virtue knowledge; [Emphasis added]

Consider what Founding Father and author of the *Declaration of Independence*, Thomas Jefferson said…

"*Educate and inform the whole mass of people. They are the only sure reliance for the preservation of our liberty.*"[642]

Portrait of Thomas Jefferson in 1791 by Charles Willson Peale [643]

This is VIRTUE

Trustworthiness	Moral excellence	Righteousness
Uprightness	Goodness	Merit
Prudence	Godly character	Charity
Respectability	Faith in God	Faithfulness
Worth	Kindness	Justice
Honor	Love	Innocence
Integrity	Purity	Temperance

---

[642] Thomas Jefferson's letter to Uriah Forrest, with Enclosure Dec 31, 1787
[643] *Wikimedia Commons, s.v.* "File:T Jefferson by Charles Willson Peale 1791 2.jpg," This work is in the public domain

> 2 Peter 1:5 ~ And beside this, giving all diligence [a constant and earnest effort to accomplish] <u>add to your faith virtue</u>; and to virtue knowledge;

What Peter was relaying was orchestrated in order, with a Holy Spirit strategy, "Add[ing] to your faith virtue" was listed first, and next listed is *knowledge*. Going on...

> 2 Peter 1:6-8 ~ ⁶ And to <u>knowledge</u> temperance; and to temperance patience; and to patience godliness; ⁷ And to godliness brotherly kindness; and to brotherly kindness charity.

Look what Peter says...

> 2 Peter 1:8-9 ~ ⁸For ***if*** these things be in you, and **abound**, they make you that ye shall neither be barren nor unfruitful in the knowledge of our Lord Jesus Christ. ⁹ <u>But he that lacketh these things is **blind**, and cannot see afar off, and hath forgotten that he was purged from his old sins</u>.

Has the pulpit been doing its job? How big are Virtue and Knowledge? Going on...

> 2 Peter 1:10 ~ Wherefore the rather, brethren, give diligence [a constant and earnest effort to accomplish] to make your calling and election sure: for <u>***if*** ye do these things, ye shall never fall</u>: ¹¹ For so an entrance shall be ministered unto you abundantly into the everlasting kingdom of our Lord and Saviour Jesus Christ.
>
> [Emphasis added]

What is this? What is Peter telling us? With all our being we must pursue Virtue and Knowledge. That's something to ponder — right?! How big is Virtue?

> Acts 14:22 ~ Confirming the souls of the disciples, and exhorting them to continue in the faith, and that we must through much tribulation enter into the kingdom of God.

Again, how big is Virtue? It is a matter of great significance that we as a people must contend for as though our lives, and the lives of those we love, depend on it.

Samuel Adams, 1834 painting[644]

Samuel Adams, *Father of the American Revolution* said that <u>liberty and happiness of the people is dependent on Virtue</u>.

"The sum of all is, if we would most truly enjoy the gift of Heaven, let us become a <u>virtuous</u> people; then shall we both deserve and enjoy it."[645]

Neither the wisest constitution nor the wisest laws will secure the liberty and happiness of a people whose manners are universally corrupt. He therefore is the truest friend to the liberty of his country who tries most to promote its <u>virtue</u> and

---

[644] *Samuel Adams in* The Works of Samuel Adams Vol I, 8th Ed., 1854, This work is in the public domain
[645] William V. Wells, *The Life and Public Services of Samuel Adams* (Boston: Little, Brown & Co., 1865) as cited in William J. Federer, *America's God and Country*, (Coppell, Texas, FAME Publishing, Inc., 1994) 23

who… will not suffer a man to be chosen into any office of power and trust who is not a wise and <u>virtuous</u> man."[646] [Emphasis added]

Edmund Burke[647]

Edmund Burke (1729-1797) was a British statesman who was known as an outstanding orator, author, and leader in Great Britain during the time of the *Revolutionary War*. Burke points out the detriment in society where virtue is absent:

"What is liberty without wisdom and without <u>virtue</u>? It is the greatest of all possible evils; for it is folly, vice, and madness, without restraint.

Men are qualified for <u>civil liberty</u> in exact proportion to their disposition to put moral chains upon their own appetites…"[648]

The *Stamp Act 1765* was an Act of the Parliament of Great Britain which imposed a direct tax on the American colonists and required that many printed materials in the colonies be produced on stamped paper from London which included an embossed revenue stamp that had to be paid for in British currency and not in colonial paper money. It was a horrendous burden imposed on the people.

Patrick Henry [649]

In May of 1765, the following was written by Patrick Henry on the back of *The Stamp Act Resolves* which was passed by the House of Burgesses (legislative body) in Virginia. Patrick Henry was the five-time governor of Virginia. What he wrote is recorded and archived in the Library of Congress. It appears that Mr. Henry wanted to impress upon future generations the final straw that caused the colonists to separate from the mother country along with the importance of Virtue in relation to the blessings of God.

"This brought on the war which finally separated the two countries and gave independence to ours. Whether this will prove a blessing or a curse, will depend upon the use our people make of the blessings, which a gracious God hath bestowed on us.

If they are wise, they will be great and happy. If they are of a contrary character, they will be miserable.

---

[646] Samuel Adams, "A political essay" printed in *The Public Advisor*, p. 1749 as cited in William J. Federer, America's God and Country Encyclopedia of Quotations, "Samuel Adams," (Coppell: FAME Publishing, Inc., 1994) 23
[647] Wikimedia s.v., "EdmundBurke1771," This work is in the public domain
[648] Edmund Burke. 1791, in "a Letter to a Member of the National Assembly." as cited in William J. Federer, America's God and Country Encyclopedia of Quotations, "Samuel Adams," (Coppell: FAME Publishing, Inc., 1994) 83
[649] *Wikimedia Commons,* s.v. "Patrick henry.JPG," This work is in the public domain

*Righteousness alone can exalt them as a nation. Reader! Whoever thou art, remember this, and in thy sphere practice **virtue** thyself, and encourage it in others."*[650]

As we practice righteousness in our individual lives, we affect our spheres of influence. When the *Body of Christ*, the *ekklesia*, practices righteousness, rather than being influenced by the world, there is a greater affect exhibited in all our spheres of influence.

John Adams[651]
"The Statesman"

In 1774, Founding Father and second President of the United States, John Adams, wrote a commentary entitled, *Novanglus: A History of the Dispute with America, from its Origin, in 1754, to the Present Time.* Adams admonished the clergy to speak out regarding public errors, saying:

> *"It is the duty of the clergy to accommodate their discourses to the times, to preach against such sins as are most prevalent, and recommend such **virtues** as are most wanted."*[652] [Emphasis added]

In review, we have looked at *frame of reference,* we have looked at *reasoning,* and the *two different wisdoms* (one earthly and one heavenly). We have also considered a teaching by the apostle Peter on Virtue. Now let's move on and consider the dream by the *Old Testament* character, Nebuchadnezzar, experienced and its recorded history in the *Old Testament*. The dream and the interpretation of to that dream were Divinely revealed to the *Old Testament* prophet, Daniel. Let's examine *Daniel 2:41-45*.

> *Daniel 2:41-42 ~ ⁴¹And whereas thou sawest the feet and toes, part of potters' clay, and part of iron, the kingdom shall be divided; but there shall be in it of the strength of the iron, forasmuch as thou sawest the iron mixed with miry clay. ⁴² And as the toes of the feet were part of iron, and part of clay, so the kingdom shall be partly strong, and partly broken.*

The ten toes are displayed as being made of both iron and clay. We will come to see and understand that this image prophetically represents the era of a kingdom that exists with the union of church and state—the Church being iron (strong) and the clay being government (weak, partly broken).

---

[650] Patrick Henry. May 1765, written on the back of the Stamp Act resolves passed in the House of Burgesses in Virginia. William Wirt Henry, *Patrick Henry—Life, Correspondence and Speeches* (NY: Burt Franklin, 1969), Vol. 1, pp. 91-91 as cited in William J. Federer, America's God and Country Encyclopedia of Quotations, "Samuel Adams," (Coppell: FAME Publishing, Inc., 1994) 289

[651] Carole Bos, "John Adams" AwesomeStories.com. giving media credit to Image online, courtesy of the abigailadams.org website

[652] John Adams, *Novanglus and Massachusettensis; or Political Essays Published in the Years 1774 AND 1775, on the Principal Points of Controversy, Between Great Britain and Her Colonies,* (Boston: Hews & Goss, 1819) 44

Moving forward with *verse 43*...

> ⁴³*And whereas thou sawest iron mixed with miry clay, they shall mingle themselves with the seed of men: but they shall not cleave one to another, even as iron is not mixed with clay.*

We can take a gallon of water and pour a quart of oil into it and be certain they will not mix. It's the same effect as iron and clay. The clay doesn't become stronger from the iron, nor does the iron become stronger from being affixed to the clay. These earthly properties do not cleave, adhere, or amalgam one to another.

Consider pondering the following very carefully. It was in 1857 when a preacher from Tennessee came to the nation's capital to present a teaching on *Daniel's Seventy Weeks*. He used a template made up of many dates that included a record of solar eclipses as well as many historical Bible dates in order to prove his point concerning the prophetic birthing of the *Declaration of Independence*.[653]

*The Old
House of Representatives*[654]

> *Church services were held in what is now called Statuary Hall from 1807 to 1857. The first services in the Capitol, held when the government moved from Philadelphia, Pennsylvania to Washington in the fall of 1800, were conducted in the "hall" of the House in the north wing of the building. In 1801 the House moved to temporary quarters in the south wing, called the "Oven," which it vacated in 1804, returning to the north wing for three years. Services were conducted in the House until after the Civil War. The Speaker's podium was used as the preacher's pulpit.*

Several members of Congress extended an invitation to this preacher to present his teaching on February 22, 1857, the anniversary of George Washington's birthday. After praise and worship, Reverend Fountain Pitts presented an astounding teaching. Because the crowd was sparse, the congressmen asked him to

---

[653] Fountain E. Pitts, *A Defence of Armageddon, or Our great country foretold in the Holy Scriptures*, (Baltimore: J.W. Bull, 1859, 1862 10th ed.)
[654] Library of Congress, Religion and the Founding of the American Republic: VI. Religion and the Federal Government, "The Old House of Representatives," This work is in the public domain

return that afternoon and present his teaching again. Reverend Pitts agreed and word was spread that afternoon as congressmen and others went throughout the city exclaiming the wonder of this astounding teaching. At 3:00 p.m. there was barely any standing room left after all seats were filled. *"Leaned theologians, civilians and statesmen have freely accredited its truthfulness, and mathematicians pronounced its chronological argument demonstration."*[655]

In addition, a newspaper reporter from the capital city's predominant newspaper, the *National Intelligencer*, wrote extensive notes and later reviewed them with Reverend Pitts. Two years later in 1859, these sermons were published as a book and the newspaper reporter's summary notes became the foreword in the book.

On February 24, 1857, you could have read in the newspaper about this astounding, amazing teaching that was presented in the Capitol building during the preceding two days. Here is an excerpt of Pitt's teaching:

> *"...so that if 70 symbolic weeks equaled 600 years and 129 days, 1290 symbolic days reached from the burning of the temple on the 189th day of the year 68, A. D., to the 4th of July, 1776; and that, making the starting-point at the occasion of the daily sacrifice, which happened, according to astronomy, at sunrise, three minutes past five o'clock, A.M., on the day the temple was burnt, the 1290 days run out at a quarter to three o'clock, P. M., on the 4th day of July, 1776; and, from the best sources of information, the Declaration of Independence was proclaimed at that hour on the glorious Fourth.*
>
> *That the United States was the fifth Government represented by the stone cut out of the mountain without hands.*
>
> *The image of Nebuchadnezzar represented the successive kingdoms of Assyria, Medo-Persia, Macedonia, and Rome;*
>
> *That the iron and clay in the feet and toes of the image, symbolized the union of Church and State under Constantine, June 19, A. D. 325;*
>
> *that the antagonism of the stone to the image smiting it on the feet, symbolized the genius of our great nation in its opposition to the union of Church and State;*
>
> *that while the stone-kingdom, or government, were not Christianity, the mountain out of which the stone was cut was Christianity.*
>
> *That the winged woman of the wilderness was an emblem of Christianity, and her man-child, to whom was given 'a rod to rule,' was an emblem of our government, arising from a pure religion;*
>
> *that this man-child, being 'caught up to heaven in the clouds,' showed the providential protection of 'our wicked should not understand.' Not only was the vision itself sealed, but the time or end of these wonders, an infant Republic."*[656]

---

[655] Fountain E. Pitts, *A Defence of Armageddon, or Our great country foretold in the Holy Scriptures*, (Baltimore: J.W. Bull, 1859, 1862 10th ed.) iii
[656] Ibid., vi-vii

Now let's look at *Daniel 2:44-45*…

> *Daniel 2:44-45 ~ ⁴⁴ And in the days of these kings [in the end times of the Last Days] shall the God of heaven set up a kingdom, which shall never be destroyed: and the kingdom shall not be left to other people, but it shall break in pieces and consume all these kingdoms, and it shall stand for ever. ⁴⁵ Forasmuch as thou sawest that the stone was cut out of the mountain without hands, and that it brake in pieces the iron, the brass, the clay, the silver, and the gold; the great God hath made known to the king what shall come to pass hereafter: and the dream is certain, and the interpretation thereof sure.* [Emphasis added]

REMEMBER — EVERY GOVERNMENT IS DERIVED FROM A PARTICULAR RELIGION!

Revelation 12: 1-2 ~ And there appeared a great wonder in heaven; a woman clothed with the sun, and the moon under her feet, and upon her head a crown of twelve stars: And she being with child cried, travailing in birth, and pained to be delivered.

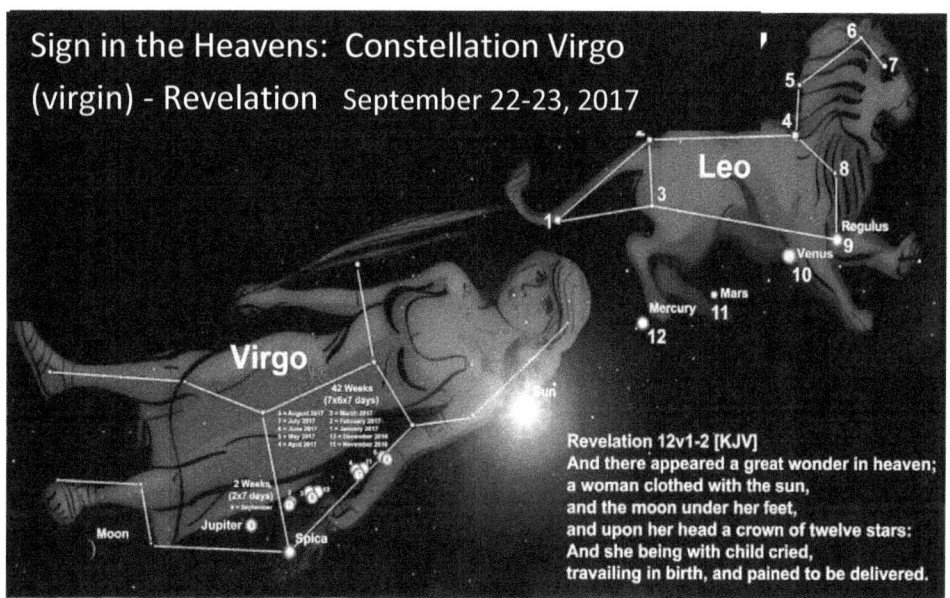

*We look to the Word of God to explain the sign in the heavens of the woman that is seen in the sun, moon, and stars, of which occurred on **September 22-23, 2017**. The Constellation of Virgo (the virgin) with the crown of twelve stars (includes Leo = King constellation, Jupiter = King planet, Regulus = King star) tells of the heavenly woman spoken of in Revelation chapter 12.* [657]

*Where it was thought that these scriptures in Revelation were meant as allegory, it wasn't until technology became available to view constellation alignments throughout all of history that revealed the intended meaning of Revelation 12:1-2 "for such a time as this." We now know that the great sign described by the Apostle John in Revelation 12 is the constellation alignment that occurred on **September 23, 2017**. This sign in the heavens has occurred only one other time – in 3 B.C. at the time*

---

[657] Luis Vega, " Luis Vega, Virgo Revelation Sign; CHARTS #26: Virgo - Comet 67p Conjunction," accessed June 10, 2016, http://www.postscripts.org/home-1.html Permission granted.

of the birth of Christ, though not to this perfection as in relation to the scriptures.[658] *According to technology projected, it will never occur again.*[659]

This co-author, David, was raised in a religious denomination that never showed him how to get saved. The schools that he attended never told him America's truthful history. They never told him who the Pilgrims were. His teachers, nor the history textbooks, ever taught what the Pilgrims believed or what they accomplished. In discovering America's truthful history with a *Providential worldview*, David felt like he was ripped-off. Many other Americans have had the same experience.

Recorded in the annals of our true history is that our Pilgrim Fathers called themselves *"the seed of Abraham, God's servants and the children of Jacob, His chosen."*[660] Throughout the next two centuries early Americans compared themselves with *Old Testament* Israel. They realized that the parallel between ancient Israel and the United States was so striking that virtually every preacher and theologian in that era recognized it and made mention of it in some way in their sermons. They called themselves the *"American Israel,"* the *"New Israel," "God's Vineyard,"* and even *"The Kingdom of God."*[661]

Reverend Abiel Abbot (1770-1828) in his *Thanksgiving Sermon*, 1799:

> *"It has been often remarked that the people of <u>the United States come nearer to a parallel with Ancient Israel, than any other nation upon the globe</u>. Hence '<u>Our American Israel</u>' is a term frequently used; and common consent allows it apt and proper."* [662]

Rev. Abiel Abbot [663]

The Founding Fathers believed they were raised up by Almighty God to establish the United States as the first free people in modern times and were stirred with conviction that they were divinely appointed in restoring His Law.[664] They structured the new nation after the principles of God's Law from the book of *Deuteronomy* to adopt the elements of "perfect law" that had been revealed to Moses. They built our nation upon the laws of God and the teachings of Christ, causing the United States of America to become the greatest nation in history!

---

[658] YouTube/chisza7, "23 September 2017 Sign in the Heaven [Revelation 12]," Published on Sep 27, 2013, https://www.youtube.com/watch?v=_1y_hLqVXf4
[659] MP, "Revelation 12 Virgo," *Daily Crow*, Sept 18, 2014, http://www.dailycrow.com/revelation-12-virgo/
[660] E. Raymond Capt, Commentary in *The U.S.A. in Bible Prophecy: Two Sermons Preached to the U.S. Congress in 1857,* (Artisan Publishers, 2003) 83
[661] Dr. Stephen Jones, *The Prophetic History of the United States,* (Fridley: God's Kingdom Ministries, 2006) p. 8
[662] Conrad Cherry, ed. *God's New Israel Religious Interpretations of American Destiny,* (Chapel Hill and London: The University of North Carolina Press, 1998), front matter page
[663] First Parish Historical Committee, Much Preached At: The Early Ministers of First Parish Church in Beverly 1667-1958: Abiel Abbot 1803-1828. [Recovered through the Internet Archive Wayback Machine http://web.archive.org/web/20181103114420/http://history.firstparishbeverly.org/archives/23] **This work is in the public domain**
[664] Dr. Stephen Jones, *The Prophetic History of the United States,* (Fridley: God's Kingdom Ministries, 2006) p. 15

Our Founding Fathers, inclusive of those forementioned, learned to read from the Holy Bible and many of them were fluent in the original Hebrew and Greek languages. They understood Biblical prophecy and identified themselves in the *Word of God* as the New Covenant people of God. [665]

Daniel Webster[666]
in his younger years

We point again to one of our revered Founding Fathers for his *wisdom from above*, Daniel Webster (1782-1852). A statesman that has been considered one of the greatest orators in American history, Daniel Webster gave a speech in honor of the Pilgrims at the *Bicentennial Celebration* at Plymouth Rock on December 22, 1820. He was intimately acquainted with the fact that our nation was built on the laws of God and teachings of Christ. He ended his speech by saying,

"Lastly our ancestors established their system of government on morality and religious sentiment. Moral habits, they believed, cannot safely be trusted on any other foundation than religious principle, nor any government be secure which is not supported by moral habits. Whatever makes men good Christians makes them good citizens.

Cultivated mind was to act on uncultivated nature and more than all a government and a country were to commence with the very first foundations laid under the divine light of the Christian religion. Happy auspices of a happy futurity; who would wish that his country's existence had otherwise begun?

Finally, let us not forget the religious character of our origin. Our fathers were brought hither by their veneration for the Christian religion. They journeyed by its light and labored in its hope, futurity, eternity.

They sought to incorporate its principles with the elements of their society and to diffuse its influence through all their institutions, civil, political, or literary.

Let us cherish these sentiments, and extend this influence still more widely; in the full conviction that that is the happiest society which partakes in the highest degree of the mild and peaceful spirit of Christianity."[667]

We recall the profound Pilgrim monument, *The National Monument to the Forefathers*, which was completed in 1888 and dedicated in 1889. On the back panel of the monument are etched the words of William Bradford, signer of the *Mayflower Compact,* and governor of the Plymouth Colony for over 30 years…

---

[665] W. Cleon Skousen, *The Majesty of God's Law, It's Coming to America*, (Salt Lake City: Ensign Publishing, 1996), 23
[666] *Wikimedia Commons,* s.v. "File:Black Dan.jpg" This work is in the public domain
[667] *The Works of Daniel Webster,* Vol. 1, 8th Ed. "FIRST SETTLEMENT OF NEW ENGLAND.: A Discourse delivered at Plymouth, on the 22d of December, 1820. (Boston: Little, Brown and Co., 1854). Edward Everett, *Biographical Memoir of the Public Life of Daniel Webster,* "The First Settlement of New England 1-50

*William Bradford (1590-1657)
a conjectural image of Bradford
produced as a postcard in 1904
by A.S. Burbank of Plymouth* [668]

"Thus out of small beginnings greater things have been produced by His hand that made all things of nothing, and gives being to all things that are; and, as one small candle may light a thousand, so the light here kindled hath shone unto many, yea in some sort to our whole nation; let the glorious name of Jehovah have all the praise."

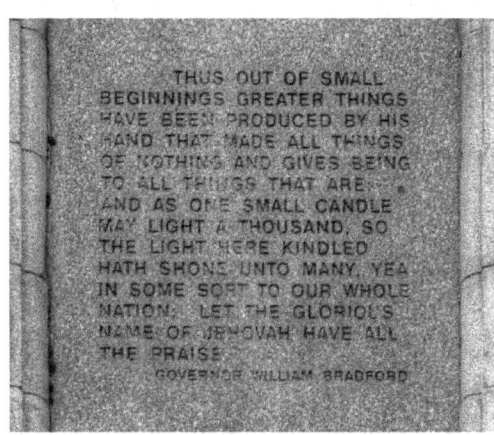

*National Monument to the Forefathers
Inscription of William Bradford quote*[669]
Courtesy of Wikimedia Commons/Dsdugan

Did William Bradford discern that the North American continent would be the land where God would gather together His New Covenant people on a land of their own,[670] that he and his fellow pilgrims were

---

[668] *Wikimedia Commons*, s.v. "Williambradford bw.jpg," This work is in the public domain
[669] *Wikimedia Commons*, s.v. "File:15 23 0513 monument.jpg," Courtesy of Dsdugan
[670] Prophesied in the *Holy Scriptures* as follows:

> *Jeremiah 31:10* ~ *Hear the word of the Lord, O ye nations, and declare it in the isles afar off, and say, He that scattered Israel will gather him, and keep him, as a shepherd doth his flock.*
> *2 Samuel 7:10* ~ *Moreover I will appoint a place for my people Israel, and will plant them, that they may dwell in a place of their own, and move no more; neither shall the children of wickedness afflict them any more, as beforetime,*
> *Hosea 2:14* ~ *Therefore, behold, I will allure her, and bring her into the wilderness, and speak comfortably unto her.*
> *Revelation 12:6* ~ *And the woman fled into the wilderness, where she hath a place prepared of God, that they should feed her there a thousand two hundred and threescore days.*
> *Isaiah 2:2* ~ *And it shall come to pass <u>in the last days</u>, that the mountain of the Lord's house shall be established in the top of the mountains, and shall be exalted above the hills; and all nations shall flow unto it.*
> *Micah 4:1* ~ *But <u>in the last days</u> it shall come to pass, that the mountain of the house of the Lord shall be established in the top of the mountains, and it shall be exalted above the hills; and people shall flow unto it.*
> *Matthew 21:42-43* ~ *42 Jesus saith unto them, Did ye never read in the scriptures, The stone which the builders rejected, the same is become the head of the corner: this is the Lord's doing, and it is marvellous in our eyes? 43 Therefore say I unto you, The kingdom of God shall be taken from you, and given to a nation bringing forth the fruits thereof.*

"one small candle" that would kindle a light to show the way for thousands more to live under the laws of God and teachings of Christ in the light of *Liberty — Civil and Religious*?

National Monument to the Forefathers
Front Panel Dedication Inscription[671]
Courtesy of Wikimedia Commons/Dsdugan

On the front panel of the Monument this is what you would read:

> "National Monument to the Forefathers. Erected by a grateful people in remembrance of their labors, sacrifices and sufferings for the cause of civil and religious liberty."

Daniel Webster[672]
(1782-1852)
In his seasoned years

In his 1820 speech at the *Bicentennial Celebration* held at Plymouth, Massachusetts where the Pilgrims first landed in America, Daniel Webster also said,

"To the free and universal reading of the Bible in the age of the Pilgrims and the Puritans, men were much indebted for right views of civil liberty."[673]

We look to the *wisdom from above* held by our nation's fathers and consider more depth and insight pertaining to *Civil and Religious Liberty*.

---

[671] *Wikimedia Commons,* s.v. "File:15 23 0519 monument.jpg," Courtesy of Dsdugan
[672] Library of Congress, "Daniel Webster," Published by E.C. Middleton & Co., Cincinnati, O. This work is in the public domain
[673] *The Works of Daniel Webster,* Vol. 1, 8th Ed. "FIRST SETTLEMENT OF NEW ENGLAND.: A Discourse delivered at Plymouth, on the 22d of December, 1820. (Boston: Little, Brown and Co., 1854). Edward Everett, *Biographical Memoir of the Public Life of Daniel Webster,* "The First Settlement of New England 1-50

Member of the Continental Congress and Signer of the *Declaration of Independence,* Reverend John Witherspoon (1723-1790), was an exceptional teacher at the College of New Jersey, today known as Princeton University. His emphasis of teaching Biblical principles impacted government offices filled with his former students during the foundation of American and attributed to him being known as "*the father of fathers.*"

Witherspoon said this:

> *It is in the man of piety [reverence for God] and inward principle that we may expect to find the uncorrupted patriot, the useful citizen, and the invincible soldier. God grant that in America <u>true religion and civil liberty may be inseparable</u> and that the unjust attempts to destroy the one, may in the issue tend to the support and establishment of both."* [Emphasis added]

John Witherspoon, c1790 [674]

Next, we consider Joseph Story (1779-1845), who was appointed as an Associate Justice of the U.S. Supreme Court by President James Madison. Justice Story wrote influential works of which included, *Commentaries on the Constitution.* In his commentary of the First Amendment's original meaning, Justice Story insures,

> *"There is not a truth to be gathered from history more certain, or more momentous, than this: that <u>civil liberty</u> cannot long be separated from <u>religious liberty</u> without danger, and ultimately without destruction to both. Wherever <u>religious liberty</u> exists, it will, first or last, bring in and establish <u>political liberty</u>."* [675]

Justice Story understood that Liberty was the fruit of a jurisdiction of God's government and laws, as well as the teachings of Christ.

Joseph Story[676]

---

[674] *Wikimedia Commons* s.v., "File:Peale, Charles Willson, John Witherspoon (1723-1794), President (1768-94)," This work is in the public domain

[675] Federer, America's God and Country Encyclopedia of Quotations, "Joseph Story," (Coppell: FAME Publishing, Inc, 1994) 575 as citing Joseph Story. Tryon Edwards, D.D., *The New Dictionary of Thoughts—A Cyclopedia of Quotations* (Garden City, NY: Hanover House, 1852; revised and enlarged by C.H. Catrevas, Ralph Emerson Browns, and Jonathan Edwards [descendent, along with Tryon, of Jonathan Edwards (1703-1758), president of Princeton], 1891; The Standard Book Company, 1955, 1963) 337

[676] *Wikimedia Commons* s.v., "Joseph Story," This work is in the public domain

America today doesn't have _Religious Liberty_ because America today doesn't have _Civil Liberty_. The American people don't even have knowledge of what _Civil Liberty_ is or where it comes from!

In *Galatians 5:13-14*, the apostle Paul says,

> ¹³ For, brethren, _ye have been called unto liberty_; only use not liberty for an occasion to the flesh, but by love serve one another. ¹⁴ For all the law is fulfilled in one word, even in this; Thou shalt love thy neighbor as thyself.
>
> [Emphasis added]

God's Solution for America!

> *Matthew 22:35-40* ~ ³⁵Then one of them [a Pharisee], which was a lawyer, asked him a question, tempting him, and saying, ³⁶ Master, which is the great commandment in the law? ³⁷Jesus said unto him, Thou shalt love the Lord thy God with all thy heart, and with all thy soul, and with all thy mind. ³⁸ This is the first and great commandment. ³⁹And the second is like unto it, Thou shalt love thy neighbour as thyself. ⁴⁰ On these two commandments hang all the law and the prophets. [Emphasis added]

Not done — keep going!

God's Solution for America!

John Eliot Preaching to the Indians[678]
Courtesy of the Presbyterian Historical Society

In 1663, a generation after the Pilgrims landed at Plymouth Rock, Puritan minister and pioneer missionary among Native Americans, John Eliot, translated the English Bible into the Wampanoag language. In 1659, John Eliot wrote *The Christian Commonwealth or the Civil Polity or the Rising Kingdom of Jesus Christ* wherein he said,

> "It is the Commandment of the Lord, that a people should enter into Covenant with the Lord to become his people, even in their _Civil Society_, as well as in their Church Society. (a) Whereby they submit themselves to be ruled by the Lord in all things, receiving from him, both the _platform of their Government_, and _all their laws_; which they do, _then Christ reigneth over them in all things_, they being ruled by his Will, and by the Word of his Mouth. Is. 33:22 The Lord is our _Judge_, the Lord is our _Law-giver_, the Lord is our _King_, he shall save us."[677]
>
> [Emphasis added]

---

[677] John Eliot, *The Christian Commonwealth, or The Civil Policy of the Rising Kingdom of Jesus Christ,* (London, 1659, reprinted by Arno Press, New York, 1972) as cited by Verna M. Hall, Rosalie J. Slater, *The Bible and the Constitution of the United States of America: A Primer of American Liberty*, (Chesapeake: The Foundation of American Christian Education, 1983) 17-18
[678] Pcusa.org, "Early American Bibles: Presbyterian Historical Society documents early scripture printing in U.S." Dec 19, 2017, https://www.pcusa.org/news/2017/12/19/early-american-bibles/

Wow! Wow! Wow! Reader! America! This is how the Pilgrims and the Puritans did it! They created a Biblical culture! Families (influence of the Family sphere) practiced Biblical virtue among themselves and brought this into their church society (influence of the Religion/Church sphere), and then into their civil society (spheres of influence: Government/Law, Education, Business/Economics, Media, Arts/Entertainment). Because of practicing a lifestyle of Biblical virtue, they enjoyed Biblical Liberty and happiness! This they did seven days a week! From this lifestyle the Pilgrims established strong righteousness in Virtue and Morality throughout their region!

One hundred fifty-six years after the Pilgrims landed, the Founding Fathers built the government of the American Republic based on the *Laws of Nature and of Nature's God* (the immutable laws of science in how His universe is to operate, and then also, the Divine revealed written *Word of God*) — God's Moral Law.

Founding Father, Dr. Benjamin Rush, said it this way.

> "[T]he only foundation for a useful education in a republic is to be laid in religion. Without this there can be no virtue, and without virtue there can be no liberty, and <u>liberty is the object and life of all republican governments</u>... But the religion I mean to recommend in this place, is <u>the religion of Jesus Christ</u>."[679]
>
> [Emphasis added]

Dr. Rush knew the Education sphere of influence had to be based on the Biblical principles of the teachings of Christ.

Benjamin Rush, 1783[680]

---

[679] Dr. Benjamin Rush, "Thoughts, Upon the Mode of Education Proper in a Republic," *A Plan for the Establishment of Public Schools and the Diffusion of Knowledge in Pennsylvania; to Which Are Added, Thoughts upon the Mode of Education Proper in a Republic*, (Philadelphia: Thomas Dobson, 1786). Reproduced in *Essays on Education in the Early Republic*, ed. Frederick Rudolph, (Cambridge, MA: The Belknap Press of Harvard University Press, 1965) 9-23
[680] Wikimedia, s.v., Benjamin Rush Painting by Peale 1783, This work is in the public domain

Samuel Adams, 1772 [681]

Samuel Adams, the *Father of the American Revolution* understood the challenge to our nation was greater from within than any external threat. In 1779 he warned:

> *"A general dissolution of Principles and Manners will more surely overthrow the Liberties of America than the whole Force of the Common Enemy."* [682]

Liberty begins internally first and works outward, externally into society, as *public Virtue*. That is how society and culture is influenced by the laws of God and the teachings of Christ in the jurisdiction of Liberty of God's Kingdom on earth.

By design, America was demoralized beginning in the early 1960s. The destruction of America came from within as our enemies crept within and influenced our society and culture.

Samuel Adams continued…

> *"While the People are virtuous they cannot be subdued; but when once they lose their Virtue they will be ready to surrender their Liberties to the first external or internal invader…If Virtue and Knowledge are diffused among the People, they will never be enslaved. This will be their great Security."* [683] [Emphasis added]

We comprehend that influencing and maintaining Virtue in our culture and society is a matter of National Security.

The position of the Church is evidenced in the sermons of the Patriot Preachers of the day who asserted that they did not hesitate to attack the great political and social evils of their day. For example,

> *"…the Fathers of the Republic, enforced by their example. They invoked God in their civil assemblies, called upon their chosen teachers of religion for counsel from the Bible, and recognized its precepts as the law of their public conduct.* **The Fathers did not divorce politics and religion, but they denounced the separation as ungodly.** *They prepared for the struggle, and went into battle, not as soldiers of fortune, but, like Cromwell and the soldiers of the Commonwealth, with the Word of God in their hearts, and trusting in him. This was the secret of that moral energy which sustained the Republic in its material weakness against superior numbers, and discipline, and all the power of England."* [684] [Emphasis added]

---

[681] *Wikimedia Commons, s.v.* "J S Copley - Samuel Adams.jpg," by artist John Singleton Copley, This work is in the public domain
[682] Rosalie J. Slater, *Teaching and Learning America's Christian Heritage* (San Francisco: Foundation for American Christian Education, American Revolution Bicentennial ed., 1975), 251
[683] Ibid.
[684] Charles T. Evans, *The Patriot Preachers of the Revolution,* (New York: Charles T. Evans, 1862) Preface

*"... England sent her armies to compel submission, and the colonists **appealed to Heaven**."*[685]

[Emphasis added]

Dr. W. Cleon Skousen[686]

We step forward for a moment in time to a modern father of our country who was a passionate patriot that has brought forward the wisdom of our nation's early fathers. Dr. Cleon Skousen (1913-2006) was a world-renowned teacher, author, lecturer, and scholar for more than 60 years. He left a tremendous legacy of books and recordings that address the principles of good government.[687] Dr. Skousen points out,

> *"In addition to specific instructions left by our Founding Fathers concerning the Constitution, there were also certain basic principles scattered among their writings which they described as 'indispensable' for America's future survival. By carefully noting each of these principles, it became apparent that these guidelines were the Founders' inspired roadmap by which they hoped to attain America's 'manifest destiny.' These principles also turned out to be the perfect litmus test by which to judge any new legislation. If an act or legislative proposal violates any of these principles, it is defective. For this reason...these 28 principles [are]... the most 'indispensable' advice the Founding Fathers could leave [for the American people]."* [688]

Dr. Skousen gleaned over 100 volumes of the Founding Fathers' original writings, minutes, letters, biographies, etc. and the knowledge of which has been instilled into his books, *The 5000 Year Leap* and *The Majesty of God's Law: It's Coming to America*. Knowledge of these 28 principles of Liberty that our Founders held as fundamental beliefs and key principles to peace, prosperity and freedom are pivotal in recovering our birthright in heritage as we work toward restoration.

An abbreviated list of these indispensable basic 28 Principles include:

~ The only reliable basis for sound government and just human relations is Natural Law.
~ A free people cannot survive under a republican constitution unless they remain virtuous and morally strong.
~ The most promising method of securing a virtuous people is to elect virtuous leaders.
~ Without religion the government of a free people cannot be maintained.
~ All things were created by God, therefore upon Him all mankind are equally dependent, and to Him they are equally responsible.
~ All mankind were created equal.
~ The proper role of government is to protect equal rights, not provide equal things.
~ Mankind are endowed by God with certain unalienable rights.

---

[685] John Wingate Thornton, A.M, *The Pulpit of the American Revolution, or, the Political Sermons of the Period of 1776,* (Boston: D. Lothrop and Company, 1876) v.
[686] Wikipedia, s.m. "File:Skousen 2.jpg," Fair use
[687] W. Cleon Skousen, "Who is Cleon Skousen?," https://wcleonskousen.com/
[688] W. Cleon Skousen, *The Majesty of God's Law: It's Coming to America,* (Salt Lake City: Ensign Publishing 1996) 494-526 and *A Miracle That Changed the World: The 5000 Year Leap,* National Center for Constitutional Studies 15th printing, 2009) 35-310

~ To protect human rights, God has revealed a code of divine law.
~ The God-given right to govern is vested in the sovereign authority of the whole people.
~ The majority of the people may alter or abolish a government which has become tyrannical.
~ The United States of America shall be a republic.
~ A Constitution should protect the people from the frailties of their rulers.
~ Life and liberty are secure only so long as the rights of property are secure.
~ The highest level of prosperity occurs when there is a free-market economy and a minimum of government regulations.
~ The government should be separated into three branches.
~ A system of checks and balances should be adopted to prevent the abuse of power by the different branches of government.
~ The unalienable rights of the people are most likely to be preserved if the principles of government are set forth in a written Constitution.
~ Only limited and carefully defined powers should be delegated to government, all others being retained by the people.
~ Efficiency and dispatch require that the government operate according to the will of the majority, but constitutional provisions must be made to protect the rights of the minority.
Strong local self-government is the keystone to preserving human freedom.
~ A free people should be governed by law and not by the whims of men.
~ A free society cannot survive as a republic without a broad program of general education.
~ A free people will not survive unless they stay strong.
~ Peace, commerce, and honest friendship with all nations—entangling alliances with none.
~ The core unit which determines the strength of any society is the family; therefore the government should foster and protect its integrity.
~ The burden of debt is as destructive to human freedom as subjugation by conquest.
~ The United States has a manifest destiny to eventually become a glorious example of God's law under a restored Constitution that will inspire the entire human race.

Within these 28 principles of Liberty lies the challenge of restoration to the American people today. It is apparent that now is the time and that we are obligated by Divine injunction and admonition to "improve and perpetuate" what the Founding Fathers began.

God's Solution for America is to have Christians with reputations of integrity that are God-fearing and full of Virtue to fill all three branches of their State governments as well as the National government. It would be endearing to see Christian governors in every State carry their Bibles to work, judges in State courts that are not ashamed of the Gospel of Christ, all members of State legislative assemblies to be upright God-fearing people!

America! God wants His righteousness to be very prevalent.

Remember, the American Republic is a Biblical Christian principle-based government with its law form based on the *Laws of Nature and of Nature's God*. From living according to *God's Word,* we obtain His character trait of Virtue. From living in Virtue, we achieve and maintain Liberty and happiness. When the righteous rule, the people rejoice! No more wickedness ruling America and our States!

In closing, we once again revert to the wisdom of an early father. It was in June 1788 when there was a speech that made an impact of lasting effect presented at New Hampshire by a preacher named Samuel Langdon. The intent of this speech was to influence the delegates of New Hampshire to vote in favor of the *Constitution for the United States*, which would also make New Hampshire become the ninth State needed to make a quorum and ratify the *Constitution* so America could start functioning by it in law form.

Samuel Langdon was an ardent patriot that graduated from Harvard College in 1740 along with his classmate, Samuel Adams. Langdon later went on to become the thirteenth president of Harvard College.

Reverend Samuel Landon, D.D.[689]

Samuel Langdon:

"Preserve your government with the utmost attention and solicitude, for it is the remarkable gift of heaven. From year to year be careful in the choice of your representatives, and all the higher powers of government.

Fix your eyes upon men of good understanding, and known honesty; men of knowledge, improved by experience; men who fear God, and hate covetousness; who love truth and righteousness, and sincerely wish the public welfare. Beware of such as are cunning rather than wise; who prefer their own interest to every thing; whose judgment is partial, or fickle; and whom you would not willingly trust with your own private interests.

When meetings are called for the choice of your rulers, do not carelessly neglect them, or give your votes with indifference, just as any party may persuade, or a sordid treat tempt you; but act with serious deliberation and judgment, as in a most important matter, and let the faithful of the land serve you.

Let not men openly irreligious and immoral become your legislators; for how can you expect good laws to be made by men who have no fear of God before their eyes, and who boldly trample on the authority of his commands? ...If the legislative body are corrupt, you will soon have bad men for counsellors, corrupt judges, unqualified justices, and officers in every department who will dishonor their stations...

...therefore be always on your guard against parties, and the methods taken to make interest for unworthy men, and let distinguished merit always determine your vote. And when all places in government are filled with the best men you can find, behave yourselves as good subjects; obey the laws; cheerfully submit to such taxation as the necessities of the public call for; give tribute to whom tribute is due, custom to whom custom, fear to whom fear, and honor to whom honor, as the gospel commands you.

Never give countenance to turbulent men, who wish to distinguish themselves, and rise to power, by forming combinations and exciting insurrections against government: for this can never be the right way to redress real grievances... I call upon you also to support schools in all your towns, that the rising generation may not grow up in ignorance. ... It is a debt you owe to your children, and that God to whom they belong...

---

[689] Samuel Langdon, "The Republic of the Israelites: An Example to the American States," obtained from The Federalist Papers Project, www.thefederalistpapers.org This work is in the public domain

I call upon you to preserve the knowledge of God in the land, and attend to the revelation written to us from heaven. If you neglect or renounce that religion taught and commanded in the holy scriptures, think no more of freedom, peace, and happiness… May the general government of these United States, when established, appear to be the best which the nations have yet known, and be exalted by uncorrupted religion and morals! And may the everlasting gospel diffuse its heavenly light, and spread righteousness, liberty, and peace, thro' the whole world.

Avoid all the vices and corruptions of the world, the judgments of heaven will pursue you. There will be a resurrection of the dead, both of the just and the unjust, and a day of solemn judgment when all mankind must give an account of their conduct in this world.

Will you permit me now to pray on behalf of the people that all the departments of government may be constantly filled with the wisest and best [people]."[690]

In the *Reconstruction Era* after the *War Between the States*, because the *Declaration of Independence* and the *Constitution* were swept under the rug and put into dormancy by the *Illuminized* Freemasons who then raised up their Corporate Democracy to run the national government, the message of Samuel Langdon's speech given 235 years ago relates to us today! Reverend Doctor Langdon's words speak to us in this current generation with experiential knowledge that will help guide us in standing up and restoring God's government once again, the Republic for the United States of America.

Our Founding Fathers held conviction that Christian principles would be part of the State governments as well as the national Federal Government. When they signed the *Declaration of Independence*, they officially separated from Great Britain which in turn dissolved every tyrannical British-ruled government in the colonies. The Founding Fathers' first task was to return to their home States and create their brand-new State constitutions to replace what they had just abolished. They created their first State governments. Not only do the State constitutions begin with "We the people," but they acknowledge the sovereignty of God. For example, Massachusetts' constitution reads in part,

"We…the people of Massachusetts, acknowledging, with grateful hearts, the goodness of the great Legislator of the universe, in affording us, in the course of His providence, an opportunity [to form a compact] …and devoutly imploring His direction in so interesting a design…establish this constitution."[691]

Another example is Connecticut:

"The People of this State…by the Providence of God…hath the sole and exclusive right of governing themselves as a free, sovereign, and independent State…and forasmuch as the free fruition of such liberties and privileges as humanity, civility, and Christianity call for us, as is due to every man in his place and proportion…hath ever been, and will be the tranquility and stability of Churches and Commonwealth, and the denial thereof, the disturbances, if not the ruin of both."[692]

---

[690] Samuel Langden, "The Republic of The Israelites An Example To The American States," sermon preached by Samuel Langdon before the New Hampshire Legislature on June 5, 1788
[691] Gary DeMar, *God and Government: A Biblical and Historical Study,* Volume I, (Atlanta, Georgia, American Vision, Inc, rev 1990, 2nd ed.) 162
[692] Ibid.

The People of their States established their civil governments by convening the legislatures and courts, drafting the laws, and writing their State constitutions — and they did it acknowledging that God made it all possible and that they, the People, were subjects and servants under His sovereign rule. This is a Biblical concept in that they recognized the sovereignty of God as delegated to all civil governments <u>through</u> the People. Furthermore, the Federal Constitution requires that...

> *"The Senators, Representatives...and the Members of the several State Legislatures, and all executive and judicial Officers, both of the United States and of the several States, <u>shall be bound by Oath or Affirmation, to support this Constitution</u>, but no religious test shall ever be required as a qualification to any office or public trust under the United States." (Article VI, Clause 3)*

The question might be asked, "A binding oath to whom?" Because the constitutional covenant was made with "We the People," we may safely assume that "We the People" are the highest authority — and that they are indeed the highest authority when the People acknowledge Creator God as their Sovereign.[693]

In addition, the Founders included what they thought was good for their States and the nation. For example, signers of the *Declaration* that returned home and wrote the Delaware constitution, included in their State governing document what everyone appointed to public office must say,

> *"I do profess faith in God the Father, and in Jesus Christ His only Son, and in the Holy Ghost, one God, blessed for evermore; I do acknowledge the holy scriptures of the Old and New Testaments to be given by divine inspiration."*[694]

Now, that's a requirement placed in the State constitution by the same men who signed the Founding Document, the *Declaration of Independence*. This reflects the clear intent of the Founding Fathers' beliefs and intentions.

A review by the U.S. Supreme Court in the 1892 case, *Church of the Holy Trinity, New York v. United States*,[695] relates to a challenge raised pertaining to Christian principles in America. In reviewing the State constitutions for the other 12 original States, plus the next 31 States that later joined the *Union of States* up to that point in time, the Court found that <u>every single State had similar requirements in its constitution</u>.[696]

Another example is New Hampshire. The New Hampshire constitution says that,

> *"...morality and piety, rightly grounded on evangelical principles, gives the best and greatest security of the government. Therefore the legislature is empowered to adopt measures for the support and maintenance of public Christian teachers of piety, religion and morality."*[697]

These examples represent the governing documents written by our Founding Fathers for their home State constitutions when they created their very first government documents. The U.S. Supreme Court pointed

---

[693] Ibid., 163
[694] Ibid.
[695] Church of the Holy Trinity v. United States, 143 U.S. 457 (1892)
[696] The John Ankerberg Show with David Barton, "How did the first state constitutions reveal a Christian foundation?," Dec 15, 2011, https://www.youtube.com/watch?v=V2u71T8TJ5Q&index=1&list=PL999A804EDC6F8B72
[697] The John Ankerberg Show with David Barton, "Was the United States founded on Christian principles?," Dec 15, 2011, https://www.youtube.com/watch?v=HBZe41uz5M8&list=PL999A804EDC6F8B72&index=5

out that at the time in 1892, there were now 44 States in the Union, and every State had a similar requirement in its constitution. Those ideas of our Founding Fathers lived long past the time of the *Founding Era*. That requirement was still in every single constitution and, to hold public office one must acknowledge *a belief in future rewards and punishments*. Not only must they believe in God, but they must also believe that they will answer to God for everything they do while in office.[698]

Where there may be cries and claims that there was a constitutional ban on religious tests to hold public office (*Article VI, Clause 3*), it's necessary to look at the Founding Father's own words to understand what they meant by "religious test." For example, Kentucky in 1796, one of the first States to join the Union after the Founding era. The Kentucky constitution says,

> *"No person who denies the being of God or a future state of rewards and punishments shall hold any office in the civil department of this state. And no religious test will be required of any officer in the government."*[699]

"Religious test" was defined by the Founding Fathers as a "denomination test." The Founding Fathers didn't want a State-run church or <u>one</u> denomination running the nation in America like they had in Great Britain. They wanted Christian principles, but they did not want one denomination.[700]

In the 1799 Maryland Supreme Court case *Runkel v Winemiller*, the Court stated,

> *"By our form of government, the Christian religion is the established religion; and all sects and denominations of Christians are placed upon the same equal footing, and are equally entitled to protection in their religious liberty."*[701]

We now have knowledge, understanding, *wisdom from above* and guidance as we proceed in the restoration process. God's Solution for America!

Righteousness exalteth "We the People" and America!

We the People must reestablish the Founding Fathers' Republic commonwealth with its foundation on the *Laws of Nature and of Nature's God*. Christ Jesus, Yeshuah HaMaschiah is the author of Creation. He is also the *Word of God* who shows us *the Way*, through His written Word so that we can learn and apply His Biblical virtue that will enable *We the People* to enjoy *Civil and Religious Liberty* with happiness! Happiness is the cause of God.

---

[698] Ibid.
[699] Ibid.
[700] Ibid.
[701] *Runkel v Winemiller, 4 Harris & McHenry 276 (Sup Ct. Md 1799)*

Re-inhabited: Republic for the United States of America
Volume II: The Story of the Re-inhabitation
Cover art by Rob Krajenke

The National Monument to the Forefathers is in Plymouth, Massachusetts. Dedicated on August 1, 1889, it is a forgotten tribute and memorial to the Mayflower Pilgrims. On the main pedestal stands the heroic figure of "Faith" with her right hand pointing toward heaven and her left hand clutching the Bible because her faith is in the God of the Bible: Jesus Christ, Yeshua HaMaschiah. The only faith that can bring true liberty is a faith in the one true God and His Word, the Holy Bible. From the Word of God comes wisdom to know how to live in this world. There are four smaller connecting statues that are tied to Faith because without faith, the liberty matrix falls apart; Faith is the beginning of it all.

In the picture going counterclockwise, starting on the right side out of view behind Jesus is "Morality." The smaller statue on the back side of the Monument is "Law." The next smaller statue is "Education," which is a young lady opening the Word of God, the book of knowledge. The last smaller statue is "Liberty." "Liberty Man" is a stud – he is the result of obeying the Matrix of Liberty as displayed on the Monument.

Pictured left of Jesus is Founding Father, Former President, and current Attorney General of the Republic for the United States of America, James Timothy Turner. The man on the left is another Founding Father, President James Buchanan Geiger, the leader of the restoration.

Jesus Christ is the great Liberator and gave us His laws which the Founders used to frame the Constitution. Christ is the foundation of the American Republic on which the whole structure rests.

John F. Kennedy, pictured to the right of Jesus, knew of the great conspiracy and deception, and wanted to bring the Republic back into operation. He exposed the tyrannical secret societies while having silver-backed certificates printed and circulated in the privately-owned Federal Reserve banks that caused disruption of the Federal Reserve Notes (FRNs). President Kennedy was assassinated on November 22, 1963.

Next pictured is President Abraham Lincoln. He was led by Divine Providence in the War Between the States to orchestrate the victory to save the Union of States; however, he didn't have time to restore the Republic. President Lincoln was assassinated on April 14th and died on April 15, 1865.

Crazy Horse, to the right of President Lincoln, took up arms against the Corporate UNITED STATES to fight against encroachments on the territories and way of life of the Lakota People. In 1877, Crazy Horse was mortally wounded when resisting imprisonment. He ranks among the most notable and iconic of Native American tribal members.

Standing to the right of Crazy Horse is Reverend Dr. Martin Luther King, Jr., a minister of the Gospel of the Kingdom of Christ and of God, and activist who led the African American Civil Rights Movement. He had a dream for the Matrix of Liberty, however, was assassinated before he could see it fulfilled.

On the horse is General George Washington, Commander-in-chief of the Continental Army during the American Revolutionary War. A Founding Father of the United States of America, General Washington presided over the convention that drafted the original United States Constitution. He is revered as the "Father of our country," and became the American Republic's first President under the Constitution.

THE GENIUS OF HISTORY RECEIVING THE RECORDS OF TIME.

The Genius of History Receiving the Records of Time
An illlustration in the children's history textbook,
"A History of the United States, on a New Plan;
Adapted to the Capacity of Youth.
To Which is Added,
The Declaration of Independence
and the
Constitution for the United States
By J. Olney, A.M.
1851

Chapter Six
Conclusion

As we conclude *God's Solution for America ~ and the Nations of the World*, we will begin with a short history about the Pilgrims, continue with an abbreviated review in what has been covered in scope and sequence, and then come to our conclusion.

*The Mayflower Compact
November 11, 1620 O.S.*

*Passengers of the Mayflower signing the "Mayflower Compact" on board the Mayflower, including
Carver, Winston, Alden, Myles Standish, Howland, Bradford, Allerton, and Fuller* [702]

Oil painting by Jean Leon Gerome Ferris (1863–1930)

The History of the Pilgrims and Settlements in the New World

There were several various explorers that ventured to the North American continent of the "New World" from Christopher Columbus on August 3, 1492, and forward in time. Having made two more return voyages, Columbus supposed what is now called Haiti to be the ancient Ophir which had been visited by the ships of King Soloman.[703] The discovery of America produced great excitement throughout the civilized world, and awakened a spirit of activity, enterprise, and inquiry never before known.[704]

The first permanent English settlement in America was at Jamestown, Virginia on May 13, 1607. The colony consisted almost entirely of men who came for the purpose of acquiring wealth and who intended to return to England. [705]

It was Jamestown where a Dutch vessel arrived with 20 Africans and offered them for sale as slaves. They were purchased by the settlers, the first slaves brought into the country and from which the foundation for

---

[702] *Wikimedia Commons*, s.v. "File:The Mayflower Compact 1620 cph.3g07155.jpg," This work is in the public domain
[703] J. Olney, A.M., *A History of the United States on a New Plan; Adapted to the Capacity of Youth, to which is Added, the Declaration of Independence, an the Constitution of the United States,* (New-Haven, Durrie & Peck, 1839) 20-21
[704] Ibid. 25-26
[705] Ibid. 41-42

that system of slavery came to exist in the United States.[706] Most of the people of Virginia were for a long time opposed to slavery and laws were passed to prevent it. The selfish policy of kings and proprietors in England (we can think of them as stockholders in the *British East India Company* which was controlled by the *Committee of 300*[707]) encouraged the introduction of slaves and the evil could not be resisted by those businessmen who were settlers.[708]

The native Indians encountered were of both a savage nature as well as many that became friends and helped the settlers.[709]

Emigrants continued to arrive from England and the settlements were widely extended. King Charles II was the ruling monarch who appointed governors over the English settlers and land tracts were granted through the monarchy. Dutch settlers came to the *New World* in 1613 to what came to be New-York.[710]

It was in 1620 when the first settlers came to New England. They were known as the *English Puritan Separatists* so known because of separating from the Church of England, which was one denomination, State-run. The *English Separatists* sought their God-given right to live and worship with a Biblical lifestyle according to the dictates of their consciences. They wanted to live according to the Holy Bible in a purer form of worship and church government. They were severely persecuted and oppressed by the English monarchs, Queen Elizabeth and then King James I, resulting in great numbers of them leaving England in 1609 and moving to Holland where there was religious freedom. It was at Leiden, Holland where these "Pilgrims" ventured and studied the *Old Testament* Hebrew Republic and its form of government under the God of Abraham, Isaac, and Jacob.

Having lived in Holland for 11 years, they became concerned with the influence of *the world* and its carnal lifestyle that was evident among their children. They were compelled to venture to the *New World* where they would have religious and civil liberties and the potential to advance the *Gospel of the Kingdom of Christ and of God* to the indigenous people.

The Pilgrims had signed a contract with the Virginia Company to sail to the *New World* and settle on land near the Hudson River, which was then part of northern Virginia. The Virginia Company was a trading company chartered by King James I with the goal of colonizing parts of the eastern coast of the *New World*. London stockholders financed the Pilgrim's voyage with the understanding they would be repaid in profits from the new settlement.

The Pilgrims and others set out for America on August 5, 1620, aboard the *Mayflower*. Of 102 passengers on the *Mayflower*, there were 50 men, 19 women, 3 of which were pregnant, 14 young adults and 19 children.[711] Only 41 men were among the Pilgrims, religious separatists seeking freedom from the Church of England that was ruled by King James I, the civil authority. The other passengers were considered common folk,

---

[706] Ibid. 42
[707] Carr, *Pawns in the Game*, 92
[708] Olney, *A History of the United States*, 45
[709] Ibid. 42
[710] Ibid. 44, 46
[711] Patricia Scott Deetz and James F. Deetz, *The Plymouth Colony Archive Project: Passengers on the Mayflower: Ages & Occupations, Origins & Connections*, 2000, http://www.histarch.illinois.edu/plymouth/Maysource.html

and included merchants, craftsmen, indentured servants, and orphaned children. The Pilgrims referred to themselves as "saints" and to the other passengers as "strangers."

There were many hardships experienced on the voyage across the Atlantic Ocean in their wooden ship. Rough seas and storms prevented the *Mayflower* from reaching its intended destination and the ship was steered northward instead toward Cape Cod. This change of course created a situation of legal uncertainty, friction, and discord between the passengers. The "strangers" argued that the Virginia Company contract was void because the *Mayflower* had landed outside the jurisdiction of the charter granted to them in England by the Virginia Company. The defiant "strangers" refused to recognize any rulers since there was no official government over them.

Pilgrim leader William Bradford later wrote, *"several strangers made discontented and mutinous speeches."* The Pilgrims knew if something wasn't done quickly it could be every man, woman, and family for themselves in the vast wilderness of the *New World*. To quell the conflict and preserve unity, before landing on shore, Pilgrim leaders drafted a set of governing laws that was agreeable to the majority of all in this colony, the *"Agreement Between the Settlers of New Plymouth."*

On November 11th 41 adult male colonists, including 2 indentured servants, signed the compact that has come to be known as the *Mayflower Compact*.

It was a short document which established that:

~ The colonists would remain loyal subjects to King James despite the circumstance of their need for self-governance.
~ The colonists would create and enact *"just and equal laws, ordinances, acts, constitutions and offices… for the general good of the colony"* and abide by those laws.
~ The colonists would create one community and work together to advance it.
~ The colonists would live in unity with the Biblical Christian faith.[712]

The brief document bound its signers into a body politic for the purpose of forming a government and pledged them to abide by any laws and regulations that would later be established *"for the general good of the colony."*[713] <u>The *Mayflower Compact* was not a constitution but rather an adaptation of a Puritan church covenant to a civil situation.</u>

After establishing their governing document in agreement to live and work together at a place they called Plymouth, they landed ashore and explored the country for several weeks to find an ideal place to settle. It was on December 22nd when they began to erect their buildings to shelter their wives and children from the piercing cold and wintry elements.[714] It was a brutal winter, ravaged by starvation, disease, and lack of shelter. More than half of the colonists died, though the Plymouth Colony survived.

---

[712] History.com Editors, "Mayflower Compact: What Was the Purpose of the Mayflower Compact?," October 29, 2009 https://www.history.com/topics/colonial-america/mayflower-compact
[713] Olney, *A History of the United States*, 55-56
[714] Olney, *A History of the United Staten*, 56

It has been claimed that the *Mayflower Compact*'s role in covenanting the colonists' dedication to each other as well as their mission was critical to their endurance that first winter. It was important because it was the first document to establish *self-government and common consent (union or unity)* in the *New World* which was an important step toward Biblical republicanism in the government of America, seeking permanent independence from British rule, and shaping the nation that would come to be the United States of America.[715]

The full text of the *Mayflower Compact* is as follows:

> *In the name of God, Amen. We, whose names are underwritten, the Loyal Subjects of our dread Sovereign Lord King James, by the Grace of God, of Great Britain, France, and Ireland, King, defender of the Faith, etc.:*
>
> *Having undertaken, <u>for the Glory of God, and advancements of the Christian faith</u>, and the honor of our King and Country, a voyage to plant the first colony in the Northern parts of Virginia; do by these presents, solemnly and mutually, <u>in the presence of God, and one another; covenant and combine ourselves together into a civil body politic</u>; for our better ordering, and preservation and furtherance of the ends aforesaid; and by <u>virtue</u> hereof to enact, constitute, and frame, <u>such just and equal laws</u>, ordinances, acts, constitutions, and offices, from time to time, as shall be thought most meet and convenient <u>for the general good of the colony</u>; unto which <u>we promise all due submission and obedience</u>.*
>
> *In witness whereof we have hereunto subscribed our names at Cape Cod the 11th of November, in the year of the reign of our dread Sovereign Lord King James, of England, France, and Ireland, the eighteenth, and of Scotland the fifty-fourth, 1620.*[716] [Emphasis added]

Memorial Bas Relief [717]
of the Signing of the Mayflower Compact

*This etched artwork
is below the Pilgrim Monument
located on Bradford Street
in Provincetown, Massachusetts
Courtesy of Peter Whitlock*

---

[715] Editors of the Britannica Encyclopaedia, "Mayflower Compact, North America [1620]," accessed on Oct 17, 2023, https://www.britannica.com/topic/Mayflower-Compact
[716] History.com Editors, "Mayflower Compact: What Was the Purpose of the Mayflower Compact?," October 29, 2009 https://www.history.com/topics/colonial-america/mayflower-compact
[717] *Wikimedia Commons*, s.v., "File:MayflowerCompactBasrelief.jpg," courtesy of Peter Whitlock, permission granted

We proceed in an abbreviated review in what has been covered in scope and sequence, and then come to our conclusion.

1 Peter 4:11 ~ *If any man speak, let him speak as the oracles of God; if any man minister, let him do it as of the ability which God giveth: that God in all things may be glorified through Jesus Christ, to whom be praise and dominion for ever and ever. Amen.*

Jesus said as recorded in *Matthew 7:24-27* ~

> *²⁴ Therefore whosoever heareth these sayings of mine, and doeth them, I will liken him unto <u>a wise man, which built his house upon a rock</u>: ²⁵ And the rain descended, and the floods came, and the winds blew, and beat upon that house; and it fell not: <u>for it was founded upon a rock</u>. ²⁶ And every one that heareth these sayings of mine, and doeth them not, shall be likened unto a foolish man, which built his house upon the sand: ²⁷ And the rain descended, and the floods came, and the winds blew, and beat upon that house; and it fell: and great was the fall of it.*

If you build a business, if you build a relationship to marriage, if you build a worship center with eager people, you have a choice. The best choice and the *wisdom from above are* to build it on the foundation of God's rock! That includes His government! Build the foundation on His Rock!

Daniel Webster[718]

On December 22, 1820, at the *Bicentennial Celebration* at the place of the Pilgrim's landing, Plymouth Rock, Massachusetts, there was dialog in plans for erecting a national monument in dedication to our forefathers, the Pilgrims. The renowned statesman and phenomenal orator, Daniel Webster, gave a profound speech. He concluded it by saying,

"<u>Lastly, our ancestors established their system of government on morality and religious sentiment</u>. Moral habits, they believed, cannot safely be trusted on any other foundation than religious principle, nor any government be secure which is not supported by moral habits… Living under the heavenly light of revelation, they hoped to find all the social dispositions, all the duties which men owe to each other and to society, enforced and performed. Whatever makes men good Christians, makes them good citizens."[719] [Emphasis added]

"Cultivated mind was to act on uncultivated nature; and, more than all, <u>a government, and a country, were to commence, with the very first foundations laid under the divine light of the christian religion</u>. Happy auspices of a happy futurity! Who would wish, that his country's existence had otherwise begun?"[720]

[Emphasis added]

---

[718] Library of Congress, "Daniel Webster," Published by E.C. Middleton & Co., Cincinnati, O. This work is in the public domain
[719] Daniel Webster, *A discourse, delivered at Plymouth, December 22, 1820. In Commemoration of The First Settlement of New-England*, (Boston: Wells and Lilly,--Court-Street, 1821) 35
[720] Ibid. 18

> "*Finally, let us not forget the religious character of our origin*. Our fathers were brought hither by their high veneration for the Christian Religion. They journeyed by its light, and laboured in its hope. *They sought to incorporate its principles with the elements of their society, and to diffuse its influence through all their institutions, civil, political, or literary*. Let us cherish these sentiments, and extend this influence still more widely; in full conviction, that that is the happiest society, which partakes in the highest degree of the mild and peaceful spirit of Christianity."[721] [Emphasis added]

Who were the Pilgrims? For many years when these authors would dine at a restaurant, David would ask every server, "Who were the Pilgrims?" Not one of them could tell him. When David was young and went to public school, the teacher had pictures of the Pilgrims with their funny looking clothes taped on the windows. The history books never told David precisely who they were, what they believed, what they stood for. David never knew that the Pilgrims created a Biblical Christian culture, a Biblical Christian foundation in civil liberty, or that they were the first to establish *self-government and common consent (unity)* that would be a steppingstone toward the founding of the American Republic.

From what was taught to school children for the first 300 years in this nation, our education system has been neutered from its true moorings while its history has been revised to a false narrative. Since the very early 1900s in the *Progressive Era*, Americans have not been taught or provided reading material about America's truthful history. For that reason, we have generations of Americans who lack knowledge of our true foundation on what this country was built — the law form of God's Moral Laws, which create the jurisdiction of Liberty — and that to maintain it is the responsibility of *We the People* to participate in their government.

The amazing monument that was erected to memorialize and significantly honor the Pilgrims, was completed in 1888 and dedicated the following year. This is the true statue of liberty in America — and it bears witness to the world of where Liberty comes from and how to get it back should it be lost. The Statue of Liberty in New York harbor is not the real and true statue of liberty. That statue was completed in the year 1886 and is a national pride of the *Illuminist* Freemasons in memorial of their mystery esoteric pagan religion of "Enlightening the World."

As was previously presented, inscribed on the back of the Pilgrim Monument above Plymouth Rock in Massachusetts is a quote by Governor William Bradford who was the Pilgrim leader and elected Governor of the Plymouth Colony for more than 30 years:

> "*Thus out of small beginnings greater things have been produced by His hand that made all things of nothing, and gives being to all things that are; and, as one small candle may light a thousand, so the light here kindled hath shone unto many, yea in some sort to our whole nation; let the glorious name of Jehovah have all the praise.*"

---

[721] Ibid. 38; Daniel Webster, *The Works of Daniel Webster* (Boston: Little, Brown and Company, 1853), Vol. I, 22-44

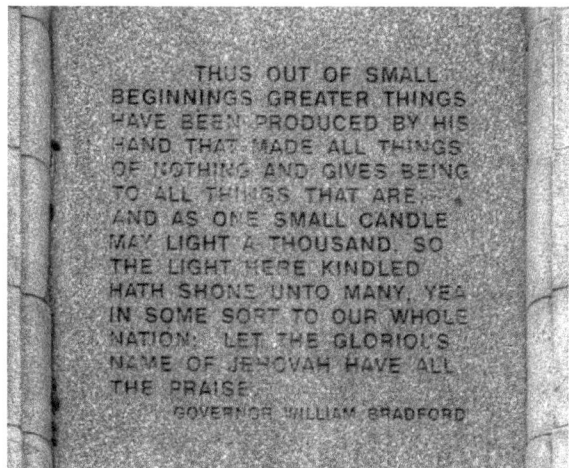

*National Monument to the Forefathers
Inscription of William Bradford quote*[722]
Courtesy of Wikimedia Commons/Dsdugan

*National Monument to the Forefathers
Front Panel Dedication Inscription*[723]
Courtesy of Wikimedia Commons/Dsdugan

On the front side of this great monument, the morning sun shines on some momentous and thought-provoking words,

> "National Monument to the Forefathers. Erected by a grateful people in remembrance of their labor, sacrifices and sufferings <u>for the cause of civil and religious liberty</u>." [Emphasis added]

The American people throughout the 50 union of States lack knowledge as to what Liberty is. They don't know what *Religious Liberty* is. They don't know or understand *Civil Liberty*. The Pilgrims created a Biblical Christian culture and because of it they had both liberties — *Civil and Religious Liberty* which are inseparable!

Daniel Webster said in his speech at the *Bicentennial Celebration* held in December 1820,

> "To the free and universal reading of the Bible in the age of the Pilgrims and the Puritans, men were much indebted for right views of civil liberty."[724]

The United States of America in Bible Prophecy

Our Pilgrim Fathers called themselves the *"seed of Abraham, God's servants, children of Jacob, His chosen."* They built our nation upon the Laws of God and the teachings of Christ, and the United States of America became the greatest nation in history.[725]

---

[722] *Wikimedia Commons*, s.v. "File:15 23 0513 monument.jpg," Courtesy of Dsdugan
[723] *Wikimedia Commons*, s.v. "File:15 23 0519 monument.jpg," Courtesy of Dsdugan
[724] *The Works of Daniel Webster*, Vol. 1, 8th Ed. "FIRST SETTLEMENT OF NEW ENGLAND.: A Discourse delivered at Plymouth, on the 22d of December, 1820. (Boston: Little, Brown and Co., 1854). Edward Everett, *Biographical Memoir of the Public Life of Daniel Webster*, "The First Settlement of New England," pp 1-50
[725] E. Ramond Capt, *The USA in Bible Prophecy*, (Muskogee: Artisan Publishers, 2003, rev. 2010) 83

National Monument to the Forefathers[726]
(formerly known as the Pilgrim Monument)
Plymouth, Massachusetts
Courtesy of Wikimedia Commons/Dsdugan

This momentous Pilgrim monument has been referred to as the "Matrix of Liberty." This monument has been a forgotten tribute and memorial to the Mayflower Pilgrims dedicated on August 1, 1889. The Monument was initially proposed as far back as 1794 and when the Pilgrim Society was founded in 1820, the bicentennial of the landing of the Mayflower Pilgrims, plans for the Monument advanced.

Formerly known as the *Pilgrim Monument*, the cornerstone was laid in 1859 just prior to the *War Between the States*, also referred to as *The Great Rebellion* and *Civil War*. It is thought to be the world's largest solid granite monument, originally imagined to be 153-feet tall though later was reduced to 81-feet probably due to lack of funds (war-related.) The Monument was designed to remind all citizens, both North and South, of their collective heritage in the cause of preserving national unity because of a shared heroic origin by the Pilgrims. In our generation, some refer to the monument as the "Matrix of Liberty" because it was left behind by our forefathers as a recipe and strategy in case their descendants would ever forget how Liberty is obtained, we would have a roadmap to restore it.[727]

On the main pedestal stands the heroic figure of "Faith" with her right hand pointing toward heaven and her left hand clutching the Bible because her faith is in the God of the Bible: *Jehovah*. The only faith that can bring true liberty is a faith in the one true God and His Word,[728] the Holy Bible. From the *Word of God* comes wisdom to know how to live in this world. There are four smaller connecting statues, each weighing nearly 20 tons with the whole monument weighing 180 tons. The smaller statues are tied to Faith because without faith, the liberty matrix falls apart. Faith is the beginning of it all.[729]

---

[726] *Wikimedia Commons* s.v. "15 23 0498 monument liberty.jpg." Courtesy of Dsdugan
[727] Hertler, *Re-inhabited, Volume II,* About the Cover
[728] *John 1:1, 14 ~ 1 In the beginning was the Word, and the Word was with God, and the Word was God. 14 And the Word was made flesh, and dwelt among us, (and we beheld his glory, the glory as of the only begotten of the Father,) full of grace and truth.*
[729] Hertler, *Re-inhabited, Volume II,* About the Cover

Statue of Morality[730]
National Monument to the Forefathers
(formerly known as the Pilgrim Monument)
Plymouth, Massachusetts
Courtesy of Wikimedia Commons/Dsdugan

If you stand in front of the Monument facing it and going counterclockwise, you will see the first small statue called, "Morality." Morality is internal liberty which is the beginning of all freedom. She has no eyes, inferring that she's looking within for internal character. It is the internal transformation of the heart first that next brings external transformation. Morality has the *Ten Commandments* in her left hand, and the scroll of *Revelation* in her right hand, signifying the Holy Bible. To have morality there has to be a standard of *Absolutes* along with internal transformation that allows Creator God to change our hearts and minds, a precondition for successful <u>self-government</u>. An external means of dictating how to live cannot effect transformation, just like being a member of a church doesn't make someone a Christian. It is the Gospel of Christ received in the heart that liberates.[731]

Throughout history there has never before been this type of government and lifestyle. There had always been kings who forced their will upon the people, whether good or bad.

Statue of Law [732]
National Monument to the Forefathers
(formerly known as the Pilgrim Monument)
Plymouth, Massachusetts
Courtesy of Wikimedia Commons/Dsdugan

The smaller statue on the back side of the Monument is "Law." To have a free civilization there has to be a civil authority or civil law that will provide a base for that freedom. In other words, there has to be a degree of order in a society which is built upon law. The principles of God's law are related to civil law, held in Law's left hand. In his right hand is extended mercy. Mercy is extended toward those he's dealing justice with, as this form of law has a degree of equity in it. Justice in equity means that when a crime is committed, punishment should be equal for everyone. Where other nations are ruled by tyrants, this law form extends mercy and grace along with the law. It is a system of law that is foundational for a free and just society that can dispense justice when crimes are committed and extend mercy to people

---

[730] *Wikimedia Commons*, s.v. "File: 15 23 0504 monument morality.jpg," Courtesy of Dsdugan
[731] Hertler, *Re-inhabited, Volume II,* About the Cover
[732] *Wikimedia Commons*, s.v. "File:15 23 0510 monument law.jpg." Courtesy of Dsdugan

while showing them grace. This is what gives the freedom. Once society is built with this foundation, then there is a civility in society and an ability to educate one's children.[733]

Statue of Education[734]
National Monument to the Forefathers
(formerly known as the Pilgrim Monument)
Plymouth, Massachusetts
Courtesy of Wikimedia Commons/Dsdugan

The next smaller statue is "Education," which is a young lady opening the *Word of God* or the book of knowledge. She wears the wreath of victory while educating her children and teaching them to pray. She sits in victory because she has trained her children in the way they should go and prepared them to do the same with their children, which continues the strategy of Truth for a free civilization. It is her responsibility to provide a *Biblical worldview* in education as to how the world works and would make her children wise in how to prevent a tyrant king or tyrannical government from enslaving them. It ensures that Liberty is passed on to the next generation.[735]

Facing the statue of Liberty Man [736]
National Monument to the Forefathers
(formerly known as the Pilgrim Monument)
Plymouth, Massachusetts
Courtesy of Wikimedia Commons/Dsdugan

The last smaller statue is "Liberty." "Liberty Man" is a stud—he is the result of obeying the *Matrix of Liberty* as displayed on the Monument. He's holding broken chains in his left hand of which he has come out of bondage and slavery to a tyrant that is represented by the lion head and skin that surrounds him. The lion head and skin represent the English tyrant in those days. Liberty Man has slain and overcome the lion, and tyranny is defeated. In his right hand is a sword which depicts protecting his family and defending the laws they have made to defend their

---

[733] Hertler, *Re-inhabited, Volume II,* About the Cover
[734] *Wikimedia Commons,* s.v. "File: 15 23 0504 monument morality.jpg." Courtesy of Dsdugan
[735] Hertler, *Re-inhabited, Volume II,* About the Cover
[736] *Wikimedia Commons* s.v. "15 23 0498 monument liberty.jpg." Courtesy of Dsdugan

values, character, and faith. Defending Liberty is imperative and Creator God's way is the only way. There exists a long-term blessing that goes with following the *Matrix of Liberty*.[737]

The Pilgrims did it God's way and they enjoyed a Biblical culture. The Pilgrims enjoyed a foreshadowing of the Kingdom of Christ and of God and His liberty, peace, and happiness.

Moving forward on the historic timeline toward the Founding Fathers and what they learned from the forefathers. Samuel Chase (1741-1811) of Maryland, was a signer of the *Declaration of Independence* and was also appointed by President George Washington as a justice on the United States Supreme Court. Justice Chase later served as the Chief Justice of the State of Maryland. In the 1799 case of *Runkel v. Winemiller*, Justice Chase gave the court's opinion and one that should be carefully considered:

"Religion is of general and public concern, and on its support depend, in great measure, the peace and good order of government, the safety and happiness of the people. By our form of government, the Christian religion is the established religion; and all sects and denominations of Christians are placed upon the same equal footing, and are equally entitled to protection in their religious liberty."[738]

Samuel Chase, 1836 [739]

America, you must know this. All government is derived from a particular religion. [740][741] America's religion was established as Biblical Christianity which was brought to and established in America by the Pilgrims. Notice and give thought to what Justice Chase declared, *"protection in their religious liberty."* Also note that Justice Chase declared that *"By our form of government, the Christian religion is the established religion."* By saying this he was not establishing a particular denomination of Christianity to be a state administered church but acknowledging that America is a Christian Nation. This is an example of "wall of separation" intended by Jefferson.

---

[737] Hertler, *Re-inhabited, Volume II,* About the Cover
[738] *Runkel v. Winemiller,* 4 Harris & McHenry 276, 288 (Sup. Ct. Md. 1799), *Runkel v. Winemiller,* 4 Harris &McHenry (MD) 429 1 AD 411, 427 (Justice Chase). David Baron, *The Myth of Separation* (Aledo, TX: WallBuilder Press, 1991), pp. 64, 151. David Barton, *America's Godly Heritage,* Video Transcript (Aledo, TX: WallBuilder, 1993), p. 13. "Our Christian Heritage," *Letter from Plymouth Rock* (Marlborough, NH: The Plymouth Rock Foundation, p. 4. as cited by William J. Federer, *America's God and Country Encyclopedia of Quotations,* "Samuel Chase," (St. Louis: Amerisearch, Inc. 2000) p. 101
[739] *Wikimedia Commons,* s.v. "Samuel Chase.jpg," This work is in the public domain
[740] S. D. Baldwin, *Armageddon: or, The Overthrow of Romanism and Monarchy; The Existence of the United States Foretold in the Bible, Its Future Greatness; Invasion by Allied Europe; Annihilation of Monarchy; Expansion into the Millennial Republic, and its Dominion Over the Whole World,* (Cincinnati: Applegate & Co., Publishers, 1864) 20
[741] Verna M. Hall, *The Christian History of the Constitution of the United States of America: Christian Self-Government,* (San Francisco: Foundation for American Christian Education, 1960 rev 1975) Preface III

John Witherspoon, c1790 [742]

John Witherspoon (1723-1794) was a signer of the *Declaration of Independence* and a member of the Continental Congress. He became a famous educator, clergyman, and president of Princeton College. Reverend Witherspoon's emphasis of Biblical principles impacting government was tremendously felt in the Colonies during the foundation of America.[743]

John Witherspoon stated:

"It is in the man of piety [reverence for God] and inward principle [self-government], that we may expect to find the uncorrupted patriot, the useful citizen, and the invincible soldier. – God grant that in America true religion and civil liberty may be inseparable and that the unjust attempts to destroy the one, may in the issue tend to support and establishment of both."[744] [Emphasis added]

So, in essence what he is stating is that someone who truly respects and reverences God and has strong moral values, is the kind of person who has potential to be a good patriot, a contributing member of their community, and a strong soldier. Let's hope that in America, we always have both real Christian faith and the freedom to live in Liberty. And when a misguided or self-serving type of people try to take away our freedom of religion, it might actually end up making our faith and freedom even stronger in the end.

Joseph Story[745]

Joseph Story (1779-1845), was a U.S. Congressman (1808-1809), was appointed in 1811 as a Justice of the U. S. Supreme Court by President James Madison who was known as *"the Chief Architect of the Constitution."* Being the youngest person ever to serve in that position, Joseph Story continued on the bench for 34 years until his death in 1845. He was instrumental in establishing federal supremacy in *Martin v. Hunter's Lessee,* 1816;[746] and in establishing the

---

[742] *Wikimedia Commons* s.v., "File:Peale, Charles Willson, John Witherspoon (1723-1794), President (1768-94)," This work is in the public domain

[743] Bill Federer, American Minute blog post American Minute with Bill Federer, "A Republic must either reserve its Virtue or lose its Liberty—Rev. John Witherspoon, Signer of Declaration of Independence," Nov 10, 2020,

[744] Federer, *America's Quotations,* "John Witherspoon," (Coppell: FAME Publishing, Inc, 1994) 703 as citing John Witherspoon. May 17, 1776, in his sermon entitled, "The Dominion of Providence over the Passions of Men." Vanum Lansing Collins, *President Witherspoon* (New York: Arno Press and *The New York Times,* 1969), I:197-98.

[745] *Wikimedia Commons* s.v., "Joseph Story," This work is in the public domain

[746] Martin v. Hunter's Lessee, 14 U.S. (1 Wheat.) 304 (1816), was a landmark decision of the Supreme Court of the United States decided on March 20, 1816. It was the first case to assert ultimate Supreme Court authority over state courts in civil matters of federal law.

illegality of the slave trade in the Supreme Court case *United States v. The Amistad*.[747]

He was a professor at Harvard Law School, 1821-1845. He wrote influential works of which included, *Commentaries on the Constitution*. In his commentary of the *First Amendment's* original meaning, Justice Story insures:

> *"There is not a truth to be gathered from history more certain, or more momentous, than this: that <u>civil liberty</u> cannot long be separated from <u>religious liberty</u> without danger, and ultimately without destruction to both. Wherever <u>religious liberty</u> exists, it will, first or last, bring in and establish <u>political liberty</u>."* [748]
>
> [Emphasis added]

Samuel Adams (1722-1803), *"Father of the American Revolution"* and signer of the *Declaration of Independence* said it this way:

> *"The sum of all is, if we would most truly enjoy the gift of Heaven, let us become a <u>virtuous people</u> then shall we both deserve and enjoy it."*[749]
>
> [Emphasis added]
>
> *"Neither the wisest constitution nor the wisest laws will secure the liberty and happiness of a people whose manners are universally corrupt."*[750]
>
> *"He therefore is the truest friend to the liberty of his country who tries most to promote its <u>virtue</u>, and who, as far as his power and influence extend, will not suffer a man to be chosen into any office of power and trust who is not a wise and <u>virtuous</u> man."*[751] [Emphasis added]
>
> *Samuel Adams, 1772* [752]

---

[747] United States v. Schooner Amistad, 40 U.S. (15 Pet.) 518 (1841)
[748] Federer, *America's Quotations*, "Joseph Story," 702-575 as citing Joseph Story. Tryon Edwards, D.D., *The New Dictionary of Thoughts—A Cyclopedia of Quotations* (Garden City, NY: Hanover House, 1852; revised and enlarged by C.H. Catrevas, Ralph Emerson Browns, and Jonathan Edwards (descendent, along with Tryon, of Jonathan Edwards (1703-1758), president of Princeton], 1891; The Standard Book Company, 1955, 1963), 337
[749] Federer, *America's Quotations*, "Samuel Adams," 23 as citing Samuel Adams. Statement. William V. Wells, *The Life and Public Services of Samuel Adams* (Boston: Little, Brown & Co., 1865).
[750] Federer, *America's Quotations,* "Samuel Adams,"23 as citing Samuel Adams. A political essay, printed in *The Public Advisor,* p. 1749. William V. Wells, *The Life and Public Service of Samuel Adams* (Boston: Little, Brown, & Co., 1865), Vol. I, p. 22.
[751] Ibid.
[752] *Wikimedia Commons, s.v.* "J S Copley - Samuel Adams.jpg," by artist John Singleton Copley, This work is in the public domain

Edmund Burke[753]

Edmund Burke (1729-1797) was a British statesman who was known as an outstanding orator, author, and leader in Great Britain during the time of the *Revolutionary War*. Burke points out the detriment in society where virtue is absent:

> *"What is liberty without wisdom and without virtue? It is the greatest of all possible evils; for it is folly, vice, and madness, without restraint.*
>
> *Men are qualified for civil liberty in exact proportion to their disposition to put moral chains upon their appetites…*
>
> *Society cannot exist, unless a controlling power upon will and appetite be placed somewhere and the less of it there is within, the more there must be without.*
>
> *It is ordained in the eternal constitution of things that men of intemperate minds cannot be free. Their passions forge their fetters"*[754]

From the Holy Bible as recorded in *Luke 8:43-48* ~

> *[43] And a woman having an issue of blood twelve years, which had spent all her living upon physicians, neither could be healed of any, [44] Came behind him, and touched the border of his garment: and immediately her issue of blood stanched [dried up]. [45] And Jesus said, Who touched me? When all denied, Peter and they that were with him said, Master, the multitude throng thee and press thee, and sayest thou, Who touched me? [46] And Jesus said, Somebody hath touched me: <u>for I perceive that virtue is gone out of me</u>. [47] And when the woman saw that she was not hid, she came trembling, and falling down before him, she declared unto him before all the people for what cause she had touched him, and how she was healed immediately. [48] And he said unto her, Daughter, be of good comfort: thy faith hath made thee whole; go in peace.* [Emphasis added]

Jesus the Christ, Yeshua HaMaschiah, was filled with VIRTUE from living in holiness and therefore enjoyed trustworthiness, uprightness, prudence, respectability, worth, honor, integrity, moral excellence, goodness, Godly character, faith, kindness, love, purity, righteousness, merit, charity, faithfulness, justice, innocence, temperance, honesty, along with all the fruits of the Spirit—love, joy, peace, long suffering, gentleness, goodness, faith, meekness, and temperance, against such there is no law (*Galatians 5:22-23*).

---

[753] Wikimedia s.v., "EdmundBurke1771," This work is in the public domain
[754] Edmund Burke, 1791, in "A Letter to a Member of the National Assembly," *The Works of the Right Honourable Edmund Burke,* Vol. III. (of 12) (London: John C. Nimmo, 1887) 560

Jesus is *the Way, the Truth,* and *the Life*[755] and leads by example. In His *First Coming* as Savior of mankind, He led *the Way* in how to live in the Kingdom and its jurisdiction of Liberty[756] by pointing out the difference between what was written in the Oracles of Creator God from the traditions of men and rudiments of the world.[757]

Courtesy of NewCREEations.org[758]

Patrick Henry [759]

Patrick Henry (1736-1799), was an American Revolutionary leader and orator who spoke the now famous phrase, *"Give me Liberty or give me death!"* He was Commander-in-Chief of the Virginia Militia, a member of the Continental Congress, a member of the Virginia General Assembly and House of Burgesses and was instrumental in writing the Constitution of Virginia. He was the five-time Governor of the State of Virginia, the only governor in United States history to be elected and reelected five times.

At the birthing of the nation this American Revolutionary leader contended against the *Stamp Act*, another grievous taxation implemented by the British (who were controlled by the *Money Changers/House of Rothschild*). Henry fought and won the *Stamp Act Resolves*, Which was passed in the House of Burgesses in May of 1765, a summary of the pivotal events preceding the American Revolution. He wrote the following words of admonition on the back of his copy of the *Stamp Act Resolves*:

---

[755] *John 14:6 ~ Jesus saith unto him, I am the way, the truth, and the life: no man cometh unto the Father, but by me.*
[756] *2 Cor. 3:17 ~ "Now the Lord is that Spirit: and where the Spirit of the Lord is, there is liberty."*
[757] *Col 2:8 ~ Beware lest any man spoil you through philosophy and vain deceit, after the tradition of men, after the rudiments of the world, and not after Christ.*
[758] NewCREEations, "Celebrate Independence Day – Galatians 5:1," https://newcreeations.org/galatians-51/
[759] *Wikimedia Commons,* s.v. "Patrick henry.JPG," This work is in the public domain

"This brought on the war which finally separated the two countries and gave independence to ours. Whether this will prove a blessing or a curse, will depend upon the use our people make of the blessings, which a gracious God hath bestowed on us.

If they are wise, they will be great and happy. If they are of a contrary character, they will be miserable.

Righteousness alone can exalt them as a nation. <u>Reader! Whoever thou art, remember this, and in thy sphere practice virtue thyself, and encourage it in others</u>."[760] [Emphasis added]

Patrick Henry before the Virginia House of Burgesses [761]
A painting of Patrick Henry's speech against the Stamp Act of 1765,
"If this be treason, make the most of it!"

We consider particular principles established in the Holy Bible according to *Psalm 19:7-11 and 14* ~

7 The law of the Lord is perfect, converting the soul: the testimony of the Lord is sure, making wise the simple. 8 The statutes of the Lord are right, rejoicing the heart: the commandment of the Lord is pure, enlightening the eyes. 9 The fear of the Lord is clean, enduring for ever: the judgments of the Lord are true and righteous altogether. 10 More to be desired are they than gold, yea, than much fine gold: sweeter also than honey and the honeycomb. 11 Moreover by them is thy servant warned: and in keeping of them there is great reward. ... 14 Let the words of my mouth, and the meditation of my heart, be acceptable in thy sight, O Lord, my strength, and my redeemer.

---

[760] William Wirt Henry, *Patrick Henry—Life, Correspondence and Speeches,* (NY: Burt Franklin, 1969), Vol. 1, pp. 91-93 as cited Federer, America's God and Country Encyclopedia of Quotations, "Patrick Henry," (Coppell: FAME Publishing, Inc, 1994) 289
[761] *Wikimedia Commons*, s.v. "Patrick Henry Rothermel.jpg," This work is in the public domain

Samuel Adams, 1772 [762]

Now let's look at what the great Christian statesman Samuel Adams says:

"A general dissolution [disintegration] of principles and manners will more surely overthrow the liberties of America than the whole force of the common enemy."[763] [Emphasis added]

Sam Adams was conveying that the demoralization of America from within, was the "Horse of Troy" that would cause the American People to lose their Virtue. By losing Virtue, they would lose their Liberty.

Samuel Adams continued,

"While the people are <u>virtuous</u> they cannot be subdued; but when they lose their <u>virtue</u> they will be ready to surrender their liberties to the first external or internal invader. ...If <u>virtue</u> and knowledge are diffused among the people, they will never be enslaved. This will be their great security.[764] [Emphasis added]

In careful study of *2 Peter chapter one*, we can see and understand why Peter wrote it. Peter's purpose in writing to the churches scattered throughout Asia Minor was to warn against false teachers. While these false teachers are not specifically identified, the danger of their teachings is sufficient to call forth a strong denunciation from the Apostle Peter and prophecy of their destruction. Peter condemns the spirit of lawlessness that false teaching had apparently begotten in the churches and warned against the spread of *antinomianism*, the heresy of belief that a Christian does not have to be moral. Because of this, some Bible scholars would identify the false teachers as the early forerunners of *Gnosticism*, a prominent heretical movement of the 2nd century Christian Church, partly of pre-Christian origin and esoteric occult in doctrine.

Peter's antidote for this poison was to urge a growth in Biblical Christian VIRTUES as the most successful method of destroying such false teaching. In fact, his antidote is established first and is also the burden of *chapter one*.

2 Peter chapter one starting at *verse three*.

³ According as his divine power hath given unto us all things that pertain unto life and godliness, through the knowledge of him that hath <u>called us to glory and virtue</u>: ⁴ Whereby are given unto us exceeding great and precious promises: that by these ye might be partakers of the divine nature, having escaped the corruption that is in the world through lust. ⁵ And beside this, giving all diligence, <u>add to your faith virtue</u>; and to virtue

---

[762] *Wikimedia Commons, s.v.* "J S Copley - Samuel Adams.jpg," by artist John Singleton Copley, This work is in the public domain
[763] Rosalie J. Slater, *Teaching and Learning America's Christian Heritage* (San Francisco: Foundation for American Christian Education, American Revolution Bicentennial edition, 1975), p. 251. Verna M. Hall, *The Christian History of the Constitution of the United States of America–Christian Self-Government with Union* (San Francisco: Foundation for American Christian Education, 1976), p.4. as cited in Federer, *America's God and Country Encyclopedia of Quotations*, "Samuel Adams," (Coppell: FAME Publishing, Inc, 1994) 23
[764] Ibid.

knowledge; ⁶ And to knowledge temperance; and to temperance patience; and to patience godliness; ⁷ And to godliness brotherly kindness; and to brotherly kindness charity. ⁸ <u>For if these things be in you, and abound, they make you that ye shall neither be barren nor unfruitful in the knowledge of our Lord Jesus Christ. ⁹ But he that lacketh these things is blind, and cannot see afar off, and hath forgotten that he was purged from his old sins</u>. ¹⁰ Wherefore the rather, brethren, give diligence to make your calling and election sure: for if ye do these things, ye shall never fall: ¹¹ For so an entrance shall be ministered unto you abundantly into the everlasting kingdom of our Lord and Saviour Jesus Christ. [Emphasis added]

Reverend Francis Grimké (1850-1937), pastor at 15th Street Presbyterian Church, Washington, DC, said this in a sermon preached in 1909:

> *"If the time ever comes when we shall go to pieces, it will …be…from inward corruption, from the disregard of right principles… from losing sight of the fact that 'righteousness exalteth a nation, but that sin is a reproach to any people.' [Proverbs 14:34] …<u>The secession of the Southern States in 1860 was a small matter compared with the secession of the Union itself from the great principles enunciated in the Declaration of Independence, in the Golden Rule, in the Ten Commandments, in the Sermon on the Mount</u>. Unless we hold, and hold firmly to these great fundamental principles of righteousness…our Union… will be "only a covenant with death and an agreement with hell."* [765]

[Emphasis added]

Reverend Francis James Grimké[766]

Reverend Grimké also points to how the righteousness of a nation is measured:

> *"How is the righteousness of a nation measured? By its public policies, and by their conformity to God's standards."*[767]

We consider *Matthew 22:36-40* ~

> ³⁶ *Master, which is the great commandment in the law?* ³⁷ *Jesus said unto him, Thou shalt love the Lord thy God with all thy heart, and with all thy soul, and with all thy mind.* ³⁸ *This is the first and great commandment.* ³⁹ *And the second is like unto it, Thou shalt love thy neighbour as thyself.* ⁴⁰ *On these two commandments hang all the law and the prophets.*

In 1663, a generation after the Pilgrims landed at Plymouth Rock, Puritan minister and pioneer missionary among Native Americans, John Eliot, translated the English Bible into the Wampanoag language. In 1659,

---

[765] Rev. Francis J. Grimke, D.D., from "Equality of Right for All Citizens, Black and White, Alike," March 7, 1909, published in *Masterpieces of Negro Eloquence*, Alice Moore Dunbar, ed. (New York: The Bookery Publishing Company, 1914) 348-349
[766] *Wikimedia Commons* s.v., "Francis James Grimke," This work is in the public domain
[767] Rev. Francis J. Grimke, D.D., from "Equality of Right for All Citizens, Black and White, Alike," March 7, 1909, published in *Masterpieces of Negro Eloquence*, Alice Moore Dunbar, ed. (New York: The Bookery Publishing Company, 1914) 348-349

John Eliot wrote *The Christian Commonwealth or the Civil Polity or the Rising Kingdom of Jesus Christ* wherein he said,

"It is the Commandment of the Lord, that a people should enter into Covenant with the Lord to becomme his people, even in their <u>Civil Society</u>, as well as in their Church Society. Whereby they submit themselves to be ruled by the Lord in all things, receiving from him, both the <u>platform of their Government, and all their laws</u>; which they do, then Christ reigneth over them in all things, they being ruled by his Will, and by the Word of his Mouth. Is. 33:22 The Lord is our <u>Judge</u>, the Lord is our <u>Law-giver</u>, the Lord is our <u>King</u>, he shall save us."[768]

[Emphasis added]

Portrait of John Eliot[769]
17th century

John Adams, 1766 portrait [770]

Founding Father John Adams wanted to structure America according to the Holy Bible. He was studied in the *Old Testament* in Latin and the *New Testament* in Greek. Adams was inspired with the hope that someday there would be a society where their only law book would be the Holy Bible.[771] On February 22, 1756, John Adams wrote in his diary:

"Suppose a nation in some distant Region, should take the Bible for their only law Book, and every member should regulate his conduct by the precepts there exhibited. Every member would be obliged in Concience to temperance and frugality and industry, to justice and kindness and Charity towards his fellow men, and to Piety and Love, and reverence towards almighty God. In this Commonwealth, no man would impair his health by Gluttony, drunkenness, or Lust – no man would sacrifice his most precious time to cards, or any other trifling and mean amusement – no man would steal or lie or any way defraud his neighbour, but would live in peace and good will with all men – no man would blaspheme his maker or prophane his Worship, but a rational and manly, a sincere and unaffected Piety and devotion, would reign in all hearts. What a Eutopa, what a Paradise would this region be."[772]

Twenty years later, one week before Thomas Jefferson was done writing the *Declaration of Independence*, John Adams wrote the following in his letter to his cousin, Reverend Zabdiel Adams pertaining to reason, honor, and love of liberty:

---

[768] John Eliot, *The Christian Commonwealth, or The Civil Policy of the Rising Kingdom of Jesus Christ,* (London, 1659, reprinted by Arno Press, New York, 1972) as cited by Verna M. Hall, Rosalie J. Slater, *The Bible and the Constitution of the United States of America: A Primer of American Liberty,* (Chesapeake: The Foundation of American Christian Education, 1983) 17-18
[769] *Wikimedia Commons* s.v., "Portrait of John Eliot," This work is in the public domain
[770] *Wikimedia Commons,* s.v. "John Adams (1766).jpg," This work is in the public domain
[771] Quoted by Norman Cousins, *In God We Trust,* (New York: Harper Brothers, 1958), p. 167 as cited by W. Cleon Skousen, *The Majesty of God's Law, It's Coming to America,* (Salt Lake City: Ensign Publishing, 1996), 4
[772] Founders Online, From the Diary of John Adams, February 1756, https://founders.archives.gov/documents/Adams/01-01-02-0002-0002

John Adams (1735-1826) [773]

"Statesmen, my dear Sir, may plan and speculate for Liberty, but it is religion [Christianity] and Morality alone, which can establish the Principles upon which freedom can securely stand… The only foundation of a free Constitution, is pure <u>virtue</u>, and if this cannot be inspired into our People, in a greater measure, than they have it now, They may change their Rulers, and the forms of Government, but they will not obtain a lasting Liberty. They will only exchange Tyrants and Tyrannies." [774]

[Emphasis added]

On July 1, 1776, John Adams spoke profoundly before the delegates from the Thirteen Colonies at the Continental Congress. Though Adams made no preparation beforehand and never committed any minutes of his to writing, there is conjecture that he eloquently presented similarly as follows:[775]

"Objects of the most stupendous magnitude. Measures which affect the lives of millions, born and unborn are now before us. We must expect a great expense of blood to obtain them, but we must always remember that a free constitution of civil government cannot be purchased at too dear a rate as there is nothing on this side of Jerusalem, of greater importance to mankind.

My worthy colleague of Pennsylvania has spoken great ingenuity and eloquence. He has given you a grim prognostication of our national future. But where he foresees apocalypse, I see hope. I see a new nation ready to take its place in the world. Not an empire, but a republic and a republic of laws not men. Gentlemen, we are in the very midst of revolution, the most complete unexpected and remarkable of any in the history of the world. How few of the human race have ever had an opportunity of choosing a system of government for themselves and their children. I am not without apprehensions, gentlemen, but the end we have in sight is more than worth all the means. I believe sirs that the hour has come, my judgement approves of this measure and my whole heart is in it. All that I have and all that I am, and all that I hope in this life, I am now ready here to stake upon it. And I leave off as I began, that live or die, survive or perish, I am for the Declaration, it is my living sentiment and by the blessing of God, it shall be my dying sentiment. Independence now, and independence forever. While I live let me have a country…a free country."

---

[773] *Wikimedia Commons*, s.v. "US Navy 031029-N-6236G-001 A painting of President John Adams (1735-1826), 2nd president of the United States, by Asher B. Durand (1767-1845)-crop.jpg," This work is in the public domain
[774] Founders Online, John Adams to Zabdiel Adams, June 21, 1776, https://founders.archives.gov/documents/Adams/04-02-02-0011
[775] John Adams *Autobiography of John Adams*, "Monday, July 1. 1776.," https://founders.archives.gov/documents/Adams/01-03-02-0016-0142

Noah Webster [776]
Painted by Samuel Finley Breese Morse, undated

Noah Webster (1758-1843) was a statesman, educator, lexicographer and the author of *Webster's Dictionary*. Known as *"the Schoolmaster of the Nation,"* Noah Webster published the first edition of his American Dictionary of the English language in November 1828. It contained the greatest number of Biblical definitions given in any secular volume. Webster's *American Spelling Book,* first written in the 1780s while he taught in New York, became the most popular book in American education. The famous *Blue-Backed Speller* set a publishing record of a million copies a year for 100 years.

In his 1828 dictionary, Noah Webster defined a "republic." He said the Latin meaning of republic is "public affairs." He defined a republic as,

> *"A commonwealth, a state in which the exercise of the sovereign power is lodged in representatives elected by the people. In modern usage, it differs from democracy or democratic state, in which the people exercise the powers of sovereignty in person.[777]*

James Wilson, U.S. Supreme Court Justice [778]

James Wilson (1742-1798), appointed as a U.S. Supreme Court Justice in 1789 by President George Washington, held the distinction of being one of six Founding Fathers to sign both the *Declaration of Independence* and the *Constitution*. In 1790, he also became the first law professor at the University of Pennsylvania. James Wilson was very active at the Constitutional Convention held in 1787; Wilson stood and spoke 168 times. One of the things he said was,

---

[776] *Library of Congress Prints and Photographs Division Washington, D.C. 20540, James Wilson, Reproduction Number: LC-USZ62-6065 (b&w film copy neg.)*, https://www.loc.gov/pictures/item/2021645231/ No known restrictions on publication.
[777] *Noah Webster's First Edition of An American Dictionary of the English Language,* 1828:
"REPUB'LIC;, n. [L. *respublica*; *res* and *publica* ; public affairs.]
1. A commonwealth ; a state in which the exercise of the sovereign power is lodged in representatives elected by the people. In modern usage, it differs from a democracy or democratic stale, in which the people exercise the powers of sovereignty in person. Vet the democracies of Greece are often called republics.
2. Common interest ; the public. [Not in use.] B. Jonson."
Republic of letters, the collective body of learned men."
[778] *Wikimedia Commons*, s.v. "JusticeJamesWilson.jpg," This work is in the public domain

"Human law must rest its authority ultimately upon the authority of that law which is divine. ...Far from being rivals or enemies, <u>religion and law are twin sisters, friends, and mutual assistants</u>. Indeed, these two sciences run into each other."[779] [Emphasis added]

Benjamin Rush, 1783[780]

Dr. Benjamin Rush (1745-1813) was a physician, signer of the *Declaration of Independence*, *"father of public schools"* and a principal promoter of the American Sunday School Union. He also served as the Surgeon General of the Continental Army, helped to write the Pennsylvania constitution, and was the treasurer of the U.S. Mint. In 1786, Dr. Rush established the first free medical clinic and later helped found the first American anti-slavery society. In 1798, after the adoption of the *Constitution for the United States*, he declared:

"[T]he only foundation for a useful education in a republic is to be laid in religion [Christianity]. Without this there can be no <u>virtue</u>, and without <u>virtue</u> there can be no liberty, and <u>liberty is the object and life of all republican governments</u>." [781] [Emphasis added]

Reverend Nathaniel Whitaker, D.D.[782]
Courtesy of Hood Museum of Art, Dartmouth College

The renowned preacher, Nathaniel Whitaker was born on February 22, 1732 — the exact same day as George Washington. Preacher Whitaker achieved extraordinary Biblical knowledge and was gifted with commanding powers of elocution; he was known as a "great political counsellor." Whitaker was born at Long Island, New York, was a graduate of Princeton, and then engaged in ministry at Norwich, Connecticut. On July 28, 1769, Reverend Whitaker agreed to preach at the Third Church in Salem, Massachusetts. It was in 1775 when the British burned down the church, so his congregation then worshipped

---

[779] James Wilson, *"The Works of James Wilson, associate justice of the Supreme Court of the United States and Professor of Law in the College of Philadelphia,"* Vol. I, ed. James De Witt Andrews, (Chicago: Callaghan and Company, 1896) , 93-95
[780] Wikimedia, s.v., Benjamin Rush Painting by Peale 1783, This work is in the public domain
[781] Dr. Benjamin Rush, "Thoughts, Upon the Mode of Education Proper in a Republic," *A Plan for the Establishment of Public Schools and the Diffusion of Knowledge in Pennsylvania; to Which Are Added, Thoughts upon the Mode of Education Proper in a Republic*, (Philadelphia: Thomas Dobson, 1786). Reproduced in *Essays on Education in the Early Republic*, ed. Frederick Rudolph, (Cambridge, MA: The Belknap Press of Harvard University Press, 1965) 9-23 ; William J. Federer, *America's God and Country Encyclopedia of Quotations*, "Benjamin Rush," (Coppell: FAME Publishing, Inc., 1994) 543
[782] Hood Museum of Art, Dartmouth College, "Reverend Nathaniel Whitaker (1730-1795), Class of 1780H," accessed April 2, 2021, https://hoodmuseum.dartmouth.edu/objects/p.866.1

in a schoolhouse. He was recognized as being uncompromising, pious, learned, and charitable.[783]

Reverend Whitaker preached a sermon in the autumn of 1777 and dedicated his sermon to General George Washington. His text was based on *Judges 5:23 ~ Curse ye Meroz, said the angel of the Lord, curse ye bitterly the inhabitants thereof; because they came not to the help of the Lord, to the help of the Lord against the mighty.*

In his sermon he touched on Natural Liberty. He said that John Locke defined Natural Liberty to be,

> *"that state or condition in which all men naturally are to order all their actions, and dispose of themselves and possessions as they think fit, within the bounds of the law of nature, without asking leave, or depending on the will of any man."*[784]

John Locke [785]
1632-1704 (England)

We interject that John Locke (1632-1704) was an English philosopher whose writings had a profound influence on our Founding Fathers and, in turn, on the writing of the *Constitution*. Of nearly 15,000 items of the Founding Fathers which were reviewed, including books, newspaper articles, pamphlets, monographs, etc., it was determined that John Locke was the third most frequently quoted author. In his *Two Treatises of Government*, 1690, he cited 80 references to the Holy Bible in the first treatise and 22 references to the Holy Bible in the second.[786]

Regarding Natural Liberty, Reverend Whitaker said,

> *"In this state all men are equal, and no one hath a right to govern or control another. And the law of nature or the eternal reason and fitness of things, is to be the only rule of his conduct; of the meaning of which everyone is to be his own judge."*[787]

Preacher Whitaker presented an outline in his sermon:

> *~ That the cause of liberty is the cause of God and truth.*
> *~ That to take arms and repel force by force when our liberties are invaded, is well-pleasing to God.*
> *~ That it is lawful to levy war against those who oppress us, even when they are not in arms against us.*
> *~ That indolence and backwardness in taking arms, and exerting ourselves in the service of our country, when called thereto by the public voice, in order to recover and secure our liberty, is a heinous sin in the sight of God.*

---

[783] Frank Moore, *The Patriot Preachers of the American Revolution: With Biographical Sketches; Nathaniel Whitaker, D.D., "An Antidote against Toryism, or the Curse of Meroz,* (New York: Charles T. Evans, 1862) 186-231
[784] Ibid., 198
[785] *Wikimedia*, s.v. "JohnLocke.png," This work is in the public domain
[786] Federer, *America's Quotations*, "John Locke," (Coppell: FAME Publishing, Inc., 1994) 397
[787] Frank Moore, *The Patriot Preachers of the American Revolution: With Biographical Sketches; Nathaniel Whitaker, D.D., "An Antidote against Toryism, or the Curse of Meroz,* (New York: Charles T. Evans, 1862) 198

> ~ *That God requires a people, struggling for their liberties, to treat such of the community who will not join them, as open enemies, and to reject them as unworthy the privileges which others enjoy.*[788]

Whitaker started his sermon with these words,

> *"The sum of the law of nature, as well as of the written law, is love. Love to God and man, properly exercised in tender feelings of the heart, and beneficent actions of life, constitutes perfect holiness."*[789]

This sermon gives serious emphasis to Creator God's Liberty! Liberty should and must be protected! Liberty pertains to <u>both</u> *Civil and Religious Liberty!*

The *Father of the American Revolution*, Samuel Adams, said it this way:

> *"The natural liberty of man is to be free from any superior power on earth, and not to be under the will or legislative authority of man, but only to have the law of nature for his rule."*[790]

If you don't have a value for life, then you don't value your own life, nor the lives of others. If you don't have a cause worth dying for, then you won't have a cause worth living for. Throughout history it has been evidenced that the nations that have had great liberty have had people who understand these principles and had enough character to give their lives for the cause of liberty. They were impassioned about others being able to live in Liberty, not just themselves.[791]

Is that the way America is today? Do you know anyone in your community that understands Liberty as they did in the 17th and 18th centuries? Are people in America ready to fight for Liberty? Does America truly have that kind of Liberty today? Do they?!

Our beloved and impassioned Founding Father Samuel Adams said,

> *"If ye love wealth better than liberty; the tranquility of servitude, [better] than the animating contest of freedom— go from us in peace. We ask not your counsels or arms. Crouch down and lick the hands which feed you. May your chains sit lightly upon you, and may posterity forget that ye were our countrymen."*[792]
>
> [Emphasis added]

It is of utmost importance to know this: The position of the Church during the American Revolution is evidenced in the sermons of the Patriot Preachers of their day, who did not hesitate to attack the great political and social evils.

> *"The voice of the Fathers of the American Republic enforced by their example. They invoked God in their civil assemblies, called upon their chosen teachers of religion for counsel from the Bible, and recognized its precepts as the law of their public conduct. The Fathers did not divorce politics and religion, but they denounced the separation as ungodly. They prepared for the struggle and went into battle…with the Word of God in their*

---

[788] Ibid. 197
[789] Ibid. 198
[790] Samuel Adams, *The Report of the Committee of Correspondence to the Boston Town Meeting*, Nov. 20, 1772, "The Rights of the Colonists," Old South Leaflets no. 173 (Boston: Directors of the Old South Work, 1906) 7: 417-428
[791] Dr. Marlene McMillan, *The Five Pillars of Liberty,* (LibertyViewMedia.com, 2011) 83
[792] *Masterpieces of American Eloquence*, "American Independence," Samuel Adams' Speech delivered at the State House in Philadelphia, August 1, 1776 (New York: The Christian Herald, 1900) 28

> *hearts and trusting in him. This was the secret of that moral energy which sustained the Republic in its material weakness against superior numbers and discipline, and all the power of England. ... The Colonists appealed to Heaven!"*[793] [Emphasis added]

Again, Patrick Henry wrote an important message to posterity, the future generations to come, on the back of his copy of the *Stamp Act Resolutions*,

> *"Righteousness alone can exalt them as a nation. Reader! Whoever thou art, remember this; and in thy sphere practise virtue thyself, and encourage it in others."*[794]

It is imperative that the American People must practice Virtue in their lifestyle and sphere of influence and teach it to others. It is an obvious conclusion in view of the crisis we experience as a nation today that virtue is missing in America. Especially in all of our worship centers across this great land. Remember! Without Virtue it is not possible to enjoy *Religious Liberty* or *Civil Liberty*.

Reflecting on historic events related to the *Organic Act of 1871*, we understand that the *Illuminist* worshipers of Satan pushed the *Declaration of Independence* and our *Constitution*, along with the *Bill of Rights* (God's tools), off to the side without giving notice to the American People while these evil ones proceeded forward with a business enterprise and masquerading as the American Republic, calling it "government."

The way or the foundation of God's Solution for America has to do with fellowship (true fellowship) with Jesus Christ and the Father. And then also true fellowship with other true believers.

Visiting the *Gospel of Matthew, chapter seven at verses 24-27* ~

> [24] *Therefore whosoever heareth these sayings of mine, and doeth them, I will liken him unto a wise man, which built his house upon a rock:* [25] *And the rain descended, and the floods came, and the winds blew, and beat upon that house; and it fell not: for it was founded upon a rock.* [26] *And every one that heareth these sayings of mine, and doeth them not, shall be likened unto a foolish man, which built his house upon the sand:* [27] *And the rain descended, and the floods came, and the winds blew, and beat upon that house; and it fell: and great was the fall of it.*

There is a freewill choice in how we build a marriage, a business, a government, or our lives (including our eternal lives). We can base the entirety of our lives on human reasoning which is equivalent to building on sand or we can base the entirety of our lives on the foundation of a solid Rock!

Revelation 3:20 ~ *Behold, I stand at the door, and knock: if any man hear my voice, and open the door, I will come in to him, and will sup with him, and he with me.*

If you are attracted to a particular person and you want to get to know that individual, then asking that person to join you for dinner at a very nice supper club would be ideal. To learn about this special person

---

[793] John Wingate Thornton, A.M., *The Pulpit of the American Revolution: or, the Political Sermons on the Period of 1776*, (Boston: D. Lothrop & Co, 1860) Preface
[794] Red Hill Patrick Henry National Memorial, "Patrick Henry's Resolutions Against the Stamp Act, May 29, 1765 to May 30, 1765," https://www.redhill.org/primary-sources/patrick-henrys-resolutions-against-the-stamp-act/

over a nice meal would be very enjoyable as well as interesting, while at the same time a relationship begins to develop.

When we visit the *sixth chapter of the Gospel of John* in the Holy Writ starting at the *twenty-fifth verse* and reading through it until the *sixty-fifth verse*, we find out that Jesus is showing the way of eternal life by having a serious fellowship with Him. Let's check it out starting at the *forty-seventh verse* in John 6.

> *47 Verily, verily, I say unto you, He that believeth on me hath everlasting life. 48 I am that bread of life. 49 Your fathers did eat manna in the wilderness, and are dead. 50 This is the bread which cometh down from heaven, that a man may eat thereof, and not die. 51 I am the living bread which came down from heaven: if any man eat of this bread, he shall live for ever: and the bread that I will give is my flesh, which I will give for the life of the world. 52 The Jews therefore strove among themselves, saying, How can this man give us his flesh to eat? 53 Then Jesus said unto them, Verily, verily, I say unto you, Except ye eat the flesh of the Son of man, and drink his blood, ye have no life in you. 54 Whoso eateth my flesh, and drinketh my blood, hath eternal life; and I will raise him up at the last day. 55 For my flesh is meat indeed, and my blood is drink indeed. 56 He that eateth my flesh, and drinketh my blood, dwelleth in me, and I in him. 57 As the living Father hath sent me, and I live by the Father: so he that eateth me, even he shall LIVE BY ME.*
>
> *58 This is that bread which came down from heaven: not as your fathers did eat manna, and are dead: he that eateth of this bread shall live for ever. 59 These things said he in the synagogue, as he taught in Capernaum. 60 Many therefore of his disciples, when they had heard this, said, This is an hard saying; who can hear it? 61 When Jesus knew in himself that his disciples murmured at it, he said unto them, Doth this offend you? 62 What and if ye shall see the Son of man ascend up where he was before? 63 It is the spirit that quickeneth; the flesh profiteth nothing: the words that I speak unto you, they are spirit, and they are life. 64 But there are some of you that believe not. For Jesus knew from the beginning who they were that believed not, and who should betray him. 65 And he said, Therefore said I unto you, that no man can come unto me, except it were given unto him of my Father.* [Emphasis added]

True fellowship with Christ is praying, reading His Word, trusting in Him by faith, and being filled with gratitude for His dying for our sins and being raised from the dead. Christ is our main being, He is our King and great Friend. He is our great Savior! He is everything, He is our eternal life!

> *Colossians 1:19* ~ *For it pleased the Father that in him should all fulness dwell;*
>
> *John 1:16-17* ~ *16 And of his fulness have all we received, and grace for grace. 17 For the law was given by Moses, but grace and truth came by Jesus Christ.*

Reverend Andrew Murray[795]

The following is taken from the 1692 posthumously published book by English Puritan pastor, Walter Marshall (1628-1680), *Sanctification; or, The Highway of Holiness,* with *An Abridgment (in the Author's Own Words) of The Gospel Mystery of Sanctification* written and published in 1884 by Reverend Andrew Murray (1828-1917). Andrew Murray was a South African pastor, missionary, and author that published over 240 books and tracts on Christian topics. This work has been praised as perhaps the single greatest work on sanctification ever composed. [796] [797]

> *"[So] the way to get Holy Endowments and Qualifications necessary to frame and enable us for the immediate practice of the Law is, to receive them out of the fullness of Christ by fellowship with Him; And that we may have this fellowship, we must be in Christ, and have Christ Himself in us, by a mystical union with Him.*[798]
>
> *Here, as much as anywhere, we have great cause to acknowledge with the apostle, that, 'without controversy great is the mystery of godliness,' even so great that it could 'not have entered into the heart of man to conceive it, if God had not made it known' in the gospel by supernatural revelation. Yea, though it be revealed clearly in the Holy Scriptures, yet the natural man has not eyes to see it there, for it is foolishness to him; and if God express it ever so plainly and properly, he will think that God is speaking riddles and parables. And I doubt not but it is still a riddle and parable even to many truly godly, who have received an holy nature in this way; for the apostles themselves had the saving benefit of it before the Comforter discovered it clearly to them (John 14:20)."*[799]
>
> *John 14:20 ~ At that day ye shall know that I am in my Father, and ye in me, and I in you.*
>
> *John 6:56 ~ He that eateth my flesh, and drinketh my blood, dwelleth in me, and I in him.*
>
> *"One great mystery is, that the holy frame and disposition, whereby our souls are furnished and enables for immediate practice of the law, must be obtained 'by receiving it out of Christ's fulness,' as a thing already prepared and brought to an existence for us in Christ, and treasured up in Him; and that, as we are justified by a righteousness wrought out in Christ, and imputed to us, so we are sanctified by such an holy frame and qualifications as are first wrought out and completed in Christ for us, and then imparted to us. And as our natural corruption was produced originally in the first Adam, and propagated from him to us, so our new nature and holiness is first produced in Christ, and derived from Him to us, or, as it were, propagated. So that we are not at all to work together with Christ in making or producing that holy frame in us, but only to TAKE IT TO OURSELVES, and use it in our holy practice, as made ready to our hands. Thus we have fellowship*

---

[795] *Wikimedia Commons* s.v. "File:Andrew Murray.JPG," This work is in the public domain
[796] Rev. Walter Marshall *Sanctification; or, The Highway of Holiness, An Abridgment (in the Author's Own Words) of The Gospel Mystery of Sanctification with an Introductory Note by* Rev. Andrew Murray (London: James Nisbet & Co., 1884) 16
[797] The Digital Puritan, "Walter Marshall," http://digitalpuritan.net/walter-marshall/
[798] Marshall, *Sanctification*, 16
[799] Ibid.

with Christ in receiving that holy frame of spirit that was originally in Him; for fellowship is when several persons have the same things in common (1 John 1:1-3)."[800] [Emphasis added]

> *1 John 1:1-3 ~ [1] That which was from the beginning, which we have heard, which we have seen with our eyes, which we have looked upon, and our hands have handled, of the Word of life; [2] (For the life was manifested, and we have seen it, and bear witness, and shew unto you that eternal life, which was with the Father, and was manifested unto us;) [3] That which we have seen and heard declare we unto you, that ye also may have fellowship with us: and truly our fellowship is with the Father, and with his Son Jesus Christ.*

If we visit a worship center one or two days a week, our conversation should not be about a favorite sports team, or the agricultural crops, or our workplace. True fellowship should be focused on Jesus Christ. Let's read *1 John 1:5-7*:

> *1 John 1:5-7 ~ [5] This then is the message which we have heard of him, and declare unto you, that God is light, and in him is no darkness at all. [6] If we say that we have fellowship with him, and walk in darkness, we lie, and do not the truth: [7] But if we walk in the light, as he is in the light, we have fellowship one with another, and the blood of Jesus Christ his Son cleanseth us from all sin.*

This is TRUE FELLOWSHIP! As we continue, read the following very carefully:

> *"This mystery is so great that, notwithstanding all the light of the gospel, we commonly think that we must get an holy frame by producing it anew in ourselves, and by forming it and working it out of our own hearts. Therefore many that are seriously devout take a great deal of pains to mortify their corrupted nature, and beget an holy frame of heart in themselves by striving earnestly to master their sinful lusts, and by pressing them vehemently upon their hearts many motives to godliness, labouring importunately to squeeze good qualifications out of them, as oil out of a flint. They account that though they be justified by a righteousness wrought out by Christ, yet they must be sanctified by a holiness wrought out by themselves. And though out of humility they are willing to call it infused grace, yet they think they must get the infusion of it by the same manner of working, as if it were wholly acquired by their endeavours. On this account they acknowledge the entrance into a godly life to be harsh and unpleasing, because it costs so much struggling with their own hearts and affections to new-frame them. If they knew that this way of entrance is not only harsh and unpleasant, but altogether impossible; and that the true way of mortifying sin and quickening themselves to holiness is by receiving a new nature out of the fulness of Christ; and that we do no more to the production of a new nature than of original sin, though we do more to the reception of it. If they knew this they might save themselves many a bitter agony, and a great deal of misspent burdensome labour, and employ their endeavours to enter in at the strait gate in such a way as would be more pleasant and successful.*[801]

> *Another great mystery in the way of sanctification is <u>the glorious manner of our fellowship</u> with Christ, in receiving an holy frame of heart from Him. It is by being in Christ, and having Christ Himself in us, -- and that not merely by His universal presence as He is God, but by such a close union as that we are one spirit and one flesh with him, -- which is a privilege peculiar to those that are truly sanctified. I may well call this a mystical union, because the apostle calleth it a great mystery, in an epistle full of mysteries (Ephesians 5:32),*

---

[800] Ibid. 16-17
[801] Ibid. 17

intimating that it is eminently great above many other mysteries. This union betwixt Christ and believers is plain from several places of Scripture, which testify that Christ is and dwelleth in believers, and they in Him (John 6:5,6 and John 14:20), and that they are so joined together as to become one spirit (1 Corinthians 6:17), and that believers are members of Christ's body, of His flesh, and of His bones; -- and that they two, Christ and the Church, are one flesh (Ephesians 5:30, 31). Furthermore, this union is illustrated in Scripture by various resemblances which would be very much unlike the things which they are made use of to resemble, and would rather seem to beguile us by obscuring the truth, than instruct us by illustrating of it, if there were no true, proper union, between Christ and believers. It is resembled by the union between God the Father and Christ (John 14:20, and John 17:21-23)..."[802]

> *John 17:21-23 ~ 21 That they all may be one; as thou, Father, art in me, and I in thee, that they also may be one in us: that the world may believe that thou hast sent me. 22 And the glory which thou gavest me I have given them; that they may be one, even as we are one: 23 I in them, and thou in me, that they may be made perfect in one; and that the world may know that thou hast sent me, and hast loved them, as thou hast loved me.*

> *"...between the vine and its branches (John 15:4, 5), between the head and the body (Ephesians 1:22, 23) ..."*[803]

> *Ephesians 1:22-23 ~ 22 And hath put all things under his feet, and gave him to be the head over all things to the church, 23 Which is his body, the fulness of him that filleth all in all.*

How can there be a government *501c3* corporation status requirement for tax exemption of worship centers for the fellowship of the saints? Scratch your chin and say, "This doesn't make sense."

> *"...between bread and the eater (John 6:51-54), it is not only resembled, but sealed in the Lord's Supper..."*[804]

There is a way to know and…

> *"...it is evidently discovered to those that have their understandings opened to discern that supernatural revelation of the mysterious way of sanctification which God hath given to us in the Holy Scriptures.*[805]

> *There are several places in Scripture that do plainly express it. Some texts show that all things pertaining to our salvation are treasured up for us in Christ, and comprehended in His fulness; so that we must have them thence or not at all (Colossians 1:19). 'It pleased the Father that in Him should all fulness dwell.' And, in the same epistle (Colossians 2:11-13), the apostle showeth that the holy nature whereby we live to God was first produced in us by His death and resurrection: 'In whom also ye are circumcised in putting off the body of the sins of the flesh; buried with him; quickened together with Him; when ye were dead in your sins.' And again in Ephesians 1:3, he testifies that 'God hath blessed us with all spiritual blessings in heavenly places in Christ.' An holy frame of spirit, with all its necessary qualifications, must needs be comprehended here in 'all spiritual blessings;' and these are given us in Christ's person in heavenly places, as prepared and treasured up in Him for us while we are upon earth; and therefore we must have our holy endowments out of Him or not at all.*[806]

---

[802] Ibid. 18
[803] Ibid. 18
[804] Ibid.
[805] Ibid. 19
[806] Ibid. 19-20

> *Other texts of Scripture show plainly that we receive our holiness out of His fulness by fellowship with Him, (John 1:16, 17): 'Of His fulness have all we received, and grace for grace' — in which Scripture the grace spoken of as received from Christ, being answerable to 'the law given by Moses' in the preceding clause, must needs include the grace of sanctification. Again we read (1 John 1:3, 5-7): 'Truly our fellowship is with the Father, and with His Son Jesus Christ. God is light. If we walk in the light, as He is in the light, we have fellowship one with another.' Whence we may infer that our fellowship with God and Christ doth include particularly out having light, and walking in it holily and righteously.*
>
> *There are other texts that reach the proof of the whole direction fully; showing, not only that our holy endowments are made ready first in Christ for us, received from Christ, but that we receive them by union with Christ: Colossians 3:10, 11, 'Ye have put on the new man, which is renewed after the image of Him that created him; where Christ is all and in all;' 1 Corinthians 6:17, 'He that is joined to the Lord is one spirit;' Galatians 2:20, 'I live; yet not I, but Christ liveth in me;' 1 John 5:11, 12, 'This is the record, that God hath given to us eternal life; and this life is in His Son. He that hath the Son hath life, and he that hath not the Son hath not life.' Can we desire that God should more clearly teach us that all the fulness of the new man, and all that spiritual nature and life whereby we live to God in holiness, is in Christ; and that they are fixed in Him so inseparably that, we cannot have them except we be joined to Him, and have Himself abiding in us."*[807]

May your eyes be opened to see and may you be blessed with a lot of spiritual understanding. Just know that...

> *"...We receive from Christ a new holy frame and nature, whereby we are enabled for an holy practice, by union and fellowship with Him; in like manner, (1.) As Christ lived in our nature by the Father (John 6:57); (2.) As we received original sin and death propagated to us from the first Adam (Romans 5:12, 14, 16, 17); (3.) As the natural body receiveth sense, motion, nourishment from the head (Colossians 2:19); (4.) As the branch receiveth its sap, juice, and fructifying virtue from the vine (John 15:4, 5); (5.) As the wife bringeth forth fruit by virtue of her conjugal union with her husband (Romans 7:4); (6.) As stones become an holy temple by being built upon the foundation and joined with the chief cornerstone (1 Peter 2:4, 5, 7); (7.) As we receive the nourishing virtue of bread by eating it, and of wine by drinking it (John 6:51, 55, 57), which last resemblance is used to seal to us our communion with Christ in the Lord's Supper."*[808]

This is what America needs! When you receive Christ, you receive all the fulness of God! You receive His holiness. You are able to practice holiness because of Christ living inside of you! You must crucify the flesh (the "Old Man"). You must in absolute surrender give Christ all of you!

> *"...By His <u>incarnation</u> there was a man created in a new holy frame, after the holiness of the first Adam's frame had been marred and abolished by the first transgression; and this <u>new frame</u> was far more excellent than ever the first Adam's was, because man was really joined to God by a close inseparable union of the divine and human nature in one person – Christ; so that these natures had communion each with other in their actings, and Christ was able to act in His human nature by power proper to the divine nature, wherein He was one God with the Father. ...[Jesus] was born Emmanuel, God with us; because <u>the fulness of the Godhead, with all holiness, did first dwell</u> in Him bodily, even <u>in His human nature</u>, that we might be filled with that fulness in Him (Matthew 1:23; Colossians 2:9, 10). Thus He came down from heaven as living bread, that, as He*

---

[807] Ibid. 20
[808] Ibid. 20-21

liveth by the Father, so those that eat Him may live by Him (John 6:51, 57); <u>by the same life of God in them that was first in Him.</u>[809] [Emphasis added]

So …

"God 'sending His own Son in the likeness of sinful flesh, for sin' (or, 'by a sacrifice for sin,' as in the margin), 'condemned sin in the flesh: that the righteousness of the law might be fulfilled in us, who walk not after the flesh, but after the Spirit' (Romans 8:3, 4). Observe here, that though Christ died that we might be justified by the righteousness of God and of faith, not by our own righteousness, which is of the law (Romans 10:4-6; Philippians 3:9), yet <u>He died also</u> that the righteousness of the law might be fulfilled <u>in</u> us, and <u>that</u> by walking after His Spirit, as those that are in Christ (Romans 8:4). He is resembled in His death to a corn of wheat dying in the earth, that it may propagate its own nature by bringing forth much fruit (John 12:24 [which says this ~ Verily, verily, I say unto you, Except a corn of wheat fall into the ground and die, it abideth alone: but if it die, it bringeth forth much fruit.])…"[810] [Emphasis added]

So then,

"…By His <u>resurrection</u> He took possession of spiritual life for us, as now fully procured for us, and made to be our right and property by the merit of His death; and therefore we are said to be quickened together with Christ. [Romans 8:11] His resurrection was our resurrection to the life of HOLINESS, as Adam's fall was our fall into spiritual death. And we are not ourselves the first makers and formers of our new holy nature, any more than of our original corruption, but both are formed ready for us to partake of them. And, by union with Christ, we partake of that spiritual life that He took possession of for us at His resurrection, and thereby we are enabled to bring forth the fruits of it; as the Scripture showeth by the similitude of a marriage union. Romans 7:4, 'We are married to Him that is raised from the dead, that we might bring forth fruit unto God.'"[811]

[Emphasis added]

So, we understand that we were born in sin and practiced sin because of our sin nature acquired at birth because of the fall of Adam. The natural man cannot be fixed or mended.

Romans 7:17-20 ~ ¹⁷ Now then it is no more I that do it, but sin that dwelleth in me. ¹⁸ For I know that in me (that is, in my flesh,) dwelleth no good thing: for to will is present with me; but how to perform that which is good I find not. ¹⁹ For the good that I would I do not: but the evil which I would not, that I do. ²⁰ Now if I do that I would not, it is no more I that do it, but sin that dwelleth in me.

This "Old Man" must be crucified and buried. You cannot fix this "Old Man" — he must be done away with.

Galatians 2:20-21 ~ ²⁰ I am crucified with Christ: nevertheless I live; yet not I, but Christ liveth in me: and the life which I now live in the flesh I live by the faith of the Son of God, who loved me, and gave himself for me. ²¹ I do not frustrate the grace of God: for if righteousness come by the law, then Christ is dead in vain.

So when Christ was crucified for all my sins, who loved me with an objective to give me a chance to be raised with Him for newness of life (eternal life), I must crucify myself daily, to die and be buried with Him,

---

[809] Ibid. 22
[810] Ibid. 23
[811] Ibid 23-24

as He died for me. The "Old Man," present because of the generational sin of Adam and Eve, must be dealt with because you can't fix the natural man as he is possessed with a spirit (our sin nature) that wants to practice sin. So, we then take on our new identity—the "New Man" as we then receive Christ and His Righteousness and live in His Spirit.

> *Ephesians 4:21, 22, 24 ~ 21 If so be that ye have heard him, and have been taught by him, as the truth is in Jesus: 22 That ye put off concerning the former conversation the old man, which is corrupt according to the deceitful lusts; ... 24 And that ye put on the new man, which after God is created in righteousness and true holiness.*

We are realizing that there are two different identities that we are observing here. One practices sin while the other, with great spiritual understanding, practices Christ's holiness. Christ's holiness is already inside of you because you have all the fulness of Christ. The only way this believer can function properly is to live by faith, walk by faith, work by faith, everything you do in the Kingdom of Christ and of God is by faith.

> *Hebrews 11:6 ~ But without faith it is impossible to please him: for he that cometh to God must believe that he is, and that he is a rewarder of them that diligently seek him.*

Hall of faith —

The just shall live by faith (*Hebrews 10:38*). They worshipped by faith as Abel. They walked by faith as Enoch. They worked by faith as Noah. They lived by faith as Abraham. They governed by faith as Moses. They followed by faith as Jacob-Israel. They fought by faith as Joshua. They conquered by faith as Gideon. They subdued kingdoms by faith as David. They closed the mouths of lions by faith as Daniel. They walked through fire by faith as the three Hebrew children. They suffered by faith as Paul. They died by faith as Stephen, the first Christian martyr. By faith they were patient in suffering, courageous in battle, made strong out of weakness, and were victorious in defeat. They were more than conquerors by faith. The faith of these saints inspires us as we look to Jesus, the author and finisher of our faith.[812]

> *Hebrews 12:2 ~ Looking unto Jesus the author and finisher of our faith; who for the joy that was set before him endured the cross, despising the shame, and is set down at the right hand of the throne of God.*

When we are "born again" we are no longer in the state of the "Old Man" to practice sin. We are in the state of the "New Man" to practice holiness.

Remember this! First of all you already have all the fulness of God inside of you. This fulness includes holiness! From holiness comes virtue! What's missing across America is virtue. With virtue, you and your worship center in true fellowship, can experience *Religious Liberty*! If you have obtained true *Religious Liberty* from virtue, then internal-to-external your community can then experience *Civil Liberty*!

> *"Holiness through faith – [we must] <u>make diligent use of your most Holy Faith, for the immediate performance of the duties of the Law</u>, by walking no longer according to your old natural State [Romans 7:1-6], or any Principles or Means of Practice that belong unto it <u>but only according to that new State which you receive by Faith</u>, and the Principles and Means of Practice that properly belong thereunto, and strive to continue and*

---

[812] *Hebrews chapter 11*

increase in such manner of practice. This is the only way to attain to an acceptable performance of these Holy and Righteous Duties, as far as it is possible in this present life."[813] [Emphasis added]

So…

"Here I am guiding you to <u>the manner of practice</u>, wherein you are to make use of faith, and of all other effectual means of holiness before treated of, which faith layeth hold on, for the immediate performance of the law; which is the great end aimed at in this whole treatise. And therefore this deserveth to be diligently considered, as the principal direction, to which all the foregoing and following are subservient. As for the meaning of it, I have already showed that our old natural state is that which we derive from the first Adam by natural generation, and it is called in the Scripture 'the old man;' and while we be in it we are said to be 'in the flesh.' And our new state is that which we receive from the second Adam, Jesus Christ, by being new born in union and fellowship with Him through faith, and it is called in Scripture 'the new man;' and when we are in it we are said to be 'in the Spirit.'"[814]

"The principles and means of practice belonging to a natural state are such as persons do, or may attain and make use of, before they are in Christ by faith. Such as belong properly to the new state, are the manifold holy endowments, privileges, and enjoyments, which we partake of in Christ by faith, such as have already appeared to be the only effectual means of a holy life. We are said to walk according to either of these states, or to the principles of means that belong to either of them, when we are moved and guided by virtue of them to such actings as are agreeable to them. The manner of the practice here directed to consists in moving and guiding ourselves in the performance of the works of the law by gospel principles and means. This is the rare and excellent art of godliness, in which every Christian should strive to be skillful and expert. The reason why many come off with shame and confusion, after they have a long time laboured with much zeal and industry for the attainment of true godliness, is because they were never acquainted with this holy art, and never endeavoured to practice it in a right gospel way."[815]

"It is a manner of practice far above the sphere of natural ability, such as would never have entered into the hearts of the wisest in the world, if it had not been revealed to us in the Scriptures. And when it is there most plainly revealed, continueth a dark riddle to those that are not inwardly enlightened and taught by the Holy Spirit. Such as many godly persons, guided by the Spirit, do in some measure walk in, yet do but obscurely discern; they can hardly perceive their own knowledge of it, and can hardly give any account to others of the way wherein they walk, as the disciples that walked in Christ the way to the Father, and yet perceived not that knowledge in themselves: 'Lord, we know not whither Thou goest, and how can we know the way?' (John 14:5) <u>This is the reason why many poor believers are so weak in Christ</u>, and attain so small a degree of holiness and righteousness. Therefore, that you may the better be acquainted with mystery of so high concernment, I shall show, in the first place, that the Holy Scriptures do direct you to this manner of practice, as only effectual for the performance of holy duties; and then I shall lay before you some necessary instructions, that you may understand how to walk aright in it; and continue and go forward therein till you be made perfect in Christ."[816]

[Emphasis added]

---

[813] Marshall, *Sanctification*, 56
[814] Ibid.
[815] Ibid. 56-57
[816] Ibid. 57

> *"For the FIRST of these the Holy Scriptures are very large and clear in directing us to this manner of practice, and to continuance and growth therein."*[817]

So let me show you…

> *"…the manner of practice in Scripture, which is expressed by 'living by faith' (Habakkuk 2:4; Galatians 2:20; Hebrews 10:38),*

Come on now, look up these Scriptures…

> *" 'walking by faith' (2 Corinthians 5:7), 'faith working by love' (Galatians 5:6), 'overcoming the world by faith' (1 John 5:4), 'quenching all the fiery darts of the wicked by the shield of faith' (Ephesians 6:16). Some make no more of living and walking by faith than merely a stirring-up and encouraging ourselves to our duty by such principles as we believe. But if this was all that was intended by these expressions, then the Jews might account that they lived by faith, because they professed and assented unto the doctrine of Moses and the Prophets, and were moved thereby to a zeal of God; yet we are expressly told of them, that they sought righteousness not by faith, but as it were by the works of the law (Romans 9:32). As it is one and the same thing to be justified by faith, and by Christ believed on (Romans 5:1), so to live, walk, and work by faith is all one with living, walking, working by means of Christ and His saving endowments, which we receive and make use of by faith, to guide and move ourselves to the practice of holiness."*[818]

> *"The same thing is commended to us by the terms of 'walking in Christ,' 'rooted and built up in Him' (Colossians 2:6, 7), 'living to God and not to ourselves, but to have Christ living in us' (Galatians 2:19, 20), 'good conversation in Christ' (1 Peter 3:16), 'putting on the Lord Jesus Christ, that we may walk honestly as in the day' (Romans 13:13, 14), 'being strong in the Lord, and in the power of His might' (Ephesians 6:10), 'doing all things in the name of Christ' (Colossians 3:17), 'walking up and down in the name of the Lord' (Zechariah 10:12), 'going in the strength of the Lord, making mention of His righteousness, even of His only' (Psalm 71:16). These phrases are frequent, and do sufficiently explain one another, and do show that we are to practice holiness, not only by virtue of Christ's authority, but also of His strengthening endowments moving us and encouraging us thereunto."*[819]

> *"It is also signified by the phrases of 'being strong in the grace that is in Christ Jesus' (2 Timothy 2:1), 'having our conversation in the world, not with fleshly wisdom, but by the grace of God' (2 Corinthians 1:12), 'having or holding fast grace, that we may serve God acceptably' (Hebrews 12:28), 'labouring abundantly,' in such a manner as that the whole work is not performed by us but 'but the grace of God that is with us' (1 Corinthians 15:10). By grace, therefore, we may well understand the privileges of our new state given to us in Christ, whereby we ought to be influenced and guided in the performance of holy duties."*[820]

> *"It is also signified, when we are taught 'to put off the old and put on the new man;' yea, to continue in so doing, though we have done it in a measure already (Ephesians 4:21, 22, 24), and to avoid sin, 'because we have put off the old and put on the new man' (Colossians 3:9, 10). I have already showed that by this twofold man is not meant merely sin and holiness; but by the former is meant our natural state, with all its*

---

[817] Ibid.
[818] Ibid. 58
[819] Ibid.
[820] Ibid. 58-59

endowments, whereby we are furnished only to the practice of sin, and by the latter our new state in Christ, whereby we are furnished with all means necessary for the practice of holiness."[821]

So to…

"…stir up and strengthen yourself to perform the duties of holiness, <u>by a firm persuasion of your enjoyment</u> of Jesus Christ, and all spiritual and everlasting benefits through Him."[822]

"Your way to a holy practice is, first to conquer and expel all unbelieving thoughts, by trusting confidently on Christ, and persuading yourselves by faith, that His righteousness, Spirit, glory, and all His spiritual benefits are yours; and that He dwelleth in you, and you in Him. <u>In the might of this confidence,</u> you shall go forth to the performance of the law; and you will be strong against sin and Satan, and able to do all things through Christ that strengthens you. <u>This confident persuasion</u> is of great necessity to the right framing and disposing our hearts to walk according to our new state in Christ. The <u>life of faith</u> principally consisteth in it. And herein it eminently appeareth, that faith is a hand, not only to receive Christ, but also to work by Him; and that it cannot be effectual for our sanctification except it contain in it some assurance of our interest in Christ, as hath been showed. Thus we act as those that are above the sphere of nature, advanced to union and fellowship with Christ. The apostle [Paul] maintained in His heart a persuasion that Christ had loved him, and given Himself for Him; and hereby he was enabled to live to God in holiness, through Christ living in him by faith. He teacheth us also, that we must maintain the like persuasion, if we would walk holily in Christ. We must know that our old man is crucified with him; and we must reckon ourselves dead indeed unto sin, and alive unto God through Jesus Christ our Lord (Romans 6:6, 11). This is the means whereby we may be filled with the Spirit, strong in the Lord and in the power of His might; which God would not require of us, if he had not appointed the means (Ephesians 6:10)."[823]

"Christ Himself walked in a constant persuasion of His excellent state; He set the Lord always before Him, and was persuaded that, because God was at His right hand, He should not be moved (Psalm 16:8)."[824]

"…If Christians knew their own strength better, they would enterprise greater things for the glory of God. But this knowledge is difficultly attained; it is only by faith and spiritual illumination. The best know but in part; and hence it is that the conversation of believers falleth so much below their holy and heavenly calling."[825]

So…

"…your hearts may be rightly fitted and framed for the performance of these principal duties, the Holy Scriptures direct you to walk in the persuasion of other principal endowments of your new state, as, that you have fellowship with the Father, and with His Son Jesus Christ (1 John 1:3); and that you are the temple of the living God (2 Corinthians 6:16); that you live by the Spirit (Galatians 5:25); that you are called to holiness, and created in Christ Jesus unto good works; that God will sanctify you wholly, and make you perfect in holiness at the last (1 Thessalonians 5:23; Ephesians 2:10); that your old man is crucified with Christ; and that through Him 'you are dead unto sin, and alive unto God; and being made free from sin, you are become the

---

[821] Ibid. 59
[822] Ibid. 66
[823] Ibid. 66-67
[824] Ibid. 67
[825] Ibid.

servants of righteousness, and have your fruit unto holiness, and the end everlasting life' (Romans 6:6, 22); "Ye are dead, and your life is hid with Christ in God. When Christ who is your life shall appear, then shall ye also appear with Him in glory' (Colossians 3:4).[826]

So, we now understand and know that all the fulness of God is in us — including His holiness, and that fulness and holiness is inside of us in our new spirit-man with all His righteousness and the gift of eternal life! The "Old Man" that was generated from the first Adam has become crucified and buried and can never be mended.

The worship centers across America must do away with the *501c3* corporate government status and involvement with secret societies — what fellowship can light have with darkness?![827] — and embrace holiness unto virtue. The worship centers must seek to stand-up the re-inhabited Republic with its foundation being Biblical Christianity (*the Laws of Nature and of Nature's God*) and be involved with putting God-fearing, virtuous people in all three branches of State government in all fifty States, as well as in the nation's capital. America (We the People) must stand-up the re-inhabited Republic and let righteousness exalt our great nation. America must once again be a "city on a hill" for the rest of the nations to see. America must be right side up and no longer upside down. "We the People" must be filled with holiness and virtue by faith and take God-given measures to make this nation a God-fearing nation with a Republic.

What is a Republic? It is a commonwealth — a state in which the exercise of the sovereign power is lodged in representatives elected by the people, in modern usage it differs from democracy and democratic state, where the people exercise the power of sovereignty in person.[828] We didn't say it, Noah Webster did!

Noah Webster, *First Edition of An American Dictionary of the English Language*, 1828:

> Virtue: Moral goodness; the practice of moral duties and the abstaining from vice, or a conformity of life and conversation to the moral law. In this sense, *virtue* may be, and in many instances must be, distinguished from *religion*. The practice of moral duties merely from motives of convenience or from compulsion, or from regard to reputation, is *virtue*, as distinct from *religion*. The practice of moral duties from sincere love to God and his laws, is virtue and religion. In this sense it is true.

> *Virtue* is nothing but voluntary obedience to truth. A particular moral excellence; as the *virtue* of temperance, of chastity, of charity. [Remember all His virtues!]

> Acting power; something efficacious.

---

[826] Ibid. 68
[827] 2 Corinthians 6:14 ~ Be ye not unequally yoked together with unbelievers: for what fellowship hath righteousness with unrighteousness? and what communion hath light with darkness?
[828] *Noah Webster's First Edition of An American Dictionary of the English Language,* 1828:
"REPUB'LIC, n. [L. *respublica; res* and *publica* ; public affairs.]
1. A commonwealth ; a state in which the exercise of the sovereign power is lodged in representatives elected by the people. In modern usage, it differs from a democracy or democratic stale, in which the people exercise the powers of sovereignty in person. Vet the democracies of Greece are often called republics.
2. Common interest ; the public. [Not in use.] B. Jonson."
Republic of letters, the collective body of learned men."

> Jesus, knowing that *virtue* had gone out of him, turned and Jesus said, *"Somebody hath touched me for I perceive that virtue is gone out of me."* (Mark 3, Luke 8:46)

Efficacy: Power to produce effects; production to the effect intended; as the *efficacy* of the gospel in converting men from sin; the *efficacy* of prayer.

Efficacious: Capable of having the desired result of effect; effective as a means of measure, remedy, effective, effectual, active, adequate, capable, competent, energetic, influential, *dunamous* power.

Synonyms for Virtue

Trustworthiness	Moral excellence	Righteousness
Uprightness	Goodness	Merit
Prudence	Godly character	Charity
Respectability	Faith in God	Faithfulness
Worth	Kindness	Justice
Honor	Love	Innocence
Integrity	Purity	Temperance

The fruits of the Spirit are nine qualities that reflect the character of God and the work of the Holy Spirit in the lives of those who receive Christ and are transformed in His image as the *New Man*: Love, joy, peace, long-suffering, gentleness, goodness, faith, meekness, temperance, against such there is no law.[829]

In summary and great conclusion, on July 4, 1776, the Founding Fathers established a Republic, a Christian commonwealth, by the *Declaration of Independence*. All governments in the world are derived from a particular religion. The American Republic sprang from Biblical Christianity, the religion of Liberty.

1 Peter 1:15, 16 calls us to holiness. *Romans 6:19-11* calls us to holiness. *Romans 7:17, 18* establishes that you cannot fix the *Old Man*, he is programmed to practice sin. When you receive Christ, you receive all the fulness of God (*Colossians 1:19, Ephesians 3:19, John 5:16, John 14:20*). You are a *New Man* in Christ with His righteousness. You are dead to sin because you are taught and enabled to crucify the *Old Man* and put him to death (*Galatians 2:20*). As a *New Man* (born again), you know that all the fulness of God is inside of you (*Colossians 1:19*). This new life is to operate only by faith in Christ (*Hebrews 11:6*). Christ's fulness is inside of you (His holy frame), including His holiness and <u>all</u> of His virtue!

When you were born from your mother's womb, you were born to practice sin!

> *Romans 7:17, 18, 19* ~ *17 Now then it is no more I that do it, but sin that dwelleth in me. 18 For I know that in me (that is, in my flesh,) dwelleth no good thing: for to will is present with me; but how to perform that which is good I find not. 19 For the good that I would I do not: but the evil which I would not, that I do.*

---

[829] Galatians 5:22-23 ~ 22 But the fruit of the Spirit is love, joy, peace, longsuffering, gentleness, goodness, faith, 23 Meekness, temperance: against such there is no law.

The first Adam gave you sin that cannot be fixed. *Galatians 2:20, I am crucified with Christ* — this sin life cannot be fixed, but must be crucified and buried, put to death. Jesus' crucifixion is your crucifixion, His death is your death, His resurrection is your resurrection!

The only way *We the People* can have *Civil and Religious Liberty* is to enjoy and practice holiness which leads to virtue. Virtue comes from living the principles of Christianity and Liberty is a result of emanating virtue!

Lyman Beecher [830]

Lyman Beecher (1775-1863) was a renowned Presbyterian minister of the Gospel in New England. He preached in Boston and Cincinnati, where he later became President of Lane Theological Seminary. He was the father of both Henry Ward Beecher, one of the most eloquent preachers of his time, and Harriet Beecher Stowe, author of the classic 1852 book, *Uncle Tom's Cabin*, which greatly precipitated the abolition of slavery.

In 1831, Lyman Beecher wrote in the newspaper, *The Spirit of the Pilgrims*:

"The government of God is the only government which will hold society, against depravity within and temptation without, and this it must do by the force of its own law written upon the heart.

This is that unity of the Spirit and that bond of peace which can alone perpetuate national purity and tranquility — that law of universal and impartial love by which alone nations can be kept back from ruin. There is no safety for republics but in self-government, under the influence of a holy heart, swayed by the government of God." [831]

The Apostle Paul wrote to the Ephesians as recorded in the scriptures at *Ephesians 4:24,*

"And that ye put on the new man, which after God is created in righteousness and TRUE holiness."

[Emphasis added]

So, our hearts may be rightly fitted and framed for the performance of these principal duties, the Holy Scriptures direct you to walk in the persuasion of other principal endowments of our new state. Our new state is to receive the holy frame of God and all His fullness — being truly born again, born anew. With holiness already inside of us we can live by Scriptures that guide us to practice holiness leading us to VIRTUE. So, most importantly, we have fellowship with the Father and His son Jesus Christ (*1 John 1:3*).

---

[830] *Wikimedia Commons*, s.v. "Lyman Beecher - Brady-Handy.jpg," his is a faithful photographic reproduction of a two-dimensional, public domain work of art. The work of art itself is in the public domain

[831] Federer, *America's Quotations*, "Lyman Beecher," 42-43 as citing Lyman Beecher. 1831. *The Spirit of the Pilgrims.* Perry Miller, *The Life of the Mind in America from the Revolutionto the Civil War-Books 1-3* (New York: Harcourt, Brace & World, 1966), p. 36.

Please don't forget *John 6:25-65*. Fellowship is very, very important! Then, fellowship with your brothers and sisters in Christ – I am talking about TRUE fellowship meaning Christ is the center of all.

> *John 17:21-23 ~ 21 That they all may be one; as thou, Father, art in me, and I in thee, that they also may be one in us: that the world may believe that thou hast sent me. 22 And the glory which thou gavest me I have given them; that they may be one, even as we are one: 23 I in them, and thou in me, that they may be made perfect in one; and that the world may know that thou hast sent me, and hast loved them, as thou hast loved me.*

That we may acknowledge that we… "

> …*"are the temple of the living God (2 Corinthians 6:16); that [we] live by the Spirit (Galatians 5:25); that [we] are called to holiness, and created in Christ Jesus unto good works; that God will sanctify [us] wholly, and make [us] perfect in holiness at the last (1 Thessalonians 5:23, Ephesians 2:10); that [our] old man is crucified with Christ and that through Him [we] 'are dead unto sin, and alive unto God, and being made free from sin, [we] are become the servants of righteousness, and have [our] fruit unto holiness, and the end everlasting life' (Romans 6:6, 22); [we]' are dead, and [our] life is hid with Christ in God. When Christ who is [our] life shall appear, then shall we also appear with Him in glory (Colossians 3:4). Such persuasions as these, when they are deeply rooted and constantly maintained in our hearts, do strongly arm and encourage us to practise universal obedience in opposition to every sinful lust; because we look upon it not only as our duty, but our great privilege, to do all things through Christ strengthening us; and God doth certainly work in us both to will and to do by these principles, because they properly belong to the gospel, …which is the ministration of the Spirit, and the power of God unto salvation (2 Corinthians 3:6, Romans 1:16)."*[832]

Now that you have been enlightened with spiritual understanding, it is time to spread this knowledge to create a movement of *We the People* in the worship centers across America to stand up and restore the RE-INHABITED REPUBLIC, the Republic for the United States of America. Next, it would be the right time, and in the best interest of America, to place God-fearing people in all three branches of government, in all 50 states! Also, in our nation's capital! With people practicing holiness and practicing VIRTUE, the RE-INHABITED REPUBLIC will become restored, will sustain and endure! Righteousness will exalt this nation once again! America will be standing right-side up and *We the People* will enjoy civil and religious liberty!

This is truly God's Solution for America ~ and for the Nations of the World! This is a spiritual revolution!

Our Founding Fathers believed that the birth of the American Republic was prophesied in the Holy Scriptures, along with a National Purpose and Prophetic Destiny this nation would have in advancing the Gospel of the Kingdom of Christ Jesus and of God the Father throughout the world. They believed from studying the Holy Scriptures that the response of those nations in receiving Christ the Messiah would be to covenant with Him as a nation of people and desire to learn His government and laws so that they too could live in His Kingdom on earth and enjoy living in His jurisdiction of Liberty. Because our Fore Fathers

---

[832] Rev. Walter Marshall *Sanctification; or, The Highway of Holiness, An Abridgment (in the Author's Own Words) of The Gospel Mystery of Sanctification with an Introductory Note by* Rev. Andrew Murray (London: James Nisbet & Co., 1884) 68-69

appealed to Heaven and trusted God to grant them their petition, they made tremendous sacrifices and endured many dangers and laborious work to birth the American Republic forth in independence, creating a national government, "the model government," and they saw those Scriptures manifest.

John Adams summed up his feelings about the American Republic and "the model government" when he wrote:

> *"I always consider the settlement of America with reverence and wonder, as the opening of a grand…design in Providence for the illumination of the ignorant, and the emancipation of the slavish part of mankind all over the earth."*[833]

When you receive Christ, all the fulness of God is inside of you. Included in the fulness of God is His holiness (you've already got it). The only way you can obtain this is by faith. The "Old Man" has to be crucified and buried.

Jude 25 ~ To the only wise God our Saviour, be glory and majesty, dominion and power, both now and ever. Amen.

*Recommended reading: *Absolute Surrender* by Andrew Murray (1897) ~ and ~

Sanctification or The Highway of Holiness by Walter Marshall (1692) reprinted with an Introductory Note by Andrew Murray (1884)

---

[833] John Adams, February 1765, in his notes for *A Dissertation on the Canon and Feudal Law*; Benjamin Franklin Morris, *The Christian Life and Character of the Civil Institutions of the United States* (Philadelphia: George W. Childs, 1864) 109; J. Eidsmoe, *Christianity and the Constitution* (Grand Rapids, MI: Baker Book House, A Mott Media Book, 1987; 6th printing, 1993) 266

Battle Hymn of the Republic

Author: Julia Ward Howe (1862)
Music: William Steffe, 1856;
arranged by James E. Greenleaf, C. S. Hall,
and C. B. Marsh, 1861
Tune: Battle Hymn of the Republic
Published in 542 hymnals[834]

Mine eyes have seen the glory of the coming of the Lord;
He is trampling out the vintage where the grapes of wrath are stored;
He hath loosed the fateful lightning of His terrible swift sword:
His truth is marching on.

(Chorus)
Glory! Glory! Hallelujah! Glory! Glory! Hallelujah!
Glory! Glory! Hallelujah! His truth is marching on.

I have seen Him in the watch-fires of a hundred circling camps;
They have builded Him an altar in the evening dews and damps;
I can read the righteous sentence by the dim and flaring lamps;
His day is marching on. [Chorus]

I have read a fiery gospel writ in rows of burnished steel:
"As ye deal with my contemners, so with you my grace shall deal!";
Let the Hero, born of woman, crush the serpent with his heel,
Since God is marching on. [Chorus]

He has sounded forth the trumpet that shall never call retreat;
He is sifting out the hearts of men before His judgment-seat;
Oh, be swift, my soul, to answer Him! Be jubilant, my feet!
Our God is marching on. [Chorus]

In the beauty of the lilies Christ was born across the sea,
With a glory in His bosom that transfigures you and me.
As He died to make men holy, let us die to make men free!
While God is marching on. [Chorus][835]

Cover of sheet music for "The Battle Hymn of the Republic," 1862 [836]

---

[834] Hymnary.org, Battle Hymn of the Republic
[835] Wikipedia, s.v. "Battle Hymn of the Republic," accessed August 17, 2023
[836] *Wikimedia Commons*, s.v. "The Battle Hymn of the Republic - Project Gutenberg eText 21566.png," This work is in the public domain

My Loving Letter to My Clergy Friends

Preachers (shepherds), Teachers, Evangelists, Prophets, and all true believers:

When a person comes to Christ and finds out that he was under the influence of the first Adam, he finds out through Scripture according to *Ephesians 4:21, 22, 24* ~

> *[21] If so be that ye have heard him, and have been taught by him, as the truth is in Jesus: [22] That ye put off concerning the former conversation the old man, which is corrupt according to the deceitful lusts; [24] And that ye put on the NEW Man, which after God is created in righteousness and true holiness.* [Emphasis added]

The one thing we learn is that from the first Adam we learned to practice sin. When we put on the NEW MAN and embrace righteousness, we should be taught to practice holiness. When we observe *Romans 7:17-20* ~

> *[17] Now then it is no more I that do it, but sin that dwelleth in me. [18] For I know that in me (that is, in my flesh,) dwelleth no good thing: for to will is present with me; but how to perform that which is good I find not. [19] For the good that I would I do not: but the evil which I would not, that I do. [20] Now if I do that I would not, it is no more I that do it, but sin that dwelleth in me.*

Therefore, we must exercise *Galatians 2:20* ~

> *I am crucified with Christ: nevertheless I live; yet not I, but Christ liveth in me: and the life which I now live in the flesh I live by the faith of the Son of God, who loved me, and gave himself for me.*

The natural man from the first Adam cannot be fixed.

When we are born again through the Spirit by accepting the work of the Second Adam (Jesus Christ), He gives us all the fulness of God (*Colossians 1:19*) including righteousness and His holiness and virtue. We partake of these Kingdom assets by faith. The only way to live in the Kingdom of Christ and of God the Father is to walk, live, work, worship, etc., by faith. We learn not to walk by sight; but to live by faith.

To move into this realm, we must have great fellowship with Jesus starting with *John 6:25-65*. Also adding *Revelation 3:20*! Also, He wants us to have true fellowship with the saints.

> *1 John 1:5-7* ~ *[5] This then is the message which we have heard of him, and declare unto you, that God is light, and in him is no darkness at all. [6] If we say that we have fellowship with him, and walk in darkness, we lie, and do not the truth: [7] But if we walk in the light, as he is in the light, we have fellowship one with another, and the blood of Jesus Christ his Son cleanseth us from all sin.*

Also,

John 17:21-23 ~ 21 That they all may be one; as thou, Father, art in me, and I in thee, that they also may be one in us: that the world may believe that thou hast sent me. 22 And the glory which thou gavest me I have given them; that they may be one, even as we are one: 23 I in them, and thou in me, that they may be made perfect in one; and that the world may know that thou hast sent me, and hast loved them, as thou hast loved me.

Fellowship with Jesus Christ and with the saints is extremely important to move into holiness. To practice holiness by faith! When we look at *Romans 6:19 and 6:22*, there is a call to holiness. When we look at,

1 Peter 1:15-16 ~ 15 But as he which hath called you is holy, so be ye holy in all manner of conversation; 16Because it is written, Be ye holy; for I am holy.

Ephesians 5:27 ~ That he might present it to himself a glorious church, not having spot, or wrinkle, or any such thing; but that it should be holy and without blemish.

Ephesians 5:30-32 ~ 30 For we are members of his body, of his flesh, and of his bones. 31 For this cause shall a man leave his father and mother, and shall be joined unto his wife, and they two shall be one flesh. 32 This is a great mystery: but I speak concerning Christ and the church.

Take time to read the last two verses of *chapter one* in the book of *Ephesians*. It is time for the worship centers to pull out of the *501c3* union of Church and State!

Paul wrote in,

1 Corinthians 15:10 ~ But by the grace of God I am what I am: and his grace which was bestowed upon me was not in vain; but I laboured more abundantly than they all: yet not I, but the grace of God which was with me.

So, by His strength and by His grace He will help us to achieve the practice of holiness!

For the same end, that your hearts may be rightly fitted and framed for the performance of these principal duties, the Holy Scriptures direct you to walk in the persuasion of other principal endowments of your new state, as that you have fellowship with the Father and with His Son, Jesus Christ (*1 John 1:3*) and that you are the temple of the living God (*2 Corinthians 6:16*) that you live by the Spirit (*Galatians 5:25*), that you are called to holiness, and created in Christ Jesus unto good works; that God will sanctify you wholly, and make you perfect in holiness at the last (*1 Thessalonians 5:23; Ephesians 2:10*); that your old man is crucified with Christ; and that through Him you are dead unto sin and alive unto God and being made free from sin, you are become the servants of righteousness, and have your fruit unto holiness, and the end everlasting life (*Romans 6:6, 22*) ye are dead and your life is hid with Christ in God. When Christ who is your life shall appear, then shall ye also appear with Him in glory (*Colossians 3:4*).

Such persuasions as these, when they are deeply rooted and constantly maintained in our hearts do strongly arm and encourage us to practice universal obedience in opposition to every sinful lust because we look upon it not only as our duty, but our great privilege, to do all things though Christ strengthening us; and

God doth certainly work in us both to will and to do by these principles because they properly belong to the gospel, or *New Testament*, which is the ministration of the Spirit, and the power of God unto salvation (*2 Corinthians 3:6, Romans 1:16*).

I take no credit for this book or this letter. I followed the prompting and lead of the Holy Spirit! I adjure all of you to embrace *God's Solution for America!* The only way that America will be saved is through repentance and a desire to be holy and practice virtue.

America (specifically, the true believers of Christ) must remove themselves from the government corporation *501c3* status — and from involvement in secret societies — and begin to embrace politics, the science of (God's) government. When I say politics, I am referring to the Re-inhabited Republic with its foundation being Biblical Christianity! Christians must put believers in every office position, in all three branches of government, in every State and in our nation's capital! Begin at the local level in the townships and counties. *We the People* must participate in our government at every level even if it be only sitting in on meetings.

Noah Webster defined this Republic as a Christian Commonwealth — a state in which the exercise of the sovereign power is lodged in representatives elected by the people. It differs from democracy or a democratic state where the people exercise the power of sovereignty in person.

We want a government with its foundation on Biblical Christianity (*Matthew 7* on a Rock), with Biblical Christians in power so that *Righteousness will exalt this nation* once again as it had from the beginning with the Pilgrims. Remember, the Republic based on Biblical Christianity will assist in producing VIRTUE (coming from holiness) and with VIRTUE we will enjoy *Religious Liberty* and *Civil Liberty*. These two Liberties are inseparable! This is what the Pilgrims brought with them to America! This is what our Founding Fathers gave us as a nation of people through the Founding Documents!

The preamble of the *Declaration of Independence*:

> *"WHEN in the Course of human Events, it becomes necessary for one People to dissolve the Political Bands which have connected them with another, and to assume among the Powers of the Earth, the separate and equal Station to which the LAWS OF NATURE and of NATURE'S GOD entitle them…*[what God created and also the 66 books in the Holy Bible]." [Emphasis added]

May God our Father bless you abundantly, and all that you love.

Respectfully,
In Christ,
David Carl Hertler

David Carl Hertler is Nebraska born and Wisconsin raised. In the early 1960s, David honorably served our country as an Aerographers Mate (weatherman) in the United States Navy. His awareness of life was expanded as he traveled our beautiful country for various schools, as well as in experiencing the Atlantic and Pacific Oceans while serving aboard ship. Upon honorable discharge, Mr. Hertler worked as a cost control accountant at IBM in Colorado and then in control data. Preferring the outdoors, he began working in construction in southern Wisconsin for a decade before briefly venturing into real estate sales. David began a U.S. Postal Service career in 1982 working as a rural mail carrier in south-central Wisconsin until his retirement 30 years later. He has faithfully served in the restoration process of the re-inhabited *Republic for the United States of America*. Throughout the first session of Republic Congress, he served in the capacity of dual roles in the House of Representatives as well as the Wisconsin free State legislative Assembly. While studying the lives of our Founding Fathers, early statesmen, the Pilgrim and Puritan fathers and preachers, David has memorized countless speeches and quotes in the last 13 years and making public presentations dressed in apropos attire. David has been a leader in education related to the American Republic's founding and operating documents, as well as teaching America's rich heritage as preserved in the writings of our early fathers and mothers. Together with his wife, Jean, David has co-authored the two-volume series, *Re-inhabited: Republic for the United States of America*.

Jean Hallahan Hertler has enjoyed living in the countryside of Wisconsin for most of her adult life. A daughter to first-generation Americans (Ireland, Italy, and England), Jean has 40 years of business experience, primarily in executive management with organizations and corporations throughout the United States. With an accomplished academic background and distinguished achievements, her love of learning has been sewn into her posterity as well as in countless others through church ministry and volunteer work. Beginning in early 2011, Jean assisted in the foundation of the interim government of Wisconsin, the re-inhabited Republic. She then began in-depth studies of the founding and operating documents of the American Republic along with American history from archived government records and documents as well as vintage out-of-print books. In 2013, Jean contributed to the American Republic by authoring *The Hertler Report, "Weekly Coverage and Reporting of Current Events, Issues, and Trends of the Republic for the United States of America."* Together with her husband David, Jean completed the research and writing of the American Republic's truthful history in a compelling two-volume series entitled, *Re-inhabited: Republic for the United States of America*.

www.ingramcontent.com/pod-product-compliance
Lightning Source LLC
Chambersburg PA
CBHW051209290426
44109CB00021B/2388